·研究生英语系列教材·

An English Course for Master Students of Engineering
工程硕士研究生英语综合教程

（第三版）

主　编：王慧莉　张　菅　安雪花
副主编：曹　硕　邱　进　马　莉
编　者：（按姓氏拼音排序）
安雪花　曹　硕　郭涵宁　郝晓争
李建嵘　李雪乔　马　莉　邱　进
王慧莉　王　宇　于风军　张　菅

北京大学出版社
PEKING UNIVERSITY PRESS

图书在版编目(CIP)数据

工程硕士研究生英语综合教程/王慧莉,张菅,安雪花主编. —3版. —北京:北京大学出版社,2016.10
(研究生英语系列教材)
ISBN 978-7-301-27766-9

Ⅰ.①工… Ⅱ.①王…②张…③安… Ⅲ.①英语—研究生—教材 Ⅳ.①H319.39

中国版本图书馆CIP数据核字(2016)第277563号

书　　名	工程硕士研究生英语综合教程(第三版)
	GONGCHENG SHUOSHI YANJIUSHENG YINGYU ZONGHE JIAOCHENG
著作责任者	王慧莉　张　菅　安雪花　主编
责任编辑	郝妮娜
标准书号	ISBN 978-7-301-27766-9
出版发行	北京大学出版社
地　　址	北京市海淀区成府路205号　100871
网　　址	http://www.pup.cn　新浪微博:@北京大学出版社
电子邮箱	编辑部 pupwaiwen@pup.cn　总编室 zpup@pup.cn
电　　话	邮购部 62752015　发行部 62750672　编辑部 62759634
印　刷　者	北京溢漾印刷有限公司
经　销　者	新华书店
	787毫米×1092毫米　16开本　18.25印张　600千字
	2007年3月第1版　2010年6月第2版
	2016年10月第3版　2023年9月第2次印刷
定　　价	55.00元(配有光盘)

未经许可,不得以任何方式复制或抄袭本书之部分或全部内容。
版权所有,侵权必究
举报电话: 010-62752024　电子邮箱: fd@pup.pku.edu.cn
图书如有印装质量问题,请与出版部联系,电话:010-62756370

前　言

《工程硕士研究生英语综合教程》自2010年第二版（2007年第一版）出版以来至今在多所高校的工程硕士研究生英语教学中使用，得到了一致的好评。第三版的教材在第二版的基础上做了很大的调整，更新了大部分的阅读内容，优化了练习形式。同时，因为工程硕士英语课程学时的减少，教材的整体内容由原来的15个单元减少到10个单元。

工程硕士研究生一般采用集中授课的形式，如何在有限的时间内让学生真正学到一些实用的东西是非常必要的。所以这一阶段的学习不应是本科英语课程的简单延续，而是让学生真正学到一些实用的东西。所以应用文体写作、实用阅读、日常和业务英语会话就显得十分重要。

工程硕士研究生英语综合教程共分为10个单元，每个单元分成五个部分。

第一部分"阅读与翻译"（Reading and Translating），旨在培养阅读能力，就相关话题进行简单的讨论，掌握使用频率较高的词汇，并设有一些英汉互译的翻译练习，英译汉练习主要以课文为主，汉译英练习主要挑选本篇主课文中一些典型句子，翻译成汉语之后让学生做一个"回译"的练习，目的是让学生能够更好地掌握课文的主要内容及表达。本部分收入两类文章：第一类为正式文体的文章；第二类为实用性的文章，力求题材多样，适合成人阅读。每篇文章均配有适量的阅读理解、词汇巩固及口头讨论等练习。

第二部分"翻译小窍门"（Tips for Translation），设有翻译理论及技巧方面的知识与练习，旨在为读者提供翻译（特别是汉译英）过程中常见问题的解决办法。

第三部分"模拟套写"（Simulated Writing），旨在培养学生参照范例用英语模拟、翻译和写作一些应用文体。本部分提供一定数量的应用文范文，同时还设计了必要的翻译、套写练习。

第四部分"听力"（Listening），听力部分提供了与本课主题相关的一个对话或者文章，旨在培养和提高学生基本的听力能力，特别是获取主要信息的能力。

第五部分"口语"（Speaking），口语部分旨在培养学生进行涉外口语交际的能力。内容涉及学术交流和涉外业务两大方面。每单元有1—2个情景对话/段落，并编配了常用表达法，供学习者学习模仿，力求"学中用，用中学"。

为了提高学生的口语表达能力，纠正发音错误，改善语音语调，养成大声朗读的习惯，每个单元的两篇阅读都提供音频，听力练习也提供的配套的音频。

为了便于使用与学习，各单元每一部分均注有生词和短语，为了让学生更好地掌握并记牢词汇，对于重复出现的词汇没有删除。

本教材得到"全国工程专业学位研究生教育2016—2017年度自选研究课题教改项目"（项目编号：2016-ZX-099）的资助。

另外，基于该教材的课程已经得到大连理工大学工程硕士专业学位研究生第一批在线课程建设项目的支持，在线课程将在2017年正式推出。

教材编写分工如下：王慧莉负责教材的整体设计、材料挑选、样章编写与统稿及第九单元的编写，曹硕编写第一单元，郝晓争编写第二单元与第六单元，马莉编写第三单元，李雪乔编写第四单元，安雪花编写第五单元，李建嵘编写第七单元，张菅编写第八单元，郭涵宁编写第十单元，邱进负责每一个单元的翻译技巧部分，王宇提供了两篇阅读文章。于风军负责整本教材的审校。

2016年10月

Contents

Unit One	Cross-Cultural Communication	1
Part One	Reading and Translating	1
	Reading A	2
	Reading B	6
Part Two	Tips for Translation	9
	翻译概述	9
Part Three	Simulated Writing	12
	Resumé	12
Part Four	Listening	18
Part Five	Speaking	20
	Business Negotiation	20

Unit Two	Social Networking	24
Part One	Reading and Translating	24
	Reading A	25
	Reading B	30
Part Two	Tips for Translation	33
	汉英语言差异	33
Part Three	Simulated Writing	36
	Instruction Manual	36
Part Four	Listening	43
Part Five	Speaking	45
	Job Hunt and Interview	45

Unit Three	Work	51
Part One	Reading and Translating	51
	Reading A	52
	Reading B	57

	Part Two	Tips for Translation	61
		词义的选择	61
	Part Three	Simulated Writing	63
		Invitation for Bids	63
	Part Four	Listening	67
	Part Five	Speaking	69
		Supplier Selection	69

Unit Four   Lifestyle   75

	Part One	Reading and Translating	75
		Reading A	76
		Reading B	81
	Part Two	Tips for Translation	83
		词的增补	83
	Part Three	Simulated Writing	85
		Writing Company Profile	85
	Part Four	Listening	89
	Part Five	Speaking	91
		Agency	91

Unit Five   Ethics   95

	Part One	Reading and Translating	95
		Reading A	96
		Reading B	101
	Part Two	Tips for Translation	104
		词的省略	104
	Part Three	Simulated Writing	106
		Patent	106
	Part Four	Listening	111
	Part Five	Speaking	112
		Technology Transfer and Cooperation	112

Unit Six   Technology   116

	Part One	Reading and Translating	116
		Reading A	117
		Reading B	122
	Part Two	Tips for Translation	124
		词类的转换	124

Contents

Part Three	Simulated Writing		126
	Minutes of a Meeting		126
Part Four	Listening		134
Part Five	Speaking		137
	Leading and Participating in a Meeting		137

Unit Seven Health 143

Part One	Reading and Translating		143
	Reading A		144
	Reading B		149
Part Two	Tips for Translation		151
	正面表达与反面表达		151
Part Three	Simulated Writing		153
	A Performance Report		153
Part Four	Listening		155
Part Five	Speaking		157
	Opening Speech		157

Unit Eight Celebrity 162

Part One	Reading and Translating		162
	Reading A		163
	Reading B		167
Part Two	Tips for Translation		171
	主动与被动		171
Part Three	Simulated Writing		174
	Proposal		174
Part Four	Listening		183
Part Five	Speaking		185
	Closing Speech		185

Unit Nine Education 188

Part One	Reading and Translating		188
	Reading A		189
	Reading B		194
Part Two	Tips for Translation		199
	合并与切分		199
Part Three	Simulated Writing		202
	Abstract		202

	Part Four	Listening	206
	Part Five	Speaking	209
		Academic Report	209

Unit Ten　Environment　214

	Part One	Reading and Translating	214
		Reading A	215
		Reading B	221
	Part Two	Tips for Translation	224
		科技文本的翻译	224
	Part Three	Simulated Writing	228
		Citations	228
	Part Four	Listening	233
	Part Five	Speaking	236
		Job Routines	236

Key to the Exercises　240

Unit One

Cross-Cultural Communication

Part One
Reading and Translating

Lead-in

Look at the visual comparisons between the western and Asian cultures. Discuss with your classmates and answer the following questions:
1. Which represents the Eastern culture in each paired pictures?
2. How much do you agree or disagree with what the pictogram intends to convey? Use examples to support your opinion.
3. Can you add more aspects of cultural differences to the pictogram?

Contact

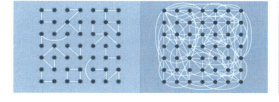

Opinion

Punctuality

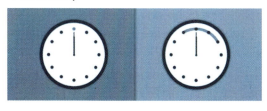

The Boss

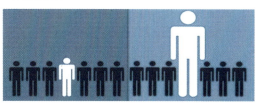

The Elderly

Reading A

Asians and North Americans See the World Differently

1   Asians and North Americans really do see the world differently. Shown a photograph, North American students of European background paid more attention to the object in the foreground of a scene, while students from China spent more time studying the background and taking in the whole scene, according to University of Michigan researchers.

2   The researchers, led by Hannah-Faye Chua and Richard Nisbett, tracked the eye movements of the students—25 European Americans and 27 native Chinese—to determine where they were looking in a picture and how long they focused on a particular area.

3   "They literally are seeing the world differently," said Nisbett, who believes the differences are cultural.

4   "Asians live in a more socially complicated world than we do," he said in a telephone interview. "They have to pay more attention to others than we do. We are individualists. We can be bulls in a china shop, but they can't afford it."

5   The findings are reported in Tuesday's issue of Proceedings of the National Academy of Sciences.

6   The key thing in Chinese culture is harmony, Nisbett said, while in the West the key is finding ways to get things done, paying less attention to others.

7   And that, he said, goes back to the ecology and economy of times thousands of years ago.

8   In ancient China, farmers developed a system of irrigated agriculture, Nisbett said. Rice farmers had to get along with each other to share water and make sure no one cheated.

9   Western attitudes, on the other hand, developed in ancient Greece where there were more people running individual farms, raising grapes and olives, and operating like individual businessmen.

10   So differences in perception go back at least 2,000 years, he said.

11   Aristotle, for example, focused on objects. A rock sank in water because it had the property of gravity, wood floated because it had the property of floating. He would not have mentioned the water. The Chinese, though, considered all actions related to the medium in which they occurred, so they understood tides and magnetism long before the West did.

12   Nisbett illustrated this with a test asking Japanese and Americans to look at pictures of underwater scenes and report what they saw.

13   The Americans would go straight for the brightest or most rapidly moving object, he said, such as three trout swimming. The Japanese were more likely to say they saw a stream, the water was green, there were rocks on the bottom and then mention the fish.

14   The Japanese gave 60 percent more information on the background and twice as much about the relationship between background and foreground objects as Americans, Nisbett said.

15   In the latest test, the researchers tracked the eye movements of the Chinese and Americans as they looked at pictures.

16   The Americans looked at the object in the foreground sooner—a leopard in the jungle for example—and they looked at it longer. The Chinese had more eye movements, especially on the background and back and forth between the main object and the background, he said.

17   Reinforcing the belief that the differences are cultural, he said, when Asians raised in North America were studied, they were intermediate between native Asians and European-Americans, and sometimes closer to Americans in the way they viewed scenes.

18   Kyle R. Cave of the University of Massachusetts at Amherst commented, "These results are particularly striking because they show that these cultural differences extend to low level perceptual processes such as how we control our eyes. They suggest that the way that we see and explore the world literally depends on where we come from."

19   Cave said researchers in his lab have found differences in eye movements between Asians and Westerners in reading, based on differences in the styles of writing in each language.

20   "When you look beyond this study to all of the studies finding cultural differences, you find that people from one culture do better on some tasks, while people from other cultures do better on others. I think it would be hard to argue from these studies that one culture is generally outperforming the other cognitively," Cave said.

New Words and Expressions

cognitively	adv.	[ˈkɔːgnətɪvli]	认知地,感知地
complicated	a.	[ˈkɔmplɪkeɪtɪd]	复杂的
ecology	n.	[ɪˈkɔlədʒi]	生态学
explore	v.	[ɪkˈsplɔː]	探测,探究
foreground	n.	[ˈfɔːgraʊnd]	前景,最显著的位置
harmony	n.	[ˈhɑːməni]	协调,融洽
illustrate	v.	[ˈɪləstreɪt]	阐明,举例说明
individualist	n.	[ˌɪndɪˈvɪdjʊəlɪst]	个人主义者,利己主义者
intermediate	a.	[ˌɪntəˈmiːdɪət]	中间的,中级的
irrigate	v.	[ˈɪrɪgeɪt]	灌溉
jungle	n.	[ˈdʒʌŋgl]	丛林
leopard	n.	[ˈlepəd]	豹,美洲豹
magnetism	n.	[ˈmægnəˌtɪzəm]	磁,磁力,吸引力
medium	n.	[ˈmiːdɪəm]	环境,媒介
object	n.	[ˈɔbdʒɪkt]	物体,目标
occur	v.	[əˈkɜː]	发生,出现
olive	n.	[ˈɔlɪv]	橄榄树,橄榄枝
outperform	v.	[aʊtpəˈfɔːm]	胜过,做得比……好
perception	n.	[pəˈsepʃən]	理解,感觉,知觉
perceptual	a.	[pəˈseptjʊəl]	知觉的,有知觉的

photograph	n.	[ˈfəʊtəɡrɑːf]	照片
proceeding	n.	[prəʊˈsiːdɪŋ]	会议录,学报
property	n.	[ˈprɒpəti]	性质,特性
reinforce	v.	[riːɪnˈfɔːs]	加强,增援
striking	a.	[ˈstraɪkɪŋ]	鲜明的,显著的
track	v.	[træk]	追踪
trout	n.	[traʊt]	鲑鱼

focus on	集中于
base on	基于……,以……为基础
pay attention to	注意
take in	获得,接受,感受
go back to	可追溯到……
be likely to	可能
close to	接近于

I. Give brief answers to the following questions.

1. What is the purpose for University of Michigan researchers to track the eye movements of European American students and native Chinese students?
2. How do North American students of European background and Chinese students see the world differently?
3. According to Nisbett, one of the researchers, why do Chinese and European Americans literally see the world differently?
4. When looking at pictures of underwater scenes, who pays more attention to the relationship between background and foreground objects?
5. Why does Cave think the results of the tests on eye movements of Asians and European Americans particularly striking?
6. What have researchers in Cave's lab found?

II. Complete the following passage by filling each of the numbered blanks with one or two suitable words using the Chinese in the brackets as the reference.

The key thing in Chinese culture is harmony, Nisbett said, while in the West the key is finding ways to get things done, ____1____ (不太关注) others. And that, he said, ____2____ (追溯到) the ecology and economy of times thousands of years ago. In ancient China, farmers ____3____ (开发了一个农业灌溉系统), Nisbett said. Rice farmers had to get along with each other to ____4____ (分享水源) and make sure no one cheated. Western attitudes, on the other hand, developed in ancient Greece where there were more people running ____5____ (个人农场), raising grapes and olives, and operating like individual businessmen. So differences in ____6____ (感知) go back at least 2,000 years, he said. Aristotle, for example, focused on objects. A rock sank in water because it had ____7____ (重力特征), wood floated because it had ____8____ (浮力特征). He would not have mentioned the water. The Chinese, though, considered all actions ____9____ (与……相关

的）the medium in which they occurred, so they understood tides and magnetism ___10___ （远远早于）the West did.

III. Complete the following sentences with one function word.

1. North American students of European background paid more attention to the object in the foreground of a scene, while students from China spent more time studying the background and taking _____ the whole scene.
2. The researchers tracked the eye movements of the students to determine where they were looking in a picture and how long they focused _____ a particular area.
3. And that, he said, goes back _____ the ecology and economy of times thousands of years ago.
4. The Japanese were more likely _____ say they saw a stream, the water was green, there were rocks on the bottom and then mention the fish.
5. Cave said researchers in his lab have found differences in eye movements between Asians and Westerners in reading, based _____ differences in the styles of writing in each language.
6. When you look _____ this study to all of the studies finding cultural differences, you find that people from one culture do better on some tasks, while people from other cultures do better on others.

IV. Complete the following sentences by translating the Chinese given in the brackets.

1. We'll _____（深入探索复杂企业业务规则的作用）in improving the issues of IT as a bottleneck. (explore, complicated)
2. If the sense of responsibility is greatly aroused, _____（人与自然的和谐）will not be far away. (harmony)
3. _____（积极向上的雇员要胜过消极的雇员）in terms of productivity, sales, energy levels, turnover rates and healthcare costs by as much as 30%. (outperform)
4. According to the experts' estimates, it will cost 100 US dollars/ sq. m to _____（加固和维修这些老住宅楼）. (reinforce)
5. Two years ago he decided that _____（公司需要把重点放在移动业务上）, so he created wechat for mobile. (focus on)
6. If you are seen as a leader rather than a follower, _____（事情也可能会按着你所期望的方向发展）. (be likely to...)

V. Translate the following sentences into English.

1. 纳兹博用一项测试说明了这一观点，他让日本人和美国人来观察水下的图像并报告他们所看到的内容。日本人给出的有关背景的信息比美国人要多60%，并且他们所指出的背景与前景物体之间的关系是美国人的两倍。
2. 美国人能更快注意到前景物体——比如丛林中的豹子——而且他们观看前景的时间更长些。中国人的视线移动得更多，他们尤其注意背景，并且在背景与主要物体间来回移动视线。

3. 亚洲人生活的世界社会关系比我们要复杂。他们要比我们更加关注他人。我们是个人主义者，我们可以像闯进瓷器店的公牛一样不管不顾，他们却不能这样做。
4. 为了测定欧洲裔美国学生和中国学生在观察图像时注意的是哪些位置以及他们的视线在某一特定区域停留的时间有多长，以理查德·纳兹博为首的研究人员追踪了这些学生眼球的移动，这些学生包括25位欧洲裔美国学生和27位中国学生。

VI. Translate the following passages into Chinese.

1. Asians and North Americans really do see the world differently. Shown a photograph, North American students of European background paid more attention to the object in the foreground of a scene, while students from China spent more time studying the background and taking in the whole scene, according to University of Michigan researchers.

2. Kyle R. Cave of the University of Massachusetts at Amherst commented, "These results are particularly striking because they show that these cultural differences extend to low level perceptual processes such as how we control our eyes. They suggest that the way that we see and explore the world literally depends on where we come from."

Reading B

Time Orientations in Different Cultures

1   As a species, our fixation with time and the power we give it are rather obvious. Over two thousand years ago, the Greek playwright（剧作家）Sophocles observed, "Time is a kindly God." As is the case with most of the issues discussed, cultures vary widely. Where they differ is in the value placed on the past, present, and future and how each influences interaction. Now let us simply highlight（强调）some of the major cultural differences in the perception（感知）of time.

2   Past-oriented cultures believe strongly in the significance of prior events. History, established religions, and traditions are extremely important to these cultures, so there is a strong belief that the past should be the guide for making decisions and determining truth. You can see this orientation in China, which because of its long and resplendent（辉煌的）history continues to respect the past. Chu and Ju found that respect for their historical heritage was considered the most important traditional value among Chinese. There is even a famous Chinese proverb that states, "The past is as clear as a mirror, the future as dark as lacquer（油漆）." In Japan, where Shintoism（日本神道教）is strong and reverence toward ancestors is important, the past still remains paramount（最重要）. Great Britain, because of its extensive devotion to tradition, including the continuation of a monarchy（君主）, resists change as it attempts to cling to（抱住）the past. France is yet another culture that can be understood by exploring its view of the past. The French, on many levels, venerate（崇敬）the past. As Hall

and Hall tell us:

3   The importance of French history to the average French person can hardly be overstated (夸大). The French live surrounded by thousands of monuments to their glorious past. Every quarter in Paris has its historically important statues(雕塑), buildings, or fountains(喷泉), daily reminders of past achievements. French villages have statues to locate heroes and important political leaders. As a result of this constant immersion(沉浸) in history, the French tend to see things in their historical context and relate contemporary events to their origins.

4   Within the United States, American Indians, in part because of their strong oral tradition, also value the past. Many Native American stories in fact use the past to set examples and to "provide moral guidelines by which one should live."

5   A culture's judgment about the past is evident in a variety of situations. For example, when conducting business with a past-oriented culture, Trompenaars and Hampden-Turner suggest you "talk about history" and "show respect for ancestors, predecessors(前辈), and older people." Lewis adds to the list by telling you that there should be "exploration of all issues before decisions are sought."

6   Present-oriented cultures hold that the moment has the most significance. For them, the future is vague, ambiguous(含糊的), and unknown, and what is real exists in the here and now. For these cultures, enjoyment comes in the present. People of Phillippines and most Latin American countries usually hold these beliefs. Mexican Americans also "prefer to experience life and people around them fully in the present." Luchmann suggests that this view is also characteristic of the African-American co-culture.

7   Future-oriented cultures, such as the U.S. dominant cultures, emphasize the future and expect it to be grander than the present. What is going to happen holds the greatest attraction for most Americans because whatever we are doing is not quite as good as what we could be doing. This does not mean that Americans have no regard for the past or no thought of the present, but it is certainly true that most of them, in thought or action, look to the future.

8   Like many other orientations(取向), our view of time is related to a host of other values. For example, Americans' view of the future makes them optimistic. This is reflected in the common proverb "If at first you don't succeed, try, try again." This optimistic view of the future also sees Americans believing they can control the future. The power to control the future was clearly spelled out(说出来) by former President Lyndon Johnson when he told all Americans that "Yesterday is not ours to recover, but tomorrow is ours to win or to lose."

9   Edward T. Hall, a famous sociologist, found that there are cultural differences in perceiving time. He distinguished between two types of cultures, monochronic and polychronic. People of monochromic cultures, such as northern Europeans and Anglo North Americans, tend to do one thing at a time. They value speed and punctuality(守时). They are efficient and focused. They are controlled by their schedules. On the other hand, those in polychronic cultures, such as Latin and Arab countries, tend to do many things at once. They value flexibility(灵活性) over punctuality and tend to change plans often and easily. They are controlled by human relationships more than their schedules.

Monochronic Culture	Polychronic Culture
· Do one thing at a time	· Do several things at a time
· Tend to be punctual	· More flexible regarding schedule
· "Time is money"	· Business is a way of socializing
Examples: USA, Germany, Japan	Examples: France, Africa, Latin America

10   The following scale is designed to measure one's monochromic and/or polychronic time orientation. In the blank before each item, indicates the degree to which you (1) strongly agree, (2) agree, (3) are neutral, (4) disagree, or (5) disagree with the statement. There is no right or wrong answer, and many of the statements are similar by design. Work quickly and record your first impression.

1. I usually feel frustrated after I choose to do a number of tasks when I could have chosen to do one at a time.
2. When I talk with my friends in as groups setting, I feel comfortable trying to hold two or three conversations at a time.
3. When I work on a project around the house, it doesn't bother me to stop in the middle of one job to pick up another job that needs to be done.
4. I like to finish one task before going on to another task.
5. At church it wouldn't bother me to meet at the same time with several different people who all had different church matters to discuss.
6. I tend to concentrate on one job before moving on to another task.
7. The easiest way for me to function is to organize my daily activities with a schedule.
8. If I were a teacher and had several students wishing to talk with me about assigned homework, I would meet with the whole groups rather than with one student at a time.
9. I like doing several tasks at one time.
10. I am frustrated when I have to start on a task without first finishing a previous one.
11. In trying to solve problems, I find it stimulating to think about several different problems at the same time.
12. I am mildly irritated when someone in a meeting wants to bring up a personal topic that is unrelated to the purpose of the meeting.
13. In school, I prefer studying one subject to completion before going on to the next subject.
14. I'm hesitant to focus my attention on only one thing because I may miss something equally important.
15. I usually need to pay attention on only one task at a time to finish it.

Scoring: For items 2, 3, 5, 8, 9, 11, reverse your response (5=1), (4=2), (3=3),(2=4), (5=1), for example, if you response to item #2 was 5, reverse it to 1. If you response to item #3 was 4, reverse it to 2. Once you have reversed your responses to those 6 items, sum the entire 15 items. Scores of approximately 30 and below indicate a monochromic orientation. Scores of approximately 42 and above indicate a polychronic orientation.

Unit One

I. Match the topics below to the eight paragraphs of the main part in the article.

Paragraph 2
Paragraph 3
Paragraph 4
Paragraph 5
Paragraph 6
Paragraph 7
Paragraph 8
Paragraph 9

Monochronic and Polychronic Time Orientations
Future Orientation
Present Orientation
Past Orientation

II. Answer the following questions.

1. What does the past-oriented culture believe in?
2. What culture holds that the moment has the most significance?
3. What culture thinks that "yesterday is not ours to recover, but tomorrow is ours to win or to lose"?
4. What is your time orientation according to the scale test? Monochronic or polychronic?

III. Questions for discussion.

1. Have you ever experienced a foreigner who deals with time differently compared with the way you do?
2. What attitudes should be adopted for communicating with those who come from different cultures of time orientations?

Part Two
Tips for Translation

翻译概述

翻译是一种跨越时空的语言活动。所谓翻译，就是把一种语言已经表达出来的东西用另一种语言准确而完整地重新表达出来。

翻译是人类社会发展和进步的需要，人类社会要发展进步就需要在不同文化的民族之间进行沟通，而这一全过程都离不开翻译，因此翻译一直都是沟通各族人民的思想，促进政治、经济、文化、科学、技术交流的重要桥梁。翻译是学习好外语的重要手段之一，也是探讨两种语言对应关系的一门学科。

一、翻译的性质

什么是翻译？由于人们认识的角度不同，所以答案也就不一样。有人认为翻译是一门科学，因为它有着自己的内在科学规律；也有人视翻译为一门艺术，因为翻译好比作画，先抓住客观人物的形态和神态，然后用画笔把它惟妙惟肖地表现在画上；还有人将翻译认作是一门技能，因为就其具体操作过程而言总是离不开方法和技巧的。但是总的看来，翻译是一门综合性的学科，因为它集语言学、文学、社会学、教育学、心理学、人类学、信息理论等学科之特点于一身，在长期的社会实践中已经拥有了它自己的一套抽象理论、原则和具体方法，形成了它自己的独立体系。

二、翻译的类别

既然翻译的性质可从不同的角度来定义，那么同样，翻译的种类也可从不同的视角来分类。一般说来，翻译可从5种不同的角度来分类：

1. 从译出语和译入语的角度来分类，翻译可分为本族语译为外语和外语译为本族语两大类；
2. 从涉及的语言符号来分类，翻译分为语内翻译、语际翻译和符际翻译；
3. 从翻译的手段来分类，翻译可分为口译、笔译和机器翻译；
4. 从翻译的题材来分类，翻译可分为专业文献翻译、文学翻译和一般性翻译；
5. 从翻译的处理方式来分类，翻译可分为全译、摘译和编译。

三、翻译标准

翻译标准就是指翻译实践时译者所遵循的原则，也是翻译批评家批评译文时必须遵循的原则。任何翻译实践总要遵循一定的翻译标准或原则，衡量一篇译文的好坏同样也离不开一定的翻译标准，因此翻译标准的确立对于指导翻译实践有着重要的意义。然而由于人们看待翻译的角度不同，自然有了不同的翻译标准。

1898年，我国清末时期的著名学者严复(1854—1921)在《天演论》(译例言)中提出了"信、达、雅"三字标准。"信"是"意义不背本文"，"达"是不拘原文形式，尽译文语音的能事以求原意明显。"信""达"互为照应，不可分割开来。"雅"在今天看来是不可取的，因为这个"雅"是用汉以前字法句法，即所谓的上等文言文。

鲁迅先生(1881—1936)曾提出"信与顺"的翻译标准。他认为："凡是翻译，必须兼顾两面，一则当然力求其易解，一则保存着原作的丰姿。"

近人在讨论文学翻译时曾提出"重神似不重形似"，"译者和原作者要达到一种心灵上的契合"，"文学翻译的标准是'化'"等主张。

目前翻译界普遍接受的，也是作为一般翻译学习者必须努力掌握的标准，简而言之是两条：忠实(Faithfulness)和通顺(Smoothness)。

所谓"忠实"，首先指忠实于原作的内容。译者必须把原作的内容完整而准确地表达出来，不得有任何篡改、歪曲、遗漏或任意增删的现象。忠实还指保持原作的风格，即原作的民族风格、时代风格、语体风格、作者个人的语言风格等，译者对原作的风格不能任意破坏和改变，不能以译者的风格代替原作的风格。

所谓"通顺"，即指译文语言必须通顺易懂，符合规范。译文必须是明白晓畅的现代语言，没有逐词死译、硬译的现象，没有语言晦涩难懂、佶屈聱牙的现象，没有文理不通、结构混乱、逻辑不清的现象。

四、对译者的要求

翻译是一门综合性学科，它集语言学、文学、心理学、信息论等于一身，涉及政治、经济、文化、科技等诸多领域，因此，翻译人员不但要具备多方面的知识、技能、修养等条件，而且要经过必要的学习和训练，掌握翻译的科学和艺术，这样才能成为合格的翻译工作者。

具体说来,翻译人员需要具备以下几个方面的条件和水平。

1. 扎实的语言基本功。译者应具有较强的驾驭译出语和译入语的能力,能正确理解原文,熟练运用本族语。

This large body of men had met on the previous night, despite the elements which were opposed to them, a heavy rain falling the whole of the night and drenching them to the skin.

这一大群人头天晚上还是聚到了一起,尽管老天与他们作对,整夜下着倾盆大雨,大家被淋得浑身透湿。

原文中的 despite the elements which were opposed to them 译作"尽管老天与他们作对",读起来未免平板滞重、佶屈聱牙,如译作"尽管天公不作美"不仅传神达意,而且文字简练、十分得体。

2. 合理的知识结构。作为一名合格的译者,要有丰富的知识,不仅要专,而且要博,要成为一名"杂家",即熟悉以英语为母语的国家的诸如历史、宗教、政治、地理、军事、外交、经济、文艺、科学、风土人情、民俗习惯等方面的社会文化。这有助于正确理解原文,完美地表达原作所要传达的思想内容。

3. 熟悉翻译理论和常用技巧,善于灵活运用各种翻译技巧。

4. 具有高度的责任感。翻译工作者应当有高度的政治责任感,即必须善于应用正确的立场、观点和方法来分析研究所译的内容,以对译文的准确性做出正确的判断;翻译者还应具备高度的职业责任感,即必须意识到自己肩负的使命,树立兢兢业业、认真负责的态度。

五、翻译的过程

西方翻译界常将翻译前的各种准备工作,甚至包括与出版商打交道也视为翻译过程的组成部分。在我们看来,翻译过程主要包括理解、表达和校核这三个方面。

(一) 理解

只有在正确理解原文的基础上,才能正确地表达译文。理解是翻译成功与否的先决条件和重要步骤,务必要求正确可靠,杜绝谬误。

理解原文词句不应脱离上下文。词义总是受上下文制约的,没有上下文就没有词义。比如说,甲乙两人见面,甲说:"上课了?"这句话的含义如果脱离了当时的环境和背景,就不好翻译。

如果是在乙夹着书本刚从教室走出来时甲对其说了这句话,那么它的意思是:"(你刚才)上课了?"译成英语便是:(Have you) Just finished your class?

如果乙是一位以前没上过课的教师,刚刚上完平生第一堂课,那么甲的这句话就可以译为:How's your first class?

如果甲和乙在路上相遇时,甲正好急急忙忙向教室走去,担心迟到,见到乙便问:"(是不是已经)上课了?"那么这句话就应译为:Has the bell gone? 或 Am I late for class?

由此可见,同样的词句在不同的语言环境里包含着不尽相同或全然不同的意思,理解和翻译时必须加以区别,不然就会造成错误,也就无法忠于原文内容。

(二) 表达

表达是理解后能否保证译文成功的又一关键步骤,是理解的深化和体现。在这一过程中,译者要注意恰到好处地再现原文的思想内容和语体色彩,使译文既忠实于原作又符合译入语的语法和表达习惯。要做到这一点,译者就必须在选词用字、组词成句、组句成篇上下工夫,在翻译技巧的运用上下工夫。

在汉英翻译的表达过程中,最需要注意的一点是必须避免机械照搬的死译和望文生义的乱译。例如:

他(听到这话)心里一跳,脸色也变了。

译文1:His heart jumped and the color of his face changed.

译文2:At this his heart missed a beat and he became pale.

译文1机械照搬了原文形式,因不符合英文语言表达习惯而不知所云;译文2将原文"心里一跳"译成missed a beat字面意思完全相反,但表达了同样的含义。在翻译时,如果不根据汉英两种语言表达上的差异做出必要的变动,而采取词与词"对号入座"的方法,往往既不能达意,又无法忠实于原文。

总之,理解和表达常常相互联系、相辅相成。译者在理解原文的同时,也在选择表达方式;在表达的同时,又会进一步加深理解。这样经过反复推敲,译文才能达到忠实和通顺的标准。

(三)校核

校核是对理解和表达质量的全面检查,是纠正错误、改进译文的极好时机,切不可认为是多余之举。优秀的译者总是十分重视校核的作用,总是利用这一良机来克服自己可能犯下的错误,初学翻译的人就更应该如此了。校核通常有以下三个步骤:

1. 初校:着重校核内容,在初稿译出后,对照原文进行校核,看有没有漏译或错译之处。

2. 复校:脱离原文,着重润饰文字,看译文是否符合英语的习惯表达法,是否符合英语规范,是否通顺。

3. 定稿:在初校和复校的基础上,再次对照原文,进行一次仔细的认真的校核,如果所有的问题均已解决,译文才能定稿。

Part Three
Simulated Writing

Resumé

简历是招聘人员了解你的第一个途径。一份好的简历,可以在众多求职简历中脱颖而出,给招聘人员留下深刻的印象。简历的主要填写方法:

1. 突出你的能力、成就以及过去经验,强调成功经验使你的简历更出众。

2. 让简历醒目。审视一下简历的空白处,用这些空白处和边框来强调你的正文,或使用各种字体和格式,如斜体、大写、下划线、首字突出、首行缩进等。用计算机来打印你的简历。

3. 尽量使你的简历简短,删除无用的东西。

4. 为你的简历定位。雇主们都想知道你可以为他们做什么。含糊的、笼统的、毫无针对性的简历会使你失去很多机会。如果你有多个目标,最好写上多份不同的简历,在每一份上突出重点,这将使你的简历更有机会脱颖而出。

5. 力求精确。要尽可能准确地阐述你的技能、能力及经验,既不夸大也不误导。确信你所写的东西与你的实际能力及工作表现相符,还要写上你曾经工作过的公司及具体时间。

6. 要注意用词,避免写错别字。使用有影响力的词汇,如:证实(prove)、分析的(analytical)、线形的(linear)、有创造力的(creative)、有组织的(well-organized)。这样可以提高简历的说服力。

7. 最后检查一遍。你的简历应该回答了以下问题:它是否清楚并能够让雇主尽快知道你的能力?是否写清了你的能力?是否写清了你要求这份工作的基础?有东西可删除吗?

Sample Reading 1 (experienced IT professional resume)

Wang Yuyang
335 Huanghe Road, Dalian, Liaoning, China
Phone: 0411-84703433 Mobile: 13904283671 E-mail: Wangyuyang309@hotmail.com

Objective	To contribute outstanding technical skills and strong commitment to achieving your company's goals in an IT consulting capacity.
Profile	MBA-level IT professional with 8 years of Information Technology experience who provides top-notch service, sets high standards, and exceeds expectations. Highly motivated, dependable troubleshooter and problem-solver. Customer-focused performer who is committed to quality in every task from personal interaction with coworkers and users to high level of service provided to company/customer. Valued contributor who performs confidently and effectively under pressure and thrives on challenge. Excellent communicator and good listener. Enthusiastic learner who quickly grasps concepts and technical skills.
Technical Skills	**Certifications**　　　**Operating Systems/Software**　　**Applications** Network + CompTIA -　　Windows　　　　　　　Internet Explorer Networking　　　　　　98/2000/XP　　　　　　Netscape Technologies　　　　　　MS Word　　　　　　　Mozilla A+ CompTIA -　　　　　MS Excel　　　　　　　Open Office Software and Hardware　MS PowerPoint Technician

Professional Experience	**PC Support Specialist,** *Solutions Center*, Haihui, Dalian. 2003 to July 2006
	
	  Responded to, evaluated, and prioritized incoming phone and email requests for technical assistance from users experiencing problems with hardware, software, networking, and other computer-related, Web, and telecom technologies.
	  Provided prompt, accurate, and respectful support to users, employing high degree of customer-service skill and technical expertise while ensuring customer satisfaction.
	  Took initiative to learn company internal organizational structure to optimize problem-resolution efficiency.
	  Applied troubleshooting techniques to verify solutions.
	  Contributed ideas to improve customer service and suggested ways for second-level support to interact with customers.
	  Frequently resolved issues with little or no supervision.
	  Quickly learned new tasks and rapidly resolved customer problems.
	  Created template server-maintenance documents to be sent out to users so new documents did not need to be created each time.
	  Logged incoming calls and email into call-tracking database.
	
	Desktop Support Analyst, *Diversified Software Solutions*, Haihui, Dalian. 2001 to 2003
	
	  Served as sole desktop analyst providing technical support for 250 users in 15 satellite offices.
	  Consistently delivered rapid, outstanding service and support, resulting in a high level of customer satisfaction; kept users updated on resolutions.
	  Supported multiple corporate-wide upgrades and office relocations.
	  Coordinated installations for 24 network printers at 15 satellite offices.
	  Instructed users on new printing system.
	  Installed and upgraded 60+ PCs in conjunction with new host system.
	  Maintained operating systems on IBM AS/400 server.
	  Assisted in configuring and rolling out PC hardware and printers for 300 users at external company job.
	  Kept knowledge of changing technology current to benefit customers.
	  Cited by supervisor as "extremely thorough, proficient and knowledgeable" about customer base and praised for frequently volunteering for assignments above and beyond daily job description, as well as delivering on-time, complete solutions, doing whatever it took to get the job done, keeping coworkers and management well informed, offering suggestions to improve teams' efficiency, and providing expedient resolutions to user problems.
	  Saved travel time to remote location office several hours away and quickly solved user problem by deploying new remote-control software package to resolve/diagnose user issue.
	
	Engineering Associate, *Diversified Software Solutions*, Haihui, Dalian.1999 to 2001

	Administered, managed, and monitored contract process.
	Earned company award.
	Played key role on project teams for the company and billing project.
Education	*Master of Business Administration with a concentration in Management Information Systems*, Dalian University of Technology, Dalian, China
	Bachelor of Arts in Business Administration, Dongbei University of Finance and Economics, Dalian, China

consulting capacity	咨询能力
top-notch service	最高级的服务
technical assistance	技术援助
telecom technologies	电信技术
trouble tickets	故障单
satellite offices	子公司
bill project	为项目做宣传

Sample Reading 2

Ma Xiaohui
9931 Zhongshan Road, Dalian, Liaoning, China
Phone: 0411-84743433 Mobile: 13904083671
E-mail: maxiaohui931@hotmail.com

OBJECTIVE
To contribute to your organization's success through the use of exceptional customer service and managerial and people skills.

QUALIFICATIONS
Exceptional versatility and adaptability.
Dedication and drive as a hard-working individual.
Ability to manage multiple tasks in a pressured environment.

PROFESSIONAL SKILLS

INTERPERSONAL AND TEAMWORK SKILLS
Entrusted to process confidential employee records such as salary changes, vacation/absenteeism reports, and performance appraisals.

Interacted with a wide variety of personalities while scheduling meetings/appointments and making travel arrangements for executives.

CUSTOMER SERVICE AND SALES SKILLS
Interacted with clients and utilized excellent organizational skills to arrange and coordinate special events.
Delivered excellent customer service and conducted in-house sales promotions.

MANAGERIAL AND SUPERVISORY SKILLS
Proved multi-tasking abilities by scheduling and supervising staff.
Served as right hand to lead managers of entertainment company in an administrative assistant capacity.

QUANTITATIVE SKILLS
Completed and submitted invoices and process for payments.
Handled expense reports with account summaries.
Consistently entrusted with large sums of money.
Maintained inventory control.
Demonstrated knowledge of and accountability for payroll and employee records, daily sales operations, and profit and loss statements, including inventories, labor, petty cash, bank deposits, change orders, and bank deposit verifications.

COMPUTER SKILLS
Proficient in using personal computer skills through CompUSA training in such programs as Microsoft Windows, Microsoft Word, Excel, Access, PowerPoint, and Visio. Additionally, use WordPerfect, Lotus 1-2-3, Peachtree, Microsoft Publisher, ClarisWorks, First Choice and First Publisher for word processing, spreadsheet, and graphic design, including internal/external correspondence, reports, procedure manuals, and presentations.
Create and distribute a variety of reports using Access and Excel.

EMPLOYMENT HISTORY
Administrative Assistant, Blue Ribbon Technologies, Inc., Dalian 2003 to Present
Office Manager, City of Entertainment, Dalian 2000—2003
Clubhouse Assistant Manager, Golden Bear Country Club , Dalian 1997—2000

EDUCATION
Bachelor of Arts in Business Administration, Dongbei University of Finance and Economics, Dalian, China
Associate in Applied Science. Specialized in Accounting, Business and Office Management. Dongbei University of Finance and Economics, Dalian, China

team-building skills	团队合作
pressured environment	压力环境
performance appraisals	执行评估
in-house sales promotions	内部促销
expense reports with account summaries	附有账目摘要的支出报告

Follow-up Writing

Complete the following resumé with the information given below.

Deng Xuewen

10 Lingshui Road, Dalian Maritime University, Dalian, China
Phone: 0411-84723433   Mobile: 13904089671
E-Mail: dengxuewen1985@yahoo.com.cn

OBJECTIVE
- To contribute strong customer-service focus in a creative, exciting marketing-oriented setting.
- Creative marketing problem-solver.
- Award-winning customer-service provider.

PROFILE
- _____1_____（良好的人际关系、优秀的监管才能和团队合作精神）.
- _____2_____（勤奋的、有献身精神的专业人员）.
- _____3_____（主动的）, good team player with fine communication skills.
- _____4_____（优秀的英语口语和书面表达能力）.

EDUCATION
Bachelor of Business Administration, Dalian University of Technology 2003. Major in General Business, minor in Marketing and Business Law

EXPERIENCE
Entrepreneur, Penghui, Dalian, 1/2002—Present
- Participated on a team of six entrepreneurs through the Quintessential Careers Entrepreneurial Program at Dalian University of Technology
- _____5_____（起积极作用）in creating business idea, formulating a business plan, and operating of business.

Server, Wanda, Dalian, China, 8/2000—Present.
- Completed extensive training course that _____6_____（促进优质服务）to every guest through both individual and teamwork.
- Voted by management as _____7_____（月份最佳雇员）for April 2001.

Assistant Manager, Eternal, Dalian, China, 8/99—8/2000

- Trained new employees on suggestive selling, creating pleasing displays, computer P.O.S. system, and servicing customers.
- Created unique clothing and accessory displays.
- _____8_____ （几次荣获客户服务和销售奖）for providing service exceeding customer expectations.
- Oversaw payroll, daily records, and ordering/receiving of merchandise.

COMPUTER SKILLS	Windows, Microsoft Word, Microsoft Excel, Lotus 1-2-3, PowerPoint, WordPerfect, and HTML programming.
REFERENCES	Available upon request.

Part Four
Listening

Lead-in

I. Discuss the following topics with your classmates.

1. Do you know something about American culture?
2. How much do you agree with the statement that America is known more than America knows?

II. Study the following vocabulary before you listen.

assume	假定	summon	召唤
curl	弯曲	troops	军队
bother	烦恼	linguistic	语言的
casualness	漫不经心	gesture	姿势
make concessions to	做出让步	multilingual	多语言的
menu	菜单	transportation	运输
cluster	聚集	condition	制约
diplomacy	外交	interpreter	口译员
ignorance	无知	distributor	分发者
poll	民意调查	the upper hand	优势

While-listening

I. Listen to the recording and supply the missing words.

    Our culture has caused most Americans to assume not only that our language is universal but that the gestures we use are understood by everyone. We do not realize that waving good-bye is the way to summon a person from the Philippines to one's side, or that in Italy and some Latin-American countries, curling the finger to oneself is a __1__.

Those private citizens who sent packages to our troops occupying Germany after World War II and marked them GIFT to escape __2__ did not bother to find out that "Gift" means __3__ in German. Moreover, we like to think of ourselves as friendly, yet we prefer to be at least 3 feet or __4__ away from others. Latinos and Middle Easterners like to come closer and touch, which makes Americans uncomfortable.

Our linguistic and cultural blindness and the casualness with which we take notice of the developed tastes, gestures, customs and languages of other countries, are losing us friends, business and __5__ in the world.

Even here in the United States, we make few concessions to the needs of __6__. There are no information signs in four languages on our public buildings or monuments; we do not have multilingual __7__. Very few restaurant menus have translations, and multilingual waiters, bank clerks and policemen are __8__. Our transportation systems have maps in English only and often we ourselves have difficulty understanding them.

When we go abroad, we tend to __9__ in hotels and restaurants where English is spoken. The attitudes and information we pick up are __10__ by those natives—usually the richer—who speak English. Our business dealings, as well as the nation's diplomacy, are conducted through interpreters.

For many years, America and Americans could get by with cultural __11__ and linguistic __12__. After all, America wastes the most powerful country of the free world, the distributor of needed funds and goods.

But all that is past. American dollars no longer buy all good things, and we are slowly beginning to realize that our proper role in the world is changing. A __13__ Harris poll reported that __14__ percent of Americans want this country to play a more significant role in world affairs; we want to have a hand in the important decisions of the next century, even though it may not always be the __15__.

II. **Listen again, stop the recording as necessary, and repeat after the speaker.**

Post-listening

Surf the Internet and find more information about the following topic areas. Then prepare a 15-minute oral presentation and deliver it in class. While preparing the presentation you need to narrow down the topic area and focus on one major point.
1. Cross-cultural communication
2. Effective methods of communicating with people from different cultures

Part Five
Speaking

Business Negotiation

Sample Dialogue 1

A: Good afternoon, may I help you?

B: Well, I'm interested in your new line of business. May I look at your CIF price sheet of auto parts?

A: Certainly. Lately we expanded our scope of business to better serve our Far East Asian customers, Chinese customers in particular. China is such an enormous market that nobody can afford to neglect. My company is willing to establish business relations with all interested Chinese parties.

B: That's very nice to hear. We would like to import auto parts from your company on a regular basis, provided your prices compare favorably with those of others. To be frank with you, your listed prices are indeed among the least competitive. I'd like to hear your most recent quotations.

A: We have just updated our prices. But of course I don't mean our offer is final. As usual, we'd like to quote our new customers the most reasonable price to start our business relationship for the future, even at the cost of substantial loss on our part.

B: But my knowledge of the auto parts market tells me that your offer is very unattractive. Besides, I need time to build up my confidence in the quality of your stuff. In any case, I'd rather wait and hunt around, if you were unable to include any reasonable discount.

A: We guarantee the quality of our supplies. And we have free samples for your inspection. As for the discount, we can reduce the listed prices by 5%. This is our floor offer and you'll have to excuse me, we're not prepared for any counter-offer.

B: I appreciate your frankness. Though there is still a gap between your rock-bottom prices and my expectations, I'm willing to sign contracts with you. I like what you said. I'm doing this for the development of our future business relations.

A: That's wonderful. Let's leave the technical details of the contract to our assistants. I'd like to invite you to a drink and celebrate the success of our first business transaction.

B: Thank you very much. I believe this initial cooperation will lead to many more in the future.

Sample Dialogue 2

A: I appreciate your inquiry. This is our list of quotations with a recent reduction on the original prices by 3.5%. I'm sure you will find our offer the most competitive one in this rising market of today.

B: I agree your offer after this reduction is attractive but excuse my frankness, in any case it is by no means the most competitive one to the best of my knowledge. I did a lot of research lately and I'm sure you'll agree with me that a growing number of suppliers in other Southeast Asian countries have joined this market. I foresee a substantial drop in price next year.

A: I'm not sure if there will be a substantial price drop. You know our products have an established fame in the world, and more importantly, we guarantee the quality of our products whatsoever. Although some new manufacturers from our surrounding countries and regions may attract their customers with lower prices, our quality guarantee policy plus this latest substantial price reduction is sure to prevail.

B: You're a real business negotiator, but if you hang on to the listed quotations, it's impossible for us to come to terms. I don't think your offer is in line with the current market. I do hope that you'll consider our counter-offer. After all, we've had a business relationship for almost ten years.

A: All right, I'm willing to grant you a special reduction of an additional 1.5% discount in honor of our ten years' business cooperation and to promote our business relation in the future. This is far below my floor offer and therefore, I'm not prepared for any counter-bid.

B: I really appreciate your concession, and I'd like to sign our papers today.

A: I'm very glad we have brought our business talk to a successful conclusion. The rest is easy. We'll take care of the paper work this afternoon.

B: Sure.

Notes

C. I. F.	Cost + Insurance + Freight 到岸价
F. O. B.	Free on Board 离岸价
price sheet	价格表
competitive	有竞争力的
quotation	报盘
offer	报盘
discount	折扣
free sample	免费样品
firm offer	实盘
floor offer	底盘
counter-offer	还盘
rock-bottom price	最低价
transaction	交易
inquiry	询价
supplier	供货商
in line with	符合
counter-bid	还价
concession	让步

USEFUL EXPRESSIONS AND PATTERNS:

1. Thank you for your quick response to our inquiry.
2. The price for this commodity has changed somewhat compared with that of last year.
3. I wonder whether there are any changes in your price.
4. I think it's better for you to quote us your price first.
5. I'd like to have your lowest quotation C.I.F. San Francisco.
6. I'd like to hear your quotation on a C.I.F. Los Angeles basis valid for 90 days.
7. Would you please tell us the quantity you require so as to enable us to work out the offer?
8. This offer is subject to market fluctuation.
9. Can you give us an indication of your price?
10. The price for this commodity is US$ 400 per piece C.I.F. San Francisco.
11. Our quotation is favorable in your interest, and there is a limit to our price adjustment. Currently we just cannot accept your counter-offer.
12. We're willing to make you a firm offer at this price.
13. We can offer you a quotation based upon the international market.
14. We'll let you have the official offer next Monday.
15. My offer was based on reasonable profit, not on wild speculations.
16. No other buyers have bid higher than this price.
17. We can't accept your offer unless the price is reduced by 5%.
18. I'm afraid I don't find your price competitive at all.
19. Let me make you a special offer.
20. We'll give you the preference of our offer.
21. This offer is based on an expanding market and is competitive.
22. The offer holds good until 5 o'clock p.m. June 23, 2008, Beijing time.
23. All prices in the price lists are subject to our confirmation.
24. Our offers are for 3 days.
25. Now we look forward to replying to our offer in the form of counter-offer.
26. Your price is too high to interest buyers in counter-offer.
27. I'll respond to your counter-offer by reducing our price by three dollars.
28. I appreciate your counter-offer but find it too low.
29. I would like to discuss the terms of payment with you.

I. **Role-play the sample dialogues.**

Unit One

II. **Match the following two columns.**

1. 到岸价　　　　A. inquiry
2. 离岸价　　　　B. rock-bottom price
3. 询价　　　　　C. floor offer
4. 报盘　　　　　D. counter-offer
5. 价格表　　　　E. C.I.F
6. 底盘　　　　　F. price sheet
7. 还盘　　　　　G. quotation
8. 最低价　　　　H. F.O.B

III. **Complete the following dialogues by making sentences with the help of the key words given in brackets.**

1. A: (Here, quotations, you, ask for).
   B: How do they compare to last year's?
   A: The price increases haven't been too bad at all.
   B: That's good to hear. (let, take a look, prices).

2. A: (when, have, C.I.F. firm offer)?
   B: We can work out the offer this evening and give it to you tomorrow morning.
   A: How long does your offer remain valid?
   B: (offer, remain open, 3 days).

3. A: (this, C.I.F. quotation)?
   B: This is our F.O.B. quotation sheet.
   A: Are the prices on the list firm offer?
   B: (all the quotations, subject to, final confirmation).

IV. **Learn to communicate in the situation given below.**

Student A:　sales manager of the Shanghai Machinery Company Inc.
Student B:　manager of the supply department of the Pacific Trading Company Ltd., Seatle, USA.

A and B are carrying on a business negotiation. B is interested in the machine tools A's company manufactures.
The following points can be referred to in your conversation:
- machine tools
- make an inquiry
- lowest quotations C. I. F. Seatle
- C. I. F. US Pacific Coastal City price list
- adjust the prices according to the quantity
- competitive
- bulk

Unit Two

Social Networking

Part One
Reading and Translating

Lead-in

Have you ever heard of the term social networking? Read the following ten reasons to know more about it.

- On social networking sites, users can develop biographical profiles, communicate with friends and strangers, do research, and share thoughts, photos, music, links, and more.
- Social networking spreads information faster and more conveniently. You can read online news and books, receive the letters, obtain the information we want to know in the shortest possible time.
- You can make more friends sharing with your interests and hobbies and create a circle of your own friendship.
- Making use of social networking will help you keep in touch with your classmates, family in a remote place.
- Social networking can cause wide public concern. Sometimes, some people may be treated illegally.
- Social networking may influence the real interpersonal relationship and make the real distance between you and me farther and farther.
- Being involved in social networking in a long term means you may waste time on frivolous activity and will weaken your eyesight.
- It can alter children's brains and behavior, making them more prone ADHD (attention deficit hyperactivity disorder).
- You may be exposed to predators like pedophiles and burglars without being aware of it.
- Social networking can spread false and potentially dangerous information and invade your privacy.

Unit Two

Reading A

Some Youth Rethink Online Communications

Martha Irvine

1 For some, it would be unthinkable—certain social suicide. But Gabe Henderson is finding freedom in a recent decision: He canceled his MySpace account.

2 No longer enthralled with the world of social networking, the 26-year-old graduate student pulled the plug after realizing that a lot of the online friends he accumulated were really just acquaintances. He's also phasing out his profile on Facebook, a popular social networking site that, like others, allows users to create profiles, swap message and share photos—all with the goal of expanding their circle of online friends.

3 "The superficial emptiness clouded the excitement I had once felt," Henderson wrote in a column in the student newspaper at Iowa State University, where he studies history. "It seems we have lost, to some degree, that special depth that true friendship entails."

4 Across campus, journalism professor Michael Bugeja—long an advocate of face-to-face communication—read Henderson's column and saw it as a "ray of hope." It's one of a few signs, he says, that some members of the tech generation are starting to see the value of quality face time.

5 As the novelty of their wired lives wears off, they're also getting more sophisticated about the way they use such tools as social networking and text and instant messaging—not just constantly using them because they're there.

6 "I think we're at the very beginning of them reaching a saturation point," says Bugeja, director of Iowa State's journalism school and author of "Interpersonal Divide: The Search for Community in a Technological Age."

7 Though he's not anti-technology, Bugeja often lectures students about "interpersonal intelligence"—knowing when, where and for what purpose technology is most appropriate.

8 He points out the students he's seen walking across campus, holding hands with significant others while talking on cell phones to someone else. He's also observed them in coffee shops, surrounded by people, but staring instead at a computer screen.

9 "True friends," he tells them, "need to learn when to stop blogging and go across campus to help a friend."

10 In the meantime, he says, many professors have begun setting their own limits, banning students from surfing the Internet during lectures.

11 Of course, these forms of communication continue to dominate. In the October issue of the journal *Pediatrics*, for instance, researchers at Stanford University released findings from an ongoing study of students at an upper-middle income high school in the San Francisco area. One written survey found that the large majority of students were members of at least one social networking site—81 percent of them on MySpace. They also found that 89 percent of those

students had cell phones, most of them with text and Web surfing capabilities.

12　　　They are more wired than ever—but they're also getting warier.

13　　　Increasingly, they've had to deal with online bullies, who are posting anything from unflattering photos to online threats.

14　　　Privacy issues also are hitting home, most recently when students discovered that personal updates on their Facebook pages were being automatically forwarded to contacts they didn't necessarily want to have the information. Facebook was forced to let users turn off the data stream after they rebelled.

15　　　Increasingly, young people also are realizing that things they post on their profiles can come back to haunt them when applying for school or jobs.

16　　　"Maybe everything we thought was so great wasn't as great as we thought," says Tina Wells, the 20-something CEO of Buzz Marketing, a New York-based firm with young advisers all over the world.

17　　　She is among those who wonder if, sometimes, simple face-to-face communication might work better.

18　　　In many instances, says 27-year-old Veronica Gross, it does.

19　　　"By and large, I would say most of my very geeky social circle prefers face-to-face interaction to mere Internet communication," says Gross, an avid online gamer who is also a doctoral student studying neuroscience at Boston University.

20　　　She sees faceless communication as a supplement to everyday interactions, not a replacement. This sentiment also was the conclusion of a study done by the Pew Internet & American Life Project. The study, released earlier this year, found that Internet users tend to have a larger network of close and significant contacts—a median of 37 compared with 30 for nonusers.

21　　　Indeed, Steve Miller, a sophomore at Rollins College in Winter Park, Fla., says social networking can be an "extremely effective" way to publicize events to large groups—and even to help build a sense of community on campus.

22　　　He joined Facebook as a way to meet people before he started school, but also quickly learned that it had limitations, too.

23　　　"I discovered, after meeting many of these (online) friends, that a good Facebook profile could make even the most boring person somewhat interesting," says Miller, who's 19 and now a sophomore.

24　　　He's also not always thrilled with text messaging via cell phones, which can be a quick way to say "have a good day" or to coordinate a plan to meet up at a noisy concert.

25　　　"Text messaging has become the easy way out," Miller says.

26　　　He's had friends cancel a night out with a text message to avoid having to explain. He's also seen some people ask for dates via text to escape the humiliation of hearing a "no" on the phone or in person.

27　　　"Our generation needs to get over this fear of confrontation and rejection," he says.

28　　　The focus, he and others say, needs to be on quality communication, in all formats.

29　　　Back in Iowa, Henderson is enjoying spending more face-to-face time with his friends and less with his computer. He says his decision to quit MySpace and Facebook was a good one.

30　　"I'm not sacrificing friends," he says, "because if a picture, some basic information about their life and a Web page is all my friendship has become, then there was nothing to sacrifice to begin with."

New Words and Expressions

accumulate	v.	[əˈkjuːmjʊleɪt]	积聚，堆积
advocate	n.	[ˈædvəkeɪt; -ət]	提倡者，鼓吹者
avid	a.	[ˈævɪd]	热衷的，渴求的
ban	v.	[bæn]	禁止，取缔
blog	n.	[blɒg]	博客
bully	n.	[ˈbʊlɪ]	恶棍，暴徒
cancel	v.	[ˈkæns(ə)l]	取消，使无效
capability	n.	[keɪpəˈbɪlɪtɪ]	能力
cellphone	n.	[ˈselˈfəun]	蜂窝式便携无线电话，手机
confrontation	n.	[ˌkɒnfrʌnˈteɪʃn]	面对，对峙，对质
coordinate	v.	[kəʊˈɔːdɪneɪt]	（使）协调，调整
dominate	v.	[ˈdɒmɪneɪt]	支配，占优势
entail	v.	[ɪnˈteɪl; en-]	牵涉，需要
enthrall	v.	[ɪnˈθrɔːl]	迷住，吸引住
format	n.	[ˈfɔːmæt]	形式
forward	v.	[ˈfɔːwəd]	转寄
geeky	a.	[ˈgiːkɪ]	〈俚〉令人讨厌的
humiliation	n.	[ˌhjuːmɪlɪˈeɪʃn]	羞辱，蒙耻
interpersonal	a.	[ɪntəˈpɜːs(ə)n(ə)l]	人与人之间的
median	n.	[ˈmiːdɪən]	中间数值；中线
neuroscience	n.	[ˈnjuːrəʊsaɪəns]	神经科学
novelty	n.	[ˈnɒv(ə)ltɪ]	新奇，新颖
ongoing	a.	[ˈɒngəʊɪŋ]	正在进行的
pediatrics	n.	[ˌpiːdɪˈætrɪks]	[医]儿科
plug	n.	[plʌg]	插头，塞子
privacy	n.	[ˈprɪvəsɪ; ˈpraɪ-]	隐私
profile	n.	[ˈprəʊfaɪl]	简介，个性及生平的简要描述
publicize	v.	[ˈpʌblɪsaɪz]	宣扬
rebel	v.	[rɪˈbel]	反抗，造反
rejection	n.	[rɪˈdʒekʃ(ə)n]	拒绝
release	v.	[rɪˈliːs]	发布
sacrifice	v.	[ˈsækrɪfaɪs]	牺牲
sentiment	n.	[ˈsentɪm(ə)nt]	观点，情绪
significant	a.	[sɪgˈnɪfɪk(ə)nt]	相当数量的
sophisticated	a.	[səˈfɪstɪkeɪtɪd]	富有经验的，老练的

sophomore	n.	[ˈsɒfəmɔː]	大学二年级生
suicide	n.	[ˈs(j)uːɪsaɪd]	自杀
surf	v.	[sɜːf]	（网上）冲浪
survey	n.	[ˈsɜːveɪ]	调查
swap	v.	[swɒp]	交换
thrill	v.	[θrɪl]	使激动，使胆战心惊
unflattering	a.	[ʌnˈflæt(ə)rɪŋ]	不顺眼的，有损形象的
unthinkable	a.	[ʌnˈθɪŋkəb(ə)l]	不可想象的
update	n.	[ʌpˈdeɪt]	更新
wary	a.	[ˈweərɪ]	谨慎的，机警的
wired	a.	[ˈwaɪəd]	接有电线的

phase out		使逐步淘汰，逐渐停止
way out		摆脱困境的办法
wear off		逐渐减弱，磨损
in the meantime		在……期间，同时
get over		克服，熬过
hit home		打中要害，触及痛处
to begin with		首先，本来
meet up (with)		遇着，碰见

I. Give brief answers to the following questions.

1. What did Gabe Henderson do to find freedom?
2. What are ways for a social networking site to achieve the goal of expanding one's circle of online friends?
3. What does Bugeja often lecture students about "interpersonal intelligence"?
4. What is online bully?
5. What was the conclusion of the study done by the Pew Internet & American Life Project about social networking?
6. What is the opinion of Steve Miller towards social networking?

II. Complete the following passage by filling each of the numbered blanks with one or two suitable words using the Chinese in the brackets as the reference.

　　Of course, these forms of communication continue to ___1___（主导）. In the October issue of the journal Pediatrics, for instance, researchers at Stanford University ___2___（发布）findings from an ___3___（不间断的）study of students at an upper-middle income high school in the San Francisco area. One written ___4___（调查）found that the large ___5___（大多数）of students were members of at least one social networking site—81 percent of them on MySpace. They also found that 89 percent of those students had cell phones, most of them with text and ___6___（上网）capabilities.

　　They are more wired than ever—but they're also getting ___7___（更焦虑）. Increasingly, they've had to deal with online bullies(网络欺凌者), who are ___8___

（发布）anything from unflattering photos to online threats.

　　Privacy issues also are hitting home, most recently when students discovered that personal updates on their Facebook pages were being automatically ___9___ （转发）to contacts they didn't necessarily want to have the information. Facebook was forced to let users turn off the ___10___ （数据流）after they rebelled.

III. **Complete the following sentences with one function word or phrase.**
1. He's also phasing out his profile on Facebook, a popular social networking site that, like others, allows users to create profiles, swap message and share photos—all with _____ expanding their circle of online friends.
2. Henderson wrote in a column in the student newspaper at Iowa State University, _____ he studies history.
3. It seems we have lost, _____, that special depth that true friendship entails.
4. "True friends," he tells them, "need to learn when to stop blogging and _____ campus to help a friend."
5. In the October issue of the journal *Pediatrics*, _____, researchers at Stanford University released findings from an ongoing study of students at an upper-middle income high school in the San Francisco area.
6. "_____, I would say most of my very geeky social circle prefers face-to-face interaction to mere Internet communication," says Gross, an avid online gamer who is also a doctoral student studying neuroscience at Boston University.

IV. **Complete the following sentences by translating the Chinese given in the brackets.**
1. Allen is _____ （在准备期末考试期间,正逐渐停止在网上写作）. (phase out, in the meantime of)
2. At the beginning, he surfed on the Internet day and night chatting with new friends. However, _____ （当逐渐失去新鲜感）, he shut down the computer and talked to his friends face to face. (wear off)
3. He was in the hospital looking after his mother when _____ （噩耗传来）—his grandma passed away. (hit home)
4. One day, John was forced to go shopping with his annoying friend. When he was _____ （试图摆脱困境,他遇到了另外一个朋友）. (way out, meet up)
5. In front of strangers, the outgoing people always _____ （有开始交流的话题）. (begin with)
6. Once we begin to try something new, we have to _____ （克服害怕失败的心理）. (get over)

V. **Translate the following sentences into English.**
1. 他说,这是标志之一,说明高科技一代中的一些人开始正视提高面对面交流质量的重要性。
2. 对网络生活不再感到新奇后,他们也开始深入思考使用社交网络、短信和即时消息这些工具的用途,而不仅仅只是为了使用而使用。

29

3. 他指出，他看到一些学生从校园走过时一边在网上与别人聊着天，一边和重要的人握手。他还观察到，这类学生在咖啡店时，即使周围坐满人，也会死死盯着电脑屏幕。
4. 隐私问题也令人堪忧，特别是近来一些学生发现，他们在脸书网上更新的个人信息会自动转发给不必要的联系人。

VI. Translate the following passage into Chinese.

"I discovered, after meeting many of these (online) friends, that a good Facebook profile could make even the most boring person somewhat interesting," says Miller, who's 19 and now a sophomore.

He's also not always thrilled with text messaging via cell phones, which can be a quick way to say "have a good day" or to coordinate a plan to meet up at a noisy concert.

"Text messaging has become the easy way out," Miller says.

He's had friends cancel a night out with a text message to avoid having to explain. He's also seen some people ask for dates via text to escape the humiliation of hearing a "no" on the phone or in person.

"Our generation needs to get over this fear of confrontation and rejection," he says.

Reading B

How to Take Care of Your Digital Legacy and Online Assets: The Steps You Should Take Now to Help Your Survivors Preserve Your Online Assets

Chris Raymond
Dying, Funerals & Grief Expert

1   In 2011, an estimated（估计的）1.78 million Facebook users were expected to die worldwide, of which 480,000 called the U.S. home. While those figures are probably skewed（扭曲的）somewhat due to the purging（清除）of duplicate（副本）Facebook pages and the classification（分类）of accounts（账户）as inactive（不活跃）if the owner didn't log in（登陆）for 30 days, one thing is certain: Your online assets（财产）will be left in limbo（处于中间的或不定的状态）if you don't specify how you want your digital legacy（遗产）handled after you die.

2   This article details（详述）several steps you should take now to help your survivors（幸存者）access and protect your online assets later.

3   Who Owns Your Online Assets?

4   According to a 2011 survey by software-security company McAfee, Americans assess（评估）the average value of their digital assets at $55,000. These assets can include personal photos and home videos, legally downloaded movies and music, and user-generated software

files detailing everything from career information to genealogical（宗谱的，家系的）records, among numerous other media-file types.

5   Unfortunately, state and federal（联邦的）laws do not advance as quickly as the pace of technologic change. As of January 1, 2013, only five U.S. states have enacted（颁布法律）laws concerning the legal right of survivors to access a deceased（已故的）loved one's social media accounts, such as Facebook, Twitter, LinkedIn（商务化人际关系网）, Google + or Pinterest — not to mention（更不用说）a host of（许多的）other account types, such as email, banking, shopping, cloud storage, entertainment, gaming, etc..

6   In addition, the "fine print" that we typically ignore when creating a Facebook, Twitter, LinkedIn, Pinterest, Google +, and most other online accounts usually spell out（讲清楚）who may legally access your online account.

7   Generally, it is illegal for anyone but you, the account creator, to access your account — even with your express permission.

8   While lawmakers on the state and federal levels currently rush to address the legislative void and various contradictions created by estate law and privacy law, one thing is certain: You should take steps now to help your survivors access and protect your online assets later.

9   How to Protect Your Digital Legacy?

10   The first step you should take is to make a list of everything you access digitally or electronically. Obviously, this should include anything that has a real monetary（货币的）value, such as digital music, book and movie files that you purchased, as well as everything that holds significant emotional worth, such as your wedding video, family photos, important emails, etc..

11   In addition, include the name and URL of every online account you access, and a brief description of the service it provides, as well as the information someone would need to login to your account. In many cases, the purpose of the site will be obvious, such as Citibank or Chase, Facebook or Flickr, but your mortgage（抵押）company or cloud-storage provider might not be readily apparent to someone else. Remember, the purpose of compiling this list is that someone whom you designate（指定）can serve as the executor of your online assets, so don't assume anything will be "obvious" to him or her.

12   CAUTION: The list you have created contains highly confidential（机密的）information. Take every precaution to keep it secure in order to prevent theft, whether monetary or identity, and to prevent unauthorized（未被授权的）access.

13   Once you have compiled your digital-asset register from memory, update your list for at least one month (six months is better). The reason for this is that you will inevitably（不可避免地）experience "Oh yeah!" moments as you access some of your less-obvious digital accounts or assets that you didn't initially include on your list. For example, did you remember to list the account information for your Xbox or Wii console? How about the online payment site for your dentist, doctor or other infrequently visited providers? Does your register include the accounts you access solely via iPhone, Nook, Kindle, Surface, iPad, etc.?

14   Another reason you should refine your list for at least a month is to ensure you add the answers to any security questions you created to verify your login identities. We routinely answer these security prompts when they pop up（突然出现）, but, again, your list needs to make it easy for your digital executor to access your accounts and digital assets.

15   Once you believe your register is complete, the next step is to determine what you want done with each of your online accounts and/or digital assets. For example, which online accounts can/should just be closed? Which accounts should be transferred to someone else for the purpose of settling your estate, such as financial accounts? Do you want to appoint a new "curator" of your online family photograph repository(仓库) so new images can be added down the road? While the state and federal laws governing online accounts and digital assets are still developing, the more detail you provide concerning how you want things handled, the better.

16   And you should definitely put your wishes in writing. Even though the laws governing online assets are still developing on both the state and federal levels, the more explicitly you express your desires/intentions in writing, the greater the chance your digital executor will be able to process your digital assets and online accounts as you wish. A good estate-plan attorney (律师,代理人) should be able to help you.

17   Next, assign someone you trust to serve as your "digital executor." Yes, this might be somebody different than the individual you legally appoint as the main executor of your will — and it probably should be. Your digital executor needs to be both trustworthy(可靠的) and tech-savvy(懂行的人) so he or she understands not only how to access your digital assets but also why each is valuable and what to do with them.

18   Finally, reference your "online account/digital asset list" in your will, but do not include the actual list. The reason for this is that keeping them separate allows you to regularly update online account/digital asset passwords (which you should be doing), and assign different beneficiaries(受益人), without needing to pay your attorney to legally authorize this updated information.

I. Match the summaries on the left column to the seven parts of the article with the number of paragraphs on the right column.

A. The explanation of who will own the digital legacy.

B. The background of why we should handle digital legacy.

C. Brief introduction to the next step regarding to determining and writing your wishes about these digital assets.

D. The last step to take to protect your online assets.

E. The reasons why you should update your list for at least one month (six months is better).

F. The first step to take to help your survivors access and protect your online assets later.

G. The way to assign someone you trust to serve as your "digital executor."

1. (Paragraph 1)
2. (Paragraphs 2—7)
3. (Paragraphs 8—12)
4. (Paragraphs 13—14)
5. (Paragraphs 15—16)
6. (Paragraph 17)
7. (Paragraph 18)

II. Answer the following questions.

1. How many steps should be taken to help the survivors access and protect your online assets later?

2. Why should you update your list for at least one month?
3. Why should the list you have created be highly confidential?

III. **Questions for discussion.**
1. Do you think it is necessary to take these steps mentioned in this article to ensure the safety of your online assets?
2. What suggestions will you give to the government if you happen to have a chance to talk to them concerning the online assets problem?

Part Two
Tips for Translation

汉英语言差异

Warm-up

Compare the following English sentence with its Chinese version and discuss about the differences between the two.

The isolation of the rural area because of the distance and paucity of transport facilities was compounded by the lack of information media.

由于距离(城镇)远,缺乏交通工具,使得广大农村地区与外界隔绝。这种状况又由于缺乏信息媒介,变得更加糟糕。

进行汉英语言对比,了解两种语言之间的异同,对于掌握翻译技巧,提高翻译质量具有十分重要的意义。下面拟从语系、文字系统、语言性质、词汇和句子等方面对汉英两种语言的差异进行简单的介绍。

一、语系
汉语是世界上使用人口最多的语言,英语是世界上使用范围最广的语言。
汉语属于汉藏语系(Sino-Tibetan family)汉语族;英语属于印欧语系(Indo-European family)日耳曼族。不同语系说明了它们形成的社会文化历史背景不同,也决定了他们在词汇、语法、表达方式、语言习惯等各个方面必然存在着显著的差异。

二、文字系统
汉语属于表意(ideographic)文字,有四种造字法:象形字(如日,水),指事字(如上、下),会意字(如从,森)以及形声字(如汤、糖、躺、烫)。汉语有音,有义,有形,或者说汉语语言的形本身记载着重要的意义,是一种三维的语言。

英语属拼音(alphabetic)文字,有音,有义,但其形无任何意义,是一种二维的语言。英语的书写符号只有二十六个字母,表音符号是四十八个国际音标。

三、语言性质

汉语属于分析型语言，或者叫意合语言，重意形契合而不太注重形态或形式，不强调思维赋形于语言时必须恪守某种以动词形态为主轴的程式要求，句中的语法关系主要靠词序（如在"学习英语"这一短语中，"学习"为动词，而在"英语学习"中则为名词）和虚词（如"我去上海"，若变成完成时只需在"去"后加副词"过"即可）来实现。语言学家形象地把汉语比喻成竹子，层次分明，严密紧凑。

英语主要属于综合型语言，也叫形合语言，特别注重形态或形式，句中的语法关系主要靠词汇的屈折变化来实现（如 I study English，要变成过去式则需将 study 变成 studied；又如 I bought a book，要变成复数则需将 book 变为 books）。语言学家形象地将英语比喻成葡萄藤，主干突出（主语＋谓语＋宾语），枝叶茂盛（借助介词、连词、分词等连接手段层层搭架，环环相扣）。

四、词汇

1. 词性

英汉两种语言都有实词和虚词之分，都有名词、动词、形容词、副词、代词、数词、感叹词，只不过英语以名词、介词见长，汉语则以动词见长。英语有冠词，汉语没有；汉语有量词，英语没有。因此，在翻译时，应充分注意英汉语言在词性上的差别。

2. 词义

英汉语中的许多专有名词、术语以及一些日常生活中的事物是完全对等的，如 Homer（荷马），Sodium（钠），helicopter（直升飞机）等，但由于历史、地理、经济、文化、政治制度、社会习俗等的不同，两种语言反映客观事物的角度、方法有着很大的差别。有许多英汉词语在词义上只是部分对应，如英语中的 uncle 和汉语中的"叔父""伯父""姑父""姨父""舅父"。还有些英汉词语在概念意义上是对应的，但在内涵意义上却是不对应的，如汉语的"醋"有"妒忌"的内涵意义，而英语的 vinegar 则有"不高兴，坏脾气"的内涵意义。另外，因为文化的差异，有时英汉语中的某些词在对方的语言中有词义空缺现象，如汉语的"文房四宝"和英语中的 congressperson。英汉语中词义上的差异往往构成了翻译中的一大难点。

3. 词序

英汉语句子的主干结构基本上相同，但附属成分的排列却有很大不同，特别是定语、状语的排列。

就定语而言，英汉语中单词作定语一般均前置，但是，英语中短语作定语时以及某些固定词组中的定语按习惯却置于中心词后，在汉译英时应引起注意。

（1）有待讨论的事情 things to be discussed

（2）经济实用的方法 a method economical and practical

（3）（联合国）秘书长 secretary general (of the United Nations)

（4）当选的总统 the president elected

英汉两种语言的状语位置也有较大差异。如果出现一系列包含时间、地点和方式的状语时，汉语的习惯顺序是：时间、地点、方式；英语的习惯顺序是：方式、地点、时间。

此外，如果一个句子里出现两个以上的时间状语或地点状语，汉语一般是按照从大到小的顺序排列；而英语恰恰相反，习惯的顺序是从小到大。

（5）新闻发布会是昨天上午大约九点在 301 会议室召开的。

The news briefing was held in Room 301 at about nine o'clock yesterday morning.

此外，在汉语里，如果一个句子有两个较长的状语，通常是一起放在句中。英语则要考虑句子的平衡关系,常常是把两个状语分别放在句首和句尾,或分别放在句首和主语之后。

(6) 中国远洋运输公司成立于1961年4月,至今已有28年的历史。28年来,在国家的大力支持下,经过不懈的努力,公司业务和船舶数量迅速发展和增长。

Established in April 1961, the China Ocean Shipping Corporation has, in the past 28 years through arduous efforts, with the support from the state, expanded its shipping business and increased its number of ships.

五、句子

(一) 句子结构

英汉两种语言属不同语系,其表达方式不尽相同,也决定了其句子结构的不同。

1. 汉语多短句和分句,英语多长句和从句

在作为形合语言的英语中,长句和从句使用的频率很高,而对于作为意合语言的汉语来说,短句和分句则更为常见。

(1) 门口放着一堆雨伞,少说有十二把,五颜六色,大小不一。

In the doorway lay at least twelve umbrellas of all sizes and colors.

(2) 我们的目的是在加纳建立一个强大、进步的社会。在这里,贫困和文盲不再存在,疾病得到控制;在这里,我们的教育机构为加纳所有的孩子提供发展他们潜力的最好机会。

Our aim is to establish in Ghana a strong and progressive society where poverty and illiteracy no longer exist and disease is brought under control; and where our educational facilities provide all the children of Ghana with the best possible opportunities for the development of their potentialities.

2. 汉语多主动,英语多被动

英语句子被动语态用得多,特别是信息性和理论性的文体;汉语被动形式用得少,有时不用被动形式也可以表示被动的含义。

(1) 如果不小心,你就会淹死。

You will be drowned if you are not careful.

(2) 大战结束时,这个组织救了800人。

By the end of the war 800 people had been saved by the organization.

3. 汉语多后重心,英语多前重心

英汉句子结构上的差异还表现为句子重心的不同。如果句子里既有叙事的部分,又有表态的部分,汉语的表达习惯往往是叙事在前,表态在后;在英语里则往往相反,表态在前,叙事在后。

(1) 双方有不同的看法不足为奇。

There is nothing surprising about the two sides having different opinions.

(2) 我原打算一月份访问中国,后来不得不推迟,这使我非常失望。

It was a keen disappointment that I had to postpone the visit which I had intended to pay to China in January.

(二) 句序

这里的句序指的是复合句中主句和从句的顺序。英汉语复合句中主句和从句之间的时间顺序和逻辑顺序不完全相同,因此它们的先后位置也不完全一样。

总的来说，英语复合句叙述顺序很灵活，一般从句可以在主句之前，也可以在主句之后，不要求按时间顺序或逻辑顺序排列。汉语则习惯于按照时间和逻辑顺序排列句子，先发生的先说，先因后果，先条件后结果。

(1) 我吃了晚饭后，出去散步。

After I had my dinner, I went out for a walk. / I went out for a walk after I had my dinner.

(2) 由于天气很好，我们决定去爬山。

As the weather was fine, we decided to climb the mountain. / We decided to climb the mountain as the weather was fine.

练习

比较下列汉语句子及其英语译文，说明每组句子分别主要反映了汉语和英语哪一方面的差异。

1. 据目击者说，凶手共开了三枪，肯尼迪显然是被第一枪击中的。

   Mr. Kennedy apparently was hit by the first of what witness believed were three shots.

2. 大夫们已经试过各种可能的办法了。

   The doctors have tried every way possible.

3. 要在这样的基础上实行改革，不是件容易的事。

   It is no easy task to try to carry out reforms on this kind of a basis.

4. 因此，我们同中国建立建设性的关系是非常重要的。

   Therefore, it is very important that we establish a constructive relationship with China.

5. 如果有人敢于预言此事的结果，那他一定是个鲁莽之徒。

   He would be a rash man if he should venture to forecast the results of this event.

6. 人们常说，电视使人了解时事，熟悉政治、科学领域的最新发展变化，并能源源不断地为观众提供各种既有教育意义又有趣的节目。

Television, it is often said, keeps one informed about current events, allows one to follow the latest developments in science and politics, and offers an endless series of programs which are both instructive and entertaining.

Part Three
Simulated Writing

Instruction Manual

产品使用说明书一般随产品交付用户，以便用户正确安装和使用产品，成为沟通产需双方的桥梁和工具。产品使用说明书因产品的不同而稍有差异，下面是软件产品使用说明书的一般结构，其他产品使用说明书应包括的内容也大同小异：

1. Introduction 产品概述（介绍产品的用途/适用范围、流程、使用惯例和术语）

Introduce the product to the user. Outline its scope/purpose, flow, conventions and glossary.

2. Installing the software 安装（声明系统要求、平台支持、安装过程中的信息和资源要求、安装步骤等）

Declare system requirements, platform support, information/resources required in the process of installation and installation steps.

At this point there is usually a decision to be made about how to depict installation procedures for different platforms. The main criterion here is how different the procedures are—if the steps are drastically different, you will have to explain the procedure separately for each platform. But if the steps are not very different, you could choose the most common platform as your base, and wherever the steps are different, indicate the steps for the different platforms as indented text.

3. Using the software 软件使用（目的、执行任务、调用方法、界面元件、任务执行的步骤等）

Introduce purpose of the software, what it does and does not do (list the exact tasks), invoking the software, interface elements and steps to perform the required tasks.

4. Administration 管理（重申并解释管理层面任务，分为管理、维护和故障修理功能）

Reiterate the administration level tasks. Segregate (if possible) into administration, maintenance and troubleshooting functions, and then get into explanations.

5. Troubleshooting 故障检修（显示器错误及含义、操作步骤、校正错误的步骤等）

For each error condition describe what happens on the display, what the error message displayed means and what is the implication with respect to the attempted action (for example, the user will have to re-enter information), and finally, steps to take to rectify the error.

6. Appendix 附录（外围信息、图表、流程图、相关软件的信息或指南等）

An appendix allows you to expound on peripheral information that would be detracting when given in the main body. Detailed diagrams, flow charts, or references to books/tutorials on related software could be included here.

产品使用说明书要简单易懂、条理清楚、语言平实。编写的时候要多用祈使句或主动句，句子简短，要用直接的、为大众所熟知的语言。编写的时候要考虑回答用户的问题：

- When, why, and how to perform a task.
- What the screen will show after performing a task.
- Examples of tasks and program operation.

因此产品使用说明书的编写过程应包括下列几点：

1. Listing the major tasks.
2. Breaking each major task into subtasks.
3. Leading the user through each subtask in a series of steps.
4. Using an "if-then" approach in explaining decisions that users can make.

USEFUL EXPRESSIONS AND PATTERNS:

1 Introduction
- This manual primarily describes precautions required in installing and operating...
- Only qualified persons trained in professional electrical procedures can be allowed to handle ...

- Before operating..., read this manual through to acquire sufficient knowledge of the Controller.
- Please read this instruction MANUAL and thoroughly familiarize yourself with the functions and characteristics of the product before use.
- ... is a ... that offers a host of advanced features amateur photographers and professionals alike will appreciate.
- It is designed to ...
- ... can regulate the room temperature, dry the room. It is convenient for your work, study and life. It can be widely used in residence, shop, hotel, office, library and laboratory, and so on.
- The following safety warning labels appear on the covers:
- The material in this manual is for information purposes only, and is subject to change without notice
- This warranty covers instruments and parts sold to end users by authorized distributors, dealers, and representatives of RKI Instruments.
- ... is built for rugged reliability and ease of use and includes the latest innovations in...
- When using..., you must follow the instructions and warnings in this manual to assure proper and safe operation of the unit and to minimize the risk of personal injury.
- Be sure to maintain and periodically calibrate... as described in this manual.

2 Installation & Administration

- Use the following to...
- ...are used for....
- Properly apply... Applying an inappropriate... or ... will cause... to fail.
- Be sure/certain/cautious (not) to...
- ...is so valuable and the improper installation of it will cause a lot of damage! Please associate the professional technician to install the unit and don't install it by yourself. Otherwise, we are not responsible for the damage like this.
- Before installation, check that the voltage of the electric supply in your home of office is the same as the voltage shown on the name plate.
- To open the battery case, press on the two tabs on the upper rear of the case then pull the two halves apart.
- Remove... from, then remove...
- To install the batteries, first ... by turning it counterclockwise, with a coin or something similar, until it can be freely removed by hand.
- Then, ...making sure that their respective plus (+) and minus (−) indications correspond with similar marks provided in the clip.
- After seating the batteries correctly, replace the lid, and secure the connection by turning it clockwise with the coin as far as it will go.
- It is advisable to remove the batteries.
- Select a location accessible to...and supply where the floor is level.
- Check... to make sure that it is closed/on/off.

Unit Two

3. Operation
   - Turn on... and check... for...
   - Slowly turn the pressure adjustment knob clockwise to set the pressure (gauge pressure) to 0.05 MPa. Then press the red stopper to lock the knob in position.
   - Operate dilution N2 selector valve, located on the side face of pump cover, in accord with the dilution N2 mode setting of dipswitch.
   - Disconnect... from the power supply before starting wiring. Devices connected to... may operate unexpectedly.
   - Before closing the switch to allow electric current to flow to the heater, make certain that... and that...
   - The... are preset to the... setting to provide a water temperature of approximately to reduce the risk of scald injury.
   - Complete failure of the heating elements will result if they are not totally immersed in water at all times.

4. Maintenance
   - Shut off the electric power whenever the water supply is turned off.
   - Shut off the electric power, water supply and drain the heater completely to prevent... whenever the building is left unoccupied during the cold weather months.
   - Check ...regularly to insure that... has not become...

5. Caution and Warning
   - Be certain/sure that... does not result in bodily injury or property damage.
   - Serious injury may possibly occur due to loss of required safety functions.
   - Wire... properly so that... do NOT touch the outputs accidentally or unintentionally.
   - Perform user testing and confirm that... configuration data and operation is correct before starting system operation.
   - Increasing the thermostat setting above the preset temperature may cause severe burns and consume excessive energy.
   - When water passes through the faucets, close them and check for possible leaks in the system.
   - Do not use or store or touch... in any of the following locations:
   - Take appropriate and sufficient measures when installing systems in the following locations. Inappropriate and insufficient measures may result in malfunction.
   - It may cause... interference, in which case the user may be required to take adequate measures to reduce interference.
   - Indicates information that, if not followed, could result in relatively serious or minor injury, property damage, or faulty operation.
   - Minor injury due to explosion may occasionally occur.
   - Serious injury may occasionally occur due to..., or.... Never attempt to...
   - Install the Time Switch only by qualified electrical workers.
   - The plug must be accessible after the appliance is positioned.

- Always wait at least 3 minutes before switching the air condition on again after you have switched it off during cooling.

6   Appendix

⚡	●Warning against electric shock Notification of possible electric shock under certain conditions.
🚫	●General warning Notification of general, unspecified prohibition items.
🚫	●Prohibition against disassembly Notification of disassembly of products, when doing so can cause possible electric shock.
❗	●General warning Notification of general, unspecified actions that users must perform.
💥	●Warning against rupture Notification of possible rupture under certain conditions.

Sample Reading

Electric Water Heater Installing and Operating Instructions

Location

Select a location accessible to water lines and power supply where the floor is level. The heater must be located in an area where leakage of the tank or connections will not result in damage to the area adjacent to the heater or to lower floors of the structure.

Installation

The hot water outlet and cold water inlet are identified on the back panel of the heater. Remove the porcelain top by sliding it toward and lifting it off the cabinet. Remove the four front panel screws. Check drain valve to make sure that it is closed. Part the top fiberglass insulation to allow access to the plumbing and electrical connections. Connect the cold water supply line and hot water outlet lines using elbows, nipples and unions as shown in the diagrams. Install a shutoff valve in the cold water inlet. Install a listed temperature-pressure relief valve in the remaining fitting.

Caution

After the installation of all water lines, open the main water supply valve and fill the heater. Open several hot water faucets to allow air to escape from the system while the heater is filling. When water passes through the faucets, close them and check for possible leaks in the system.

Electrical Connections

Before any electrical connections are made, be sure that the heater is full of water and that the valve in the cold water supply line is open. Check the rating plate and wiring diagram before proceeding. The heater must be well grounded. A green ground screw is provided at the electrical connection point for connecting a ground wire.

Operation

Before closing the switch to allow electric current to flow to the heater, make certain that the heater is full of water and that the cold water inlet valve is open. Complete failure of the heating elements will result if they are not totally immersed in water at all times. When the switch is closed, the operation of this electric water heater is automatic. The thermostats are preset to the "HOT" setting to provide a water temperature of approximately 120°F to reduce the risk of scald injury.

Caution

Increasing the thermostat setting above the preset temperature may cause severe burns and consume excessive energy. Hotter water increases the risk of scald injury.

Maintenance

Shut off the electric power whenever the water supply is turned off.

Shut off the electric power, water supply and drain the heater completely to prevent freezing whenever the building is left unoccupied during the cold weather months.

Check the temperature-pressure relief valve regularly to insure that the valve has not become incrusted with lime.

Safety Warning

Be certain that any released water does not result in bodily injury or property damage.

Service

The temperature limiting devices on this heater will cut off all power to heater if temperature of water exceeds 190°F. If there is no hot water after a reasonable period of time, check the main fuse box. In the event that the fuses have not blown, call a serviceman; have him check the entire circuit including the elements and thermostats before resetting the temperature limiting device. Consult the plumber or electric service company in your area for all service. Replacement parts or any questions you might have regarding this heater, insist on factory inspected and approved replacement parts. Contact manufacturer listed on rating plate[6] for replacement information.

Notes

drain valve 排水阀
ground wire 地线,避雷线
scald injury 烫伤

relief valve 安全阀
fuse box 保险丝盒
rating plate 定额牌,标牌

Check Your Understanding

Answer the following questions according to the above instruction manual.

1. Where should the heater be located?
2. When the machine is installed, in what position should the drain valve be?

3. What should we use to connect the cold water supply line and hot water outlet lines?
4. What should we do after the installation of all water lines?
5. What is the consequence if we increase the thermostat setting above the preset temperature?
6. Who should we refer to if we need replacement parts?

Follow-up Writing

The following is part of a digital camera instruction manual. Complete it with the information given below.

Starting the software
For Windows:
*_____1_____.（打开电脑开始视窗程序）
*Select "Start"—"Programs (P)"—"Dimage Image Viewer Utility", double click "Dimage Image Viewer Utility"
*_____2_____.（主应用视窗出现）
For Macintosh:
*Turn on your Macintosh to start Mac OS
*_____3_____.（打开你安装应用程序的文件夹）(the folder that you selected or created during the software installation), and open the "Dimage Image Viewer Utility" folder in the same way.
*_____4_____.（双击"Dimage Image Viewer Utility"应用软件图标）
*The main window of the Utility appears.
Operating the software
*Set the CF card to the digital camera according to the digital camera's instructions. _____5_____（将数码相机设置为电脑连接模式）, and then connect it to your computer using the USB cable.
*_____6_____.（开始"Dimage Image Viewer Utility"应用软件）
*Click the "Load All Image" button of the main window.
*_____7_____（选择保存图像文件的文件夹）and then click select.
*_____8_____.（可以阅读选择的图像文件）

Unit Two

Part Four
Listening

Lead-in

I. Discuss the following topics with your classmates.

1. Do you know something about social networking? If yes, say something about it.
2. Which kind of communication do you prefer? Face-to-face communication or online communication? Why?

II. Study the following vocabulary before you listen.

terrorism	恐怖主义
Homeland Security Secretary	国土安全部长
phase	阶段
ABC News	美国广播公司
self-declared	自称的，自命的
Islamic State	伊斯兰国家
launch	发动（战争等），实施（措施、调查等）
reach out	联系
recruit	招募
open fire on...	朝……开火
Curtis Culwell Center	德州加兰柯蒂斯展演中心
Garland	加兰（美国城市）
Texas	美国德克萨斯州
Prophet Muhammad	先知穆罕默德
vigilant	警惕的
Federal Bureau of Investigation	（美）联邦调查局
disrespectful	无礼的，失礼的
Minneapolis	明尼阿波里斯市(美国城市)
counter	反对
militant	激进分子
gone viral	像病毒般迅速扩散

While-listening

I. Listen to the recording and supply the missing words.

A top Obama administration official says the fight against __1__ has entered what he calls a new __2__. Homeland Security Secretary Jeh Johnson spoke to ABC News on Sunday. He said groups like the __3__ Islamic State are successfully using social media to interest new members or to __4__ attacks in the United States. His comments followed reports that federal law enforcement officials have __5__ hundreds of investigations to identify likely __6__ nationwide. Mr. Johnson says the terrorist threat has changed because of the successful use of social media by the Islamic State. He says the group has shown the ability to __7__ and __8__ members in the United States.

Police shot and killed two gunmen.	Police shot and killed two gunmen after they __9__ a security officer outside Curtis Culwell Center in Garland, Texas, Monday, May 4, 2015. The center was hosting a __10__ for Prophet Muhammad cartoons. "Because of the use of the Internet, we could have little, or no, notice in advance of an independent actor (attacker) attempting to __11__ . And so that's why law enforcement at the local level needs to be ever more __12__ , and we're constantly reminding them to do that." Mr. Johnson says federal, state and local law enforcement officials are cooperating more closely now than they were before the terrorist attacks of September 11, 2001.
There might be thousands of Islamic State followers online in the United States.	Last week, the head of the Federal Bureau of Investigation warned there might be thousands of Islamic State followers __13__ in the United States. FBI Director James Comey said it is not easy to know who among them is a threat. Earlier this month, two gunmen attacked what has been called a "free speech" event in Garland, Texas. The event's organizers offered a $10,000 prize for the best cartoon of Islam's Prophet Mohammad. For Muslims, any image of the Prophet is considered __14__ . The gunmen were killed in an exchange of gunfire with police. Mr. Comey said the FBI had warned the Garland police to __15__ the two men hours before the attack.
Federal officials are fighting social media recruitment efforts.	Secretary Johnson says federal officials are fighting social media recruitment efforts by talking to members of the Muslim community in the United States. "Since I've been secretary, I have personally participated in __16__ with community leaders in the Islamic community and elsewhere. I've been to New York, Boston, Minneapolis, Chicago, Los Angeles and other places where I personally meet with community leaders about __17__ violent extremism in their communities. That has to be part of our efforts in this new phase." Mr. Johnson admits the Islamic State seems to be effective in its communications. He says Muslim communities must help federal, state and local officials fight the recruiting efforts. "It has to come from Islamic leaders who, __18__ , can talk the language better than the federal government can and so, when I meet with community leaders, Islamic leaders, it's one of the things we __19__ them to do. Some have begun it. We've seen some good __20__ , but there's a lot more than can be done."

Terrorism has gone viral.	Mr. Johnson supported the decision by U.S. military officials to increase __21__ at bases across the country. The FBI had warned that Islamist __22__ could attack troops or local police. Michael McCaul is the chairman of the House Homeland Security Committee. He told Fox News on Sunday there had been an increase in threats __23__ local police and military bases in the US. "We're seeing these on an almost daily basis. It's very __24__. I'm over here with the French counter-terrorism experts on the *Charlie Hebdo* case (trying to learn) how we can stop foreign fighters coming out of Iraq and Syria to Europe. But then, we have this __25__ in the United States where they (terrorists) can be activated by the Internet. And, really, terrorism has __26__."
The possible threat from terrorism is worse than the FBI has said it is.	Representative McCaul says the possible threat from terrorism is __27__ than the FBI has said it is. He says the United States faces two threats: one from fighters leaving the Middle East, and the other from thousands __28__ the country who will __29__ when the Islamic State sends a message on the Internet. He warns that __30__ from the terrorists will increase because of the many failed states in the Middle East and North Africa.

II. **Listen again, stop the recording as necessary, and repeat after the speaker.**

Post-listening

Surf the Internet and find more information about the following topic areas. Then prepare a 15-minute oral presentation and deliver it in the class. While preparing the presentation you need to narrow down the topic area and focus on one major point.
1. We-chat communication
2. Argument on whether we should post our inner sound on the Internet

Part Five
Speaking

Job Hunt and Interview

Sample Dialogue 1

Interviewer: I've just looked over your resume and I must admit I am quite impressed.
Interviewee: Thank you. I've worked pretty hard to be able to list those accomplishments.
Interviewer: You've got plenty of training and experience. I wonder if you could tell me something about your goals. Where do you see yourself ten years from now?

Interviewee:	To be honest, I don't plan in that much detail. My goals tend to be general; I define success according to the job at hand. I see myself advancing as I succeed, but I don't necessarily dwell on the timing of each step.
Interviewer:	Interesting! And how do you feel about decision-making? Are you an independent thinker, or do you depend more on your superior for direction?
Interviewee:	That depends a bit on the problem at hand. There are certain situations in which a manager can give a general directive, and expect his employees to know how to take the initiative on the details. I am known for taking the initiative, but I believe I also have the discernment to wait for direction when the situation calls for that.
Interviewer:	Sounds good. Everyone is talking about teams these days. Can you describe your role as a member of a sales team?
Interviewee:	I see myself as an encourager. Of course, sales can be quite competitive and sometimes people in this field have a secret desire for others to fail. In my last job, each representative handled a different region. I developed a system for sharing sales gimmicks that worked. Soon the whole sales team started saving up stories, not just to brag, but to share.
Interviewer:	So, your experience is as impressive in practice as it is on paper.

Sample Dialogue 2

Interviewer:	From reviewing your resume I can see that you have ample experience for this position. What I want to know is why you think you're right for the job.
Interviewee:	Well, I'm impressed with what the company has done in the past and I think by hiring me the company's future can only be brighter. I find that my personal goals and ideas about business operations match perfectly with this company's goals and mission statement.
Interviewer:	So you've acquainted yourself with the company. It's refreshing to interview someone who's sure of what they want.
Interviewee:	Yes, I believe that it's crucial for me to know if a company is right for me, not just if I'm right for the company. I've only been impressed by what I've read and heard and I see myself having a very rewarding and successful career here.
Interviewer:	Commitment to the company and the team is very important to us here.
Interviewee:	Well, I'm definitely a team player as well as being highly self-motivated. I believe this company can fulfill my long-term goals and offer me great upward mobility. Therefore you will find in me a very loyal employee.

Notes

look over	察看	save up	储存起来
dwell on	老是想着	mission statement	使命宣言
decision-making	决策	team player	有团队精神的人，合作意识强的人

Unit Two

general directive   大致的指示   self-motivated   自我激励的
take the initiative   采取主动   upward mobility   晋升

USEFUL EXPRESSIONS AND PATTERNS:

1. I have come here for an interview by appointment, nice to meet you.
2. Did you have any difficulty finding our company?
3. I wanted challenges in my career.
4. When I read your ad., I said to myself that this is the one opportunity I shouldn't pass up. I'm very enthusiastic about the job.
5. It's always a challenge to find a job. I will work at it and believe that ultimately I'll succeed.
6. What do you think is your biggest weakness?
7. Maybe I'm too aggressive for a Chinese. But that will be a big plus when I develop more maturity.
8. I am learning every day in every way.
9. What salary would you expect to get?
10. I would expect the standard rate of pay at your company for a person with my experience and educational background.
11. I'm cheerful when challenged.
12. You're high on my list.
13. We require the applicant to have some experience in advertising projects and a good knowledge of English.
14. I've been working at an advertising company for over two years now.
15. Would you please tell me a bit about yourself?
16. I am a graduate of a technical university and have been employed as a technician with IBM for approximately 10 years.
17. Please explain why you are interested in leaving your current position and please elaborate on your technical skills.
18. I am looking for a growth opportunity, which I feel is not available at my current employer. In terms of skills, I am Microsoft certified in Windows XP and several other operating systems.
19. Where do you see yourself five years from now?
20. I see myself in a management position.
21. I can see from your resume you were in charge of sales for Corporate World Unlimited from 2005 to 2008. Can you please tell me about your responsibilities?
22. I was in charge of profit and loss for the northwest region of Canada. As a manager, I was directly responsible for a 50% increase in sales over a four-month period.
23. What, do you believe, are some of the key attributes that helped you to achieve such an outstanding increase in sales?
24. I believe persistence and perseverance are key attributes.

25. Can you tell me what training you have had that would specifically relate to the cable television Industry?
26. I've attended some conferences in this field. But the most relevant training I've had was in computer design. I believe I could integrate that knowledge with my college degree to design a program for your company.

I. Role-play the sample dialogues.

II. Match the following two columns.

1. 采取主动   A. team player
2. 使命宣言   B. general directive
3. 有团队精神的人，合作意识强的人   C. self-motivated
4. 自我激励   D. decision-making
5. 晋升   E. upward mobility
6. 大致的指示   F. take the initiative
7. 决策   G. look over
8. 储存起来   H. mission statement
9. 察看   I. save up

III. Read through this outline of the responses of three applicants to the same questions asked of them in an interview. Consider their answers carefully.

Q: *Good morning, my name is Ms Martin. You've applied for the Laboratory Assistant's position right?*

A. Yes.

B. Yes, Ms Martin, I have.

C. Yes, Ms Martin. When I saw it advertised I thought it would really suit me.

Q: *Can you tell me why you replied to our advertisement?*

A. I ... I'm not really sure ... ahh ...

B. Well, I've always enjoyed science and felt that this position would offer me an opportunity to extend my skills in this area.

C. I think that I'd be really good at this kind of work. In fact I learn so fast that I'd be looking for promotion very shortly.

Q: *Do you know exactly what you would be doing as a Laboratory Assistant?*

A. Well, I don't really know for sure, but I think it's got something to do with helping out the scientists in the laboratory, hasn't it?

B. A Laboratory Assistant helps to maintain scientific equipment, keeping a check on the supplies in the store, and preparing the chemicals for experiments.

C. Oh, a Lab. Assistant helps make sure that all the experiments are done properly.

Unit Two

Q: *What sort of student do you regard yourself as ... did you enjoy studying while you were at school?*
  A. I wasn't the best student. I didn't really like study all that much, but I did it when I had to.
  B. I suppose I'm a reasonable student. I passed all my tests and enjoyed studying subjects that interested me.
  C. I'm a really great student. I didn't have to study much because I always seemed to get by without worrying too much about it.

Q: *What were your favorite subjects at school?*
  A. I liked Science—it was O.K. . . well, at least the bits I understood were O.K.
  B. Maths and Science were my favorite subjects at school. I also enjoyed doing History.
  C. I'm afraid that I only liked the ones I was good at. The others were so boring that I found them to be a thorough waste of my time.

Q: *Do you have any further plans for further study?*
  A. I hadn't really thought much about it . . .I don't know what courses I could do.
  B. Well, I've thought about doing the part-time Chemistry Certificate course at Technical College. I think I would really benefit from doing that.
  C. Well, if I had to do it I suppose I would, but now I've finished school I'd much rather try to get my social life back into full swing again.

Q: *Suppose our company wanted you to attend an institution to further your skills, how would you feel about this?*
  A. Attend a what?
  B. If the course would help me improve my prospects for promotion and help me to be better at my job I would definitely do it.
  C. Attend a course? When? I hope it would be in the day time? Would I get time off from work to attend it? I hope it's not at night—my social life would be ruined.

Q: *Have you ever had a job before?*
  A. No I haven't. I've never really been game enough to get one.
  B. Yes. I have worked part-time at a take away food store—the one just round the corner. . .
  C. No. I've really been too busy, what with all the study I've had to do to get a good result. . .

Q: *We have a lot of other applicants for this position. Why do you think that you deserve to get the job?*
  A. I can't think of any special reason—I suppose I'm no different from most other people.
  B. Well, I've found out a lot about this type of work and my research suggests that I would be quite capable of doing the work involved. I also think that I would be able to handle any training course reasonably well.

C. I reckon I'd probably be the best applicant you're likely to get for the job.

Q: *Now, do you have any questions you'd like to ask me about the position?*
   A. No thank you. I don't think so.
   B. Yes. Ms Martin, could you tell me what hours I'd have to work, and for whom I'd be working?
   C. Yes... What's the pay like?

Q: *I think I have asked you everything I wanted to. Thank you for coming along to the interview.*
   A. Thank you Ms Martin. Goodbye.
   B. Thank you. When will I know if I am successful?
   C. Oh, think nothing of it... Could I see where I'll be working?

Questions

For each applicant, choose three words/phrases from the list below, which best describes their answers to the interviewer's questions.

has done some research; confident and prepared; ill-prepared; unsure; arrogant; hesitant; doubts ability to cope; lazy; not interested in the job; an upstart (presumptuous); modest but sure of him/ herself; adequate; pushy; polite; rude; interested; keen; under confident; energetic; has good study habits; has sound attitude to study.

1. Applicant A _____ _____ _____
2. Applicant B _____ _____ _____
3. Applicant C _____ _____ _____
4. Which applicant do you think would be successful? Why?

IV. Learn to communicate in the situation given below.

Interviewer: a personnel manager from Smith and Sons Company.
Candidate: an experienced applicant applying for a job at Smith and Sons Company.
A and B are having a job interview.
The following points can be referred to in your conversation:
- financial consultant
- entry level (beginning) position
- a full-time or part-time position
- greatest strength
- work well under pressure

Unit Three

Work

Part One
Reading and Translating

Lead-in

Work efficiency in the office is very important. Here are some tips for you to maintain efficiency in the office.

- Write your daily schedule. A list makes it impossible to forget tasks.
- Filter your e-mails. Learn to discard unimportant e-mails, not only spam. Set your priorities straight.
- Don't check your personal e-mail in the morning. It's so nice to waste time reading all the jokes, interesting articles and videos sent by your friends... till you realize you have lost about an hour... Do it during the break to relax a little. And answer to all those messages after finishing the program.
- Ignore sites with jokes, sport news and blogs. They only serve to make you waste some more precious time.
- Limit the duration of personal phone calls while at work. Telling your friend what you did yesterday after you got home from work is definitely not an emergency.
- Always keep a bottle of water on your desk. If every 30 minutes you go get some water, there's the risk of starting some long "discussions" around the same habit of yours: never wasting any change of killing time.
- If you have to ask something or talk with your colleagues, establish short breaks for this. If all the time you interrupt your work to ask, laugh, talk with the others... at the end of the day you'll realize you haven't worked at all.
- Use your headphones. This way, you'll be "immune" to all the background noise made by typing, phones ringing, printers. Since songs with too many lyrics can distract your attention, jazz or chill out music genres are recommended.
- Close programs you do not use: many open applications will make searching for those you need at a certain moment much more difficult, plus: they eat a lot of RAM, which slows down your computer.
- You may get bored of doing the same long tasks. Work for one hour on a certain task, then continue with another, especially if you have no urgent task to finish.

Reading A

How Rumor and Gossip Oil the Wheels of Office Life

Naomi Shragai

1   Gossip and rumor are part of the fabric of working life — they entertain, inform and connect people, but they can also ruin reputations, destroy trust, create bad attitudes and even reduce productivity.

2   What distinguishes the helpful consequences from the harmful is the intention behind what is said, how the information is perceived and acted on, and the length of time it is allowed to spread and fester.

3   As well as providing informal communication networks, gossip and rumor act as psychological spaces for perceived unfairness and power imbalances, or emotions such as jealousy, resentment, boredom and even hatred. When it is not possible to confront an issue or person directly, chats with colleagues become a way of offloading frustrations. People's anxieties heighten at times of change and uncertainty, such as when an organization restructures, changes leadership or undertakes a merger or acquisition.

4   Such situations lead people to worry about how they will be affected. Who will be promoted or demoted, whose job will disappear or be changed, and who will be paid what?

5   In the absence of adequate information from management, people naturally create narratives to fill the void. The longer executives take to make decisions, the more anxious people become and the more rumors fill the vacuum and make sense of the uncertainty.

6   Nicholas DiFonzo, professor of psychology at Rochester Institute of Technology and co-author of *Rumor Psychology*, says, "The common denominator seems to be fear — we're afraid of what this person in the organization will do to us; we're afraid of how the engineering department is going to get more money and we in marketing are going to get less money; we're afraid of what this rival company is doing — and so we spread rumors about them."

7   Spreading negative rumors can make us feel better in the short term, but means we are less likely to take responsibility for either our predicament or obtaining the information we need from the powers that be.

8   Professor DiFonzo nevertheless believes organizations could not survive without informal information spread by word of mouth. "There's a wealth of information that is not in the procedural manual and nobody is going to write it down," he says.

9   "It's the kind of information you have to hear through the grapevine: what the organizational norms are, who you should approach and who you should not approach, and who gets paid what, the kind of information that is often secret." Studies have shown that while rumors reduce trust in management and harm the attitudes of staff, they do not necessarily affect productivity.

10   Prof DiFonzo explains, "If I hear rumors about my company being downsized and the

management won't talk to me, there's a great deal of uncertainty. I may feel worse about the management, I may trust them less, but I may work harder so that if there is a downsizing I will be retained."

11   A senior executive of a large UK technology company, however, found that rumors left unchecked affected sales when disparaging stories spread about a product, resulting in staff being reluctant to sell it.

12   "When rumors spread across the sales teams that a product doesn't work or is difficult to implement, there may be an element of truth in them. But often the rumor is exaggerated and means that no one wants to deal with it... and so sales decrease."

13   Although rumors often hold some truth, people's interpretation of events tends to avoid complexity and personal responsibility, and is often directed towards an individual, a department or an outside rival.

14   Mannie Sher, director of the group relations program at the Tavistock Institute and adviser to companies and organizations, believes rumors are often a larger systemic phenomenon that often targets an individual. He says, "Rumors are about 'an individual who acted badly' because individualizing a systemic problem is easier than to say to an organization, 'we have a problem which as a team we have to resolve'."

15   "Very often the route taken is to identify an individual who may have acted badly, and for the group to use him to project the group's incompetence. We can say the CEO is a control freak and it's because of him that we're in this mess."

16   Gossip, as opposed to rumor, is often about social networking and bonding and can be entertaining, irresistible and even witty. Because it is so pleasurable, people tend not to consider the harm it causes.

17   Although positive gossip occurs, it is the negative gossip most people enjoy more because it makes us feel better about ourselves and reassures us, because we are not the subject of it.

18   There are many motives for malicious gossip. Projecting our own feelings of inadequacy on others by putting them down rids us of our bad feelings and makes us feel superior. Gossip allows us to retaliate against perceived unfairness, act out passive-aggressive and envious feelings and redress power imbalances. People revert to gossip when they believe they cannot confront an issue directly.

19   There is cachet to be gained from it. The office gossip gains influence as he or she collects valuable information while also creating a wealth of contacts. "In" and "out" groups then form around those "in the know" and those not.

20   A woman who came to me for psychotherapy related how a colleague who was also a friend denied she was having an affair with the boss despite overwhelming evidence to the contrary.

21   The betrayal she felt was aggravated by feelings of unfairness, powerlessness and distrust because of privileges her colleague was enjoying as a result.

22   Because she could not confront either party directly, she joined in the office gossip to clear her confusion, but primarily to have an outlet for her feelings.

23   "I had my head messed up when she told me it wasn't happening and I wanted to know what evidence people had, which was pretty compelling," she says. "When it's the boss, it is not bad behavior that you can confront." Joining in the gossip eventually left her feeling even worse

when she was verbally attacked for spreading the news by a colleague who did not believe it.

24   There is a positive element to gossip, though. It acts as a safety valve for grievances, allowing pent-up feelings to be released in a way that minimizes potential damage. Rushing to a quiet corner with a colleague for a whispered rant is preferable to a flare-up with your boss.

New Words and Expressions

acquisition	n.	[ˌækwɪˈzɪʃ(ə)n]	收购
aggravate	v.	[ˈægrəveɪt]	使加重,使恶化
aggressive	a.	[əˈgresɪv]	好斗的,侵略性的
betrayal	n.	[bɪˈtreɪəl]	背叛
boredom	n.	[ˈbɔːdəm]	厌倦
cachet	n.	[ˈkæʃeɪ]	声望
compelling	a.	[kəmˈpelɪŋ]	令人信服的
confront	v.	[kənˈfrʌnt]	面对,对抗
denominator	n.	[dɪˈnɒmɪneɪtə]	共同特征,共同性质
deny	v.	[dɪˈnaɪ]	否认,否定
disparaging	a.	[dɪˈspærɪdʒɪŋ]	毁谤的
envious	a.	[ˈenvɪəs]	羡慕的,嫉妒的
exaggerated	a.	[ɪgˈzædʒəˈreɪtɪd]	夸大的,言过其实的
fester	v.	[ˈfestə]	引起怨恨
flare-up	n.	[ˈfleərˌʌp]	怒气发作
freak	n.	[friːk]	怪人,狂热的人
gossip	n.	[ˈgɒsɪp]	八卦,流言蜚语
grapevine	n.	[ˈgreɪpvaɪn]	小道消息,秘密情报网
grievance	n.	[ˈgriːv(ə)ns]	不满,委屈
inadequacy	n.	[ɪnˈædɪkwəsɪ]	不足
incompetence	n.	[ɪnˈkɒmpɪt(ə)ns]	无能,不胜任
interpretation	n.	[ɪntɜːprɪˈteɪʃ(ə)n]	解释,诠释
irresistible	a.	[ɪrɪˈzɪstɪb(ə)l]	不可抗拒的
jealousy	n.	[ˈdʒeləsɪ]	妒忌,猜忌
malicious	a.	[məˈlɪʃəs]	恶意的,蓄意的
merger	n.	[ˈmɜːdʒə]	合并,并购
overwhelming	a.	[ˌəʊvəˈwelmɪŋ]	压倒性的
pent-up	a.	[ˈpentˌʌp]	被压抑的
phenomenon	n.	[fɪˈnɒmɪnən]	现象
predicament	n.	[prɪˈdɪkəm(ə)nt]	窘况,困境
privilege	n.	[ˈprɪvəlɪdʒ]	特权,优待
psychological	a.	[saɪkəˈlɒdʒɪk(ə)l]	心理(学)的,精神上的
psychotherapy	n.	[saɪkə(ʊ)ˈθerəpɪ]	心理疗法,精神疗法
rant	n.	[rænt]	抱怨

reassure	v.	[riːəˈʃʊə]	使安心,使消除疑虑
redress	v.	[rɪˈdres]	纠正
resentment	n.	[rɪˈzentm(ə)nt]	愤恨
resolve	v.	[rɪˈzɒlv]	解决
restructure	v.	[riːˈstrʌktʃə]	重组,调整结构
retaliate	v.	[rɪˈtælɪeɪt]	报复,回敬
rumor	n.	[ˈruːmə]	谣言
superior	a.	[suːˈpɪərɪə]	优越的
valve	n.	[vælv]	阀,阀门
void	n.	[vɔɪd]	空隙,空白
whispered	a.	[ˈhwɪspəd]	低声的,耳语的
witty	a.	[ˈwɪtɪ]	诙谐的

reluctant to	不甘心情愿做……
opposed to	反对
project ... on	投射到……上
revert to	诉诸,恢复为
have an affair with	与……有染
mess up	搞得乱七八糟

I. Give brief answers to the following questions.

1. What distinguishes the helpful consequences of gossip and rumor from the harmful?
2. According to Nicholas DiFonzo, what is the common denominator of gossip and rumor?
3. What kind of information has to be heard through the grapevine?
4. What are the motives for malicious gossip?
5. Why do most people enjoy the negative gossip more?
6. What is the positive element to gossip?

II. Complete the following passage by filling each of the numbered blanks with one suitable word using the Chinese in the brackets as the reference.

Gossip and rumor are part of the fabric of working life — they ___1___ (娱乐), inform and connect people, but they can also ruin reputations, ___2___ (摧毁) trust, create bad attitudes and even reduce productivity.

What distinguishes the helpful consequences from the harmful is the intention behind what is said, how the information is perceived and acted on, and the length of time it is allowed to ___3___ (传播) and fester.

As well as providing informal communication networks, gossip and rumor act as psychological spaces for perceived ___4___ (不公平) and power imbalances, or emotions such as jealousy, resentment, boredom and even ___5___ (仇恨). When it is not possible to confront an issue or person directly, chats with colleagues become a way of offloading frustrations. People's ___6___ (焦虑) heighten at times of change and uncertainty, such as when an organization restructures, changes leadership or undertakes a merger or acquisition.

Such situations lead people to worry about how they will be ___7___ （影响）. Who will be promoted or demoted, whose job will disappear or be changed, and who will be paid what?

In the absence of ___8___ （充足的） information from management, people naturally create narratives to fill the void. The longer executives take to make ___9___ （决策）, the more anxious people become and the more rumors fill the vacuum and make sense of the ___10___ （不确定）.

III. Complete the following sentences with one function word.

1. People's anxieties heighten _____ times of change and uncertainty, such as when an organization restructures, changes leadership or undertakes a merger or acquisition.
2. _____ the absence of adequate information from management, people naturally create narratives to fill the void.
3. We can say the CEO is a control freak and it's because _____ him that we're in this mess.
4. Spreading negative rumors can make us feel better in the short term, but means we are less likely to take responsibility for either our predicament or obtaining the information we need _____ the powers that be.
5. The betrayal she felt was aggravated _____ feelings of unfairness, powerlessness and distrust because of privileges her colleague was enjoying as a result.
6. It acts as a safety valve _____ grievances, allowing pent-up feelings to be released in a way that minimizes potential damage.

IV. Complete the following sentences by translating the Chinese given in the brackets.

1. It not only causes us to be unhappy, but can strain or ruin relationships, distract us from work and family and other important things, _____（使得我们不愿意敞开胸怀去接受新的事物或者新的人）. (reluctant to)
2. _____（如果他们反对这一工作法案）, I'd like to know what exactly they're against. (oppose to)
3. When you find yourself thinking "I never would have expected such behavior from her", you know _____（你已经犯了一个错误,把自己的想法投射到别人身上）. (project on)
4. Maintaining history is also important so you can compare the current work against previous versions, and if needed, _____（可以恢复到先前的工作）. (revert to)
5. Eighty-two percent of the 210 unfaithful partners I've treated _____（与他人有过暧昧关系）who was, at first, "just a friend". (have an affair with)
6. _____（使人们生活陷入困境的一个主要原因）is that they have no godly friends to give them feedback. (mess up)

V. Translate the following sentences into English.

1. 共同的要素似乎是恐惧——我们担心组织里的这个人会对我们做什么;我们担心工程(部)将得到更多资金,而我们市场部的人得到的资金将会变少;我们害怕对手公司正在做的事情——因此我们传播关于它们的谣言。
2. 研究表明，尽管谣言降低了员工对管理层的信任，对员工的心态造成了不良影响，但谣言并不一定会影响生产率。
3. 尽管谣言往往包含了一些真相，人们对事件的诠释往往会回避复杂性和个人责任，通常会指向一个人、一个部门或者一个外部竞争对手。
4. 和谣言不同的是，八卦通常与社交网络和人际关系相关。八卦可以是富有娱乐性、不可抗拒，甚至诙谐的。因为八卦如此令人愉悦，人们往往不考虑八卦引起的害处。

VI. Translate the following passage into Chinese.

Gossip and rumor are part of the fabric of working life — they entertain, inform and connect people, but they can also ruin reputations, destroy trust, create bad attitudes and even reduce productivity.

What distinguishes the helpful consequences from the harmful is the intention behind what is said, how the information is perceived and acted on, and the length of time it is allowed to spread and fester.

As well as providing informal communication networks, gossip and rumor act as psychological spaces for perceived unfairness and power imbalances, or emotions such as jealousy, resentment, boredom and even hatred. When it is not possible to confront an issue or person directly, chats with colleagues become a way of offloading frustrations. People's anxieties heighten at times of change and uncertainty, such as when an organization restructures, changes leadership or undertakes a merger or acquisition.

Such situations lead people to worry about how they will be affected. Who will be promoted or demoted, whose job will disappear or be changed, and who will be paid what?

In the absence of adequate information from management, people naturally create narratives to fill the void. The longer executives take to make decisions, the more anxious people become and the more rumors fill the vacuum and make sense of the uncertainty.

Reading B

Data-Crunching (数据分析) Is Coming to Help Your Boss Manage Your Time
David Steritfeld

1　You might be at work, but that hardly means you are working.

2　Mitesh Bohra thought that projects at his software company, InfoBeans, were taking too long. "Something was supposed to be done in a thousand hours and it would end up taking 1,500," he said. "We were racking (榨取) our brains to figure out where the time went."

3　Increasingly, bosses have an answer. A new generation of workplace technology is allowing white-collar jobs to be tracked, tweaked (调整) and managed in ways that were difficult even a few years ago. Employers of all types — old-line manufacturers, nonprofits(非营利性组织), universities, digital start-ups(创业公司) and retailers — are using an increasingly wide range of tools to monitor workers' efforts, help them focus, cheer them on and just make sure they show up on time.

4   The programs foster connections and sometimes increase productivity among employees who are geographically(在地理上) dispersed(分散的) and often working from home. But as work force management becomes a factor in offices everywhere, questions are piling up. How much can bosses increase intensity? How does data, which bestows(给予) new powers of vision and understanding, redefine who is valuable? And with half of salaried workers saying they work 50 or more hours a week, when does working very hard become working way too much?

5   "The massive forces of globalization(全球化) and technological progress are removing the need for a lot of the previous kind of white-collar workers," said Andrew McAfee, associate director of the Center for Digital Business at the M.I.T. Sloan School of Management. "There's a lot of competition, global labor pools of pretty good quality, automation to make you more productive and make your job more 24/7. These are not calming(缓和) forces."

6   One way employees are pushed to work harder is by tethering(拴住) them to the office outside of normal business hours. Nearly a third of workers in a Gallup poll last year said they were expected to "check email and stay in touch" when they were not working.

7   "People in sales are continually measured and always know where they stand. Now this is happening in the rest of the white-collar work force," said Paul Hamerman, a workplace technology analyst with Forrester Research. "Done properly, it will increase engagement. Done in the wrong way, employees will feel pressured or micromanaged(管得太细)."

8   Myrna Arias, a Southern California saleswoman for Intermex, a money-transfer company based in Miami, was required to download an app(应用程序) on her cellphone that tracked her whereabouts(行踪) 24 hours a day, she claims in a lawsuit now pending(等待审理) in federal court. Ms. Arias's suit quotes her manager as saying, perhaps jokingly, that he knew how fast she was driving at all times.

9   "Ms. Arias believed it was akin(近似) to wearing a felon's(重罪犯) ankle bracelet(脚镣)," said her lawyer, Gail A. Glick. She deleted the app and was fired. Her suit, which accuses Intermex of invasion of privacy and wrongful termination(解雇), seeks $500,000 in lost wages. Neither Intermex nor its lawyers responded to requests for comment.

10 Companies making work force technology that relies more on engagement than enforcement(强制) say it increases transparency and fairness.

11 "In the office of the future," said Kris Duggan, chief executive of BetterWorks, a Silicon Valley start-up founded in 2013, "you will always know what you are doing and how fast you are doing it. I couldn't imagine living in a world where I'm supposed to guess what's important, a world filled with meetings, messages, conference rooms, and at the end of the day I don't know if I delivered anything meaningful."

12 BetterWorks is focused less on measuring how employees spend their time at the office than in making them more connected to it. One way to do that: Make it feel more like Facebook.

13   One of its clients, Capco, a financial services consultant, is seeking to make the millennials（千禧一代）happy. "They are looking for gigs（临时工作）, not careers," said Patrick Gormley, the chief operating officer. "The things that would keep them tied to a job in years gone past — a mortgage（按揭）, a car loan — have evaporated（消失）. That really challenges us to create an outstanding employee experience, so we can retain the best."

14   Capco's 3,000 employees, who are spread out geographically, post their most ambitious goals for the year electronically for all colleagues to see and they, as well as executives, can issue "nudges" and "cheers" to each other.

15   Other work force developers are enhancing the traditional process of evaluating employees, which used to be annual and backward-looking. Now it is more spontaneous（自发性的）.

16   Amazon, the e-commerce giant（巨头）, uses an internal tool called Anytime Feedback, which allows employees to submit praise or criticism to management. The company says most of the remarks are positive, though some Amazon employees complain that the process can be hidden and harsh.

17   Workday, which is based in the Bay Area, has developed a tool called Collaborative Anytime Feedback. Colleagues use it to salute each other — everyone in the company can see who is saying what.

18   "People wouldn't put something negative in a public forum, because it would reflect poorly on them," said Amy Wilson, Workday vice president of human capital management products.

19   The software also enables employees to comment privately, however, to a colleague's manager. Workday says these remarks range from positive to at least constructive.

20   Workday also sells an employee time-tracking program, which it advertises as being able to increase worker productivity, along with reducing labor costs — presumably in human relations departments — and minimizing compliance（遵从）risks.

21   Some say time tracking simply replaces a manual time sheet and encourages honesty.

22   "We tell people not to focus on the Big Brother aspect. This is all about efficiency," said Joel Slatis, founder of Timesheets.com, which makes clock-in software used by 1,400 small companies. "If you fill out a paper timecard and write down 8 a.m. when you come in at 8:02, no one is going to bat an eye. But if you do that when you leave too, that means you're getting 5 minutes more a day."

23   Jamie Clausen, who clocks in and out of her job in customer service at a State Farm insurance office in Silicon Valley from her home using Timesheets, says she accepts it as a modern reality.

24   "It shouldn't be an option to just show up at 9:15," she said. Ms. Clausen, 29, previously worked in a call center, where she was closely monitored. She added that she had been watching "Mad Men," and its portrayal of freewheeling（随心所欲的）1960s office life "seemed crazy." "It was a totally different world, back then."

25   At InfoBeans, an Indian company whose United States headquarters is in the Bay Area, managers feared that workers' inefficiency would lead to financial losses and client defections（背叛）. So it began to use a software system called Buddy, which is made by Sapience, an

Indian firm that is expanding into the American market.

26   Khiv Singh, a Sapience vice president, noted that data surrounded workers. "We have pedometers(计步器) to measure how far we walk, apps to monitor our blood pressure, stress level, the calories we're taking in, the calories we're burning. But the office is where we spend the majority of time, and we don't measure our work."

27   When InfoBeans began using Buddy, Mr. Bohra was surprised by what he found.

28   "Engineers would write on their time sheets that they were doing development for eight hours, but we started to see a very different set of activities that people are performing," Mr. Bohra said. "Meetings. Personal time. Uncategorized time. Performing research on something that maybe already should be a part of our knowledge repository(知识库)."

29   Mr. Bohra declined to let any of his employees be interviewed. But he said the work was more focused now, which meant smaller teams taking on bigger workloads. Eliminating(消除) distractions(干扰), including some meetings, lets people go home earlier, he added.

I. Match the companies with the description according to the article.

1. Intermex   A. a financial services consultant
2. BetterWorks   B. insurance company in Silicon Valley
3. Capco   C. a money-transfer company based in Miami
4. Amazon   D. an Indian software company
5. State Farm   E. an Indian firm expanding into the American market
6. InfoBeans   F. the e-commerce giant
7. Sapience   G. a Silicon Valley start-up founded in 2013

II. Answer the following questions.

1. What do managers at InfoBeans fear? What do they do to deal with it?
2. According to Kris Duggan, chief executive of BetterWorks, what will happen in the office of the future?
3. How did Khiv Singh, a Sapience vice president, note the data surrounded workers?

III. Questions for discussion.

1. Do you agree that creating, inventing, and innovating are essential skills for engineers? Why or why not?
2. What can you learn from the Invention Studio at Georgia Tech? What are the implications for engineering education in China?

Part Two
Tips for Translation

词义的选择

Warm-up

Compare the following Chinese sentences and their English versions. Pay special attention to the different ways of translating the same character "头".

（1）她正在梳头。She was combing her hair.
（2）一辆小车停在桥西头。A car was parked at the west end of the bridge.
（3）让我从头讲起吧。Let me tell the story from the very beginning.
（4）这还是我头一次来杭州呢。This is the first time I came to Hangzhou.

正确选词是保证译文质量的重要前提。汉英两种语言都有一词多类和一词多义的现象。在汉英翻译过程中，句式选定之后最大量的工作是从英语中选择恰当的词汇来表达汉语中的词义。词的选择主要应从两方面着手：

一、根据上下文正确理解原文的词义

词的正确选择首先取决于对原文词义的确切理解，而对原文词义的确切理解又取决于对原文上下文的推敲，英译汉时情况如此，汉译英时也是如此。

例如"情况"这个词的基本含义与英语中的 circumstances, situation, condition 等词相近，但是究竟怎样翻译，还需要根据具体的上下文来定。

（1）这种情况必须改变。This state of affairs must change.
（2）现在情况不同了。Now things are different.
（3）前线有什么情况？How is the situation at the front?
（4）可是在其他地方，情况却完全两样了。
But the picture outside this place is quite another story.
（5）我们可能去那儿，不过得看情况而定。
We may go there, but that depends.（或...it all depends.）

由以上例句中可以看出，因为汉语和英语在用词方面有不同的习惯，有的词在某种场合下可以译成英语的某个词，而在另一种场合下则不能这么译，经常出现汉语一个词表达的地方，译成英语要换成不同的词的情况。这时，根据上下文确定词义是关键。

二、辨析词义和正确选词

（一）注意词的广义和狭义

英语中不少同义词有广义和狭义的区别，运用范围也各不相同。

（1）农业是国民经济的基础。
Agriculture is the foundation of the national economy.
（2）农林牧副渔相结合的方针
the principle of combining farming, forestry, animal husbandry, side-occupations and fishery.

例(1)原文中的"农业"一词是广义,指一切农业经济,包括农业、畜牧业、林业和渔业,所以译作 agriculture。而在例(2)中,原文中的"农"与"林牧副渔"并列,是指耕作的农业,而不是整个农业经济,所以译为 farming。

(二)注意词的褒贬
由于人们对事物的态度不同,就会使用含有不同感情色彩的词,或肯定、赞扬,或否定、鄙视。这种感情色彩需要相应地在译文中表达出来。例如:
他们讲唯心论,我们讲唯物论。
They preach idealism whereas we advocated materialism.
同是一个"讲"字,译文中一处用 preach,另一处用 advocate,一贬一褒,反映了对两种世界观的不同态度。

(三)注意词的语体色彩
语体是同一语言使用者在不同场合使用的该语言的变体,其实质是根据场合选用同义词,它们或是随便,或是亲昵,或是刻板,或是典雅,或是商谈式的,或是命令式的等等。汉译英选词时应注意词的语体色彩。
(1) 禁止赌博。Gambling is prohibited.
(2) 这小伙干活真冲。This young fellow does his work with vim and vigor.
例(1)中原文的"禁止"一词语体色彩较为正式,故译为 prohibit。例(2)中原句的"真冲"是口语体,译文也相应地用了口语化的 vim。

(四)注意词的搭配
汉英两种语言在长期使用过程中形成了各自的固定词组和搭配用法,翻译时必须注意两者的不同,而不能把汉语词的搭配用法生搬硬套到译文中。
1. 定语和中心词的搭配
淡茶/淡酒/淡水/淡季 weak tea / light wine / fresh water / slack season
同是一个"淡"字,与不同的名词搭配,译成英语需选用不同的词。
2. 动词和宾语的搭配
(1) 下车/下面条/下结论/下决心/下命令/下棋
   to get off a car / to cook noodles / to draw a conclusion / to make a decision / to issue orders / to play chess
由于与不同的宾语搭配,同是一个"下"字,译成英语选用了不用的动词。
(2) 他把他的全部书籍都献给了图书馆。
   He presented all his books to the library.
(3) 教师应当献身于教育事业。
   A teacher should devote himself to the cause of education.
(4) 谨以此书献给王教授以表敬慕和感激之情。
   To Prof. Wang I dedicate this volume in token of affection and gratitude.
以上例句中,一个"献"字根据具体情况被译成了不同的词或词组,取得了很好的效果。

Unit Three

练习

翻译下列各句,注意词的选择。
1. 他醉心于医学研究。
2. 那个人醉心于名利。
3. 我借一下你的电话好吗?
4. 借光、借光。
5. 他把自己的一生献给为人民服务的事业。

Part Three
Simulated Writing

Invitation for Bids

投标招标是市场经济下进行大宗货物的买卖、工程建设项目的发包与承包,以及服务项目的采购时,所采用的一种交易方式。招标公告的作用是让潜在投标人获得信息,以便进行项目筛选,确定是否参与竞争。招标公告或投标邀请函的具体格式可由招标人自定,内容一般包括:招标单位名称;建设项目资金来源;工程项目概况和本次招标工作范围的简要介绍;购买资格预审文件的地点、时间和价格等有关事项。

Sample Reading

Invitation for Bids (IFB)

Date: November 26, 2005
Loan No.: 1543-PRC
IFB No.: ITC991508

1. The People's Republic of China (PRC) has received a loan from the Asian Development Bank (ADB) towards the cost of Tongchuan Environment Improvement Project, of which Xi'an Xijiao Cogeneration Plant is a component as Subproject 1 and it is intended that part of the proceeds of this loan will be applied to eligible payments under the contract for Electric Feed Water Pump, 110kv Electric Equipment and Circulating Water Pump & Raw Water Pump.

2. The China International Tendering Company (hereinafter referred to as ITC) is authorized by Xi'an Xijiao Cogeneration Plant to invite sealed bids from eligible bidders from member countries of ADB for the supply of the following Goods by way of International Competitive Bidding:

Package No.5. Electric Feed Water Pump

Package No.8. 110kv Electric Equipment
Package No.9. Circulating Water Pump & Raw Water Pump

3. Interested eligible bidders may obtain further information on the bid form and inspect the bidding documents at the office of China International Tendering Company.

    Room 514
    China International Tendering Company
    Jiuling Building (North Wing)
    No. 21 Xi San Huan Bei Lu
    Beijing, 100089

4. A complete set of bidding documents may be purchased by any interested bidder on the submission of a written application to the above address between 9:00 a.m.—11:00 a.m. and 1:30—4:00 p.m. (Beijing Time) starting from November 26, 2005 (Sunday and Holidays expected) upon payment of nonrefundable fee of RMB 1,000 for each set of bidding documents.

5. Bids must be delivered to the above office at or before 9:30 a.m. (Beijing Time) on January 18, 2006 and must be accompanied by a security of not less than 2% of the total bid price.

6. China International Tendering Company will not be responsible for any costs or expenses incurred by bidders in connection with the preparation or delivery of bids.

    Procurement Agent: China International Tendering Company
    Mailing Address:
        Jiuling Building (North Wing)
        No. 21 Xi San Huan Bei Lu
        Beijing, 100089

    Tel: (0086-10) 68991383
    Fax: (0086-10) 68991366

Notes

Invitation for Bids (IFB)	招标公告
Asian Development Bank	亚洲发展银行
environment improvement	环境治理
electric feed water pump	电力给水泵
110kv electric equipment	110千伏电力设备
circulating water pump	循环水泵
raw water pump	原水泵
China International Tendering Company	中国国际招投标公司
hereinafter referred to as	以下称
sealed bids	密封标单
member countries of ADB	亚洲发展银行成员国
International Competitive Bidding	国际公开竞争性招标

Unit Three

interested eligible bidders	有意参加投标的合格投标者
further information on the bid form	进一步的关于投标格式的信息
a complete set of bidding documents	完整的招标文件
the submission of a written application	递交书面申请
upon payment of nonrefundable fee	所付款项，一概不退
a security	投标保证金
any costs or expenses incurred by bidders in connection with the preparation or delivery of bids	投标者项目投标过程所发生的各种准备或邮寄费用

Check Your Understanding

Supply the missing information in the following table according to the sample of invitation for Bids you have just read.

procurement agent 代理机构	1.
date of the notice of IFB 招标公告日期	2.
bid number 招标编号	3.
loan number 贷款编号	4.
finance source 资金来源	5.
name of the project 项目名称	6.
buyer 买方	7.
contract(s) to be signed 拟签署的合同	8.
time and date of obtaining bidding documents 领取招标文件的时间和日期	9.
address of obtaining bidding documents 领取招标文件的地点	10.
payment for each set of bidding documents 每套招标文件的价格	11.
deadline of delivering the bids 投标文件递交截止日期	12.

Follow-up Writing

Complete the following Invitation for Bids by filling in the following items in proper places.

Procurement agent: CMC International Tendering Company (CMC-ITC)
Date of the notice of IFB: August 28, 2006
Bid number: CMC991511
Loan number/credit number: 4325-CHA

Finance source: World Bank
Name of the project: The Pipeline at Jetty Project
Buyer: Shengli Petroleum Administrative Bureau, the People's Republic of China
Contract(s) to be signed: tubing, welded line pipe
Time and date of obtaining bidding documents: between 8:30 and 11:00 a.m. /1:30 and 4:00 p.m. starting from August 28, 2006 (except Sundays and holidays)
Address of obtaining bidding documents: CMC International Company,
No 2110, the West Wing of Sichuan Mansion
1 Fuchengmenwa Dajie
Beijing, China
Payment for each set of bidding documents: RMB 1,000 or US$120
Deadline of delivering the Bids: 10:30 a.m. on October 12, 2006 (Beijing Time)
Time of bid opening ceremony: 10:30 a.m. on October 12, 2006 (Beijing Time)
Postcode: 100037
Tel: 0086-10-68991383
Fax: 0086-10-68991366

Invitation for Bids (IFB)

Date: _____
Loan No.: _____
Bid No.: _____

1. The Government of the People's Republic of China (PRC) has received a loan from _____ in various currencies towards the cost of _____ _____. It is intended that part of the proceeds of this credit will be applied to eligible payments under the Contract(s) for _____.

2. The procurement agent — _____ (hereinafter referred to as _____) for and on behalf of the buyer — The World Bank Loan Projects Management Center of the State Forestry Administration of the People's Republic of China invites sealed bids from eligible bidders for the supply of the following goods: tubing, welded line pipe.

3. Interested eligible bidders may obtain further information from and inspect the bidding documents at the office of CMC-ITC:
Address: _____
Tel: _____ Fax: _____

4. A complete set of bidding documents may be purchased by any interested bidder on the submission of a written application to the above address between _____ _____ upon payment of nonrefundable fee of _____ for one set of

bidding documents.

5. Bids must be delivered to the above office _____ and must be accompanied by a security of not less than 2% of the total bid price.
6. Bids will be opened in the presence of bidders' representatives who choose to attend _____ at the address given below:

Rm 2110, the West Wing of Sichuan Mansion
1 Fuchengmengwai Dajie, Beijing 100037, China

Procurement Agent: CMC International Tendering Company
Mailing Address: 2110, West Wing of Sichuan Mansion
1 Fuchengmenwai Dajie, Beijing 100037, China
Tel: (0086-10)68991383   Fax: (0086-10)68991366

Part Four
Listening

Lead-in

I. Discuss the following topics with your classmates.

1. Do you know something about remote work or virtual workplace? If yes, say something about it.
2. What do you imagine about the workplace in the year 2050?

II. Study the following vocabulary before you listen.

remote work	远程办公
virtual workplace	虚拟办公室
infrequent	不经常的
U.S. Census Bureau	美国人口调查局
hybrid	混合
scenario	情境
pros and cons	正反两方面
personal assets	个人资产
inventory	存货清单
intranet portal	公司内部系统
undeniable	不可否认的
propinquity	接近,邻近
serendipity	机缘

While-listening

I. Listen to the recording and supply the missing words.

The Workplace of the Future Is Still the Office

Every time I read about the future of work, I see a focus almost entirely on remote work, virtual workplaces and stories of people working from coffee shops. Yes, overall, this is a rapidly __1__ trend, increasing by over 60% in recent years. I personally have worked __2__ for almost two decades, but in general this is still pretty infrequent. What we need to realize is that the overall number is still quite __3__. According to Global Workplace Analytics' *State of Telework in the U.S.* and based on the U.S. Census Bureau, the total __4__ of people who work solely from home is still only around 3 million.

On the other hand, those who work only part of their time from home, or on the road, are __5__ to be a much larger 45% of all U.S. jobs. So, the idea of organizations with most of their employees working from practically anywhere they want is still a distant __6__ for the broader economy. More accurately, the idea of a significantly virtual __7__ with no need for office space, or everyone sitting in co-working spaces, is not the reality for the __8__ of companies. And it won't be for a while, if ever.

While you will need to __9__ more remote workers, the hybrid office-plus-remote worker scenario will continue to be the biggest __10__ for office, IT and HR managers. The pros and cons of what this does for __11__ aside, consider the complexity in managing resources for such situations.

In one view, you could gain some efficiencies by sharing office rooms, or desks. That idea __12__ to office managers more than employees—what employee wouldn't __13__ people to not mess around with their desk space, files, or __14__ just as they have left them?

Yet, "mobility desks" or offices are gaining popularity in larger companies. What makes this more __15__ is a mind shift away from the primary view of "my office" as a specific __16__ in their company building, to seeing it more as a virtual space they access from a laptop or smartphone.

This shift from the physical to virtual is made possible by __17__: powerful laptops or mobile devices, high speed wireless networks, VPNs, enterprise portals, and, most of all, employee __18__ management tools in software.

I recently spoke to Elizabeth Dukes, co-author of Wide Open Workspace, and EVP & CMO at iOffice, Inc. on how __19__ are managing resources in this hybrid future.

Office and Facilities Managers today are typically responsible for all the resources that keep the office running and employees __20__: coordinating office space use, assigning and tracking laptops and personal assets, managing common resources such as network printers and devices, keeping office supply inventory, building __21__, the mailroom chase, etc..

In a connected business, these are easily accessible and __22__ by the employee through the intranet portal, to see how much they have used as well as to request and track resources—e.g., every time you need to book a __23__ room, find quick directions to a local office in another town, have a package shipped to a salesperson, etc. Similarly, it is critical to operations all around to see __24__ of any of these resources, forecast the demand for resources as the organization grows, moves or pivots.

Unit Three

As mentioned in the beginning, while new forms such as co-working is a __25__ trend, it is still far from the norm. According to Ms. Dukes, this seems to be growing faster in the tech centers of the West and East coast, and less so in other __26__ of the U.S.. While large companies have an undeniable need to manage facilities, she also sees growth in mid-market organizations.

The analytics from facilities management software offer a new __27__ of capabilities and issues. Propinquity—the outcomes of being __28__ near others—is gaining more significance as more start moving towards remote work. This is the property of collaborating in a physical office space that creates new serendipities and __29__ that you don't really get when working entirely virtual or remote. Without it, you don't run into your peers, or come across new __30__ and ideas that may lead to new ideas, collaboration or innovation.

II. **Listen again, stop the recording as necessary, and repeat after the speaker.**

Post-listening

Surf the Internet and find more information about the following topic areas. Then prepare a 15-minute oral presentation and deliver it in the class. While preparing the presentation you need to narrow down topic area and focus one major point.
1. Remote work
2. My ideal workplace in the future

Part Five
Speaking

Supplier Selection

Sample Dialogue 1

A: One of the critical challenges faced by purchasing managers is the selection of strategic partners that will furnish them with the necessary products, components, and materials in a timely and effective manner to help maintain a competitive advantage. But how to choose the right supplier?

B: Choosing the right supplier involves much more than scanning a series of price lists. Your choice will depend on a wide range of factors such as value for money, quality, reliability and service.

A: How do you weigh up the importance of these different factors?

B: It is based on your business' priorities and strategy. For example, if you want to cut down the time it takes you to serve your customers, suppliers that offer you faster delivery will rate higher than those that compete on price alone.

A: I see. The most effective suppliers are those who offer products or services that match—or exceed—the needs of your business. So when you are looking for suppliers, it's best to be sure of your business needs and what you want to achieve by buying, rather than simply paying for what suppliers want to sell you.

B: Yeah, that's right. And it's well worth examining how many suppliers you really need. Buying from only one supplier can be dangerous—where do you go if they let you down, or even go out of business? It's always worth having an alternative supply source ready to help in difficult times. On the other hand, it's a waste of time for you and the potential supplier if you approach them when there's little chance of them fulfilling your requirements. You can find suppliers through a variety of channels. It's best to build up a shortlist of possible suppliers through a combination of sources to give you a broader base to choose from.

A: What factors should be considered when choosing the firms on the shortlist?

B: Once you have a manageable shortlist, ask yourself the questions like: Can these suppliers deliver what you want, when you want it? Are they financially secure? How long have they been established? Do you know anyone who has used and can recommend them? Are they on any approved supplier lists from trade associations, local or central government? Do some research and try to slim your list down to no more than four or five candidates.

A: And then you can approach the potential suppliers and ask for a quotation.

B: Exactly, when you've got the quotation, compare the potential suppliers in terms of what matters most to you. For example, the quality of their product or service may be most important. Price is important, but it shouldn't be the only reason you choose a supplier.

A: Signing the contract is the last step, is it?

B: You hit the point. Once you've settled on the suppliers you'd like to work with, you can move on to negotiating terms and conditions and drawing up a contract. Choosing the right suppliers is essential for your business. It is always a good idea to do research with regard to what you expect from a supplier, how much you're willing to pay for your supplies and the balance you want to strike between cost, reliability, quality and service.

selection of strategic partners	战略合作伙伴的选择
competitive advantage	竞争优势
weigh up	权衡
manageable shortlist	便于管理的决选名单
trade association	贸易协会
slim... down	瘦身,缩减
draw up a contract	拟订合同
with regard to	关于
strike a balance between	在……和……间取得平衡

Unit Three

Sample Dialogue 2

Importer: I'm interested in your satellite receivers.

Exporter: Our TVROs are one of our best-selling products. In fact we occupy about 50% of the world market on this item. We specialize in microwave technology.

Importer: Taiwan has certainly gained a place in the high-tech market.

Exporter: We used to lack R & D so we found it hard to innovate. That's the reason our company now invests 10% of our revenues in R & D.

Importer: You used to have trouble with quality control too. Can you tell me how your company insures that your receivers meet a uniform high standard?

Exporter: At first we had to station one of our engineers at the factories we used to forge the parts for our TVROs. But by now these factories have stringent quality control of their own.

Importer: Well, we're looking for a supplier who can give us a lower price with no reduction in quality.

Exporter: May I ask how many TVROs you were thinking of ordering?

Importer: I would estimate that we'd buy about 1,000 per month.

Exporter: Well, since you'd be placing a large order, we can give you a discount on the price.

Importer: That would certainly encourage us to order from you. Let me discuss what you offer with my home office.

Exporter: I'll be expecting your call then.

Notes

satellite receiver	卫星接收器
best-selling product	热销产品
quality control	质量控制
home office	总公司

USEFUL EXPRESSIONS AND PATTERNS:

1. One of the critical challenges faced by purchasing managers is the selection of strategic partners that will furnish them with the necessary products, components, and materials in a timely and effective manner to help maintain a competitive advantage.

2. Your choice will depend on a wide range of factors such as value for money, quality, reliability and service.

3. The most effective suppliers are those who offer products or services that match—or exceed—the needs of your business.

4. The quality of their product or service may be most important. Price is important, but it shouldn't be the only reason you choose a supplier.

5 Once you've got a clear idea of what you need to buy and you've identified some potential suppliers, you can build a shortlist of sources that meet your needs.

6 Lower prices may reflect poorer quality goods and services which, in the long run, may not be the most cost effective option. Be confident that your supplier can make a sufficient margin at the price quoted for the business to be commercially viable.

7 Wherever possible it is always a good idea to meet a potential supplier face to face and see how their business operates. Understanding how your supplier works will give you a better sense of how it can benefit your business.

8 We ought to focus on education, technology and innovation. It's our ace card.

9 Buyer-supplier relationships based solely on price are no longer acceptable for suppliers of critical materials or for organizations that wish to practice the latest innovations in supply chain management.

10 Recent emphasis has also been on other important strategic and operational factors such as quality, delivery, and flexibility.

11 Strategic relationships also play a vital role for the long-term well-being of a supply chain.

12 We now have a new Quality Assurance program.

13 We will have to terminate the contract and find a new supplier.

14 We're looking for a supplier who can give us a lower price with no reduction in quality.

15 We supply many leading companies.

16 We also have a good reputation. And that reputation is built upon reliability and good relationships with our customers.

17 We can re-negotiate with Southford Components or we can work with MAGL or Parkview.

18 A crucial factor is how quickly they can deliver.

I. **Role-play the sample dialogues.**

II. **Match the following two columns.**

1. 便于管理的决选名单　　　　A. with regard to
2. 拟订合同　　　　　　　　　B. selection of strategic partners
3. 关于　　　　　　　　　　　C. strike a balance between
4. 在……和……间取得平衡　　D. competitive advantage
5. 权衡　　　　　　　　　　　E. weigh up
6. 战略合作伙伴的选择　　　　F. manageable shortlist
7. 瘦身　　　　　　　　　　　G. slim down
8. 竞争优势　　　　　　　　　H. draw up a contract
9. 热销产品　　　　　　　　　I. quality control
10. 总公司　　　　　　　　　　J. satellite receiver
11. 质量控制　　　　　　　　　K. best-selling product
12. 卫星接收器　　　　　　　　L. home office

Unit Three

III. Complete the following dialogues by making choices from the sentences given.

Jenny: There's a problem with the circuitry on some of the units that went to Japan last week. Derek flew to Tokyo to look at the problem.
Kate: So it's serious.
Jenny: Yes. (1)_____.
Kate: Jenny, I need to talk to Don as soon as possible, contact him right now.
...
Kate: Hello, Don. We have three options. (2)_____.
A crucial factor is how quickly they can deliver.
Don: MAGL certainly claim to be the fastest. But I'm worried that although they are fast they may not have the best quality control. (3)_____.
Kate: Exactly. Although they have promised that their system is improved.
Don: Looking at these quotations from Parkview, I don't think Parkview are the best option.
Kate: They offer a very fast delivery time, they have a very high reputation and they are the nearest supplier to the assembly line. (4)_____.
But, price can't be a factor at this stage.
Don: I don't agree with you. (5)_____. I think we can re-negotiate a far better deal with Southford Components. I'm working hard for this now.
Kate: If so, we must move fast.

A: But they are very expensive compared with Southford.
B: We can re-negotiate with Southford Components or we can work with MAGL or Parkview.
C: I think we have to get the best service at the best price.
D: And Don's gone to the component supplier to find out how it happened.
E: And quality control was the problem with Southford Components.

IV. Read the dialogue given below and translate the sentences into English. Refer to Useful Expressions and Patterns if necessary.

Smith: Buyer   Jeff: Supplier
Smith: I'm sorry to have to say this, Jeff. But we have got a problem. The problem is with the product itself. It looks like batch numbers 993 and 994 all have the same problem.
Jeff: I will send someone to see to it right now, please wait a minute.
...
Jeff: We have tracked down the problem. There was a localized problem in quality control which we have isolated and rectified. We can guarantee that it won't happen again. (1)_____.（我们现在用的是一套新的质保程序。）
Smith: That's all very well but you have failed to meet the terms of the contract. I am afraid we have no option. (2)_____.（我们不得不终止

合约，另找供应商。)

Jeff: Mr. Smith, I understand your concern and recognize that it's a very unsatisfactory situation, but may I point out it was just two batches that were defective...

Smith: It may have been just two batches but we now have two hundred defective products on the market with my company name on them.

Jeff: Mr. Smith, we appreciate that the situation has damaged your reputation. And we are very sorry. But (3)_____. (我们也有着良好的声誉。我们的声誉是建立在产品的可靠性和良好的客户关系上的。) We supply many leading companies and we are very embarrassed by this incident. I must assure you that it won't happen again.

Smith: I want to know what you're going to do to remedy the situation. (4)_____. (这会损坏我们的市场声誉，使我们很尴尬。)

Jeff: I am terribly sorry for what has happened, we always enjoy good relationship with each other. (5)_____. (我们准备给予你们百分之五的特别折扣，以补偿给你方所造成的不便。)

Unit Four

Lifestyle

Part One
Reading and Translating

Lead-in

How many books did you read last year? Read the following information to know more about books.

- The word book comes from Old English "bōc", which in turn comes from the Germanic root "*bōk-", cognate to "beech".
- The first books used parchment or vellum (calfskin) for the pages. The book covers were made of wood and covered with leather. Because dried parchment tends to assume the form it had before processing, the books were fitted with clasps or straps.
- The term e-book is a contraction of "electronic book"; it refers to a book-length publication in digital form. An e-book is usually made available through the internet, but also on CD-ROM and other forms. E-Books may be read either via a computer or by means of a portable book display device known as an e-book reader, such as the Sony Reader, Barnes & Noble Nook, Kobo eReader, or the Amazon Kindle. These devices attempt to mimic the experience of reading a print book.
- Throughout the 20th century, libraries have faced an ever-increasing rate of publishing, sometimes called an information explosion. The advent of electronic publishing and the internet means that much new information is not printed in paper books, but is made available online through a digital library, on CD-ROM, or in the form of e-books. An on-line book is an e-book that is available online through the internet.
- In the words of Jan Tschichold, book design "though largely forgotten today, methods and rules upon which it is impossible to improve have been developed over centuries. To produce perfect books these rules have to be brought back to life and applied." Richard Hendel describes book design as "an arcane subject" and refers to the need for a context to understand what that means.

- The size of a modern book is based on the printing area of a common flatbed press. The pages of type were arranged and clamped in a frame, so that when printed on a sheet of paper the full size of the press, the pages would be right side up and in order when the sheet was folded, and the folded edges trimmed.
- During the 20th century, librarians were concerned about keeping track of the many books being added yearly to the Gutenberg Galaxy. Through a global society called the International Federation of Library Associations and Institutions(IFLA), they devised a series of tools including the International Standard Bibliographic Description (ISBD).
- Commercial publishers in industrialized countries generally assign ISBNs to their books, so buyers may presume that the ISBN is part of a total international system, with no exceptions. However, many government publishers, in industrial as well as developing countries, do not participate fully in the ISBN system, and publish books which do not have ISBNs.

Reading A

Let's Come out of the Kindle Closet and Reveal What We're Really Reading

Lists of top-selling paper and electronic books show that while on paper we prop up great literary careers, on ebooks we cater to our basest instincts

Bidisha[①]

1   The British reading public are a bunch of hypocrites. A recent list of Waterstones top-selling paper books of 2015, compared with the top 20 ebooks purchased from Amazon in the same period, has revealed the gulf between what we are seen to be reading and what we're really reading. The real book versus ebook list is like seeing Dorian Grey's public face right up against his portrait.

2   While on paper we dole out our wages to prop up the careers of Colm Tóibín, Ian McEwan and Richard Flanagan, what we read on our Kindles is very different. We're like American winos, hiding our cheap, nasty, yet oh-so-satisfying liquor in brown paper bags—or the dead grey plastic of a Kindle. We sip fine literary wine in public and neck any old drain-clearing hooch when we're left to our own (e-reading) devices: harrowing first-person accounts of abuse, marshmallow love stories, gritty killings, true crime, contemporary commuting-based psychodramas with "girl" and "train" in the title.

3   We like our fictional characters to be multidimensional (except for Ana Steele from Fifty

---

① Bidisha is a regular guest on the BBC shows *Front Row*, *The Review Show* and *Saturday Review* and guest presents the World Service books show *The Word*. She is also a regular contributor to *the Guardian* and *the Observer*.

Shades of Grey, who's as thick as a post), but as readers we remain resolutely two-faced. I'm not surprised, though. Who wouldn't be desperate to find out the ending of *Dare She Date Again?* by Amy Ruttan, in the Mills & Boon Medical Romance line? It's about a widow, — a paramedic turned air ambulance pilot — who falls for her hunky trainee. Genius.

4   And right now in the Amazon Kindle top 100 I am excited to see *Stone Deep: An Alpha Bad Boy Romance* by Tess Oliver and Anna Hart at number 86, and *Cover Model* by Devon Hartford at number 89. Both feature striking cover images of nameless, faceless, oiled beefcake — and, no, I'm not talking about a late-summer barbecue platter from Lidl.

5   Meanwhile, copies of untouched prize-winning novels languish on our shelves, impressive but remote, like an exhibition of Elizabeth Taylor's evening dresses. The hardbacks are what we feel we ought to buy, or better yet give as gifts, which show our high-mindedness while ensuring that we pass the reading burden on to someone else.

6   We tout our beautiful Edwardian-green Virago Classics or zingy orange Penguin Classics, giving a little eye-sparkle of recognition to the other person on the train reading that year's much-admired novel-that-proves-the-novel-isn't-dead. We pay for hardback editions of thoughtful, exquisitely written meditations on something or other, which took years to write.

7   But they only take a few seconds to shelve and forget. What we really respond to is the old kiss-kiss-bang-bang, the thrill of the penny dreadful, the glitter of the music hall, the big-screen swoon. Well, we yearn in our imaginations; perhaps not in life, where kiss-kiss etc. would disrupt the school run. Your Kindle library is like your personal dark web, the place where your basest instincts and truest, rawest, subconscious urges settle like slime at the bottom of a forbidding lake. Indeed, *Slime at the Bottom of a Forbidding Lake* is the title of my forthcoming enovel, which I am generously releasing on to the market for 99p, complete with authentic spelling mistakes, a cover image ripped from Shutterstock and the promise of a sex scene on every page that doesn't have a murder on it.

8   Let's embrace the truth. In our hands we have highly wrought prose about highly wrought characters and their personal, political and cultural issues. In our heads it's all bums, willies, magic amulets and blood-soaked corpses. I think it's time to come out of the Kindle closet and admit the strain of maintaining a double life. Time to upload venerable and worthy works on to our e-readers, place them carefully in a drawer and forget about them, then hit WH Smiths at Heathrow Terminal 5 and go crazy buying what we really want.

9   The fine literary novels can wait for our retirement years, when natural resources will be low and we can burn them for fuel. In the meantime, we need to liberate ourselves, reclaim the misery memoirs, overripe pseudo-medieval swords and sorcery bunk and PG-rated romantic fantasies, and flash that trash with pride.

New Words and Expressions

beefcake	n.	[ˈbiːfkeɪk]	男子健美照片
bum	n.	[bʌm]	狂欢作乐
corpse	n.	[kɔːps]	尸体
desperate	adj.	[ˈdesp(ə)rət]	极度渴望的
drain	n.	[dreɪn]	下水道
exquisitely	adv.	[ekˈskwɪzɪtli]	精致地
glitter	n.	[ˈglɪtə]	闪光；灿烂
gritty	adj.	[ˈgrɪti]	勇敢的，刚毅的
gulf	n.	[gʌlf]	分歧；深渊
hardback	adj.	[ˈhɑːdbæk]	精装的；硬封面的
harrow	vt.	[ˈhærəʊ]	耙地；开拓
hooch	n.	[huːtʃ]	烈酒
hunky	n.	[ˈhʌŋki]	匈牙利人；来自中欧的移民
hypocrite	n.	[ˈhɪpəkrɪt]	伪君子；伪善者
languish	vi.	[ˈlæŋgwɪʃ]	憔悴；失去活力
liquor	n.	[ˈlɪkə]	烈酒；液体
marshmallow	n.	[ˈmɑːʃmeləʊ]	棉花软糖
meditation	n.	[medɪˈteɪʃ(ə)n]	冥想；沉思
multidimensional	adj.	[ˌmʌltɪdɪˈmenʃənl]	多维的；多面的
neck	vt.	[nek]	与……搂着脖子亲吻
paramedic	n.	[ˌpærəˈmedɪk]	伞兵医务人员
platter	n.	[ˈplætə]	大浅盘
pseudo	n.	[ˈsjuːdəʊ]	伪君子
psychodrama	n.	[ˈsaɪkəʊdrɑːmə]	心理剧
reclaim	vt.	[rɪˈkleɪm]	回收再利用
resolutely	adv.	[ˈrezəluːtlɪ]	坚决地；毅然地
sip	vt.	[sɪp]	啜
slime	n.	[slaɪm]	烂泥
sorcery	n.	[ˈsɔːs(ə)rɪ]	巫术
strain	n.	[streɪn]	负担
swoon	n.	[swuːn]	神魂颠倒
thrill	n.	[θrɪl]	激动；紧张
tout	vt.	[taʊt]	兜售
venerable	adj.	[ˈven(ə)rəb(ə)l]	珍贵的
wino	n.	[ˈwaɪnəʊ]	酒鬼
zingy	adj.	[ˈzɪŋɪ]	极吸引人的
a bunch of			一群；一堆
be desperate to			渴望做某事
cater to			迎合

Unit Four

dole out	少量发放
fall for	迷恋
ought to	应该
pass on to	传给
penny dreadful	廉价的惊险小说或杂志
prop up	支持
release on to	发表,发布
school run	上学交通高峰期

I. Give brief answers to the following questions.

1. Who is Dorian Grey? What is the meaning of "The real book versus ebook list is like seeing Dorian Grey's public face right up against his portrait."?
2. According to the author, what are we seen to be reading?
3. According to the author, what are we really reading?
4. Why does the author say "Your Kindle library is like your personal dark web"?
5. What's the title of the author's forthcoming enovel?
6. According to the whole article, what is the author's suggestion about reading?

II. Complete the following passage by filling each of the numbered blanks with one suitable word using the Chinese in the brackets as the reference.

Let's __1__（接受）the truth. In our hands we have highly __2__（精炼的）prose about highly wrought characters and their personal, political and cultural issues. In our heads it's all bums, willies, magic __3__（护身符）and __4__（浴血的）corpses. I think it's time to come out of the Kindle closet and __5__（承认）the __6__（负担）of maintaining a double life. Time to upload __7__（珍贵的）and worthy works on to our e-readers, place them carefully in a drawer and forget about them, then hit WH Smiths at Heathrow Terminal 5 and go crazy buying what we really want.

The fine literary novels can wait for our retirement years, when natural resources will be low and we can burn them for fuel. In the meantime, we need to liberate ourselves, __8__（回收）the misery memoirs, __9__（腐朽的）pseudo-medieval swords and __10__（巫术）bunk and PG-rated romantic fantasies, and flash that trash with pride.

III. Complete the following sentences with one function word.

1. While on paper we dole _____ our wages to prop _____ the careers of Colm Tóíbin, Ian McEwan and Richard Flanagan, what we read on our Kindles is very different.
2. Lists of top-selling paper and electronic books show that while on paper we prop up great literary careers, on ebooks we cater _____ our basest instincts.
3. I'm not surprised, though. Who wouldn't be desperate _____ find out the ending of *Dare She Date Again*?
4. The hardbacks are what we feel we ought _____ buy, or better yet give as gifts, which show our high-mindedness while ensuring that we pass the reading burden _____ to someone else.

5. It's about a widow, — a paramedic turned air ambulance pilot — who falls _____ her hunky trainee.

6. Indeed, *Slime at the Bottom of a Forbidding Lake* is the title of my forthcoming enovel, which I am generously releasing _____ to the market for 99p...

IV. **Complete the following sentences by translating the Chinese given in the brackets.**

1. Kodak, for example, failed because _____（让数码摄影的核心专利失去活力）in its vaults for decades. (languish)

2. If so, _____（这个伪君子真的打从心底相信）, what he is saying? (hypocrite)

3. Although he has enjoyed the job, he has always hated the months he has to spend in Washington, calling it "the world's worst city" and _____（毅然地远离交际圈）. (resolutely)

4. This technology reveals a picture of the subterranean environment using _____（极其灵敏的传感器）. (exquisitely)

5. _____（定期的锻炼和冥想）help promote relaxation and may offer relief to those with stress-related bruxism. (meditation)

6. These processes have on direct impact on the user experience, and the system can kill them _____（在任何时间回收内存）for a foreground visible, or service process. (reclaim)

V. **Translate the following sentences into English.**

1. 水石书店2015年最畅销纸质书排行与同一时期在亚马逊被购买的前20名电子书相比，已经显露出我们被认为所阅读的与我们真正阅读的书目之间的鸿沟。

2. 精装书是我们觉得我们应该买的，或者更好是当礼物送人的，这不仅能显示我们的高尚情操，同时也确保我们把阅读负担传递给别人。

3. 同时，一册册没碰过的获奖小说在我们的书架上失去生气，令人印象深刻却又偏远，犹如展览中的伊丽莎白·泰勒的晚礼服。

4. 精巧准确表达那些经过深思熟虑的思想通常需要经年累月的时间，为此我们愿意购买其精装版本。

VI. **Translate the following passage into Chinese.**

Let's embrace the truth. In our hands we have highly wrought prose about highly wrought characters and their personal, political and cultural issues. In our heads it's all bums, willies, magic amulets and blood-soaked corpses. I think it's time to come out of the Kindle closet and admit the strain of maintaining a double life. Time to upload venerable and worthy works on to our e-readers, place them carefully in a drawer and forget about them, then hit WH Smiths at Heathrow Terminal 5 and go crazy buying what we really want.

The fine literary novels can wait for our retirement years, when natural resources will be low and we can burn them for fuel. In the meantime, we need to liberate ourselves, reclaim the misery memoirs, overripe pseudo-medieval swords and sorcery bunk and PG-rated romantic fantasies, and flash that trash with pride.

Reading B

Can Craft Beer Really Be Defined? We're about to Find out

A newly formed United Craft Brewers is attempting to define what craft beer is in the UK. Is that possible? And, if so, is it a good thing?

Tony Naylor

1   Next month, possibly in a secret underground bunker, but more likely in a pub, the leading lights of new wave British brewing（酿造）will meet to do something that, so far, beer geeks（怪人）have found impossible. They will define what craft beer is in the UK.

2   This attempt by the new United Craft Brewers (UCB) to codify craft is essential in their mission to, "promote and protect the interests of British craft brewers, their beers and beer enthusiasts." UCB has been established by the scene's big guns — Brewdog, Beavertown, Magic Rock and Camden Town Brewery are among its founders — but, nonetheless, and despite the upbeat "Hey guys!" tone of their first public statement, I cannot help but think they have set themselves a thankless task, and a pointless one.

3   Defining what is and isn't craft beer is notoriously difficult. You cannot restrict it to a list of ingredients（原料）, like the historic German purity laws, because modern brewers want to use everything from coffee grounds to chillies in their beers. You cannot define craft beer in terms of how it is packaged, as Camra did with real ale（麦芽酒）, because it already comes in cask（木桶）, keg, can, bottle and — who knows? — probably Tetrapak cartons and PET bottles soon, too. Nor is an ambitious company such as Brewdog (it is poised to hugely increase its brewing capacity and already owns 35 bars) likely to signup to something that restricts craft breweries to a certain size, be that in terms of volume production — as craft breweries are primarily regulated in the US — financial turnover or diversification（多样化）of the company's interests.

4   Yes, a definition of craft could outlaw certain practises, such as the addition of cheap adjuncts（附属物）such as corn and rice to beers, or pasteurization（巴氏灭菌法）, but even that would run contrary to the spirit of craft which has, repeatedly, overturned the shibboleths（口令）around beer. Tell a craft brewer you cannot do something and, invariably（不变地）, they will come back next week with a flavour-packed beer that proves you can. Craft beer is antithetical（对立的）to rules. Even those things which UCB should logically demand of its members (a ban on third-party contract brewing; no-membership for "small breweries" that are owned / funded by multinationals), would pose immediate issues for its founders. Brewdog is about to (albeit as a one-off stunt), effectively contract brew a beer in the UK on behalf of the US brewery Stone while fellow UCB founders James Clay distribute Founders' beers, a company 30% owned by Mahou San Miguel.

5   You can see the thinking behind UCB. Loads of big breweries are piling into the sector with sub-standard beers that trade on the language and design of craft. They are cashing in on a

scene they did nothing to cultivate（培养）and exploiting a cachet（优良标志）they have not earned. If left unchecked, some argue, they will devalue, if not destroy, what craft — in terms of encouraging experimentation, craftsmanship, big flavours, a quality product — has achieved. In principle, trying to stymie that infiltration（渗透物）is a good thing. Except that, legally, how will you ever stop big breweries using the term "craft beer"? And what if Guinness or Molson Coors suddenly produced a stunning mass market beer? It is unlikely, but not impossible.

6 Being ultra-cynical, moreover, at a point when tiny microbreweries are multiplying like wild yeast, UCB could be seen as an attempt by its founders to portray themselves as the defenders of the true craft faith, precisely because it will give them a timely marketing boost. True, UCB is being promoted as an inclusive, collaborative entity, but, in the short term, it is more good publicity for a group of established breweries that already dominate UK craft beer. For instance, if some of the gloss has recently come off Brewdog, UCB will help reassert（重复主张）its legitimacy.

7 Technical problems aside, however, I cannot help but think that any attempt to define craft beer is a retrograde（倒退的）step. The great thing about the craft upsurge（高潮）is that it has made beer fans question everything. After years of lazy real ale dogma (cask beer is morally superior; lager is evil), flavour has become the paramount（最重要的）issue in beer. That is craft's one guiding aim: the maximisation of flavour. You do not need to know how the beer is made. You just need a mouth and a modicum of curiosity. Just trust your tastebuds.

8 The obvious danger in trying to define craft beer — in turning this subjective byword for quality into something objectively quantifiable（可以计量的）— is that such innovation will be swapped（交换）for the pettifogging（诡辩）of a UCB rulebook. Even now, some Camra militants will defend the most boring brown bitter, simply because it is a regulation, box-ticking cask ale. People like rules. They like simplicity. They like not having to think. Define craft beer and it can only encourage a similarly conservative（保守的）mindset.

9 Will some breweries knockout ersatz craft beers? Of course. Will some people be fooled by them? Naturally. But only until they try the genuine article, which, given the unprecedented（空前的）growth of craft beer, is only a matter of time.

10 Fundamentally, beer fans may not be able to define craft beer, but they certainly know what it is when they taste it. Do you agree? Or do you think the formation of the UCB is long overdue?

I. Match the summaries (A–J) on the left column with the number of paragraphs on the right column.

  A. Beer breweries will recognise the truth sooner or later. Paragraph 1
  B. Defining craft beer is pettifogging. Paragraph 2
  C. Defining craft beer may bring the UCB a timely marketing boost. Paragraph 3
  D. Beer fans know what craft beer is. Paragraph 4
  E. The UCB has set a thankless and pointless task. Paragraph 5
  F. Defining craft beer is a retrograde step. Paragraph 6
  G. Big breweries make a profit without cultivation and exploiting a cachet. Paragraph 7

Unit Four

H. It's hard to define what craft beer is.   Paragraph 8
I. Craft beer is antithetical to rules.   Paragraph 9
J. The UCB will give a definition to craft beer.   Paragraph 10

II. Answer the following questions.
1. According to the author, what's the most important issue in beer?
2. What is the purpose to establish the new United Craft Brewers according to their announcement?
3. Why does the author say "Defining what is and isn't craft beer is notoriously difficult"?

III. Questions for discussion.
1. How do you define what craft beer is? Do you agree with the author's idea that "craft beer is antithetical to rules"?
2. In your opinion, what's "the thinking behind UBC"? Do you agree with the author's idea?

Part Two
Tips for Translation

词的增补

Warm-up

Compare the following pairs of sentences and discuss what have been added during the process of translation.

(1) 小不忍则乱大谋。
    If one is not patient in small things, one will never be able to control great ventures.
(2) 虚心使人进步,骄傲使人落后。
    Modesty helps one to go forward, whereas conceit makes one lag behind.

汉英两种语言由于用词造句的规律不同,在表达同一个思想时常需在译文中增补一些原文中没有的词语。通常增补词语是出于以下两方面的需要。

一、为了保证译文语法结构的完整

英汉两种语言在语法上差异较大,例如:英语有冠词,而汉语却没有;英语重形合、连接词较多,汉语重意合、连接词较少;英语中介词丰富,多达280多个,汉语中介词则较少,只有30来个;英语中经常使用代词,尤其是经常使用人称代词、关系代词等,而汉语中代词则用得较少;因此,汉译英时可根据具体情况增补冠词、连接词、介词、代词,使译文更符合英语习惯。

(一) 代词

交出翻译之前,必须读几遍,看看有没有要修改的地方。这样你才能把工作做好。

Before handing in your translation, you have to read it over and over again and see if there is anything in it to be corrected or improved. Only thus can you do your work well. (增加作主语的代词和物主代词)

(二) 连词

(1) 我是半路出家,可能干不好这工作。

I have not received regular training for the job, so I may not do it well.

(2) 留得青山在,不怕没柴烧。

So long as green hills remain, there will never be a shortage of firewood.

(三) 介词

(1) 咱们机场见吧。

Let's meet at the airport.

(2) 你是白天工作还是晚上工作?

Do you work in the daytime or at night?

(四) 冠词

耳朵是用来听声音的器官,鼻子用来嗅气味,舌头用来尝滋味。

The ear is the organ which is used for hearing. The nose is used for smelling. The tongue is used for tasting.

二、为了保证译文意思的明确

(一) 原文中暗含而无须明言的词语

汉语和英语的习惯用法不同。汉语中某一说法本来是很清楚的,谁也不会误解,可是如果生搬硬套,逐字译成英语,就很可能不达原意,甚至还会引起误解,因此往往需要在译文中增补适当的词,把原文中暗含的意思明确表示出来。例如:

一个篱笆三个桩,一个好汉三个帮。

A fence needs the support of three stakes, an able fellow needs the help of three other people.

(二) 概括性词语

汉语里有时不用表明事物范畴的概括性词语,译成英语时却往往需要增补进去,不然译文含义就不清楚,或者语法结构上有缺陷,或行文不流畅。例如:

黄金白银,坚甲利兵,并非构成大国的要素。

Gold and silver, a strong army and powerful weapons — these are not the elements that constitute a great nation.

(三) 注释性词语

汉语中的典故、谚语和在一定历史、政治条件下形成的某些名词、术语和简化说法,汉语读者熟悉,一看就明白,但是英语读者就不见得能懂,所以翻译时就得适当地添加一点注释性词语。例如：

这对年轻夫妇并不相配，一个是西施，一个是张飞。

This young couple is not well-matched, one is a Xishi, a famous Chinese beauty, while the other is a Zhangfei, a well-known ill-tempered brute.

练习

翻译下列句子，根据需要增补适当的词语。

1. 接到你的来信，非常高兴。
2. 她用手蒙住脸，好像是为了保护眼睛。
3. 请把这张表填一下，填完给我。
4. 下午6点开晚饭。
5. 我们对问题要做全面的分析，才能解决得妥当。
6. 三个臭皮匠，顶个诸葛亮。

Part Three
Simulated Writing

Writing Company Profile

良好的企业简介可以吸引潜在客户，有利于企业宣传。

企业简介应该包括以下信息：企业历史、主要职员、公司产品或服务。这不意味不可以加入复杂的行业信息，但介绍一定要通俗易懂。

除了对产品的描述，企业简介还应该反映出该企业的文化个性。解释企业的主旨，说明得到了哪些社会支持，具体介绍员工的教育、培训和工作经历，都可以使简介更加人性化，更能吸引读者。

Company profiles usually include:

1. Name of company or organization
2. Age of company or organization
3. Products or services of company or organization
4. Growth history of company or organization
5. Anticipated growth of company or organization
6. Current challenges faced by company or organization
7. Location of plants, offices, and stores of company or organization
8. Parent company of company or organization
9. Subsidiaries of company or organization
10. Major activity of company or organization

Sample Reading 1

The Philips Story

The foundations of the world's biggest electronics company were laid in 1891 when Gerard Philips established a company in Eindhoven, the Netherlands, to manufacture light bulbs and other electrical products. In the beginning, it concentrated on making carbon-filament lamps and by the turn of the century was one of the largest producers in Europe. Developments in new lighting technologies fuelled a steady programmed of expansion and, in 1914, it established a research laboratory to stimulate product innovation.

In the 1920s, Philips decided to protect its innovations in X-ray radiation and radio reception with patents. This marked the beginning of the diversification of its product range. Since then, Philips has continued to develop new and exciting product ideas like the compact disc, which it launched in 1983. Other interesting landmarks include the production of Philip's 100-millionth TV set in 1984 and 250-millionth Philishave electric shaver in 1989.

The Philips Company

Philip's headquarters are still in Eindhoven. It employs 256,400 people all over the world, and has sales and service outlets in 150 countries. Research laboratories are located in six countries, staffed by some 3,000 scientists. It also has an impressive global network of some 400 designers spread over twenty-five locations. Its shares are listed in nine countries and it is active in about 100 businesses, including lighting, monitors, shavers and color picture tubes; each day its factories turn out a total of 50 million integrated circuits.

The Philips People

Royal Philips Electronics is managed by the Board of Management, which looks after the general direction and long-term strategy of the Philips group as a whole. The Supervisory Board monitors the general course of business of the Philips group as well as advising the Board of Management and supervising its policies. These policies are implemented by the Group Management Committee, which consists of the members of the Board of Management, chairmen of most of the product divisions and some other key offices. The Group Management Committee also serves to ensure that business issues and practices are shared across the various activities in the group.

The company creed is "Let's make things better". It is committed to make better products and systems and contributing to improving the quality of people's work and life. One recent example of this is its "Genie" mobile phone. To dial a number you just have to say it aloud. Its web TV Internet terminal brings the excitement of cyberspace into the living room. And on travels around the world, whether passing the Eiffel Tower in Paris, walking across London's Tower Bridge, or witnessing the beauty of the ancient pyramids of Giza, you don't have to wonder any more who lit these world famous landmarks, it was Philip.

Notes

carbon-filament lamp	炭丝灯泡
diversification	多样化
compact disc	压缩碟
electric shaver	电动剃须刀
radio reception	无线电接收
color picture tube	彩色显像管
integrated circuit	集成电路
mobile phone	移动电话

Sample Reading 2

The Shell Company

We are best known to the public for our service stations and for exploring and producing oil and gas on land and at sea; but we deliver a much wider range of energy solutions and petrochemicals to customers.

These include transporting and trading oil and gas, marketing natural gas, producing and selling fuel for ships and planes, generating electricity and providing energy efficiency advice. We also produce and sell petrochemical building blocks to industrial customers globally and we are investing in making renewable and lower-carbon energy sources competitive for large-scale use.

We operate in over 140 countries and territories and employ approximately 109,000 people. Around the globe, Shell companies work in partnership with industry, government and society to deliver what is expected of us—economically, socially and environmentally. We invest and collaborate in the development of new technologies that will keep improving our performance. We try to ensure that our employees continuously acquire new skills and capabilities, through training and experience in their own countries and on secondments and assignments abroad. And we constantly check how well we're doing, with internal and independent audits of every aspect of our business.

The Shell Story

In 1833 Marcus Samuel opened a small shop in London, selling seashells to Victorian natural history enthusiasts. It soon became a thriving import-export business. Throughout the early twentieth century, the Group expanded with acquisitions in Europe, Africa and the Americas. The two World Wars years saw many of Shell's operations closed down or confiscated; but others were added or expanded, particularly in North America. Throughout the 1950s and 1960s, Shell's oil output and sales increased dramatically, to the point where Shell supplied almost one-seventh of the world's oil products. In the 1970s, Shell made major oil & gas discoveries in the North Sea, just off the coast of Scotland. In the 1980s, Shell companies installed advanced technology, launched new products and services, and explored solutions to environmental concerns. Shell began to sell unleaded petrol, and subsequently gained a worldwide leadership position. With the 1990s came lower oil prices, and a concentration on Shell's core businesses—mainly oil, gas and chemicals. Fundamental changes have occurred and continue to be made in the Shell Group to ensure that it retains its competitive advantage. These changes include the unification, in July 2005, of the parent companies of Royal Dutch and Shell Transport under a single parent company, Royal Dutch Shell plc.

The Shell People

Royal Dutch Shell has a single tier Board of Directors chaired by a Non-executive Chairman, Jorma Ollila. The executive management is led by the Chief Executive, Jeroen van der Veer. The members of the Board of Royal Dutch Shell meet regularly to discuss reviews and reports on the business and plans of Royal Dutch Shell.

The objectives of the Shell Group are to engage efficiently, responsibly and profitably in oil, oil products, gas, chemicals and other selected businesses and to participate in the search for and development of other sources of energy to meet evolving customer needs and the world's growing demand for energy.

We believe that oil and gas will be integral to the global energy needs for economic development for many decades to come. Our role is to ensure that we extract and deliver them profitably and in environmentally and socially responsible ways.

Notes

petrochemicals	石化产品
generating electricity	发电
lower-carbon energy source	低二氧化碳能源
confiscate	充公
launch new products	推出新产品

Check Your Understanding

Match the items listed in the following two columns.

1. electrical products   A. 长期战略
2. unleaded petrol   B. 全球网络
3. product range   C. 生产
4. global network   D. 无铅汽油
5. turn out   E. 电子产品

6. long-term strategy　　　　　F. 管理委员会
7. Board of Management　　　　G. 倒闭
8. acquire new skills　　　　　　H. 获得新技术
9. import-export business　　　　I. 进出口交易
10. close down　　　　　　　　　J. 产品系列

Follow-up Writing

Complete the following Company Profile with the information given below.

Name: The Textron Company, one of the largest and most successful multi-industry companies

Establishment: in 1923

Revenue: $10 billion

Staff: 37,000 employees in nearly 33 countries

Headquarters: in Providence, Rhode Island

Rank: 190th on the FORTUNE 500 list of largest U.S. companies.

Organization: numerous subsidiaries and operating divisions

Part Four
Listening

Lead-in

I. **Discuss the following topics with your classmates.**

　　1. Have you ever cooked? If yes, say something about it.

　　2. In your opinion, what are the main advantages of cooking?

II. **Study the following vocabulary before you listen.**

dub	授予称号	popularise	推广,使通俗化
conceit	自负	soufflés	[法语] 起酥的
bacteria	细菌	fermentation	发酵
conundrum	难题	paradox	悖论
microbes	微生物	edible	可食用的
detoxify	使解毒	hymn	赞美诗
obesity	肥胖	E. coli	大肠杆菌
frontier	前沿,进展	Pasteurian	巴氏消毒法
gut	肠胃	durian	榴莲

maize	玉米	stew	炖汤
harness	利用	sterilise	消毒，灭菌
quaint	新奇有趣的	alternative	供替代的选择

While-listening

I. Listen to the recording and supply the missing words.

Humanity's Relationship with Cooking Is Unique—and Shouldn't Be Lost

Before Michael Pollan came along, eating as a form of politics was a __1__ activity. Dubbed the "liberal foodie intellectual" by the *New York Times*, the American activist and author has spent the last two decades writing bestselling books, such as "In Defence of Food" (2008) and "The Omnivore's Dilemma" (2006), in an effort to popularise cooking and __2__ the defects of the food industry and the rich world's bad eating habits.

Mr. Pollan's latest book, "Cooked", is divided into four sections: fire, water, air and earth. Although something of an authorly conceit, these __3__ allow him to explore a range of __4__ topics from the joy of making soufflés that rise to why bacteria are needed in fermentation. He also returns to a conundrum he has previously described as the "cooking paradox": why it is that people now spend less time preparing food from __5__ and more time reading about cooking or watching cookery programmes on television.

Mr. Pollan explores the same way a __6__ might, by studying the animals, plants and microbes involved in cooking, and delving into history, culture and chemistry. With help from experts he masters the "whole hog" barbecue, a __7__ of bread and the cooking pot. He describes the remarkable transformations that take place in the humble saucepan, where __8__ are broken down, seeds softened and rendered edible, plants detoxified, and __9__ brought together from far-flung taxonomic kingdoms.

Side by side with Mr. Pollan the __10__ is the author as activist. Although the fruit and vegetable areas of supermarkets have grown ever bigger over the past two decades, cooking has expanded to take in heating up a tin of soup, microwaving ready-meals and frozen pizzas or breaking open a bag of mixed __11__ leaves. Mr. Pollan places great __12__ on the work of Harry Balzer, an expert on food, diet and eating patterns in America. Collecting data from thousands of food diaries, Mr. Balzer concludes that, since the 1980s, fewer and fewer people have been cooking their evening meal. (The most popular meal in America, at lunch and dinner, is a sandwich accompanied by a __13__ drink.)

Mr. Pollan is __14__ for this trend to be reversed and his book is a hymn to why people should be enticed back into the kitchen. Cooking, he believes, creates bonds between humans and the web of living creatures that __15__ and __16__ them. Turning away from this means that foods that are tasty and healthy (as bread once was) are being taken off the menu with far-reaching __17__. Industrially produced food almost always trades in quality __18__ for higher amounts of sugar, salt and fat—with a __19__ rise in levels of obesity.

Before __20__, bad food often killed people. Bacteria, such as E. coli, __21__ still do. In recent decades a great deal of research has been done on the __22__ of good microbes humans carry within them and which they need in order to stay healthy. "Cooked" is particularly informative about the rapidly moving scientific frontier of microbial __23__ and how, in a post-Pasteurian world, the live-culture foods which used to make up a large part of the human diet are good for people and for the microbes that live inside the gut.

The book __24__ on fermented foods, for example. These have largely __25__ from supermarkets but many cultures have developed such __26__, including Malaysian tempoyak, (fermented durian fruit), Russian kefir (similar to yogurt) and Mexican pozole (a maize stew). Even bread, cheese and chocolate all depend on harnessing the power of microbes. These invisible forces travel alongside humans, Mr. Pollan says, in a "dance of __27__ symbiosis", cleverly transforming, sterilising or even adding __28__.

Mr. Pollan recognises that cooking today is very different from what it was in his grandmother's time, and that decades from now even a limited desire to cook may be seen as quaint. This would be a shame. Real cooking (not just heating up) allows people to create, to put their own values into food, to escape the __29__ eating that has created health crises all over the world. Cooking is part of being human. The alternative is to evolve into passive consumers of __30__ commodities that promise more than they deliver. Best of all, argues Mr. Pollan, cooking makes people happy.

II. **Listen again, stop the recording as necessary, and repeat after the speaker.**

Post-listening

Surf the Internet and find more information about the following topic areas. Then prepare a 15-minute oral presentation and deliver it in the class. While preparing the presentation you need to narrow down topic the area and focus on one major point.
1. food or cooking
2. Introduction to a festival dish in English speaking country

Sample Dialogue 1
M: Mr. Wan, we've spoken before this matter, and I hope we can come to some agreement this time. As you know, Jackson Co. Ltd. would very much like to act as the agent of China Chemical Product Import and Export Company in the U. S. and South America.

W: Yes, indeed. I have spoken to the relevant branches of our organization, and we are willing to appoint Jackson as our sole agent for the U.S.

M: Excellent news. Once the agreement is signed, we'll be able to promote your products more vigorously. Giving sole agency to us will also reduce the number of rivals, which is beneficial for business development. And, as you are aware, we have a broad customer base and deal with many retailers not only in the U. S. but all over South America. So we feel that the agency agreement should cover South America as well as the U. S.

W: I see. But we also have a well-established customer base in South America, and don't really feel the need for an agent to cover America on our behalf. Besides, we have many old customers in Canada and Brazil. If we signed up with you, we would undoubtedly lose these old and valued customers.

M: Okay. Well, let's bear that in mind. I would suggest that the duration of the agreement should be 3 years and then after that, if it proves satisfactory to both sides, we can extend the agreement.

W: Sounds fine. You've clearly given this a lot of thought. What quantity do you propose to sell?

M: I would suggest 3,000 tons in Year One, 4,000 tons in Year Two and 5,000 tons in Year Three.

Sample Dialogue 2

W: Good morning, Mr. Black.

M: Good morning, Miss Wu. First of all, I'd like to thank you for your kind invitation to visit your beautiful country. I hope my visit will help promote a friendly relationship between us.

W: We've been looking forward to your visit. It is a great pleasure for us to have you as our guest. And it is always more convenient to discuss things face to face.

M: I have good news for you, Miss Wu. Your PC pumps can find a ready market in our country. My clients are very satisfied with the last delivery of your PC pumps. The models are very much to the taste of our market.

W: Thank you for your efforts.

M: We've spared no efforts in promoting the sales of your PC pumps. Advertisements have been made both in newspaper and on TV programs. Our salesmen have worked hard to push sales of your products here and there. All these have cost us a lot.

W: Thank you for all the work you've done to promote the sales of our products.

M: Not at all. I am honored to be able to help you. But to most effectively promote your products, I believe you need the services of a well-established firm, one which can guarantee you the sales you deserve.

W: You mean, we should appoint an agent.

M: Yes, to be frank, to appoint us. I understand you are selling the same products to some other Canadian importers. But this tends to complicate my business. As you know, I'm experienced in the business of PC pumps and enjoy a good business relationship with all the leading wholesalers and retailers in that line. So, one of the reasons for my visit here is to sign a sole agency agreement with you on this item for a period of three years. As it is to our mutual interest and profit, I'm sure you'll have no objection to it.

act as	充当	appoint...as	任命,指定
sole agent	独家代理	PC pump	螺杆泵
to the taste of...	合……口味	spare no efforts	不遗余力

Unit Four

USEFUL EXPRESSIONS AND PATTERNS:

1. As you know, Jackson & Co. Ltd. would very much like to act as the agent of China Chemical Product Import and Export Company in the U. S. and South America.
2. We are willing to appoint Jackson as our sole agent for the U.S.
3. Once the agreement is signed, we'll be able to promote your products more vigorously.
4. Giving sole agency to us will also reduce the number of rivals, which is beneficial for business development.
5. And, as you are aware, we have a broad customer base and deal with many retailers not only in the U. S. but all over South America. So we feel that the agency agreement should cover South America as well as the U. S.
6. I would suggest that the duration of the agreement should be 3 years and then after that, if it proves satisfactory to both sides, we can extend the agreement.
7. In fact only 20% — 25% of our sales are to U. S. retailers.
8. That would be fair enough. And, there is one more point we should discuss, and that is our commission.
9. You know, we'll have to put in a lot of extra work and do a lot of advertising now we have the responsibility of agency.
10. But to most effectively promote your products, I believe you need the services of a well-established firm, one which can guarantee you the sales you deserve.
11. One of the reasons for my visit here is to sign a sole agency agreement with you on this item for a period of three years.
12. According to our records, the total amount of your orders last year was moderate, which does not warrant an agency appointment.
13. Unless you increase the turnover we can hardly appoint you our sole agent.
14. Don't you think this annual turnover is rather conservative for a sole agent?
15. Our price is the lowest among all similar products, and, with the Sole Agency in your hand, there will be no competition and you could easily control the market, which would naturally result in bigger sales.

I. **Role-play the sample dialogues.**

II. **Complete the following dialogue by translating Chinese into English orally.**
A: I've come to talk about an agency agreement.
B: What do you have in mind?
A: Ever since your products entered our market two years ago, _____1_____ (它一直显示出极大的市场潜力). But you can do even better if you develop some kind of sales network there.
B: To tell you the truth, I was just thinking of that.
A: As you know, we are a well-established firm in the line of chemical products, and _____2_____ (我们与加拿大的所有的批发商、连锁店、销售商保持良好的关系). You'll find most worthwhile if you appoint us as your sole agent.

93

B: Thank you for your intention to _____3_____ (有助于我们的产品的促销), and we are quite satisfied with your performance in the last two years. But honestly, an annual sales volume of $500, 000 does not justify a sole agency agreement.

A: _____4_____ (如果你指定我们做独家代理), we can assure you that we'll double the turnover.

B: Do you mean to say that if we entrust you with the agency, you will sell $1, 000, each year?

A: I couldn't have said it any better. But we expect a 10% commission, of course.

B: _____5_____ (我们在其他地区的代理通常可以得到10%的佣金).

A: But your product is still new to our market, and _____6_____ (我们需要在促销上做很多的工作, 花很多时间). A 10% commission won't leave us much.

B: What duration are we talking about?

A: Let's say three years to start with. After that the agreement can be renewed if we both agree.

B: Let's put it this way, we'll allow you a 10% commission if you guarantee an annual of $100, 000, starting from $1, 000, 000 for the first year.

A: You certainly drive a hard bargain, Mr. Li. But I agree.

B: The territory will be confined to the Canadian market only.

A: Of course. Within the validity of the agency agreement, _____7_____ (你不能将产品提供给其他任何买主) in Canada, and we, on our part, shall not handle competitive products by other suppliers either.

B: Sure. Let's call it a deal.

III. **Learn to communicate in the situation given below.**

Student A: a representative from a petrochemical company in China

Student B: Mr. Anderson, a foreign businessman

A is discussing with B about an agency agreement. Make a conversation with the following expressions.

- So I wonder if you'd be willing to take the job?
- Then let me propose an annual sales volume of 10, 000 dozen for three years. Is this all right?
- Well, how about the commission?
- What about other terms?

Unit Five

Ethics

Part One
Reading and Translating

Lead-in

Case Study: Evaluate the following case and discuss the questions.

The Cost of Integrity

Dr. X, a distinguished structural engineer, received a phone call from an engineering student at a nearby college. The student expressed concern that Dr. X's famous skyscraper had a serious technical design flaw. At first, Dr. X dismissed the student's concerns outright but the conversation gets him thinking. Over the weekend, Dr. X sifts through his data and realizes the student is indeed correct — strong winds could cause this famous landmark to topple and in the process kill thousands of innocent people. Rectifying the problem would be no small task and would require notifying the building's owners, city officials, and the press and might negatively impact Dr. X's professional reputation.

1. What is the action or inaction that is the cause for concern?
2. Who or what may be affected?
3. How will they be affected? (i.e., what are the possible consequences?)
4. Are there any laws, regulations written or unwritten that may apply?
5. What actions might be taken and what would the consequences of these actions be?
6. Can anything be done to prevent this from reoccurring or to minimize the severity of the consequences?

Reading A

Basic Principles of Environmental Ethics

1   Many traditional western ethical perspectives, however, are anthropocentric or human-centered in that either they assign intrinsic value to human beings alone (i.e., what we might call anthropocentric in a strong sense) or they assign a significantly greater amount of intrinsic value to human beings than to any nonhuman things such that the protection or promotion of human interests or well-being at the expense of nonhuman things turns out to be nearly always justified (i.e., what we might call anthropocentric in a weak sense). For example, Aristotle maintains that "nature has made all things specifically for the sake of man" and that the value of nonhuman things in nature is merely instrumental. Generally, anthropocentric positions find it problematic to articulate what is wrong with the cruel treatment of nonhuman animals, except to the extent that such treatment may lead to bad consequences for human beings. Immanuel Kant, for instance, suggests that cruelty towards a dog might encourage a person to develop a character which would be desensitized to cruelty towards humans. From this standpoint, cruelty towards nonhuman animals would be instrumentally, rather than intrinsically, wrong. Likewise, anthropocentrism often recognizes some non-intrinsic wrongness of anthropogenic (i.e. human-caused) environmental devastation. Such destruction might damage the well-being of human beings now and in the future, since our well-being is essentially dependent on a sustainable environment.

2   Biocentrism states that nature does not exist simply to be used or consumed by humans, but that humans are simply one species amongst many, and that because we are part of an ecosystem, any actions which negatively affect the living systems of which we are a part, adversely affect us as well, whether or not we maintain a biocentric worldview. Biocentrists believe that all species have inherent value, and that humans are not "superior" in a moral or ethical sense. Paul Taylor, one of the major early proponents of biocentrism, maintains that biocentrism is an "attitude of respect for nature", whereby one attempts to make an effort to live one's life in a way that respects the welfare and inherent worth of all living creatures. Taylor states that:

  ＊Humans are members of a community of life along with all other species, and on equal terms.

  ＊This community consists of a system of interdependence between all members, both physically, and in terms of relationships with other species.

  ＊Every organism is a "teleological center of life", that is, each organism has a purpose and a reason for being, which is inherently "good" or "valuable".

  ＊Humans are not inherently superior to other species.

3   Deep ecology is a contemporary ecological philosophy that recognizes an inherent worth of all living beings, regardless of their instrumental utility to human needs. The philosophy

emphasizes the interdependence of organisms within ecosystems and that of ecosystems with each other within the biosphere. It provides a foundation for the environmental, ecology and green movements and has fostered a new system of environmental ethics. Deep ecology's core principle is the belief that, like humanity, the living environment as a whole has the same right to live and flourish. Deep ecology describes itself as "deep" because it persists in asking deeper questions concerning "why" and "how" and thus is concerned with the fundamental philosophical questions about the impacts of human life as one part of the ecosphere, rather than with a narrow view of ecology as a branch of biological science, and aims to avoid merely anthropocentric environmentalism, which is concerned with conservation of the environment only for exploitation by and for humans purposes, which excludes the fundamental philosophy of deep ecology. Deep ecology seeks a more holistic view of the world humans live in and seeks to apply to life the understanding that separate parts of the ecosystem (including humans) function as a whole.

4 In the literature on environmental ethics the distinction between instrumental value and intrinsic value has been of considerable importance. The former is the value of things as means to further some other ends, whereas the latter is the value of things as ends in themselves regardless of whether they are also useful as means to other ends. For instance, certain fruits have instrumental value for bats who feed on them, since feeding on the fruits is a means to survival for the bats. However, it is not widely agreed that fruits have value as ends in themselves. We can likewise think of a person who teaches others as having instrumental value for those who want to acquire knowledge. Yet, in addition to any such value, it is normally said that a person, as a person, has intrinsic value, i.e., value in his or her own right independently of his or her prospects for serving the ends of others. For another example, a certain wild plant may have instrumental value because it provides the ingredients for some medicine or as an aesthetic object for human observers. But if the plant also has some value in itself independently of its prospects for furthering some other ends such as human health, or the pleasure from aesthetic experience, then the plant also has intrinsic value. Because the intrinsically valuable is that which is good as an end in itself, it is commonly agreed that something's possession of intrinsic value generates a prima facie direct moral duty on the part of moral agents to protect it or at least refrain from damaging it.

5 Ecofeminism, a pluralistic, nonhierarchical, relationship-oriented philosophy that suggests how humans could reconceive themselves and their relationships to nature in nondominating ways, is proposed as an alternative to patriarchal systems of domination. It is concerned not so much with rights, obligations, ownership, and responsibilities as with care, appropriate reciprocity, and kinship. This worldview promotes a richly textured understanding or sense of what human life is and how this understanding can shape people's encounters with the natural world. According to ecofeminist philosophy, when people see themselves as related to others and to nature, they will see life as bounty rather than scarcity, as cooperation rather than isolated egos. Ecofeminists reject the view of a single, ahistoric, context-free, neutral observation stance. Instead, they favor multiple understandings, context relationships, and "embodied objectivity".

6 Environmental racism is inequitable distribution of environmental hazards based on race. Evidence of environmental racism can be seen in lead poisoning in children. The Federal Agency

for Toxic Substances and Disease Registry considers lead poisoning to be the number one environmental health problem for children in the United States. Some 4 million children—many of whom are African American, Latino, Native American, or Asian, and most of whom live in inner-city areas—have dangerously high levels of lead in the house paint, contaminated drinking water from lead pipes or lead solder, and soil polluted by industrial effluents and automobile exhaust. The evidence of racism is that at every income level, whether rich or poor, black children are two to three times more likely than whites to suffer from lead poisoning.

New Words and Expressions

acquire	v.	[əˈkwaɪə(r)]	获得,取得,学到
adversely	adv.	[ədˈvɜːsli]	逆地,反对地;不利地,有害地
ahistoric	a.	[ˌeɪhɪsˈtɒrɪk]	无历史记载的
aesthetic	a.	[iːsˈθetɪk]	美的,美学的;审美的
anthropocentric	a.	[ˌænθrəpəˈsentrɪk]	人类中心说的
articulate	v.	[ɑːˈtɪkjuleɪt]	清晰地发(音);言语表达
assign	v.	[əˈsaɪn]	分派,选派,分配;归于,归属
biocentrism	n.	[baɪəʊˈsentrɪzəm]	生物中心论
biosphere	n.	[ˈbaɪəʊsfɪə(r)]	生物圈,生物界,生物层
consequence	n.	[ˈkɒnsɪkwəns]	结果,成果;[逻]结论;重要性
considerable	a.	[kənˈsɪdərəbl]	相当大(或多)的;相当数量的
contaminate	v.	[kənˈtæmɪneɪt]	弄脏,污染;损害,毒害
contemporary	a.	[kənˈtemprəri]	当代的,现代的;同时代的
core	n.	[kɔː(r)]	中心,核心,精髓
desensitize	v.	[ˌdiːˈsensətaɪz]	减少感光性,使不敏感
devastation	n.	[ˌdevəˈsteɪʃn]	毁坏,荒废
ecofeminism	n.	[iːkəʊˈfemənɪzəm]	生态女性主义
ecology	n.	[iˈkɒlədʒi]	生态学,社会生态学
ecosphere	n.	[ˈiːkəʊsfɪə]	生物圈,生态层
ecosystem	n.	[ˈiːkəʊsɪstəm]	生态系统
effluent	n.	[ˈefluənt]	(注入河里的)污水,工业废水
ego	n.	[ˈiːɡəʊ]	自我,自负,自尊心,自我意识
embody	v.	[ɪmˈbɒdi]	表现,象征;包含
essentially	adv.	[ɪˈsenʃəli]	本质上,根本上,本来
ethical	a.	[ˈeθɪkl]	伦理学的,道德的,伦理的
flourish	v.	[ˈflʌrɪʃ]	茂盛,繁荣;活跃,蓬勃;挥舞
foster	v.	[ˈfɒstə(r)]	培养,抚育;促进;代养
holistic	a.	[həʊˈlɪstɪk]	全盘的,整体的;功能整体性的
impact	n.	[ˈɪmpækt]	碰撞,冲击;影响;冲击力
ingredient	n.	[ɪnˈɡriːdiənt]	(构成)要素;(烹调)原料
inherent	a.	[ɪnˈhɪərənt]	固有的,内在的,天生的

intrinsic	a.	[ɪnˈtrɪnsɪk]	内在的,本质的
justified	a.	[ˈdʒʌstɪfaɪd]	有正当理由的,合理的
kinship	n.	[ˈkɪnʃɪp]	亲属关系
merely	adv.	[ˈmɪəli]	仅仅,只不过,只是
negatively	adv.	[ˈneɡətɪvlɪ]	否定地,消极地,负地
nonhierarchical	a.	[ˌnɒnˌhaɪəˈrɑːkɪkl]	无级的
patriarchal	a.	[ˌpeɪtriˈɑːkl]	家长的,族长的;父权的
persist	v.	[pəˈsɪst]	坚持,固执;存留;继续存在
pluralistic	a.	[ˌplʊərəˈlɪstɪk]	兼职的;多元论的,多元化的
prima facie	a.	[ˌpraɪməˈfeɪʃi]	乍看的,据初步印象的
proponent	n.	[prəˈpəʊnənt]	支持者,拥护者,提倡者
racism	n.	[ˈreɪsɪzəm]	种族主义,种族偏见
reciprocity	n.	[ˌresɪˈprɒsəti]	相互性,相互作用;互给;互惠
reconceive	v.	[ˌriːkənˈsiːv]	重构
registry	n.	[ˈredʒɪstri]	记录,登记;登记处
scarcity	n.	[ˈskeəsəti]	不足,缺乏,稀少
superior	a.	[suːˈpɪərɪə(r)]	(级别、地位)较高的;(在质量等方面)较好的;上等的
survival	n.	[səˈvaɪvl]	幸存,生存;幸存者
sustainable	a.	[səˈsteɪnəbl]	可持续的;可以忍受的;可支撑的
teleological	a.	[ˌtiːliːəˈlɒdʒɪkl]	目的论的
texture	n.	[ˈtekstʃə(r)]	质地,结构,本质
toxic	a.	[ˈtɒksɪk]	有毒的,中毒的;因中毒引起的

assign ... to	指定,分配给,归因于
in ... sense	从……意义上说
at the expense of	以……为代价
from ... standpoint	从……角度,从……观点看
attempt to	尝试,企图;试图做某事
along with	和……一起,随着
in terms of	用……的话,就……而言
regardless of	不管,无论
aim to	旨在,打算,目的
refrain from	忍住,制止,控制,克制不要

I. Give brief answers to the following questions.

1. How does anthropocentric perspective interpret the relationship between human beings and non human beings?
2. What is the key point of biocentrism?
3. Why is the "deep ecology" philosophy deep?
4. What are the differences between instrumental value and intrinsic value?

5. What does "ecofeminism" philosophy denote?
6. What does "environmental racism" mean?

II. Complete the following passage by filling each of the numbered blanks with one suitable word using the Chinese in the brackets as the reference.

   Ecofeminism, a pluralistic, nonhierarchical, relationship-oriented philosophy that suggests how humans could reconceive themselves and their relationships to nature in nondominating ways, is proposed as an alternative to patriarchal systems of __1__（控制）. It is concerned not so much with rights, obligations, ownership, and __2__（责任）as with care, __3__（适当的）reciprocity, and kinship. This worldview __4__（促进）a richly textured understanding or sense of what human life is and how this understanding can shape people's __5__（对抗）with the natural world. According to ecofeminist philosophy, when people see themselves as related to others and to nature, they will see life as bounty rather than __6__（稀缺）, as cooperation rather than __7__（孤立的）egos. Ecofeminists __8__（反对）the view of a single, ahistoric, context-free, __9__（中立的）observation stance. Instead, they favor multiple understandings, context relationships, and "embodied __10__（客观性）."

III. Complete the following sentences with one function word.

1. For example, Aristotle maintains that "nature has made all things specifically _____ the sake of man" and that the value of nonhuman things in nature is merely instrumental.
2. Such destruction might damage the well-being of human beings now and in the future, since our well-being is essentially dependent _____ a sustainable environment.
3. Humans are members of a community of life along _____ all other species, and on equal terms.
4. Humans are not inherently superior _____ other species.
5. However, it is not widely agreed that fruits have value as ends _____ themselves.
6. Toxic Substances and Disease Registry considers lead poisoning _____ be the number one environmental health problem for children in the United States.

IV. Complete the following sentences by translating the Chinese given in the brackets.

1. Also unclear is how much debt Time Warner _____（将会选择让这家子公司承担）. (assign ... to)
2. _____（严格上讲）, even if it does produce some short-term effects, they will come _____（长期代价也很大）. (in ... sense, at the expense of)
3. _____（从费用的方面看）, the underlying principle applicable to planning is simple. (from ... standpoint)
4. You need to take into account the initial cost of the software, _____（以及相关的长期成本）. (along with)
5. Practitioners often think that having courage means they can forge ahead with a plan, _____（而不管这样做的后果）. (regardless of)
6. _____（这发出一个强烈的信号，制止通过施加不正当贸易限制来竞争）and takes us one step closer to a level playing field for raw materials. (refrain from)

Unit Five

V. Translate the following sentences into English.

1. 然而，很多传统的西方伦理观都是人类中心说或者以人类为中心的，这一观点或者仅赋予人类以内在价值，或者赋予人类的内在价值远远高于非人类生物的价值，以至于为了保护人类的利益和福利，牺牲非人类事物的做法都是正当合理的。
2. 生物中心论者认为，所有物种都具有内在价值，并且，无论从道德还是伦理意义上讲，人类并不比其他生物"高级"。
3. 这一哲学观点强调生态系统物种的互相依赖性，和在生物圈中生态系统间的互相依赖性。
4. 生态女性主义哲学认为，当人们认为自己与他人及自然有联系和互动时，他们便可以感受到生命的慷慨而非匮乏，感受到和谐共存而非独立自我。

VI. Translate the following passage into Chinese.

Biocentrism states that nature does not exist simply to be used or consumed by humans, but that humans are simply one species amongst many, and that because we are part of an ecosystem, any actions which negatively affect the living systems of which we are a part, adversely affect us as well, whether or not we maintain a biocentric worldview. Biocentrists believe that all species have inherent value, and that humans are not "superior" in a moral or ethical sense. Paul Taylor, one of the major early proponents of biocentrism, maintains that biocentrism is an "attitude of respect for nature", whereby one attempts to make an effort to live one's life in a way that respects the welfare and inherent worth of all living creatures.

Reading B

Can Ethics Be Taught?
Manuel Velasquez, Claire Andre, Thomas Shanks, S.J. and Michael J. Meyer

1　In a recent editorial（社论）, the *Wall Street Journal* announced that ethics courses are useless because ethics can't be taught. Although few people would turn to the *Wall Street Journal* as a learned expert on the teaching of ethics, the issue raised by the newspaper is a serious one: Can ethics be taught?

2　The issue is an old one. Almost 2,500 years ago, the philosopher Socrates debated the question with his fellow Athenians. Socrates' position was clear: Ethics consists of knowing what we ought to do, and such knowledge can be taught.

3　Most psychologists（心理学家）today would agree with Socrates. In an overview of contemporary research in the field of moral development, psychologist James Rest summarized the major findings as follows:

   • Dramatic changes occur in young adults in their 20s and 30s in terms of the basic

problem-solving strategies they use to deal with ethical issues.
- These changes are linked to fundamental changes in how a person perceives society and his or her role in society.
- The extent to which change occurs is associated with the number of years of formal education (college or professional school).
- Deliberate(故意的,深思熟虑的)educational attempts (formal curriculum) to influence awareness of moral problems and to influence the reasoning or judgement process have been demonstrated to be effective.
- Studies indicate that a person's behavior is influenced by his or her moral perception and moral judgements.

4 Much of the research that Rest alludes to(提到)was carried on by the late Harvard psychologist, Lawrence Kohlberg. Kohlberg was one of the first people to look seriously at whether a person's ability to deal with ethical issues can develop in later life and whether education can affect that development.

5 Kohlberg found that a person's ability to deal with moral issues is not formed all at once. Just as there are stages of growth in physical development, the ability to think morally also develops in stages.

6 The earliest level of moral development is that of the child, which Kohlberg called the preconventional(成规前期)level. The person at the preconventional level defines(规定)right and wrong in terms of what authority figures say is right or wrong or in terms of what results in rewards and punishments. Any parent can verify(证实,证明)this. Ask the four or five year old why stealing is wrong, and chances are that they'll respond, "Because daddy or mommy says it's wrong" or "Because you get spanked(挨揍,打屁股)if you steal." Some people stay at this level all of their lives, continuing to define right and wrong in terms of what authorities say or in terms of reaping(收获)rewards or avoiding unpleasant consequences.

7 The second level of moral development is the level most adolescents(青少年)reach. Kohlberg called this the conventional(常规的,传统的)level. The adolescent at the conventional level has internalized(内化)the norms(标准,规范)of those groups among whom he or she lives. For the adolescent, right and wrong are based on group loyalties: loyalties to one's family, loyalties to one's friends, or loyalty to one's nation. If you ask adolescents at this level why something is wrong or why it is right, they will tend to answer in terms of what their families have taught her, what their friends think, or what Americans believe. Many people remain at this level, continuing to define right and wrong in terms of what society believes or what laws require.

8 But if a person continues to develop morally, he or she will reach what Kohlberg labeled the postconventional(成规后期)level. The person at the postconventional level stops defining right and wrong in terms of group loyalties or norms. Instead, the adult at this level develops moral principles that define right and wrong from a universal point of view. The moral principles of the postconventional person are principles that would appeal to any reasonable(通情达理的,合理的)person because they take everyone's interest into account. If you ask a person at the postconventional level why something is right or wrong, she will appeal to what promotes or doesn't promote the universal ideals of justice or human rights or human welfare.

Many factors can stimulate a person's growth through the three levels of moral development. One of the most crucial factors, Kohlberg found, is education. Kohlberg discovered that when his subjects took courses in ethics and these courses challenged them to look at issues from a universal point of view, they tended to move upward through the levels. This finding, as Rest points out, has been repeatedly supported by other researchers.

Can ethics be taught? If you look at the hard evidence psychologists have amassed(积累，积聚), the answer is yes. If you read the *Wall Street Journal*, you wouldn't have thought so.

I. **Match the philosophers or psychologists with their claims or ideas mentioned in the article.**

1. Considerable changes take place in young adults in their 20s and 30s in terms of the basic problem-solving strategies they use to deal with ethical issues.
2. The adolescent at the conventional level has internalized the norms of the groups among whom he or she lives.
3. The extent to which change occurs is associated with the number of years of formal education, college or professional school, for example.
4. Ethics consists of knowing what we ought to do, and such knowledge can be taught.
5. Of the many factors that can stimulate a person's growth, is education, which is a crucial factor.
6. Moral development consists of different levels, namely the preconventional level, the conventional level, and the postconventional level.

A. Socrates _____
B. James Rest _____
C. Lawrence Kohlberg _____

II. **Answer the following questions.**

1. What is the serious issue proposed by *Wall Street Journal*?
2. On what most psychologists today will agree?
3. What are the features of postconventional level development according to Kohlberg?

III. **Questions for discussion.**

1. What can be inferred about Athenians' viewpoint, according to the article?
2. What is your own point of view as to the issue "whether ethics can be taught"?

Part Two
Tips for Translation

词的省略

Warm-up

Compare the following pairs of sentences and discuss what have been omitted during the process of translation.

(1) 所有的物体都由分子组成，而分子又由原子组成。
　　All bodies consist of molecules and molecules of atoms.
(2) 根据水的蒸发现象，人们知道液体在一定的条件下能变成气体。
　　From the evaporation of water people know that liquids can turn into gases under certain conditions.

词的省略也是汉译英时常见的现象。与词的增补情况相反，原文中有些词语从译文的角度来看往往是多余的，可以或必须删去，决不能只字不漏地生搬硬套过来，不然会引起文理不通、意思含糊等弊病。词的省略的目的是为了使译文符合英语的表达习惯和修辞特点。

汉译英中所省略的词语可分为以下几类：

一、省略英语中没有的词类

（一）省略量词

汉语中有量词，而英语中没有专门的量词，因此在汉译英时常常省略量词。如"一辆自行车""一轮满月"和"一场噩梦"对应的英文分别是 a bike, a full moon, a bad dream。

(1) 一轮红日从风平浪静的海面升起。
　　A red sun rose slowly from the calm sea.
(2) 这纯粹是一派胡言。
　　This was a complete lie.

（二）省略语气助词

汉语中有许多语气助词，如"啊""啦""呢""吧""罢了"等，而英语中没有语气助词，因此汉译英时可以省去这些语气助词。

(1) 我呢，从一开始就不赞成。
　　As for me, I don't agree from the very beginning.
(2) 不要认真嘛！我不过开开玩笑罢了。
　　Don't take it seriously. I'm just making fun of you.

二、省略原文中重复出现的词语

汉语中为了讲究句子的平衡，常使用排比、对仗、重复等修辞手段，英语则不同。因此，汉译英时，原文中含义重复的词往往只译出其中一个。

（1）所有的物体都由分子组成，而分子又由原子组成。

All bodies consist of molecules and molecules of atoms.

（2）每条河流都有上游、中游和下游。

Every river has its upper, middle and lower reaches.

（3）这件事要抓紧快办。

This matter needs immediate action.

三、省略原文中表示范畴的词语

汉语里有些名词像"工作""任务""状态""问题""情况""制度""途径""事业""局面"等等通常有具体的含义，自然应当照译，但是它们用来表明范畴时，则失去了具体含义，一般可以省略不译而并不影响意义。如"分析问题"中的"问题"一词，就有具体含义，非译出不可；而"人民内部矛盾问题"中的"问题"则是表明范畴，不必译出，只需译作 contradictions among the people 就可以了。

（1）他的朋友们听到她家中的困难情况后，都主动伸出援助之手。

After her friends heard about her family difficulties, they offered her an helping hand.

（2）论文总结了电子计算机、人造卫星和火箭三方面的新成就。

The thesis summed up the new achievements made in electronic computers, artificial satellites and rockets.

四、省略可能影响译文修辞效果的词语

汉语中，有时为了语言生动，常用四字词组做比喻；有时为了加强语气，可以连续使用好几个短句。在翻译这类句子时，某些词语往往可以省去不译或加以简化和压缩，不然译文势必拖泥带水，松散无力，反而失去了原文的特色。例如：

花园里面是人间的乐园，有的是吃不了的大米白面，穿不完的绫罗绸缎，花不完的金银财宝。

The garden was a paradise on earth, with more food and clothes than could be consumed and more money than could be spent.

原文中的"大米白面""绫罗绸缎""金银财宝"等四字词组分别指"吃的"、"穿的"、"花的"，可直截了当地译成 food, clothes, money，虽然丧失了原文四字词组的特点及其比喻性，却不失简洁明了，反而更符合英文的习惯。如果按原文逐字译出，句子就会显得臃肿、累赘。

练习

翻译下列句子，根据需要省略适当的词语。

1. 这纯粹是一派胡言。
2. 他们是亲密无间的朋友。
3. 质子带正电，电子带负电，而种子既不带正电，也不带负电。
4. 人们利用科学去了解自然，改造自然。
5. 多年来那个国家一直有严重的失业现象。

Part Three
Simulated Writing

Patent

　　专利说明书是申请人用以说明发明的内容和要求取得的权力要求范围的文件。用英文出版的专利说明书有美国、英国、加拿大、澳大利亚等国。此外,国际专利申请说明书(PCT)和欧洲专利说明书(EPO)也有相当数量是用英文出版的。

　　专利说明书的扉页上是标头部分,通常载明各著录项目、专利摘要和主要附图。

　　标头部分各项之前的编号是"专利局间情报检索国际合作委员会"制定的统一代码。目的是便于识别和进行计算机检索。这种代码从1973年起开始施行。

　　各国专利说明书的标头部分采用了统一的代码,这样,根据代码就可知道该项的内容,这对于计算机检索特别方便。下面将标头部分的各种英文表示法做一总结。

[12] (UK Patent Application)	文件类别
[15] Publication Number	文件号,专利号
[19] (GB)	国别
[21] Application Number: Appl. No.; Ser. No.	申请号
[22] Date of Filing; Filed	申请日期
[23] Claims Files	专利权利要求登记日期
[30] Priority Data; Foreign Application Priority Data	国际优先案项目
[31] Priority Application Number; Convention Application No.	优先申请号
[32] Priority Date; Filed	优先申请日期
[33] Priority Country	优先申请
[43] Date of Publication of Application; Application Published	未经审查和未批准专利权的说明书出版日期
[44] Complete Specification Published	专利说明书全文公布日期
[45] (Sept. 26, 1972)	获准专利权的说明书的出版日期
[51] International Classification Number; Int. CL	国际专利分类号
[52] Domestic Classification; Index at Acceptance	本国专利分类号
[54] Title	专利题目
[56] Documents Cited; Reference Cited	参考文献
[57] Abstract	专利摘要
[58] Field of Search	检索范围
[60] Patent Application or Grants	与申请案有法律关联的文件
[62] Division of Ser. No. ...	分案专利
[63] Constitution-in-part of Ser. No. ...	接续专利
[71] Applicant	申请人

Unit Five

[72] Inventor 发明人
[73] Assignee(Assignor) 受让人
[74] Agents; Representative 律师或代理人
[81] Designated States 指定国
[84] Designated Contracting States 指定协约国
    Primary Examiner 主审查员
    Assistant Examiner 助理审查员
    Attorney, Agent, or Firm 专利代理人,专利代理所

Sample Reading 1

United States Patent   [15] 3,670,030
Sparks   [45] June 13, 1972

[54] ALKYLATION OF PHENOLIC COPOUND
[72] Inventor: Allen K. Sparks, Des Plaines, III
[73] Assignee: Universal Oil Products, Des Plaines, III.
[22] Field: Feb. 20,1970
[21] Appl. No.: 13,196
[52] U.S.CI ... 260/613 D,260/624 C, 260/613 13R 260/619 F, 260/619 F, 260/571
[51] Int.CL ... C07c 37/571

[58] Field of Search ... 260/624 C, 613 D, 613R, 619 F 260/619 D, 609 F, 571

[56] References Cited
    UNITED STATES PATENTS
3,290,389   12/1966   Hahn ... 260/624 C UX
    OTHER PUBLICATIONS
Kaiser, Aluminas from Kaiser (Pamphlet) 1965 Pages 8 and 9

Primary Examiner—Bernard Helfin
Attorney—James R. Hoatson, Jr. and Bernard L. Kramer

[57]   ABSTRACT
Water in a controlled concentration is added in the alkylation of a phenolic compound with an olefin in contact with alumina catalyst. This serves to prolong the activity of the catalyst to effect the alkylation reaction and particularly ortho-alkylation.

9 Claims, No Drawings

专利题目:酚类化合物的烷基化反应
专利摘要:一个酚类化合物同一个与铝催化剂接触过的烯烃发生烷基化反应,在该体系中加入一定浓度的水有助于提高催化剂的反应活性,从而保证烷基化反应(尤其是邻位烷基化)的顺利实施。

Notes

a phenolic compound 酚类化合物
alumina catalyst 铝催化剂
alkylation reaction 烷基化反应
ortho-alkylation 邻位烷基化

Sample Reading 2

(12) UK Patent Application (19) GB (15) 2018236 A

(21) Application No 7905828

(22) Date of filing 19 Feb 1979

(23) Claims filed 19 Feb 1979

(30) Priority data

(31) 25807/78

(32) 28 Feb 1978

(33) United Kingdom (GB)

(43) Application published

(51) INT CL2 C06F 3/04

(52) Domestic classification
　　C1D 1B
　　F3D

(56) Documents cited
　　GB 213590 GB 213544

(58) Field of search
　　C1D F3

(71) Applicant
　　Wilkinson Sword Limited
　　Sword House
　　High Wycombe
　　Buckinghamshire

(72) Inventors
　　Robert Lyall
　　Ian Maxwell-Valerie Ann Buckle
　　Michael Graham Carey
　　Cox

(54) Sintering Ferroeilectric materials such as brarium titanate in a vacuum

(57) Abstract

The dielectric properties of ferroelectric materials such as barium titanate are upgraded by sintering the dry pressed shapes in a vacuum having partial air pressures of 1 to 1000 micros. Maintaining the vacuum during cooling is optional.

(74) Agents
　　Marks & Clark, 57—60
　　Lincoln's Inn Fields
　　London, WC2A 3LS

Unit Five

> 专利题目:真空烧结钛酸钡等铁电材料
>
> 专利摘要:提高钛酸钡等铁电材料介电性能的一种方法是在真空度1至1000微米空气分压下煅烧干压成形的制品。在冷却期间,是否保持真空可任意选择。

in a vacuum	真空
dielectric properties	介电性能
barium titanate	钛酸钡
ferroelectric materials	铁电材料
sintering the dry pressed shapes	煅烧干压成形的制品
during cooling	在冷却期间

Check Your Understanding

Match the items listed in the following two columns.

1. date of filing   A. 专利题目
2. claims files   B. 律师
3. priority data   C. 主审查员
4. Appl. No.   D. 优先申请日期
5. priority application number   E. 优先申请号
6. priority date   F. 本国专利分类号
7. priority country   G. 申请日期
8. primary examiner   H. 检索范围
9. Int.CL   I. 专利权利要求登记日期
10. domestic classification J. 国际优先案项目
11. field of search   K. 申请号
12. title   L. 国际专利分类号
13. U. S. CL   M. 优先申请国
14. attorney   N. 美国专利分类号

Follow-up Writing

Complete the following Patent with the information given below.

专利号	3,694,513
获准专利权的说明书的出版日期	Sept. 26, 1972

109

国际专利分类号	C07c 79/24
申请日期	June 8, 1970
申请号	44,666
美国专利分类号	260/622 R
专利题目	DIRECT NITRATION OF ALKYPHENOLS
检索范围	260/622 R
发明人	Stephen W. Tobey, Sudbury, Mass. 01776; Marilyn Z. Lourandos, Ashland, Mass. 01721
受让人	The Dow Chemical Company, Midland, Mich.
主审查员	Howard T. Mars
律师,代理	Griswold & Burdick, Herbert D. Knudsen & C. E. Rehberg

United States Patent [15] __1__
Tobey et al [45] __2__

[54] __3__

[72] Inventor: __4__

[73] Assignee: __5__

[22] Field: __6__
[21] Appl. No.: __7__
[52] U.S.CI __8__
[51] Int.CL __9__

[58] Field of Search __10__

Reference Cited

UNITED STATES PATENTS

2,868,844 1/1959 Coffield et al .... 260/622 R
2,802,833 8/1957 Dietzler .... 260/622 R
3,557,159 1/1971 Gruber .... 260/622 R

FOREIGN PATENTS OF APPLICATIONS
1,294,254 4/1962 France ... 260/622 R
1,142,300 2/1969 Great Britain ... 260/622 R

OTHER PUBLICATIONS
Arnall, J. Chem. Soc., (1942) 125 pp. 811-816
QDIC6

Primary Examiner— __11__
Attorney— __12__

[57] ABSTRACT
Alkylphenols are nitrated with nitric acid in the presence of a secondary or tertiary alcohol, a secondary alkyl nitrate, an aldehede or a ketone. Use of such inhibitor decreases the quantity of oxidation products formed, especially quinine formation, and increases the conversion of the starting phenols to the desired nitrated products

8 Claims, No Drawings

Unit Five

Part Four
Listening

Lead-in

I. Discuss the following topics with your classmates.

1. Do you know anything about ethics? If yes, say something about it.
2. How would you classify ethics?

II. Study the following vocabulary before you listen.

ethics	道德准则,伦理标准
caste	种姓制度,社会等级制度
creed	信条,教义,纲领
professional ethics	职业道德准则
common morality	共同道德
personal ethics	个人伦理

While-listening

I. Listen to the recording and supply the missing words.

Ethics

Ethics is the word that refers to morals, values, and beliefs of the ___1___, family or the society. The word has several meanings. ___2___ it is an activity and process of inquiry. Secondly, it is different from non-moral problems, when dealing with issues and ___3___. Thirdly, ethics refers to a particular set of beliefs, attitudes, and habits of individuals or family or groups ___4___ with morals. Fourth, it is used to mean 'morally correct'.

The study on ethics helps to know the people's beliefs, values, and morals, learn the good and bad of them, and practice them to ___5___ their well-being and happiness. It ___6___ the inquiry on the existing situations, form judgments and ___7___ the issues. In addition, ethics tells us how to live, to ___8___ to issues, through the duties, rights, responsibilities, and obligations. In religion, similar principles are ___10___, but the reasoning on procedures is limited. The principles and practices of religions have 10 from to time to time (history), region (geography, climatic conditions), religion, society, language, caste and creed. But ethics has grown to a large ___11___ beyond the barriers listed above. In ethics, the ___12___ is to study and apply the principles and practices, universally.

II. Match the following terms with their related items.

1. common morality   A. Parallel to the principles of common morality

     B. A set of standards adopted by professionals

2. personal morality   C. Differing from common morality in some areas

     D. A set of moral beliefs shared by all

3. professional ethics   E. A set of moral beliefs that a person holds

F. Basis for the other types of morality

III. Listen to the passage again, and answer the following questions based on the passage.

1. What is the definition of ethics?
2. What are the three types of ethics or morality?

Part Five
Speaking

Technology Transfer and Cooperation

Sample Dialogue 1

M: I see we've got a nice foundation for our project, but the technical problems are considerable.

W: You're right. We have a lot of hard work ahead.

M: Shall we discuss technology transfer now?

W: O.K. If you want the product to compete successfully on the international market, you'll have to acquire advanced technology.

M: Sure, and the imported technology should be of top class in the world.

W: Excuse me, what does "technology" mean when you say imported technology?

M: Naturally it does not only refer to industrial property, know-how should also be included.

W: We agree, but the know-how we promise to transfer is what we are adopting in our production. And you'll pay for it in the form of royalties apart from a certain initial down payment, right?

M: Yes and no. We'll certainly pay for the imported technology. But we expect that for the duration of the joint venture, you will continue offering us your improved technological expertise without extra charges.

W: Oh, no, we can't go that far. Surely you know that technology has a price tag. How could the achievements of our future research be committed in this agreement?

M: Well, both of us should consider ourselves as partners. The higher the technology, the better the product. Your share is 40% of the registered capital of the JV. That means, nearly half of the profit would go to you.

W: I admit there's something in what you say, but I must point out that technology itself creates value and needs to be compensated. Free transfer is out of the question.

M: Let's suspend this discussion for the time being. We think that we are partners and share developments and costs fairly.

W: OK, let's keep it.

Sample Dialogue 2

M: As to our existing technology, the minimum accepted royalty is 5 percent of the net sales price of all licensed items made and sold during the term of the agreement, in addition to an initial payment of US$ 100,000.

W: I'm afraid both the royalty rate and the initial down payment are too high. As you know, the company will have a tough time in the initial stage of operation. How could a joint venture bear such a heavy additional load?

M: The initial down payment can not be reduced, but we may consider lowering the royalty rate a little bit.

W: We suggest the rate come down to 4% of the net sales price.

M: This can be considered. We'd like to have the samples of the first production sent to us. Our technical department will make sure the products meet the necessary specifications.

W: Will you issue a surveyor's report after the inspection, or suggest measures for improvement if the samples fall short of the requirements?

M: Yes, we'll do that. I think things are quite clear now.

W: Not quite, not before we've prepared the feasibility report and drafted the contract.

Notes

feasibility report	可行性报告
imported technology	引进技术
royalty	提成费
industrial property	工业产权
initial down payment	起始预付款
licensed items	许可商品
net sales price	纯销售额
technology transfer	技术转让
fall short of	不符合

USEFUL EXPRESSIONS AND PATTERNS:

1. Strengthening cooperation with China is one of our important strategies.
2. It will help expand our influence in China.
3. Could you be a little more explicit (明确) about your plans?
4. We plan to offer you an initial funding (启动资金) of US $200, 000.
5. I'd like to express our sincere gratitude to your company on behalf of …
6. It's our great honor to be able to join hands with …
7. We have decided to introduce your technological know-how.
8. We would like to talk with you about the possibility of importing some of your technology.

⑨ The technology acquired shall be appropriate and advanced.
⑩ The technology imported shall enable the products to be competitive on the international market.
⑪ The technology provided must be integrated, precise and reliable.
⑫ The technology acquired must meet the requirements of the company's purpose of operation.
⑬ Expenses for the use of know-how shall be fair and reasonable.
⑭ The royalty rate shall be 50% of the net sales value of the products.
⑮ The royalty rate shall not be higher than the standard international rate.

I. **Role-play the sample dialogues.**

II. **Match the following two columns.**

1. 先进技术　　　　A. technology transfer
2. 可行性报告　　　B. know-how
3. 技术转让　　　　C. royalty
4. 提成费　　　　　D. initial down payment
5. 工业产权　　　　E. industrial property
6. 专有技术　　　　F. advanced technology
7. 起草合同　　　　G. draft the contract
8. 起始预付款　　　H. feasibility report

III. **Complete the following dialogues by making sentences with the help of the key words given in brackets.**

1. A: Enhancing cooperation with China is one of our important strategies.
   B: (this, certainly, wise, strategy).
   A: We have decided to donate some chemical products to your research center.
   B: (wish, extend, thanks, your help).

2. A: If you want the product to be competitive on the international market, you'll have to acquire advanced technology.
   B: Yes, besides, (integrated, precise, reliable).
   A: You need to pay for the imported technology in the form of royalties apart from a certain initial down payment.
   B: Yes, we know. But (expense, fair, reasonable).

3. A: The initial down payment cannot be reduced, but we may consider lowering the royalty rate a little.
   B: (suggest, come down to, 3%, net sales price).
   A: I think everything is clear now.
   B: Not yet, not before we (finish, feasibility report, draft, contract).

IV. Learn to communicate in the situation given below.

Student A: a manager from a petrochemical company.
Student B: the president of US the Dow Chemical Company.
A and B are talking about technological transfer and cooperation.
The following points can be referred to in your conversation:
world market
technological cooperation
imported advanced technology
advanced world level

Unit Six

Technology

Part One
Reading and Translating

Lead-in

Have you ever heard of the term high technology? Read the following ten reasons to know more about it.

- High technology makes communication easier. With things such as Internet, we can now talk to our family and friends on the other side of the earth.
- High technology makes transportation a lot quicker. With vehicles like planes and jets, we can now go to anywhere we want much faster.
- With high technology we can now achieve what human workers alone cannot. Machines can go where humans can't (e.g. undersea).
- High technology brings convenience. While machine helps us do our work, our time will be saved, and we can spend that time on more meaningful things.
- It has become very easy for you to get access to relevant information at any time anywhere.
- Since high technology is challenging, it will inspire you to spark your brain to work to its full potential.
- Modern transportation technology makes it very easy for you to travel long distances either in our lives or in the business world.
- Modern technology has played a big role in changing the entertainment industry. Thanks to the high technology, our home entertainment has been improved with the invention of video games and advance music and visual systems like smart televisions which can connect live to internet so that we can share what we're watching with friends.
- High technology will make it simple for students to learn from anywhere through online education and mobile education. Also students now use modern technology in classrooms to learn better.
- It helps the business community develop health applications which can enable us monitor our health and weight. These applications can be used on mobile phones, so we can have them at any time of the day.

Reading A

Technology Must Let Doctors Be Doctors

Jonathan Bush

1 When my doctor walks into the exam room, I want her to pay attention to me, not the computer. Not only is that what all patients want, but it's what doctors want, too. Yet doctors today are under pressure to feed the digital beasts.

2 Health care's latest best-selling M.D. author, Bob Watcher, says that in a 10-hour shift a single doctor might record 4,000 clicks. Worse, much of this activity is routine census taking, driven by insurers and regulators who assume digitization makes it easy to gather statistical data, regardless of whether it contributes to the quality of care.

3 Doctors are not Luddites. Many were initially enthusiastic at the thought of automating their practices, expecting the same kind of usability and productivity they enjoyed with, say, the software they use to do their taxes. The expectation was that software for medical professionals would at least be that good. The reality is that the more "digital" physicians go, and the longer they use software, the less satisfied they become.

4 That's the kicker: Health care is the only industry that has managed to lose productivity while going digital.

5 The typical electronic medical records software is a maze of tabs and dialog boxes that doctors must navigate to record the same information they used to be able to handle with a few notes in a file folder. And what do they get back for their effort? Sadly, consumer apps are much better at volunteering helpful information and unexpected insights.

Fixing the Unfixable

6 Health care's software problem will not be solved with a user interface overhaul — EMRs need to be smarter, not just prettier. Think networks, not software alone. We need to bring together the intelligence of doctors, nurses, patients, hospitals, laboratories, insurers and everyone else who contributes to the continuum of care.

7 Too many doctors document care in disconnected software that doesn't know if a patient had an adverse reaction to a medicine, saw a different doctor down the road last week for a related aliment, or has had countless tests done over the years for similar symptoms. Expecting that intelligence from an isolated EMR would be like hoping your CD player will start to play *Isaac Hayes* because you like James Brown. Unlike your favorite digital music service, it just isn't wired that way.

8 For the past four years, my company, Athenahealth, has been working to reimagine the EMR. We want to take the hassle out of technology, making it useful for the physician and seamless for the patient. We're not done, but we're making progress. Ultimately, we are focused

on delivering EMRs that provide rich clinical information, while still allowing doctors to be fully present at meaningful moments of care. In other words, we believe technology must let doctors be doctors.

9   In our quest to make the EMR smarter, one of our primary tactics is to simplify every process where clinicians are presented with an overwhelming number of choices. Because we operate a network that more than 67,000 providers, serving more than 69 million patients, are plugged into, we can aggregate what we learn from every interaction. That's on the order of 330 million data exchanges per month. We're studying health care in the wild, as well as listening to doctors and care staffs.

10   Complexity is the enemy. Medicine is necessarily complex, but the administrative complexity surrounding it can be reduced. For more than 15 years, we have managed the byzantine world of reimbursement to help providers get paid faster. More recently, we've been applying the same discipline to making electronic health records more useful. Our goal is to prompt providers to gather the data they need to gather in the least intrusive way.

11   Wherever possible, delegation should happen from doctors to nurses and administrative staff, and even to patients. Instead of patients answering a whole series of routine questions with their knickers down in the exam room, let them do it on a mobile app from home the night before. If a doctor is prescribing a prescription for a diabetes patient, rather than being presented with all possible medications, why can't the EMR surface those most likely to be appropriate based on a doctor's past choices, but also based on what's trending and in use across the network?

12   If we expect information technology to help us achieve a more efficient, more effective, higher quality health care system, we not only need to gather data efficiently but make sure we learn from it and translate it into meaningful moments of care.

13   We need make EMRs serve providers, rather than the other way around.

14   That's why we're launching the social engagement campaign *Let Doctors Be Doctors*. We are hopeful that all in the provider community that similarly believe there is a better way, share their EMR stories and recommendations at letdoctorsbedoctors.com. We will bring that feedback to Washington to help influence developing Health IT policy initiatives, including legislative efforts currently underway to improve the interoperability and usability of EMRs.

New Words and Expressions

automate	v.	[ˈɔːtəmeɪt]	使……自动化
aggregate	v.	[ˈæɡrɪɡət]	使……聚集
adverse	a.	[ˈædvɜːs]	相反的，不利的
aliment	n.	[ˈælɪm(ə)nt]	滋养品，食物
byzantine	a.	[baɪˈzæntaɪn; ˈbaɪzəntaɪn]	错综复杂的
clinician	n.	[klɪˈnɪʃn]	临床医生
continuum	n.	[kənˈtɪnjʊəm]	连续统一体
delegation	n.	[delɪˈɡeɪʃ(ə)n]	代表团

diabetes	n.	[ˌdaɪəˈbiːtiːz]	糖尿病
digitization	n.	[ˌdɪdʒɪtɪˈzeɪʃən]	数字化
disconnected	a.	[dɪskəˈnektɪd]	不系统的,不连续的
effective	a.	[ɪˈfektɪv]	有效的
hassle	n.	[ˈhæs(ə)l]	困难,麻烦
insurer	n.	[ɪnˈʃʊərə]	保险公司
interoperability	n.	[ˈɪntərˌɒpərəˈbɪləti]	协同工作的能力
intrusive	a.	[ɪnˈtruːsɪv]	打扰的
kicker	n.	[ˈkɪkə]	爱发牢骚的人
knickers	n.	[ˈnɪkəz]	短裤
launch	v.	[lɔːntʃ]	发起
legislative	a.	[ˈledʒɪslətɪv]	合法的
Luddite	n.	[ˈlʌdaɪt]	卢德派,卢德分子
navigate	v.	[ˈnævɪgeɪt]	操控
overwhelming	a.	[ˌəʊvəˈwelmɪŋ]	巨大的
overhaul	n.	[əʊvəˈhɔːl]	彻底检查,大修
physician	n.	[fɪˈzɪʃ(ə)n]	医生
provider	n.	[prəˈvaɪdə]	提供者;(尤指)维持家庭生计者
prompt	v.	[prɒm(p)t]	促进,激起
reimbursement	n.	[ˌriːɪmˈbɜːsmənt]	补偿,赔偿
seamless	a.	[ˈsiːmlɪs]	无伤痕的
symptom	n.	[ˈsɪm(p)təm]	症状
tactics	n.	[ˈtæktɪks]	方法,策略
underway	a.	[ˈʌndəˈweɪ]	在进行中的
usability	n.	[juzəˈbɪləti]	可用性

in the wild	在自然环境下
plug into	把(电器)插头插入;接通
the other way around	相反地
manage to do ...	成功做……
a maze of	像迷宫般的……
make progress	取得进步
in other words	换句话说
an overwhelming number of	很多的……
go digital	变得数字化
EMR (Electronic Medical Record)	电子病历

I. **Give brief answers to the following questions.**

1. What does a patient want when a doctor walks into the exam room even the technology is highly improved?
2. What is the only industry that has managed to lose productivity while going digital according to the article? And why?

3. Will the health care's software problem be solved with a user interface overhaul? Why or why not?

4. What does it mean by saying "we believe technology must let doctors be doctors"?

5. In the quest to make the EMR smarter, what is one of the primary tactics?

6. What is the company's goal of applying the same discipline to making electronic health records more useful?

II. **Complete the following passage by filling each of the numbered blanks with one or two suitable words using the Chinese in the brackets as the reference.**

In our ___1___ (寻求) to make the EMR smarter, one of our primary ___2___ (方法) is to ___3___ (简化) every process where ___4___ (临床医生) are presented with an ___5___ (巨大的) number of choices. Because we operate a network that more than 67,000 providers, serving more than 69 million patients, are ___6___ (接通), we can ___7___ (使……聚集) what we learn from every interaction. That's on the order of 330 million data exchanges per month. We're studying health care in the wild, as well as listening to doctors and care staffs.

Complexity is the enemy. Medicine is necessarily complex, but the administrative complexity surrounding it can be reduced. For more than 15 years, we have managed the ___8___ (错综复杂的) world of ___9___ (补偿) to help providers get paid faster. More recently, we've been applying the same discipline to making electronic health records more useful. Our goal is to prompt providers to gather the data they need to gather in the least ___10___ (打扰的) way.

III. **Complete the following sentences with one function word.**

1. Not only is that what all patients want, but it's what doctors want, too. _____ (然而) doctors today are under pressure to feed the digital beasts.

2. Worse, much of this activity is routine census taking, driven by insurers and regulators who assume digitization makes it easy to gather statistical data, _____ (不管) of whether it contributes to the quality of care.

3. We need to bring together the intelligence of doctors, nurses, patients, hospitals, laboratories, insurers and everyone else who contributes to the _____ (连续统一体) of care.

4. Too many doctors document care in disconnected software that doesn't know if a patient had an adverse reaction to a medicine, saw a different doctor down the road last week for a related _____ (食物), or has had countless tests done over the years for similar symptoms.

5. We want to take the _____ (困难, 麻烦) out of technology, making it useful for the physician and seamless for the patient.

6. That's why we're _____ (发起) the social engagement campaign *Let Doctors Be Doctors*. We are hopeful that all in the provider community that similarly believe there is a better way, share their EMR stories and recommendations at *letdoctorsbedoctors.com*.

Unit Six

IV. **Complete the following sentences by translating the Chinese given in the brackets.**

1. Under California law, the most visited ports in the state are now working towards providing shore power for certain types of ships so they can _____ (有效地接通电源) supply and reduce emissions. (effective, plug into)
2. After years of efforts, Ella _____ (成功地成为了一名临床医生) in this hospital. (manage to do, clinician)
3. The 21th century is a magical time. _____ (很多东西都变得数字化) in all walks of life. (an overwhelming number of, go digital)
4. Conservationists said that with none in zoos and almost nothing known about how to keep them in captivity, if the species vanish _____ (在自然环境下) they will be extinct. (in the wild)
5. After days' negotiation, the Ronan said rebels would not make pace with the government. They will continue to _____ (对市民发动大规模的攻击). (overwhelming, launch)
6. Too many students' personal files _____ (不系统的软件不知道学生是否会对一个新老师产生相反的反应) after having been adapted to the former one. (disconnected, converse)

V. **Translate the following sentences into English.**

1. 更糟糕的是，此类活动的大部分内容都是常规的统计调查，是由自认为数字化能使统计数据收集更容易的保险公司和校准器控制的。他们并不会理会这样做是否会对治疗质量起到什么作用。
2. 现实是，医生使用软件的时间越长，他们会变得越"智能"，也会越来越不满足。
3. 我们需要集大家的智慧为一体，既包括医生、护士、医院、实验室、保险公司，也包括所有对医疗统一体有贡献的人。
4. 我们需要把电子病历变得更智能，方法之一就是要把每个过程中呈现给医生的诸多选项一一简化。

VI. **Translate the following passage into Chinese.**

Too many doctors document care in disconnected software that doesn't know if a patient had an adverse reaction to a medicine, saw a different doctor down the road last week for a related aliment, or has had countless tests done over the years for similar symptoms. Expecting that intelligence from an isolated EMR would be like hoping your CD player will start to play Isaac Hayes because you like James Brown. Unlike your favorite digital music service, it just isn't wired that way. For the past four years, my company, Athenahealth, has been working to reimagine the EMR. We want to take the hassle out of technology, making it useful for the physician and seamless for the patient. We're not done, but we're making progress. Ultimately, we are focused on delivering EMRs that provide rich clinical information, while still allowing doctors to be fully present at meaningful moments of care. In other words, we believe technology must let doctors be doctors.

Reading B

History and Future of 3D Printer
Jeremy Hsu

1   3D printing, also known as additive(附加的，添加的) manufacturing, is any of various processes used to make a three-dimensional object. In 3D printing, additive processes are used, in which successive(连续的) layers of material are laid down(放置) under computer control. These objects can be of almost any shape or geometry(几何学), and are produced from a 3D model or other electronic data source. A 3D printer is a type of industrial robot.

2   3D printing in the term's original sense refers to processes that sequentially(循序地) deposit(存放) material onto a powder bed with inkjet(喷墨打印机) printer heads. More recently the meaning of the term has expanded to encompass(包含) a wider variety of techniques such as extrusion(喷出，挤压) and sintering(烧结) based processes. Technical standards generally use the term additive manufacturing for this broader sense.

3   A 3D printer cannot make any object on demand like the "Star Trek" replicators(复制器) of science fiction. But a growing array of(大量的) 3D printing machines has already begun to revolutionize(革命化) the business of making things in the real world.

4   3D printers work by following a computer's digital instructions to "print" an object using materials such as plastic, ceramics(制陶术) and metal. The printing process involves building up an object one layer at a time until it's complete. For instance, some 3D printers squirt(喷射) out a stream of heated, semi-liquid plastic that solidifies as the printer's head moves around to create the outline of each layer within the object.

5   The instructions used by 3D printers often take the form of computer-aided design (CAD) files — digital blueprints for making different objects. That means a person can design an object on their computer using 3D modeling software, hook the computer up to(连接到) a 3D printer, and watch the 3D printer build the object right before his or her eyes.

6   Manufacturers(制造商) have quietly used 3D printing technology—also known as additive manufacturing—to build models and prototypes(原型) of products over the past 20 years.

7   Charles Hull invented the first commercial 3D printer and offered it for sale through his company 3D Systems in 1986. Hull's machine used stereo(立体的) lithography(平版印刷术), a technique that relies upon a laser(激光) to solidify(凝固) an ultraviolet(紫外线)—sensitive polymer material wherever the ultraviolet laser touches.

8   The technology remained relatively unknown to the greater public until the second decade of the 21st century. A combination of U.S. government funding and commercial startups has created a new wave of unprecedented(空前的) popularity around the idea of 3D printing since that time.

9   First, President Barack Obama's administration awarded $30 million to create the National Additive Manufacturing Innovation Institute (NAMII) in 2012 as a way of helping to revitalize

（使……复兴）U.S. manufacturing. NAMII acts as an umbrella organization for a network of universities and companies that aims to refine 3D printing technology for rapid deployment in the manufacturing sector.

10   Second, a new wave of startups has made the idea of 3D printing popular within the so-called "Maker" movement that emphasizes do-it-yourself projects. Many of those companies offer 3D printing services or sell relatively cheap 3D printers that can cost just hundreds rather than thousands of dollars.

11   3D printing probably won't replace many of the usual assembly-line methods for building standard products. Instead, the technology offers the advantage of making individual, specifically tailored（定制的）parts on demand—something more suited to creating specialized parts for military aircraft rather than making thousands of trash cans for sale at Wal-Mart. Boeing（波音客机）has already used 3D printing to make more than 22,000 parts used on civilian and military aircraft flying today.

12   The medical industry has also taken advantage of 3D printing's ability to make unique objects that might otherwise be tough to build using traditional methods. U.S. surgeons（外科医生）implanted a 3D-printed skull piece to replace 75 percent of a patient's skull during an operation in March 2013. Researchers also built a 3D-printed ear mold that served as the framework for a bioengineered ear with living cells.

13   The spread of 3D printing technology around the world could also shrink geographical distances for both homeowners and businesses. Online marketplaces already allow individuals to upload 3D-printable designs for objects and sell them anywhere in the world. Rather than pay hefty（重的）shipping fees and import taxes, sellers can simply arrange for a sold product to be printed at whatever 3D printing facility is closest to the buyer.

14   Businesses won't be alone in benefiting from 3D printing's print-on-demand-anywhere capability. The U.S. military has deployed 3D printing labs to Afghanistan（阿富汗）as a way to speed up the pace of battlefield innovation and rapidly build whatever soldiers might need onsite. NASA has looked into 3D printing for making replacement parts aboard the International Space Station and building spacecraft in orbit.

15   Most 3D printers don't go beyond the size of household appliances such as refrigerators（冰箱）, but 3D printing could even scale up in size to build objects as big as a house. A separate NASA project has investigated the possibility of building lunar bases for future astronauts（宇航员）by using moon "dirt" known as regolith.

16   But 3D printing still has its limits. Most 3D printers can only print objects using a specific type of material—a serious limitation that prevents 3D printers from creating complex objects such as an Apple iPhone. Yet researchers and commercial companies have begun developing workarounds（变通方案）. Optomec, a company based in Albuquerque（阿尔伯克基，美国新墨西哥州中部大城）, New Mexico, has already made a 3D printer capable of printing electronic circuitry（电路）onto objects.

17   The 3D printing boom could eventually prove disruptive（破坏的）in both a positive and negative sense. For instance, the ability to easily share digital blueprints online and print out the objects at home has proven a huge boon for do-it-yourself makers. But security experts worry about 3D printing's ability to magnify（夸大）the effects of digital piracy（剽窃）and the sharing of knowledge that could prove dangerous in the wrong hands.

I. Match the summaries (A–E) on the left column to the five parts of the article with the number of paragraphs on the right column.

A. The history of the 3D printing.
B. The general introduction of 3D printing.
C. The working principles of 3D printing.
D. Some limitations of the 3D printing.
E. The future of the 3D printing.

1. (Paragraphs 1—2)
2. (Paragraphs 3—5)
3. (Paragraph 6—10)
4. (Paragraphs 11—15)
5. (Paragraph 16)

II. Answer the following questions.

1. What does 3D printing mean in the original sense and in a broader sense respectively?
2. What are the possible applications in this article?
3. Does 3D printing have some limitations? If any, what are they?

III. Questions for discussion.

1. Do you agree that the 3D printing is more good than bad? Why or why not? Give some of your reasons and evidences.
2. What can you learn from this article? Can you imagine any more applications or changes might brought by the 3D printing?

Part Two
Tips for Translation

词类的转换

Warm-up

Each Chinese sentence below is followed by its English version. Compare each pair of sentences and discuss what changes might have been made in the translation process.

（1）这个实验很成功。

This experiment was a great success.

（2）多喝水有利于减肥。

Water works for weight loss.

（3）这块表一个月的误差从不超过一秒钟。

This watch never varies more than a second in a month.

在英汉互译实践中，有些句子可以逐词对译，有些句子则由于英汉两种语言的表达方式不同，要做到既忠实于原文又符合译文语言规范，就不能机械地用"一个萝卜一个坑"的方法来逐词对译，而需要适当改变一些词类，即把原文中属于某种词类的词在译文中转换成另一词类。这就是翻译上通常所说的"词类转换"。

Unit Six

词类转换是汉译英中很重要的手段之一,运用得当,可使译文通顺流畅,符合英语习惯;否则译文可能变得生硬累赘。

一、汉语的动词转换成英语的名词

汉语中动词用得较多,除大量的动宾结构外,还有连动式、兼语式等两个以上动词连用的现象。而英语则不然,一句话往往只用一个谓语动词,而且英语的名词也比汉语的名词用得多。由于两种语言各自所具有的这种特点,汉译英时常常需要把汉语动词转换成英语名词。有时,随着汉语动词的这种转换,修饰该动词的副词也自然需要转换。

(1) 你必须好好地照顾病人。

You must take good care of the patient.

(2) 他在讲话中特别强调提高产品质量。

In his speech he laid special stress on raising the quality of the products.

二、汉语的动词转译成英语的形容词

汉语中一些表示知觉、情感等心理状态的动词,往往可以转换成英语形容词,通常多以"be+形容词"结构来表达。

(1) 获悉贵国遭受地震,我们极为关切。

We are deeply concerned at the news that your country has been struck by an earthquake.

(2) 我们决不满足于现有的成就。

We are not content with our present achievements.

三、汉语的动词转换成英语的介词或介词词组

与汉语相比,英语用介词较多,而且有一些英语介词本是由动词演变而来的具有动词的特征。因此在汉译英时,汉语的一些动词常常可用英语的介词或介词词组来翻译。

(1) 我们全体赞成他的建议。

We were all in favour of his suggestion.

(2) 他们不顾一切艰难险阻,勇往直前。

They kept going forward courageously in spite of all dangers and difficulties.

四、汉语的形容词或副词转换成英语的名词

在汉译英时,有时由于语法结构和修辞上的需要,也可以把汉语的一些形容词或副词转译成英语的名词。

(1) 独立思考对学习是绝对必需的。

Independent thinking is an absolute necessity in study.

(2) 他的新书十分成功。

His new book is a great success.

五、汉语的名词转换成英语的动词

在汉译英中,比较普遍的现象是汉语的动词转换成英语的名词。但也有相反情况,即汉语的名词转换成英语的动词。与此同时,原来修饰该名词的形容词也常随之而转换成英语的副词,作为状语来修饰由汉语名词转换成的英语动词。

（1）他的讲演给听众的印象很深。
   His speech impressed the audience deeply.
（2）该厂产品的主要特点是工艺精湛,经久耐用。
   The products of this factory are chiefly characterized by their fine workmanship and durability.

练习

翻译下列句子,注意黑体部分词类的转换。
1. 我既不**喝酒**,也不**抽烟**。
2. 政府号召**建立**更多的技术学校。
3. 我非常感激父亲,因为在我小时候他总是不断地**鼓励**我。
4. 他长期以来习惯于在最后一分钟**做出决定**。
5. 我们觉得解决这个问题并不**难**。
6. 会上透露了许多**信息**。
7. 十一点时,他已**睡**在被窝里。
8. 我国科学研究发展的**特点**是理论**联系**实际。

Part Three
Simulated Writing

Minutes of a Meeting

会议记录是会议的正式书面记录,其主要目的是准确地记录会议中讨论的重点,以及做出的方案或决议。通常在正式会议上,有指定的人员负责撰写会议记录,例如公司的秘书,但如果是非正式的会议,则需要每次指派负责人,或轮流负责。会议记录必须简明、完整、清楚和易于理解(concise, complete, clear, understandable)。以下是会议记录中通常应该包含的内容:

- Title and nature of the meeting 会议的名称、性质
- Time, date and place of meeting 会议的召开日期、时间和地点
- List of people attending 参会人员
- List of absent members of the group 缺席会议的人员
- Approval of the previous meeting's minutes 通过往届会议记录
- Any matters arising from those minutes 由以往会议记录引发的问题
- For each item in the agenda, a record of the principal points discussed and decisions taken; actions and the persons vested with the responsibilities 记录每项会议议程中所讨论的要点、做出的决定、将采取的行动及负责人
- Time, date and place of next meeting 下次会议的日期、时间和地点
- Name of person taking the minutes 会议记录人

Sample template

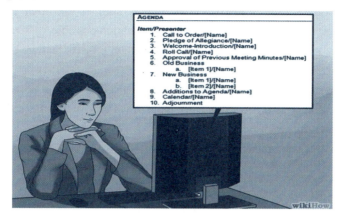

Check Your Understanding

1. **General introduction (title, date, place & participants)**
   - Date: September 13, 2006
   - Venue: conference room 3B, the ITS office, 3900 Wake Forest Road
   - Board Members: Present: Sandy Hermann, (Chair), John Burgess, Terry Smith, Kelly Hickok, Susan Neal for Lee Price, Monica Smyth, Shirley Hicks, Mark Russell
   - Members Absent: Sherry Confer
   - Staff Present: Katherine Lawson
   - TO ORDER: 8:40AM
   - APPROVAL OF COMMITTEE MINUTES: The Community Integration Committee unanimously approved the minutes of the June meeting without amendments. /Minutes from March 8, 2002 were approved as distributed.
   - Several appointments and dismissals were announced at the meeting.
   - Minutes of the last meeting were approved as an accurate record.
   - The chairman called the meeting to order at 10:00 a.m.

2. **Old business**
   - Discussion regarding increasing membership and conference participation
   - Consideration of updating, publishing and re-distribution of directory
   - Utilize a theme in conferences
   - ...will initiate a survey of larger institutions to see if they have units that might want to join the organization
   - Survey was distributed to evaluate conference.
   - Possibility of a summer/fall mini institute was considered.
   - Consideration of proximity of conference program
   - Hold conference meetings on campuses
   - Review of the Agenda. Review and approval of the draft agenda of the September 2006 meeting occurred.

- Cynthia Jones, Executive Director of Medical Home Plus (MHP) presented the organization's mission, values and various initiatives that support families and their family members to ensure the greatest degree of choice and self determination possible.
- Discussion of the Achievement of Community Integration projects that are currently ongoing in this area of emphasis.
- With the consent of the meeting, the chairman made a speech and proposed that a gold metal be given to Mr. Zhang as a reward for his industrious and successful service in the past 2 years.
- The following points were raised in discussion.

3. New business
    - Future Annual Meeting sites and dates were planned:
    - The president noted the following information concerning...
    - The president noted a letter dated...from...stating that...
    - Gift for...
    - Held election of new officers.
    - Katherine Lawson and Susan Neal provided an update regarding the status of the Improving Community Living Options (ICLO) grant (CI-04-01).
    - Katherine Lawson updated the committee regarding the Consumer Choice in Community Living Grant (CI-05-2).
    - Any Other Business: There was no other business.
    - With the plan to rebuild 5 state of the art institutions in Virginia by the Department of Mental Health Mental Retardation and Substance Abuse Services, (DMHMRSAS) and the lack of sufficient community supports, urgent waiting lists for institutions are anticipated to grow.
    - A second RFP was envisioned to expand outreach mechanisms to educate family members of children who are at risk of or currently living in institutional settings or in institutions about formal and informal community supports.
    - One other new issue was mentioned by Peter Motavalli for informational purposes. He noted that ...
    - Mr. Smith made a brief report on...
    - ...was nominated for...
    - ...was appointed/promoted to...

4. Adjournment
    - The meeting was adjourned at 11: 45 a. m.

5. The ending
    - There being no further business, the chairperson closed the meeting.
    - It was agreed that the next meeting will be held on 1st July, 2016, at 10:00 a.m. in the conference room.
    - The focus of the paper is to be a meta analysis of carbon sequestration by cropping systems such as no-till.

Unit Six

- The issue was raised about whether or not the paper should have a regional focus because of region-specific factors and the availability of published data.
- Respectfully submitted, B. Thomas Lowe, Secretary.
- Prepared by...
- The next meeting was scheduled for...
- A further meeting was provisionally scheduled for..., dependent upon...

Sample Reading 1

Virginia Board for People with Disabilities
Community Integration Committee Meeting

Date: September 13, 2006
Venue: conference room 3B, the ITS office, 3900 Wake Forest Road
Board Members Present: Sandy Hermann, (Chair), John Burgess, Terry Smith, Kelly Hickok, Susan Neal for Lee Price, Monica Smyth, Shirley Hicks, Mark Russell
Members Absent: Sherry Confer
Staff Present: Katherine Lawson
TO ORDER: 8:40AM

APPROVAL OF COMMITTEE MINUTES: The Community Integration Committee unanimously approved the minutes of the June meeting without amendments.

AGENDA ITEM 1:	Review of the Agenda. Review and approval of the draft agenda of the September 2006 meeting occurred. Sandy Hermann highlighted the planned activities for the meeting, including a speaker from Medical Home Plus. The final activity planned included discussion of RFP development for 2007.
AGENDA ITEM 2:	Cynthia Jones, Executive Director of Medical Home Plus (MHP) presented the organization's mission, values and various initiatives that support families and their family members to ensure the greatest degree of choice and self determination possible. She indicated their work would support home medical service, which are increasingly available and alternative to nursing home and institutional placements.
AGENDA ITEM 3:	Discussion of the Achievement of Community Integration projects that are currently ongoing in this area of emphasis.

- Katherine Lawson and Susan Neal provided an update regarding the status of the Improving Community Living Options (ICLO) grant (CI-04-01). The overall concept of the original $250,000 grant was to provide "seed money" for innovative ideas for people with disabilities to help them overcome barriers to community integration. As the original intent of the large grant was not met in having multiple initiatives take place throughout Virginia a portion of the grant was returned to the agency. More recently, in August, the Department of Mental Health Mental Retardation and Substance Abuse Services, (DMHMRSAS) requested in a letter that the grant be returned to the agency as well as associated administrative funds. In this process Board staff would manage the grant directly. This was recommended to occur on October 1, 2006. The CI voted to recommend to the Board acceptance of this proposed grant return.

- Katherine Lawson updated the committee regarding the Consumer Choice in Community Living Grant (CI-05-2). The grant steering committee was actually meeting on the same day as this Community Integration Committee. Ms. Lawson provided a copy of an e-mail that outlined the agenda for the meeting that was taking place in Richmond, and she indicated she would provide any updates to the board that were necessary prior to the December meeting as necessary. She indicated that current focus at the steering committee level is on developing a protocol of best practices for going into nursing homes and informing consumers of choice.

AGENDA ITEM 4: Consider RFP Development: The Community Integration Committee began discussion of the broader community of individuals who are living successfully independently of institutions. With the plan to rebuild 5 state of the art institutions in Virginia by the Department of Mental Health Mental Retardation and Substance Abuse Services, (DMHMRSAS) and the lack of sufficient community supports, urgent waiting lists for institutions are anticipated to grow.

A second RFP was envisioned to expand outreach mechanisms to educate family members of children who are at risk of or currently living in institutional settings or in institutions about formal and informal community supports. This initiative would encompass two years, and a total investment of $75,000 for an 18 month initiative.

AGENDA ITEM 5: Any Other Business: There was no other business
The meeting adjourned at 11:15 a.m.

Notes

people with disabilities 残疾人士
board members 理事会成员
unanimously 全体一致地
amendments 修正
Executive Director 执行理事
update 更新

grant steering committee 基金管理委员会
protocol 草案,协议
mental retardation 智障
initiative 初始阶段

Sample Reading 2

Minutes of Business Meeting
Association of Deans and Directors of University Colleges and Under Graduate Studies
March 14, 2003

1. Call to order: Meeting was called to order by President Elizabeth Guertin, Ph.D., at 10:00 a.m., in the Department of Labor and Workforce Development Building, Room 208, 3301 Eagle St., Anchorage.
2. Approval of Minutes: Minutes from March 8, 2002 were approved as distributed.
3. Approval of Report: The Treasurer's Report was approved as distributed.
4. Old Business
   a. Discussion regarding increasing membership and conference participation.
      Consideration of updating, publishing and re-distribution of directory.
      Members are encouraged to recruit additional attendees at next meeting.
      Utilize a theme in conferences.
      Peter White will initiate a survey of larger institutions to see if they have units that might want to join the organization.
      Survey was distributed to evaluate conference.
      Possibility of a summer/fall mini institute was considered.
      Consideration of proximity of conference program.
      Hold conference meetings on campuses.
   b. It was moved to reconstitute the committee on producing occasional position papers.
      The motions was seconded and passed.
      The committee members are Eric White, Shelly Potts, Kriss Boyd, Lettie Raab, Sue Weaver, Dorothy Muller, Jayne Richmond, Cubie Ward.
   c. Promotion of exchanges and consultant-ships were discussed to assist programs.
      Elizabeth Guertin and Karla Muggler were appointed to that committee.
5. New Business
   a. Future Annual Meeting sites and dates were planned
      2004 Philadelphia, PA, March 24—27, 2004, Host: Eric White
      2005 Albuquerque, NM, Host: Peter White
      2006 New Orleans
      Possibilities include Indianapolis, Indiana and Savannah, Georgia
   b. Gift for Jolanna Erickson
   c. Held election of new officers.
      President for 2003—2004 is Carolyn Collins
      President elect for 2003—2004 is Sally Roden
      The group thanked Cubie Ward for all his hard work to make the Ft. Worth conference a success.

6. Adjournment: The meeting was adjourned at 11: 45 a. m.
   Respectfully submitted
   B. Thomas Lowe, Secretary

call to order	宣布开会
Treasurer's Report	财务总管的报告
updating, publishing and re-distribution of directory	更新、出版及重新发行通讯录
recruit dditional attendees	征募更多参会者
consideration of proximity of conference program	考虑大致会议日程
the motions was seconded and passed	议案得到支持并得以通过
promotion of exchanges and consultant-ships	促进协商、交流
annual meeting sites and dates	年会的时间及地点

Check Your Understanding

Match the items listed in the following two columns.

1. members present   A. 开会
2. members absent   B. 会议地点
3. call to order   C. 以往事宜
4. approval of committee minutes   D. 审议并通过议案草案
5. review and approval of draft agenda E. 休会
6. old business   F. 出席会议成员
7. new business   G. 会议日期
8. adjourn the meeting   H. 缺席会议成员
9. date   I. 通过委员会会议记录
10. venue   J. 新增事宜

Follow-up Writing

Complete the following abstract with the information given below.

会议地点：Conference Room, 48/F, Immigration Tower, Wan Chai, Hong Kong
开会日期：26 April 2006 (Wednesday)
会议记录者：Peter Vireck, Secretary
会议开始时间：3:00 p.m.
出席会议成员：Prof. HO Kin Chung, Chairman; Mr. CHAN Chi Chiu, Vice-Chairman, Director of Water Supplies; Prof. TSO Wung Wai, The Chinese University of

Hong Kong; Dr. CHAN Hon Fai, Cinotech Consultants Limited; Ms. LEE Yoke Shum, Sam World Wide Fund for Nature Hong Kong

会议第二项活动：会议主席向已退休的委员会创始人FANG Hung, Kenneth主席致谢。
会议议程第一项：批准上次会议记录
会议议程第二项：讨论新事项
会议议程第二项第二点：公布水质数据
会议第五项活动：讨论其他事项
会议第六项活动：休会

Advisory Committee on the Quality of Water Supplies
Minutes of Meeting No. 14
Date: _____1_____
Time: _____2_____
Venue: _____3_____
Members Present: _____4_____

1. The Chairman announced that this was the first meeting of the fourth two-year term of the Advisory Committee on the Quality of Water Supplies (ACQWS).
2. _____5_____, who laid a solid foundation of the ACQWS, and the other six retired Members for their contributions in the past.
3. The Chairman welcomed all Members for attending the meeting, and, in particular, the five new Members, for attending the meeting of the ACQWS for the first time.
4. Agenda
   Item 1 : _____6_____
   The minutes were confirmed without any amendment.
   Item 2 : _____7_____

A: Quality of water in buildings
   Fresh Water Plumbing Quality Maintenance Recognition Scheme
   WSD briefly introduced the background and development of the Fresh Water Plumbing Quality Maintenance Recognition Scheme.
   He reported that up to March 2006, a total of about 4,400 certificates had been issued since the launch of the Scheme in July 2002 and the number of valid certificates was about 1,600, which covered about 450,000 residential flats, representing 19% of the territorial total.
   A Member commented that the figures presented did not show the trend or progress of the Scheme as the number of certificates issued each year was not presented. The Chairman suggested WSD to compile the necessary figures and carry out a detailed analysis for the reference of Members in the next meeting.

B: _____8_____

WSD reported that to promote transparency of information to the public, WSD had been publishing the water quality data for Dongjiang water received in Hong Kong at Muk Wu Pumping Station and for drinking water in the Internet via WSD's Homepage two times each year. The latest data published in the Internet in November 2005 was the 10th publication covering the period from 1 October 2004 to 30 September 2005. Full compliance with the Guidelines for Drinking-water Quality published by the World Health Organisation (WHO) in 1993 was achieved.

A Member suggested that the substantial improvement in the Dongjiang water quality after commissioning of the dedicated aqueduct system should be announced to the public through the media. WSD replied that a press conference had already been arranged after the last visit to Guangdong in November 2005 to report the situation to the public through the media. The Chairman added that WSD had presented the quality data of Dongjiang water in graphical form, which helped the public understand the trend or changes more easily.

5. _____9_____

WSD reported that the Government had concluded negotiations with the Guangdong Provincial Government on the new supply arrangements for Dongjiang water on 12 April 2006. The new arrangement would guarantee a fully flexible supply of Dongjiang water up to 2008 based on the actual needs of Hong Kong.

A Member stated that the emphasis of "Water Safety" and "Water Security" was somewhat different: the concern of the former was water quality while that of the latter was mainly water availability.

6. There being no other business, _____10_____ 5:00 p.m.

Minutes submitted by Secretary Peter Vireck.

Part Four
Listening

Lead-in

I. **Discuss the following topics with your classmates.**

1. Would you like to ride in a self-driving car?
2. Do you think self-driving cars will become the standard?

Unit Six

II. **Study the following vocabulary before you listen.**

automotive	自动的,机动的	supplier	供应商
automobile	汽车	steering wheel	方向盘
pedal	踏板	violate	违反,违背
autopilot	自动驾驶仪	brake	刹车
bend	转弯处	lane	航线
sensor	传感器	intersection	十字路口
transport	运送	costly	昂贵的
priced	定价的		

While-listening

I. **Listen to the recording and supply the missing words.**

Will Your Next Car Drive Itself?

You know how much your __1__ has changed over the past 10 years? Your __2__ will change even more than that in the next 10 years. One of the big __3__ is that cars will drive themselves. Some day you may not need to drive a car. You will just tell the car where you want to go and it will drive itself.

"We __4__ have the technology for it now," says Andrew Poliak of __5__ technology supplier QNX. "We expect __6__ cars to be a __7__ thing between 2020 and __8__." The American company Google has been working on a self-driving automobile for years. These cars are already on the roads in the United States, mainly in California.

Will Your Next Car Drive Itself?	Last week, police ordered one of Google's cars to stop for driving too slowly on a public road. The car was not __9__ any law, so no one was punished. But police did speak with the __10__ of the vehicle. According to Google, its __11__ cars have been driven nearly 2 million kilometers. That is equal to the distance the average person drives in 90 years. So far, no Google self-driving car has gotten a traffic ticket. Some of them have been in accidents when other cars hit them.
Tesla Model S	Another American company, Tesla, added an "Autopilot" feature to its cars last month. Tesla put the feature, a computer software program, in cars that were built after September 2014. With the __12__ turned on, the vehicle drives itself. The car will speed up, slow down, __13__ and __14__ by itself. You can take over driving any time by turning the steering wheel or touching a __15__. Your car will __16__ if the vehicle in front of you gets closer. It will turn at bends and change __17__ if you use the turn signal. The car uses sensors to know when lane changing is safe and whether it should speed up or slow down. Tesla Autopilot

	takes over driving at speeds over 29 kilometers per hour when you press a button twice. Autopilot is made for cross-country driving. It keeps you in the lane and helps you __18__ hitting other cars. Autopilot does not work as well on local roads. It will not stop at a red light or stop sign or turn at intersections. Reporter Carolyn Nicander Mohr tried the Autopilot feature of a Tesla earlier this month. She had a hard time __19__ the car to do what it should do. She thought about disabling the Autopilot feature many times during her trip. She wanted to take control at every bend in the road and hit the brake when the car in front of her slowed down. Yet the car drove __20__ .
Advantages of Self-Driving Cars Safety	According to The Auto Insurance Center, 81% of car crashes result from human __21__ . Many lives could be saved if cars drove more safely without human drivers. With fewer accidents, insurance costs may be lower for self-driving cars than other vehicles.
Efficiency	In a self-driving car, you would not have to be worried about talking on the phone or sending a text message. You could do other things while getting to where you need to go. __22__ may be reduced. Cars could flow more __23__ , with fewer cars on the road during busy times. Fewer accidents mean improving traffic conditions, and reducing delays, repairs and injuries. Speed __24__ could rise with more people using self-driving cars. When self-driving cars prove they can __25__ at higher speed limits, speed limits could be __26__ . Self-driving cars could drive people who are unable to drive themselves. They could travel without depending on others. Businesses could use self-driving cars to bring goods to your home. Order food and have a self-driving car __27__ it. Send the store your shopping list and wait for the store's self-driving car to bring your order to you.
Criticism of Self-Driving Cars Cost	Self-driving cars may cost a lot more than other cars. The self-driving __28__ may first be offered on the most __29__ cars. Lower __30__ vehicles may take longer to offer the feature. But the cost of technology usually drops over time. Expect that self-driving cars could become less costly in the future.

II. Listen again, stop the recording as necessary, and repeat after the speaker.

Post-listening

Surf the Internet and find more information about the following topic areas. Then prepare a 15-minute oral presentation and deliver it in the class. While preparing the presentation you need to narrow down topic area and focus one major point.
1. Self-driving cars
2. Introduction to a high-technology you find interesting

Part Five
Speaking

Leading and Participating in a Meeting

Sample Dialogue 1

Background Information: In this meeting, the Business Conduct Committee of a company discusses the first of three incidents that have been brought to its attention for review. The Committee has the benefit of viewing videotapes of the incidents. The videotape shows the interaction between Betty, a proposal manager, and her supervisor, Bill, at a large meeting. Bill is using Betty as an example to his group to make the point that losing proposal results are not acceptable.

Grant: Good morning. It looks like everyone is here, so let's get started. We have several helpline calls to be discussed today. One has to do with a report of abusive management practices. Jill, would you please brief us on this?

Jill: This arises out of our night vision goggle division. The report was made by several employees who observed a manager, Bill Smith, who was allegedly abusive in public of Betty Wright, who worked for Bill doing proposal preparation. Here's part of what happened. Keep in mind this was a large meeting, or sort of training session.

(Scene cuts to videotape.)

Jill: Well, that shows you about as much as you need to see. Apparently, it went on like this for about five minutes until everyone was embarrassed for Betty and resentful of Bill. In fact, two colleagues of Betty's called the helpline to complain, and Betty called as well.

Pat: HR has investigated this carefully. We have found these episodes with Bill are not common, but this is not the first. When we spoke with Bill, he said that he had to get the attention of people in his group that these kinds of losing results simply were unacceptable. That's why he chose a public discussion.

Jill: Well, Pat, what's your recommendation on this?

Pat: I think we should have Bill's manager counsel him that any public disparagement of an employee is inconsistent with the spirit in our vision statement.

Jill: That seems pretty mild to me. I mean, I think it's a pretty fundamental part of our culture and values not to beat up on our people in public in this company. Bill obviously doesn't get that. I mean, if we don't do something stronger, he's not going to believe that anyone truly cares about this.

Pat: Jill, I'm not sure that discipline is necessary here. I just think Bill needs a little coaching. And Jill, there's really another issue here. This isn't an ethical concern. This type of management style question is exactly the kind of thing HR should handle.

...

Grant: Thank you all for attending. This meeting is finished. We'll see everyone next Wednesday.

Sample Dialogue 2

Joe: I'd like to reach a decision today about item 1. The issue is falling sales in the Italian market. Henry will explain the background to this, and the present situation.

Henry: Thanks. Well, as you know, in Italy we've always... So that's how things are at the moment.

Joe: Thank you, Henry. Now, let's look at possible courses of action.

Sophia: Could I just say something? The Italian market isn't as important to us as the Russian orders. I was in Moscow last week, and learnt some pretty interesting things about the way things are moving out there.

Joe: Let's keep to the immediate subject, which is the Italian market.

Bob: My own feeling is this: in years of experience, in many different markets throughout the world, I've often found that, when... and you know, if I could pass on my experience to the younger people here, I'd say that the only way to sell in Italy is to go there and see the market for yourself, instead of asking your agents to do it.

Joe: Sorry to interrupt you, Bob, but I'd like to know if the others agree. What do you think about this, Watson?

Watson: I'm not too sure about this. My own feeling is that if...

Bob: I don't know why you don't ask me. I've been to Italy so many times recently.

Joe: Could you let Watson finish? I'd like to have his view on this.

Watson: Well, I'd like to say that for the last two years we haven't had a stand at the Milan Trade Fair. I understand that the Fair has produced lots of contacts in the past.

Joe: That's an interesting point, Watson. Let's summarize what we've said so far. Bob thinks we depend on the agents too much, and Watson suggests that the Trade Fair is important.

Unit Six

Business Conduct Committee	业务规范委员会
helpline call	热线服务电话
abusive management practices	污辱性管理方式
allegedly	据称的
episode	事件
agent	代理
stand	展位
Milan Trade Fair	米兰商品交易会

USEFUL EXPRESSIONS AND PATTERNS:

1. It looks like everyone is here, so let's get started.
2. We have several helpline calls to be discussed today.
3. Would you please brief us on this?
4. This arises out of our night vision goggle division.
5. That shows you about as much as you need to see.
6. HR has investigated this carefully.
7. What's your recommendation on this?
8. And there's really another issue here.
9. Thank you all for attending. This meeting is finished. We'll see everyone next Wednesday.
10. I'd like to reach a decision today about item 1. The issue is...
11. Henry will explain the background to this, and the present situation.
12. So that's how things are at the moment.
13. Now, let's look at possible courses of action.
14. Let's keep to the immediate subject, which is...
15. Sorry to interrupt you, but I'd like to know if the others agree.
16. What do you think about this?
17. Could you let Watson finish? I'd like to have his view on this.
18. That's an interesting point. Let's summarize what we've said so far.
19. Now, let's switch gears and talk about how to turn off the stress response and return to a calm state.
20. Chronic stress is a known risk and contributing factor to many physical diseases.
21. The relaxation response is why a normal load of daily stress does not affect our health.
22. Long-term stress results in chronic, day-to-day activation of the stress response.
23. Let's look at an example.
24. Right now we'll learn ways to strengthen our innate prevention factors.

25 Our number one stress buffer is coping skills.
26 Here are three main coping styles.
27 The first coping type is called appraisal focused coping, meaning people who seek and interpret the meaning in events.
28 The second type of coping is problem-focused coping, finding practical solutions to problems.
29 The second innate stress buffer is psychological resilience.
30 The fourth and final stress buffer is self-care strategies such as exercise and good diet and adequate sleep.

I. **Role-play the sample dialogues.**

II. **Match the following two columns.**
1. 依靠代理   A. brief on...
2. 目前议题   B. proposal preparation
3. 与……不一致   C. HR
4. 管理方式   D. inconsistent with
5. 人力资源部   E. management style
6. 准备建议书   F. reach a decision
7. 简单介绍……   G. depend on the agents
8. 做出决定   H. immediate subject

III. **Below is what was said in a meeting of the Board of Directors of a bus company, "Crazy Bus Company." Complete the dialogue with the help of the Chinese information given.**

A: Yes, we had decided to come to some agreement today on whether or not to allow drunks on our buses. _____1_____ (询问参会人员的意见)?

B: Of course we can't allow drunks! They are noisy and smelly and frighten the other passengers.

C: I agree. But _____2_____ (提出问题), how do we know how drunk someone is?

D: Well, how about just not allowing extremely drunken people on the buses? I mean, if they are too drunk to climb on?

B: Yes, _____3_____ (表示同意)! How about instructing our drivers to drive off at full speed if a drunk tries to get onto a bus?

A: Excellent idea! _____4_____ (询问其他人的意见)?

All: Yes, we all agree.

A: Good! _____5_____ (提出开始讨论第一项事宜): to consider taking all the seats out of our entire bus fleet. Any opinions?

B: _____6_____ (表示完全赞同). That way, we can cram as many passengers as possible into our buses, upstairs and down.

C: Yes, I like the idea. Who needs to sit down? Hong Kong is small, journey times are short. During rush hours especially, it is very difficult to get a seat on any bus. Hong Kong people are used to standing and shouldn't mind having no chance to sit.

D: What about old people, pregnant ladies and the handicapped?

E: Yes, this might be a problem. But the percentage of passengers in these categories is very small. Many old people and even some pregnant women will not mind standing. If they really want to sit down, they can take another company's bus.

A: _____7_____ （询问大家是否表示完全赞同）?

All: Yes.

A: Good, _____8_____ （要求继续讨论第二项）. To consider employing ex-racing car drivers for our entire fleet.

E: Yes, it's time we did this. We have very serious competition here from the other bus companies in Hong Kong. To put it simply, we are just not fast enough. I know for a fact that our most serious competitor, Deathwish Buses, has hired eight of Macau's top ex-racing champions.

A: Well, if this is the case, we are behind the times. Hong Kong is a fast-moving city, and our buses must be fast too. As they say, time is money, and if we can save passengers time by faster speeds than Deathwish buses, it will be a good thing for the company.

B: Yes, everybody will want to ride our buses!

All: Yes, I agree!

A: Excellent! _____9_____ （指派C负责打广告招聘前赛车车手）? Remember, we want the fastest.

C: _____10_____ （表示乐于接受任务）.

A: Ok then, _____11_____ （表示今天的会议到此结束）. Our next meeting?

B: Next week, same place, same time.

IV. Learn to communicate in the situation given below.

You are the Managing Director of a manufacturing company. Over the past 12 months, you see that the company does not need so many design engineers, because your company had reduced its product lines. There are four design engineers in the company, but two of them must go. You meet with three of your top managers to decide on which two design engineers to retrench（辞退）and which two to keep. Divide into equal groups of four. Together, decide on and write the dialogue for this meeting, using the information about the four engineers given below.

1. Mr. Chung
   Age: 26
   Education: university degree in design engineering
   Experience: two years with the company after leaving university
   Marital Status: to be married soon
   Personality: very friendly, sociable
   Work: first class
   Other information: eager to climb to the top

2. Mr. Lee

   Age: 55

   Education: F5 graduate（中五毕业）; self-trained from apprenticeship with the company

   Marital Status: married with four children, two at university in the United States

   Personality: friendly, quiet

   Work: slow but steady, reliable

   Other information: due to retire in 5 years

3. Mr. So

   Age: 37

   Education: F5 then tutorial college, diploma in engineering; learned through experience

   Experience: 18 years with the company

   Marital status: married with two children

   Personality: prefers to work alone, not sociable

   Work: excellent

   Other information: just bought a flat with a heavy mortgage commitments

4. Mr. Cheuk

   Age: 31

   Education: Engineering Degree, Swiss M.B.A.

   Marital Status: single

   Personality: unpleasant, bossy, does not like dealing with people

   Work: refuses to work overtime; careless, not a hard worker

   Other information: the nephew of one of the directors in the company; worked as a funds manager before joining the company

Unit Seven

Health

Part One
Reading and Translating

Lead-in

Are you happy now? Emotional world can have a remarkable power to our health. Here are five positive emotions that have been shown to improve physical health and prevent disease.
- Optimism may protect the heart.

　　A growing body of research has suggested that cultivating this quality can have a protective effect on the heart. Optimism's benefits for physical health also extend beyond heart health. Here are a few other ways that a sunny disposition may improve health outcomes, including improved immune system function and increased longevity.
- Experiencing awe reduces inflammatory markers associated with autoimmune disease.

　　According to new research from the University of California at Berkeley, awe is not only pleasurable but also enormously beneficial for one's physical and mental health.
- Compassion and care for others can improve vagus nerve function（迷走神经功能）.

　　Positive psychologist Barbara Frederickson has conducted research on the effects of lovingkindness meditation (LKM), a traditional Buddhist practice that involves meditating on love and extending compassion to oneself and a progressively large group of others. Frederickson found just six weeks of LKM training to have a positive impact on the vagus nerve.
- Gratitude may also benefit heart health and immune system function.

　　Like optimism, an "attitude of gratitude" an appreciation and feeling of thankfulness for the blessings one has in life which is carries significant mental and physical health benefits.
- Self-compassion improves health-related behaviors.

　　A study published in the Personality and Social Psychology Bulletin examined the relationship between self-compassion, reactions to illness, and a range of health-related behaviors, finding that self-compassionate people sought medical attention sooner for symptoms that they were experiencing than people who were lacking in self-compassion. Self-compassionate people also tended to be less depressed about health problems they were experiencing, and also to take a more proactive approach towards their own health.

Reading A

New Study Claims to Find Genetic Link Between Creativity and Mental Illness

Ian Sample

Results imply creative people are 25% more likely to carry genes that raise risk of bipolar disorder and schizophrenia. But others argue the evidence is flimsy.

1 The ancient Greeks were first to make the point. Shakespeare raised the prospect too. But Lord Byron was, perhaps, the most direct of them all: "We of the craft are all crazy," he told the Countess of Blessington, casting a wary eye over his fellow poets.

2 The notion of the tortured artist is a stubborn meme. Creativity, it states, is fuelled by the demons that artists wrestle in their darkest hours. The idea is fanciful to many scientists. But a new study claims the link may be well-founded after all, and written into the twisted molecules of our DNA.

3 In a large study published on Monday, scientists in Iceland report that genetic factors that raise the risk of bipolar disorder and schizophrenia are found more often in people in creative professions. Painters, musicians, writers and dancers were, on average, 25% more likely to carry the gene variants than professions the scientists judged to be less creative, among which were farmers, manual labourers and salespeople.

4 Kari Stefansson, founder and CEO of deCODE, a genetics company based in Reykjavik, said the findings, described in the journal *Nature Neuroscience*, point to a common biology for some mental disorders and creativity. "To be creative, you have to think differently," he told the Guardian. "And when we are different, we have a tendency to be labelled strange, crazy and even insane."

5 The scientists drew on genetic and medical information from 86,000 Icelanders to find genetic variants that doubled the average risk of schizophrenia, and raised the risk of bipolar disorder by more than a third. When they looked at how common these variants were in members of national arts societies, they found a 17% increase compared with non-members.

6 The researchers went on to check their findings in large medical databases held in the Netherlands and Sweden. Among these 35,000 people, those deemed to be creative (by

profession or through answers to a questionnaire) were nearly 25% more likely to carry the mental disorder variants.

7   Stefansson believes that scores of genes increase the risk of schizophrenia and bipolar disorder. These may alter the ways in which many people think, but in most people do nothing very harmful. But for 1% of the population, genetic factors, life experiences and other influences can culminate in problems, and a diagnosis of mental illness.

8   "Often, when people are creating something new, they end up straddling between sanity and insanity," said Stefansson. "I think these results support the old concept of the mad genius. Creativity is a quality that has given us Mozart, Bach, Van Gogh. It's a quality that is very important for our society. But it comes at a risk to the individual, and 1% of the population pays the price for it."

9   Stefansson concedes that his study found only a weak link between the genetic variants for mental illness and creativity. And it is this that other scientists pick up on. The genetic factors that raise the risk of mental problems explained only about 0.25% of the variation in peoples' artistic ability, the study found. David Cutler, a geneticist at Emory University in Atlanta, puts that number in perspective: "If the distance between me, the least artistic person you are going to meet, and an actual artist is one mile, these variants appear to collectively explain 13 feet of the distance," he said.

10   Most of the artist's creative flair, then, is down to different genetic factors, or to other influences altogether, such as life experiences, that set them on their creative journey.

11   For Stefansson, even a small overlap between the biology of mental illness and creativity is fascinating. "It means that a lot of the good things we get in life, through creativity, come at a price. It tells me that when it comes to our biology, we have to understand that everything is in some way good and in some way bad," he said.

12   But Albert Rothenberg, professor of psychiatry at Harvard University is not convinced. He believes that there is no good evidence for a link between mental illness and creativity. "It's the romantic notion of the 19th century, that the artist is the struggler, aberrant from society, and wrestling with inner demons," he said. "But take Van Gogh. He just happened to be mentally ill as well as creative. For me, the reverse is more interesting: creative people are generally not mentally ill, but they use thought processes that are of course creative and different."

13   If Van Gogh's illness was a blessing, the artist certainly failed to see it that way. In one of his last letters, he voiced his dismay at the disorder he fought for so much of his life: "Oh, if I could have worked without this accursed disease—what things I might have done."

14   In 2014, Rothernberg published a book, "Flight of Wonder: an investigation of scientific creativity", in which he interviewed 45 science Nobel laureates about their creative strategies. He found no evidence of mental illness in any of them. He suspects that studies which find links between creativity and mental illness might be picking up on something rather different.

15   "The problem is that the criteria for being creative is never anything very creative. Belonging to an artistic society, or working in art or literature, does not prove a person is creative. But the fact is that many people who have mental illness do try to work in jobs that have to do with art and literature, not because they are good at it, but because they're attracted to it. And that can skew the data," he said. "Nearly all mental hospitals use art therapy, and so when patients come out, many are attracted to artistic positions and artistic pursuits."

New Words and Expressions

aberrant	a.	[əˈber(ə)nt]	异常的,脱离常轨的
accursed	a.	[əˈkɜːsɪd; əˈkɜːst]	被诅咒的,讨厌的,可憎的
bipolar	a.	[baɪˈpəʊlə]	两级的
concede	v.	[kənˈsiːd]	承认
creativity	n.	[ˌkriːeɪˈtɪvɪtɪ]	创造力,创造性
culminate	v.	[ˈkʌlmɪneɪt]	达到高潮
deem	v.	[diːm]	认为,视作
diagnosis	n.	[ˌdaɪəɡˈnəʊsɪs]	诊断
dismay	n.	[dɪsˈmeɪ]	沮丧,灰心
disorder	n.	[dɪsˈɔːdə]	紊乱,失调
fanciful	a.	[ˈfænsɪfʊl; -f(ə)l]	想象出来的,虚构的
flair	n.	[fleə]	天资,天分
flimsy	a.	[ˈflɪmzɪ]	不足的,不足信的
insane	a.	[ɪnˈseɪn]	疯狂的,精神病的
laureate	n.	[ˈlɒrɪət; ˈlɔː-]	获得荣誉者,获奖者
meme	n.	[miːm]	文化基因
molecule	n.	[ˈmɒlɪkjuːl]	分子
overlap	n.	[ˈəʊvəˌlæp]	重叠,重复
psychiatry	n.	[saɪˈkaɪətrɪ]	精神病学
reverse	n.	[rɪˈvɜːs]	相反,反面
schizophrenia	n.	[ˌskɪtsə(ʊ)ˈfriːnɪə]	精神分裂症
skew	v.	[skjuː]	曲解,歪曲
straddle	v.	[ˈstræd(ə)l]	跨越(不同时期、群体或领域)
struggler	n.	[ˈstrʌɡlə]	奋斗者,斗争者
stubborn	a.	[ˈstʌbən]	顽固的
therapy	n.	[ˈθerəpɪ]	治疗,疗法
torture	v.	[ˈtɔːtʃə]	折磨
wary	a.	[ˈweərɪ]	谨慎的,小心的
wrestle	v.	[ˈres(ə)l]	斗争,搏斗
variant	n.	[ˈveərɪənt]	变体,变种

cast an eye over sth.	粗略地看一下;匆匆地看
on average	平均
draw on	利用
culminate in	(以某种结果)告终;(在某一点)结束
end up	结束
pick up on	领略,意识到
come at a price	付出代价
happen to	偶然发生

Unit Seven

I. Give brief answers to the following questions.

1. Illustrate some ancient notions about artists and creativity.
2. What do scientists in Iceland report about the relationship between creativity and mental illness?
3. What does Stefansson think of the small overlap between the biology of mental illness and creativity?
4. What are the artists like according to the romantic notion of the 19th century?
5. What are the Rothernberg's findings after interviewing 45 science Nobel laureates about their creative strategies?
6. What can be the reasons for the link between mental illness and artistic pursuits?

II. Complete the following passage by filling each of the numbered blanks with one suitable word using the Chinese in the brackets as the reference.

Stefansson believes that scores of __1__ (基因) increase the risk of schizophrenia and bipolar disorder. These may __2__ (改变) the ways in which many people think, but in most people do nothing very harmful. But for 1% of the population, genetic factors, life experiences and other influences can __3__ (达到高潮) in problems, and a __4__ (诊断) of __5__ (精神的) illness.

"Often, when people are creating something new, they end up __6__ (跨越) between sanity and insanity," said Stefansson. "I think these results __7__ (支持) the old concept of the mad genius. __8__ (创造力) is a quality that has given us Mozart, Bach, Van Gogh. It's a quality that is very important for our society. But it comes at a __9__ (危险) to the individual, and 1% of the __10__ (人口) pays the price for it."

III. Complete the following sentences with one function word.

1. But Lord Byron was, perhaps, the most direct of them all: "We of the craft are all crazy," he told the Countess of Blessington, casting a wary eye _____ his fellow poets.
2. The scientists drew _____ genetic and medical information from 86,000 Icelanders to find genetic variants that doubled the average risk of schizophrenia, and raised the risk of bipolar disorder by more than a third.
3. These may alter the ways _____ which many people think, but in most people do nothing very harmful.
4. But it comes _____ a risk to the individual, and 1% of the population pays the price for it.
5. Most of the artist's creative flair, then, is down to different genetic factors, or to other influences altogether, such as life experiences, that set them _____ their creative journey.
6. He just happened _____ be mentally ill as well as creative.

IV. Complete the following sentences by translating the Chinese given in the brackets.

1. Tom _____ (屋里环视了一周), to find that there were about ten people and sitting at the head of a long conference table was the boss. (cast an eye over)

2. No matter how tough and difficult life can be, one should always _____（用自己的天赋,勇气和创造力克服生活中的重重困难）. (draw on, creativity)

3. Months of hard work _____（终于取得了成功）, and researchers held a party to celebrate the great findings. (culminate)

4. Tom shared an interesting story with his friends, but they failed _____（领悟他话中的幽默）. (pick up on)

5. Sam _____（跨越两种文化）, having been brought up in the United States and later converted to Islam. (straddle)

6. He finally _____（承认南希做出了正确的决定）after thinking carefully. (concede)

V. Translate the following sentences into English.
1. 斯蒂芬森教授认为大量的基因会增加患精神分裂症和躁郁症的风险。这可能会改变人们思考问题的方式,不会有什么坏处。
2. 科学家通过对八万六千个冰岛人的基因和医疗信息分析,发现基因变异会使患精神分裂的风险加倍并且使患躁郁症的风险增加三分之一。
3. 大多数艺术家的创造力天赋来源于基因或其他诸如生活经历等各种因素的影响。这开启了他们的创造之旅。
4. 但是事实上,许多患有精神病的人尝试从事艺术和文学方面的工作,不是因为他们擅长做这些工作而是因为他们被其吸引。

VI. Translate the following passage into Chinese.

For Stefansson, even a small overlap between the biology of mental illness and creativity is fascinating. "It means that a lot of the good things we get in life, through creativity, come at a price. It tells me that when it comes to our biology, we have to understand that everything is in some way good and in some way bad," he said.

But Albert Rothenberg, professor of psychiatry at Harvard University is not convinced. He believes that there is no good evidence for a link between mental illness and creativity. "It's the romantic notion of the 19th century, that the artist is the struggler, aberrant from society, and wrestling with inner demons," he said. "But take Van Gogh. He just happened to be mentally ill as well as creative. For me, the reverse is more interesting: creative people are generally not mentally ill, but they use thought processes that are of course creative and different."

Reading B

How Stressful Work Environments Hurt Workers' Health

Teresa Tritch

1 A lot of people would not work in a place where co-workers smoke. And most people will never be faced with that decision because smoking is typically banned(禁止) in the workplace on the sensible(明智的) ground that secondhand smoke is dangerous to everyone.

2 Should long and unpredictable hours, excessive(过多的) job demands, capricious(反复无常的) management and other aspects of the modern workplace be banned on the same ground?

3 That is the question raised by a new study from researchers at Stanford and Harvard, who found that workplace stress is about as dangerous to one's health as secondhand smoke.

4 The study, published recently in the peer-reviewed journal *Behavioral Science & Policy*, examined 10 workplace conditions. Five were presumed(推测) to harm health: long working hours; shift(改变) work; work-family conflict(冲突); high job demands; and low job control, which refers to the level of discretion employees have over their work. Another four were presumed to mitigate(减轻) those stressors: social support; social networking opportunities; availability of employer-provided health care and organizational justice(公正), defined as the perceived fairness of a workplace.

5 The last workplace condition, and arguably the most important, was whether the person was employed at all. The researchers acknowledged that employers are not responsible for macro-economic(宏观经济) forces that influence unemployment. But, they noted, employers are responsible for decisions about layoffs(解雇), which increase economic insecurity even among workers who keep their jobs.

6 The researchers calculated the effects of each of the 10 conditions on four health outcomes: self-rated poor health; self-rated poor mental(精神的) health; physician-diagnosed(医生诊断的) health problems and death. Among the findings:

• Work-family conflict more than doubled the odds(可能性) of an employee reporting poor mental health and increased the odds of self-reported poor physical health by about 90 percent.

• Job insecurity raised the odds of self-reported poor physical health by about 50 percent.

• Low organizational justice increased the odds of having a physician-diagnosed condition by about 50 percent.

• High job demands raised the odds of a physician-diagnosed illness by 35 percent.

• Long work hours increased mortality(死亡率) by nearly 20 percent.

7 In addition, unemployment and low job control significantly upped the odds of all of the outcomes, while adverse(不利的) psycho-social situations at work — lack of fairness, low

social support and low job control — were as strongly associated with poor health as concrete（具体的）factors like long hours and shift work.

8   In all, the researchers calculated that workplace stress contributes to at least 120,000 deaths each year — comparable to the annual（每年的）number of accidental deaths in the United States — and accounts for up to $190 billion in health care costs.

9   The researchers give many reasons that employers should care. If the human right to health does not resonate, employers have a bottom line interest in a healthy workforce. Better health is associated with greater productivity（生产力）. Better health would presumably lower（减少）the costs for employer-provided health insurance and health-care related taxes.

10   The study, however, ends on a cautionary（警告的）note: "Unless and until companies and governments more rigorously measure and intervene（干预）to reduce harmful workplace stressors, efforts to improve people's health — and their lives — and reduce health care costs will be limited in their effectiveness（有效性）."

I. **Match the summaries (A–J) on the left column with the number of paragraphs on the right column.**

   A. Effects of 10 workplace conditions on four health outcomes.   Paragraph 1
   B. Workplace stress can cause deaths and large health care costs.   Paragraph 2
   C. The reasons for employers to provide a healthy environment.   Paragraph 3
   D. Smoking ban in workplace.   Paragraph 4
   E. Companies and governments should work together to improve people's health.
                                                                      Paragraph 5
   F. Workplace stress is dangerous to one's health.   Paragraph 6
   G. Other issues that should be banned in workplace.   Paragraph 7
   H. The effects of unemployment and low job control on health.   Paragraph 8
   I. The most important workplace condition was whether the person was employed.
                                                                      Paragraph 9
   J. Results of examination of 10 workplace conditions.   Paragraph 10

II. **Answer the following questions.**

   1. What kinds of workplace can be harmful for workers' health?
   2. What are the effects of high job demands and long work hours?
   3. What can be the reasons for employers to reduce workplace stress?

III. **Questions for discussion.**

   1. Paying more attention to a healthy workplace such as cutting working hours can influence working efficiency to some extent. What do you think of it?
   2. Do you have some concrete suggestions for companies and governments to improve workplace environments?

Unit Seven

Part Two
Tips for Translation

正面表达与反面表达

Warm-up

Compare each Chinese sentence given below with its English version and discuss what changes have been made in the translation process.

(1) 他知道他得的是不治之症。
   He knew he was mortally ill.
(2) 调查结果清清楚楚说明病人死于癌症。
   The examination left no doubt that the patient had died of cancer.

人们在叙述同一事物或表达同一思想时,可以正说,也可以反说。汉语如此,英语也如此。在翻译时,对原文某个词语或句子,在译文中既可采用正说,也可采用反说。例如:
(1) 他是外乡人。(正说;译文可正说,也可反说)
   He is a stranger here.
   He is not a native.
但是由于思维方式的不同,汉语中有些从正面表达的词或句子,在英语中习惯从反面来表达;而汉语里有些从反面表达的词或句子,在英语中则习惯从正面来表达。因此,英译汉时常常有必要进行转换。这就是通常所说的"正说反译、反说正译"法。
(2) 油漆未干 Wet paint
这是一句招贴用语。搭配"油漆"一词,汉语习惯用"未干",而英语却习惯用wet搭配paint。用意相同,表达各异。如果汉语说成"湿的油漆",英语说成Paint Not Dry,就都不合乎各自的习惯用法了。
(3) 到目前为止,联合国辜负了世界人民所寄予的希望。
   The United States has not, so far, justified the hopes which the people of the world place in it.
原文是正说的"辜负",没有否定词,译文转换成了反说 has not ... justified。

在汉译英中,为了正确处理正说和反说的转换,可以灵活变换句型,也可以利用反义词。此外,英语中有许多含有否定或半否定语气的词语,在翻译中可充分利用,以便使译文符合英语习惯,并使句子结构多样化。

一、借助英语动词

(1) 一天我和他坐车转了一转,看看船怎么卸货。
   I rode around with him one day seeing how the ships unloaded. (汉语正说,英语反说)
(2) 甲:飞机什么时候起飞?乙:要是三两天内天气保持不变,就可以起飞了。
   A: When will the plane take off? B: If the weather holds a couple of days. (汉语反说,英语正说)

二、借助英语名词

(1) 他开车时心不在焉,几乎闯祸。

His absence of mind during the driving nearly caused an accident. (汉语正说,英语反说)

(2) 他未能履行诺言,大家都很失望。

His failure to carry out his promise has disappointed everyone. (汉语反说,英语正说)

三、借助英语形容词

(1) 博物馆内一切展品禁止触摸。

All the articles are untouchable in the museum. (汉语正说,英语反说)

(2) 甚至只要有一点点风声漏出去,结果就不堪设想。

It would be most disastrous if even a rumor of it were given out. (汉语反说,英语正说)

四、借助英语副词

(1) 他马马虎虎地看了看那张便条就走了。

He carelessly glanced through the note and got away. (汉语正说,英语反说)

(2) 甲:这孩子很聪明。乙:一点不错。

A: The boy is quite clever. B: Exactly. (汉语反说,英语正说)

五、借助英语介词

这个问题我不懂(我解决不了)。

This problem is above me. (汉语反说,英语正说)

练习

请根据给出的汉语句子填写出对应英语句子中缺少的词或词组。所需要的词性已在括号中给出。

1. 第一批导弹没有击中目标。

   The first bombs _____ the target. (动词)

2. 我们这样说万无一失(错不了)。

   We may _____ say so. (副词)

3. 他这个人优柔寡断,而且总是反复无常。

   He was an _____ sort of person and always capricious. (形容词)

4. 他无权签订这种合同。

   It was _____ his power to sign such a contract. (介词)

5. 岛上的居民发现自己远远没有做好作战准备。

   The islanders found themselves _____ ready to fight the war. (介词词组)

Unit Seven

Part Three
Simulated Writing

A Performance Report

工作报告是工作过程中向上级、同事或客户等不同对象报告情况的一种书面材料,常被用来阐述对某些问题进行调查得出的结论、就某些问题提出的意见和建议、分析与评估,总结工作进展情况等。

工作报告格式多样,有时可以采用便笺的形式,将接收人、报告人和报告日期写在报告前面。也可以使用信函的形式,只将报告人的姓名写在报告的结尾。

报告必须写明标题,正文内容可以根据需要分段叙述。报告通常包括以下几个部分:

1. Introduction 这部分主要介绍写报告的原因、目的或背景,简要概括报告内容。
2. Findings 这部分包括所发现的问题,已有的应对措施等。
3. Conclusion 本部分主要对相关问题进行分析和论证,阐述结果。
4. Recommendations 报告的最后一部分在前述分析论证的基础上进一步提出建议和意见。

Sample Reading

A Report on Recruitment Services

(A) Introduction

CrazyOne Electronics Ltd. has experienced difficulty in recruiting suitable employees. The Human Resources Manager made a request to investigate the services offered by local employment agencies. Based on his findings, he hoped to recommend a suitable agency to use to fill the posts of Webmaster, CFO and 5 Programmers for his own company.

(B) Findings

The manager visited ten agencies during the week. He selected the following three agencies as being the most reliable:

a) Green's Communications Inc.

   Staff trained in telecommunications work: IP telephone, telecommunication, Web technicians

   Commission: 10% of annual salary

b) The Abacus People

   A wide range of accountants, computing workers with good references

   Commission: 15% of annual salary

c) Software Creators Reservoir

   Experienced applicants above 21 years old with good qualifications. Largely applicants returning to full- or part-time work.

Commission: 15% of annual salary

(C) Conclusion

It can be concluded that the three agencies listed above provide trained personnel resources suitable for the three vacant positions at CrazyOne Electronics Ltd.

(D) Recommendations

It is recommended that these three agencies be used to fill the following vacant positions:

a) Webmaster: Green's Communications Inc.

b) CFO: The Abacus People

c) 5 Programmers: Software Creators Reservoir

The management shall make its own decision on the final choice or choices from among the three.

employment agencies 职业介绍所
Web technician 网络技术人员
commission 佣金
personnel resources 人力资源
vacant position 空缺职位

Check Your Understanding

Answer the following questions.

1. What kind of difficulty has CrazyOne Electronics Ltd. experienced?
2. Who made a request to investigate the services offered by local employment agencies?
3. How many most reliable agencies have been chosen? What are they?
4. What are the three vacant positions at CrazyOne Electronics Ltd.?

Follow-up Writing

Complete the following report with the words given below. Be sure to use the correct form of each word.

(1) finding, (2) conclusion, (3) recommendation, (4) recommend, (5) summarize, (6) aim, (7) approach, (8) identify

Report on Effective Team Leadership Workshop

The __(1)__ of this report is to __(2)__ issues arising from the recent Team Leadership Workshop at Ekstrom and __(3)__ appropriate action.

__(4)__

The workshop began with an assessment of how the Ekstrom team leaders understood their roles. Perceptions ranged from assigning and checking other people's work to motivating others to do the work. This disparity clearly showed that the team leaders had different understandings of their roles and that Ekstrom therefore needed communicate its expectations more explicitly.

In order to do this, Ekstrom identified key tasks and used WorkSet colors to illustrate the precise level of responsibility which could be allocated to each. A task such as communicating with the team, for example, might be __(5)__ in a variety of ways:
- I give my staff instructions every morning. (Blue work)
- I let my staff decide on the best approach for themselves. (Yellow work)
- My team and I discuss how to do each job. (Orange work)

Having __(6)__ the different possible approaches to each key task, the company was able to select which was most appropriate and communicated its expectations in terms of the skills and behavior required.

__(7)__

It is clear that Ekstrom needs to ensure that its team leaders are capable of performing key tasks in a manner compatible with company expectations. However, whilst the appropriate skills can be developed through in-company training, changing behavioral attributes is much more difficult.

__(8)__

We strongly recommend, therefore, that Ekstrom sets up assessment centres where existing team leaders and new applicants can be screened to ensure that they have the appropriate attributes for effective team leadership.

Barrie Watson
Belbin Associates, February 2000

Lead-in
I. Discuss the following topics with your classmates.
1. Do you know something about obesity? What can be the reasons for obesity?
2. A good diet is central to avoid obesity. Which are the best foods to include in your meals, and which ones are best avoided?

II. **Study the following vocabulary before you listen.**

symposium	研讨会	obesity	肥胖
engender	产生，引起	tackle	处理
endocrinology	内分泌学	diabetes	糖尿病学
metabolic	新陈代谢的	calorie	卡路里
intake	摄取量	bariatric	肥胖症治疗学
fizzy drinks	汽水	prospect	前途，预期
unrefined	未提炼的	carbohydrate	碳水化合物
epidemic	流行的	commercially	商业上地
Ice Age	冰河时代	fiber	纤维
protein	蛋白质	radically	彻底地
indigenous	土著的，本土的	intervention	介入，干预

While-listening

I. **Listen to the recording and supply the missing words.**

For the last 15 years, Plymouth, England has held a symposium on obesity. It's ___1___ that more than half the city's adults are overweight or obese. The rest of Britain is not fairing much better.

Professor Jonathan Pinkney said, "No one health issue has the most ___2___ on human health, or engenders more ___3___ about how to tackle it, than obesity." Pinkney, a professor of Endocrinology and Diabetes, took part in the annual Plymouth Symposium on Obesity, Diabetes and Metabolic Syndrome on May 21st.

He said, "obesity is a ___4___ issue that involves more than calorie intake. I ___5___ feel that this is such a wide field. There are so many issues. There's politics. There's ___6___. There's everything you can imagine. There's the food industry. And I think that sometimes we're all a bit ___7___ of just maybe concentrating on one of those areas. And you can go to a ___8___ anywhere in the world where they spend days just talking about bariatric surgery or fizzy drinks. So, I think it's right to talk about everything under one umbrella." He thinks that many issues are concerned with source.

Going to the source means how eating habits are formed. Poor eating ___9___ can be a learned ___10___ passed down by parents to their children. "I think a lot of things start very early in life. You know, it's difficult to ___11___ the habits of a lifetime, isn't it?" he said. "Solving the problem," he said, "is a lot harder than simply trying to ___12___ prevention. There isn't a kind of medical way to prevent the problem. It really does look as if it's down to politics, policy, marketing, food industry and ___13___ children from being exposed to all of this. And I think that's the ___14___ thing that we face in the world. It's very, very difficult." Professor Pinkney said too many ___15___ carbohydrates — sugars — were to blame for much of the ___16___ epidemic. He said that they didn't ___17___ a person's hunger for long and people ate their next meal sooner.

"___18___ produced processed food with large ___19___ of carbohydrates — sweeteners, short acting carbohydrates — and it just sets us up to fail. And I think there are big problems with carbohydrates in the Western ___20___," he said. While it may be difficult to

Unit Seven

__21__ better eating habits, Pinkney said, "there is __22__ for large scale behavior change. Other things have changed. I mean one really interesting thing, I think, was what's happened over __23__ smoking. And how people complained about not being able to smoke in pubs and restaurants and have to go outside. But it didn't take very long for that to translate into clear health benefits. So, you know, maybe you can get these things through in time, little by little."

"Some lessons," he said, "can be learned from our hunter-gatherer __24__. The hunter-gatherers going right back to last Ice Age and before that would have had a __25__ that was rich in complex, sort of, fiber kind of carbohydrates. There would be protein in it now and again. But it didn't have all the sugar. So, the diet that is, of course, followed by traditional peoples is __26__ different." He said studies of __27__ peoples took a step back from __28__ health problems. A __29__ of prevention methods, medical __30__ and policy will be needed to stop the obesity epidemic.

II. Listen again, stop the recording as necessary, and repeat after the speaker.

Post-listening

Surf the Internet and find more information about the following topic areas. Then prepare a 15-minute oral presentation and deliver it in the class. While preparing the presentation you need to narrow down the topic area and focus on one major point.
1. Solutions to obesity
2. Best diets for healthy eating

Part Five Speaking

Opening Speech

Sample 1

First Meeting of the Ad-hoc Group of Experts on Science and Technology for Food Security and Sustainable Development
K.Y. Amoako Executive Secretary of the Economic Commission for Africa

Distinguished Ladies and Gentlemen,

It gives me great pleasure to welcome you to this inaugural meeting of experts invited to make a contribution to the efforts of the United Nations Economic Commission for Africa, by helping bring Science and Technology (S&T) to bear on the Food Security and Sustainable Development of Africa. On behalf of the Executive Secretary of this commission, I wish to thank you for honouring our invitation in spite of your very busy schedules.

As you are well aware, Africa is the only continent where per capita food production has been stagnating or declining in the last three decades. This poor trend has been further compounded by a population growth rate that exceeds food production. Worse still, the food problem and the population pressure have led to an alarming rate of environmental degradation as a result of soil erosion, widespread depletion of soil nutrients and deforestation...

...

Before I end this keynote address, permit me to underscore the appreciation of ECA for the generosity of the Carnegie Corporation of New York whose grant has made your meeting possible.

I wish you very fruitful deliberations and a very exciting time in Addis Ababa. Thank you.

Sample 2

Thank you, Mr. Chairperson, Mr. Director-General, distinguished members of the ILO's Governing Body and friends. I welcome this opportunity to be here today, with an Organization which in many ways belongs to all of us workers. In fact, I can think of no other international body that one can claim as one's own so unambiguously.

I have also had a longstanding formal association with the ILO. Many of my early pieces on women and technological change and on land rights were published by the ILO, as well as was the work of many other scholars. It is therefore a pleasure for me to be here on this important Symposium.

The canvas of the Symposium is very large. I will focus on two aspects of gender inequality that centrally affect millions of women as workers but perhaps have failed to receive the attention they deserve. First, the gender gap in command over property and productive assets and, second, gender biased social perceptions and social norms.

ad-hoc group	特别小组
bear on	有关,瞄准
sustainable development	可持续发展
per capita	每人
environmental degradation	环境恶化
Addis Ababa	亚的斯亚贝巴(埃塞俄比亚首都)
canvas	背景
symposium	研讨会
gender gap	性别差距
command over	指挥
productive asset	生产性资产,经营性资产
social perception	社会知觉
social norm	社会规范

Unit Seven

USEFUL EXPRESSIONS AND PATTERNS:

1. Thank you very much, Prof. Fawcett, for your very kind introduction. Mr. Chairman, Ladies and gentleman, Good morning! I consider it a great honor to be asked to speak about ...on this session of our symposium.

2. Ladies and gentleman. It's an honor to have the opportunity to address such a distinguished audience.

3. Good morning. Let me start by saying just a few words about my own background.

4. Mr. Chairman, thank you very much for your kind introduction. President, Distinguished colleagues, Ladies and Gentleman, Good morning! Is my voice loud enough?

5. Good morning, everyone. I appreciate the opportunity to be with you today. I am here to talk to you about...

6. Good morning, everyone. I am very happy to have this chance to give my presentation. Before I start my speech, let me ask you a question. By a show of hands, how many of you own a car?

7. I consider it a great honor to be asked to speak about ...on this session of our symposium/ at this conference.

8. It is a great pleasure to be given the honor of first speaker on this important topic.

9. It's a very great pleasure for me to be able to attend this conference.

10. I am honored/privileged to be here (with you this afternoon).

11. On behalf of...I wish to convey our warmest congratulations, and I now ask you to step forward to receive the ... Prize from the hands of ...

12. I would like to start by briefly reviewing the history of open heart surgery.

13. Let us start with the theoretical basis of this new technique.

14. The first thing I would like to talk about is the definition of the terms I shall use in my lecture.

15. I would like to concentrate on the problem of antibiotic abuse in hospitals.

I. Read the sample opening speeches.

II. Match the following two columns.

1. 每人   A. symposium
2. 特别小组   B. environmental degradation
3. 研讨会   C. social norm
4. 社会规范   D. sustainable development
5. 背景   E. canvas
6. 环境恶化   F. per capita
7. 社会知觉   G. social perception
8. 可持续发展   H. ad-hoc group

III. The following is the opening speech by Dr Yaacob Ibrahim, Minister for the Environment and Water Resources in Singapore, at the 1st IWA-ASPIRE Conference, at Pan Pacific Hotel. Fill in the blanks with the following expressions.

key to success	sustainable water resources	a robust exchange of views
warm welcome	so many of you	as many of you as possible
for organizing a conference	to declare	
managing our water resources	a fruitful discussion	

Distinguished Guests, Ladies and Gentlemen:

A very ___1___ to all our distinguished guests and participants of the first IWA-ASPIRE Conference in Singapore. Singapore is indeed honored to host this inaugural IWA-ASPIRE conference. The presence of ___2___ here today is testimony to the value of this forum to all in the water industry.

I would also like to thank IWA-ASPIRE ___3___ which encompasses both water and wastewater. I see this as a step in the right direction. Given that water-related issues are complex and inter-connected in nature, it is important that we look at the entire water cycle in a holistic manner—especially when we are looking for better and more sustainable approaches in ___4___.

...

To conclude, I would like to emphasize that managing water resources in a holistic manner is ___5___ to ensure that our people get and continue to enjoy good potable water. We have to strive to look carefully at our unique needs and overcome each of our limitations by careful planning and implementation. During this conference, many distinguished speakers will be sharing their experiences and expertise on various water issues. I therefore encourage you to use this opportunity to engage one another on new ideas and approaches on water-related issues. Let us learn from one another to create a better world. Through ___6___, I am certain that all of us will find this conference an enriching and fruitful engagement.

Let me now take the opportunity to wish everyone ___7___ and an enjoyable stay in Singapore. Perhaps you also will find some time to visit our NEWater Visitor Centre, which showcases the high-grade production process of NEWater. I hope to meet ___8___ again in September for the International Desalination Association World Congress to be held here in Singapore.

I started off relating how critical water has been to the thriving of many civilizations. It is incumbent upon us that we seize the day, look ahead to put in place tangible plans that help ensure that future generations are supplied with good ___9___. On this note, it is now my pleasure ___10___ the IWA-ASPIRE Conference open.

Thank you!

Unit Seven

IV. Complete the following speech by translating the Chinese into English.

Opening Speech at the University of Cambridge by Wen Jiabao, Premier of the State Council of the People's Republic of China

Feb. 2, 2009

Vice Chancellor Alison Richard, Ladies and Gentlemen,

  It gives me great pleasure to come to Cambridge, a world-renowned university that I have long wanted to visit. Cambridge has produced many great scientists and thinkers Isaac Newton, Charles Darwin and Francis Bacon, to name but a few, and _____1_____ (对人类文明做出了重要贡献). This year marks the 800th anniversary of the university. Please _____2_____ (接受我热烈的祝贺).

  This is my fourth visit to your country. Despite the great distance between China and Britain, _____3_____ (两国人民友好的交流) have been on the rise. The successful resolution of the question of Hong Kong and fruitful cooperation between our two countries in areas such as economy, trade, culture, education, science and technology have cemented the foundation of our comprehensive strategic partnership. Here, I wish to pay high tribute to all those who have been working tirelessly to promote friendly ties between our two countries.

  ...

  In the 21st century, _____4_____ (经济全球化和信息网络化) have linked us all together. Different cultures live together and influence each other. _____5_____ (没有一种文化可以孤立地发展繁荣). How much a country or a nation contributes to the culture of humanity is increasingly determined by her ability to absorb foreign cultures and renew herself. That is why China will remain open and receptive, value her own traditions while drawing on others' successful experience, and _____6_____ (取得经济繁荣和社会进步) in a civilized and harmonious way. I hope more of you will turn your eyes to China, see my country in the light of her development, and act as ambassadors of China-Britain friendship. I believe that as long as you, the young people of China and Britain learn from each other and strive for progress hand in hand, you will add a brilliant new chapter to the annals of our relations.

  Thank you!

Unit Eight

Celebrity

Part One
Reading and Translating

Lead-in

In Western culture, people are obsessed by the concept of celebrity. Celebrities are like royalty—glamorous and untouchable. Read the following terms to be familiar with the major Hollywood movie producer/distributor studios where many shining celebrities are cultivated.

- MGM/UA Pictures（米高梅公司）
- 20th Century Fox Pictures（20世纪福克斯公司）
- Sony Pictures（索尼公司）
- Warner Bros Pictures（华纳兄弟公司）
- Paramount Pictures（派拉蒙公司）
- Universal Pictures（环球公司）
- Disney Pictures（迪士尼公司）

Unit Eight

Reading A

A Real Number
A Beautiful Mind's John Nash Is Nowhere Near As Complicated As The Real One

Chris Suellentrop

1   Here's what's true in Ron Howard's movie *A Beautiful Mind*—or, at least, here's what corresponds to Sylvia Nasar's biography of the same name: The mathematician John Forbes Nash Jr. attended graduate school at Princeton, where he was arrogant, childish, and brilliant. His doctoral thesis on the so-called "Nash equilibrium" revolutionized economics. Over time, he began to suffer delusions. He was hospitalized for paranoid schizophrenia, administered insulin shock therapy, and released. Afterward, Nash became a mysterious, ghostlike figure at Princeton. Eventually, through the support of his loving wife, his friends, and the force of his own will, he experienced a dramatic remission. In 1994, he won the Nobel Prize in economics, and to this day he keeps an office at Princeton.

2   A few things in the movie, of course, are just plain wrong—characters and scenes are compressed, events prettied up—but the fudges are mostly forgivable, given the difficulty of whittling a nearly 400-page book into a two-hour biopic. Nasar herself believes that the filmmakers have "invented a narrative that, while far from a literal telling, is true to the spirit of Nash's story." More troubling, though, are the filmmakers' lies of omission. Among the many important events from Nash's life they dropped:

3   1. Homosexual experiences. Nash had recurring liaisons with other men. As an undergraduate, he once climbed into a friend's bed while the friend was sleeping and "made a pass at him," Nasar writes. Nash also made a sexual overture toward John Milnor, a fellow mathematician with whom Nash lived one summer while working for the RAND Corporation think tank in Santa Monica, Calif. According to Nasar, "What Nash felt toward Milnor may have been something very close to love."

4   Nash's first loves were one-sided infatuations with other men. He once kissed another friend, Donald Newman, on the mouth. According to Newman, "He tried fiddling around with me. I was driving my car when he came on to me." Nash also had "special friendships," in his own words, with two men. One of these was Nash's "first experience of mutual attraction," Nasar writes. Of the other, she writes that they were "friends—and then more than friends."

5   In 1954, Nash was arrested for indecent exposure in a bathroom in Santa Monica, which cost him his position at RAND. (He told his bosses that he was "merely observing behavioral characteristics.")

6   2. An illegitimate child. Nash's other "special friendship" was with Eleanor Stier, a Boston nurse. In 1953, when Nash was 25, Eleanor bore him a son, John David Stier. (Nash's other son,

who is depicted in the movie, is also named John.) Though single, Nash was unwilling to care for Eleanor or John, and John had to be placed in foster care for a time. In 1956, Eleanor was forced to hire a lawyer in order to get Nash to pay child support.

7   Nash saw John David occasionally until the child was six. Around John's senior year of high school, he and Nash began communicating by letter. Six years later, they met in person. Nash was still ill at the time and thought John Stier would play "an essential and significant personal role in my personal long-awaited 'gay liberation,'" according to a letter Nash wrote to a friend. The reunion "petered out," Stier told Nasar. "Having a mentally ill father was rather disturbing."

8   After a 17-year estrangement, John Stier and Nash met again. Nash criticized Stier's decision to become a nurse and urged him to go to medical school. He told Stier that it would be beneficial for his other son John (who also developed schizophrenia) to know his "less intelligent older brother."

9   3. Divorce. John Nash and Alicia Larde married in February 1957. Their son, John Charles Martin Nash, born May 20, 1959, remained nameless for a year. On the day after Christmas in 1962, Alicia filed for divorce. Her papers stated that Nash blamed her for twice committing him to a mental institution. He had moved into another room and refused to have sex with her for more than two years. By 1965, she hoped to marry another math professor, John Coleman Moore.

10 Nash moved in with Alicia again in 1970, and it's true that her patience and concern played a critical role in his recovery from schizophrenia. But she referred to him as her "boarder," Nasar writes, and "they lived essentially like two distantly related individuals under one roof" until he won the Nobel Prize, when they renewed their relationship.

11 In the movie, Nash uses his Nobel Prize acceptance speech to pay tribute to Alicia. In reality, Nash was not asked to give a Nobel lecture, presumably because of his instability. He did, however, give a short speech at a small party in Princeton. Here is Nasar's synopsis:

12 He was not inclined to give speeches, he said, but he had three things to say. First, he hoped that getting the Nobel would improve his credit rating because he really wanted a credit card. Second, he said that one is supposed to say that one is glad he is sharing the prize, but he wished he had won the whole thing because he really needed the money badly. Third, Nash said that he had won for game theory and that he felt that game theory was like string theory, a subject of great intrinsic intellectual interest that the world wishes to imagine can be of some utility. He said it with enough skepticism in his voice to make it funny.

13 Are these episodes the whole story of John Nash? No. But neither is the movie.

New Words and Expressions

administer	v.	[ədˈmɪnɪstə]	执行,用(药)
arrogant	a.	[ˈærəg(ə)nt]	自大的,傲慢的
compress	v.	[kəmˈpres]	压缩,精简
delusion	n.	[dɪˈl(j)uːʒ(ə)n]	幻想,错觉
depict	v.	[dɪˈpɪkt]	描述,描画

Unit Eight

dramatic	a.	[drəˈmætɪk]	戏剧性的,激动人心的
drop	v.	[drɒp]	漏掉
episode	n.	[ˈepɪsəʊd]	插曲,一段情节
estrangement	n.	[ɪˈstreɪn(d)ʒm(ə)nt; e-]	疏远,失和
eventually	ad.	[ɪˈventʃʊəli]	最后
exposure	n.	[ɪkˈspəʊʒə; ek-]	暴露
fudge	v.	[fʌdʒ]	捏造,粗制滥造
given	prep.	[ˈgɪv(ə)n]	考虑到
hospitalize	v.	[ˈhɒspɪtəlaɪz]	使住院
indecent	a.	[ɪnˈdiːs(ə)nt]	有伤风化的,不雅的
infatuation	n.	[ɪnˌfætʃʊˈeɪʃ(ə)n; -tjʊ-]	迷恋
instability	n.	[ɪnstəˈbɪlɪtɪ]	不稳定
insulin	n.	[ˈɪnsjʊlɪn]	胰岛素
intrinsic	a.	[ɪnˈtrɪnsɪk]	固有的
liaison	n.	[lɪˈeɪz(ə)n; -zɒn]	联络,关系
omission	n.	[ə(ʊ)ˈmɪʃ(ə)n]	省略,遗漏
overture	n.	[ˈəʊvətj(ʊ)ə]	提议,主动示爱
paranoid	n.	[ˈpærənɒɪd]	偏执狂患者,患妄想狂的人
plain	ad.	[pleɪn]	绝对地
presumably	ad.	[prɪˈzjuːməblɪ]	大概,推测起来
recurring	a.	[rɪˈkɜːrɪŋ]	重复发生的
remission	n.	[rɪˈmɪʃ(ə)n]	缓解
schizophrenia	n.	[ˌskɪtsə(ʊ)ˈfriːnɪə]	精神分裂症
synopsis	n.	[sɪˈnɒpsɪs]	概要,大纲
skepticism	n.	[ˈskeptɪsɪzəm]	怀疑的态度,怀疑论调
utility	n.	[juːˈtɪləti]	用处,效用
whittle	v.	[ˈwɪt(ə)l]	削减

correspond to	与……符合
over time	久而久之
to this day	至今
pretty up	美化
fiddle around	玩弄,调戏
foster care	看护所,养育院
peter out	逐渐消失,逐渐减少
file for	申请,起诉
blame sb. for	因为……责备某人
play a critical role	起到至关重要的作用
refer to someone as	称某人为
pay tribute to	表示敬意、称赞
be inclined to	倾向于做
credit rating	信用评价,信用额度

I. **Give brief answers to the following questions.**
   1. Who is John Nash?
   2. Who is Nasar?
   3. Are there stories in the movie true to the book?
   4. How did Nasar comment on the movie?
   5. What are the major omissions that the filmmakers deliberately made?
   6. What did Nash say in his short speech made for a small party of celebration in Princeton?

II. **Complete the following passage by filling each of the numbered blanks with one or two suitable words using the Chinese in the brackets as the reference.**

   He was not __1__（倾向于）to give speeches, he said, but he had three things to say. First, he hoped that __2__（获得）the Nobel would improve his __3__（信用等级）because he really wanted a credit card. Second, he said that one is __4__（应该）to say that one is glad he is sharing the prize, but he wished he had won the whole thing because he really needed the money __5__（非常）. Third, Nash said that he had won for game theory and that he felt that game theory was like __6__（弦理论）, a subject of great __7__（固有的）intellectual interest that the world wishes to imagine can be of some __8__（用处）. He said it with enough __9__（怀疑论调）in his voice to make it __10__（风趣的）.

III. **Complete the following sentences with one function word.**
   1. He was hospitalized _____ paranoid schizophrenia, administered insulin shock therapy, and released.
   2. I was driving my car when he came on _____ me.
   3. Around John's senior year of high school, he and Nash began communicating _____ letter.
   4. _____ the day after Christmas in 1962, Alicia filed for divorce.
   5. Her papers stated that Nash blamed her for twice committing him _____ a mental institution.
   6. Nash moved in _____ Alicia again in 1970, and it's true that her patience and concern played a critical role in his recovery from schizophrenia.

IV. **Complete the following sentences by translating the Chinese given in the brackets.**
   1. The report of the _____（养育院不符合）the reality. (foster care, correspond to)
   2. Timor-Leste strongly supports the creation of a Peacebuilding Commission, which _____（应该发挥至关重要的作用）in post-conflict situations (be supposed to, play a critical role).
   3. Plans for a biomass power station are under threat after the consortium behind it _____（申请破产）as it cannot pay for debts of £3m. (file for)
   4. Should Ukraine's tottering economy collapse, the country's ability to resist Russian aggression would _____（最终丧失殆尽）. (over time, peter out)

5. The local people and the doctors in the local primary level hospital send a letter, _____（称赞董和王两位医生在援甘帮扶期间医德高尚医术精湛）. (pay tribute to)
6. The UK government _____（希望增加）the amount of aid it gives Yemen, according to ministers in a press conference. (be inclined to)

V. Translate the following sentences into English.

1. 纳什为加州圣莫妮卡的兰德公司智库打工期间的某个夏天，向同住的一个数学家约翰米尔纳主动表示性爱。
2. 1954年纳什因为在圣莫妮卡的洗浴中心不雅暴露而被捕，这件事使他失去了在兰德公司的工作。
3. 尽管纳什尚未再婚，他也不愿意赡养艾莉诺或者抚养儿子约翰，以至于约翰不得不一度被寄养在养育院里。
4. 纳什当时仍然在病中，在他给朋友写的信中他说，约翰施蒂尔会起到至关重要的私人作用，将他从他本人一直期待摆脱的同性恋爱中解脱出来。

VI. Translate the following passage into Chinese.

A few things in the movie, of course, are just plain wrong—characters and scenes are compressed, events prettied up—but the fudges are mostly forgivable, given the difficulty of whittling a nearly 400-page book into a two-hour biopic. Nasar herself believes that the filmmakers have "invented a narrative that, while far from a literal telling, is true to the spirit of Nash's story." More troubling, though, are the filmmakers' lies of omission. Among the many important events from Nash's life they dropped.

Reading B

Bertrand Russell
First published Thu Dec 7, 1995; substantive revision Tue Mar 10, 2015

1   Bertrand Arthur William Russell (1872—1970) was a British philosopher, logician, essayist and social critic best known for his work in mathematical logic and analytic philosophy. His most influential contributions include his championing of logicism (the view that mathematics is in some important sense reducible（可简化）to logic), his refining of Gottlob Frege's predicate calculus（微积分学）(which still forms the basis of most contemporary systems of logic), his defense of neutral monism（中立一元论）(the view that the world consists of just one type of substance（物质）which is neither exclusively mental nor exclusively physical), and his theories of definite descriptions and logical atomism（原子论）.

2　　Together with G.E. Moore, Russell is generally recognized as one of the main founders of modern analytic philosophy. Together with Kurt Gödel, he is regularly credited with being one of the most important logicians of the twentieth century.

3　　Over the course of a long career, Russell also made significant contributions to a broad range of other subjects, including the history of ideas, ethics（伦理学）, political theory, educational theory and religious studies. In addition, generations of general readers have benefited from his many popular writings on a wide variety of topics in both the humanities and the natural sciences. Like Voltaire, to whom he has been compared, he wrote with style and wit and had enormous influence.

4　　After a life marked by controversy（争论）—including dismissals（免职）from both Trinity College, Cambridge, and City College, New York—Russell was awarded the Order of Merit in 1949 and the Nobel Prize for Literature in 1950. Noted also for his many spirited anti-nuclear protests and for his campaign against western involvement in the Vietnam War, Russell remained a prominent（著名的）public figure until his death at the age of 97.

5　　Attempts to sum up Russell's life have been numerous. One of the more famous comes from the Oxford philosopher A.J. Ayer. As Ayer writes, "The popular conception of a philosopher as one who combines universal learning with the direction of human conduct was more nearly satisfied by Bertrand Russell than by any other philosopher of our time" (1972a, 127). Another telling comment comes from the Harvard philosopher W.V. Quine, "I think many of us were drawn to our profession by Russell's books. He wrote a spectrum of（一系列）books for a graduated public, layman（外行）to specialist. We were beguiled（陶醉）by the wit and a sense of new-found clarity with respect to central traits of reality" (1966c, 657).

6　　Despite such comments, perhaps the most memorable encapsulation（包装）of Russell's life and work comes from Russell himself. As Russell tells us, Three passions, simple but overwhelmingly strong, have governed my life: the longing for love, the search for knowledge, and unbearable pity for the suffering of mankind. These passions, like great winds, have blown me hither and thither, in a wayward course, over a great ocean of anguish（苦闷）, reaching to the very verge of despair.

7　　I have sought love, first, because it brings ecstasy（狂喜）— ecstasy so great that I would often have sacrificed all the rest of life for a few hours of this joy. I have sought it, next, because it relieves loneliness — that terrible loneliness in which one's shivering consciousness looks over the rim of the world into the cold unfathomable（深不可测的）lifeless abyss（深渊）. I have sought it finally, because in the union of love I have seen, in a mystic miniature, the prefiguring（预想）vision of the heaven that saints and poets have imagined. This is what I sought, and though it might seem too good for human life, this is what — at last — I have found. With equal passion I have sought knowledge. I have wished to understand the hearts of men. I have wished to know why the stars shine. And I have tried to apprehend the Pythagorean power by which number holds sway（支配）above the flux（通量）. A little of this, but not much, I have achieved. Love and knowledge, so far as they were possible, led upward toward the heavens. But always pity brought me back to earth. Echoes of cries of pain reverberate（回响）in my heart. Children in famine, victims tortured by oppressors, helpless old people a hated burden to their sons, and the whole world of loneliness, poverty, and pain make a mockery of what human life should be. I long to alleviate(缓解)this evil, but I cannot, and I too suffer. This has been my life. I have found it worth living, and would gladly live it again if the chance were offered me.

8   By any standard, Russell led an enormously full life. In addition to his ground-breaking intellectual work in logic and analytic philosophy, he involved himself for much of his life in politics. As early as 1904 he spoke out frequently in favour of internationalism and in 1907 he ran unsuccessfully for Parliament. Although he stood as an independent, he endorsed(支持)the full 1907 Liberal platform. He also advocated extending the franchise(公民权)to women, provided that such radical political change was introduced only through constitutional means (Wood 1957, 71). Three years later he published his *Anti-Suffragist Anxieties* (1910).

9   With the outbreak of World War I, Russell became involved in anti-war activities and in 1916 he was fined 100 pounds for authoring an anti-war pamphlet(小册子). Because of his conviction, he was dismissed from his post at Trinity College, Cambridge (Hardy 1942). Two years later, he was convicted(定罪)a second time, this time for suggesting that American troops might be used to intimidate(恐吓)strikers(罢工者)in Britain (Clark 1975, 337—339). The result was five months in Brixton Prison as prisoner No. 2917 (Clark 1975). In 1922 and 1923 Russell ran twice more for Parliament, again unsuccessfully, and together with his second wife, Dora, he founded an experimental school that they operated during the late 1920s and early 1930s (Russell 1926 and Park 1963). Perhaps not surprisingly, some of Russell's more radical activities — including his advocacy of post-Victorian sexual practices — were linked in many people's minds to his atheism, made famous in part by his 1948 BBC debate with the Jesuit philosopher Frederick Copleston over the existence of God.

10   Although Russell became the third Earl Russell upon the death of his brother in 1931, Russell's radicalism continued to make him a controversial figure well through middle-age. While teaching at UCLA in the United States in the late 1930s, he was offered a teaching appointment at City College, New York. The appointment was revoked following a series of protests and a 1940 judicial decision which found him morally unfit to teach at the College (Dewey and Kallen 1941, Irvine 1996, Weidlich 2000). The legal decision had been based partly on Russell's atheism(无神论)and partly on his fame as an advocate of free love and open marriages.

11   In 1954 Russell delivered his famous "Man's Peril" broadcast on the BBC, condemning the Bikini H-bomb tests. A year later, together with Albert Einstein, he released the *Russell-Einstein Manifesto* calling for the curtailment(削减)of nuclear weapons. In 1957 he became a prime organizer of the first Pugwash Conference, which brought together a large number of scientists concerned about the nuclear issue. He became the founding president of the Campaign for Nuclear Disarmament in 1958 and Honorary President of the Committee of 100 in 1960.

12   In 1961, Russell was once again imprisoned, this time for a week in connection with anti-nuclear protests. The media coverage surrounding his conviction only served to enhance Russell's reputation and to further inspire the many idealistic youths who were sympathetic to his anti-war and anti-nuclear message. Beginning in 1963, he began work on a variety of additional issues, including lobbying(游说)on behalf of political prisoners under the auspices

（支持）of the Bertrand Russell Peace Foundation.

13   Interestingly, throughout much of his life, Russell saw himself primarily as a writer rather than as a philosopher, listing "Author" as his profession on his passport. As he says in his Autobiography, "I resolved not to adopt a profession, but to devote myself to writing" (1967, 125). Upon being awarded the Nobel Prize for Literature in 1950, Russell used his acceptance speech to emphasize themes relating to his social activism.

REFERENCES:

Ayer, A.J., 1972a, "Bertrand Russell as a Philosopher," *Proceedings of the British Academy*, 58: 127—151; repr. in A.D. Irvine (ed.) (1999) *Bertrand Russell: Critical Assessments,* 4 vols, London: Routledge, vol. 1, 65—85.

Clark, Ronald William, 1975, *The Life of Bertrand Russell,* London: Jonathan Cape and Weidenfeld & Nicolson.

Dewey, John, and Horace M. Kallen (eds.), 1941, *The Bertrand Russell Case,* New York: Viking.

Hardy, Godfrey H., 1942, *Bertrand Russell and Trinity,* Cambridge: Cambridge University Press, 1970.

Irvine, A.D., 1996, "Bertrand Russell and Academic Freedom," *Russell,* 16: 5—36.

Park, Joe, 1963, *Bertrand Russell on Education*, Columbus: Ohio State University Press.

Quine, W.V., 1966c, "Russell's Ontological Development," *Journal of Philosophy,* 63: 657—667; repr. in E.D. Klemke, Essays on Bertrand Russell, Urbana, Chicago, London: University of Illinois Press, 3—14.

Russell, B. 1926, *On Education, Especially in Early Childhood, London: George Allen and Unwin; repr. as Education and the Good Life,* New York: Boni and Liveright, 1926; abridged as Education of Character, New York: Philosophical Library, 1961.

Russell, B. 1967, 1968, 1969, *The Autobiography of Bertrand Russell,* 3 vols, London: George Allen and Unwin; Boston: Little Brown and Company (Vols 1 and 2), New York: Simon and Schuster (Vol. 3).

Weidlich, Thom, 2000, *Appointment Denied: The Inquisition of Bertrand Russell,* Amherst, New York: Prometheus Books.

Wood, Alan, 1957, *Bertrand Russell: The Passionate Sceptic,* London: Allen and Unwin.

I. Match the summaries below with the thirteen paragraphs of the article.

A. The most important contributions of Russell.

B. The rest life of Russell after being regarded controversially.

C. The basic information of Russell.

D. Russell's life as a writer.

E. The radicalism of Russell leads to the revoke of a teaching appointment.

F. Two kinds of famous comments on Russell.

G. The three passions of Russell's life in his own words.

H. The political life of Russell before the WWI.

I. The description of Russell's life by himself.

J. The contributions of Russell on other ranges.

K. The career of Russell on nuclear issue.

L. The political life of Russell after WWI.

M. Other political issues besides the anti-nuclear protests.

II. **Answer the following questions.**

1. What are the three passions in Russell's self comment?

2. Why was Russell's teaching appointment at City College revoked?

3. How did Russell contribute to the nuclear issues in 1957?

III. **Questions for discussion.**

1. How do you understand the three passions that have governed Russell's life?

2. What can you learn from Russell? What kind of characteristics that Russell has in common with other celebrities that you know?

Part Two
Tips for Translation

主动与被动

Warm-up

Please compare the following pairs of sentences and discuss what are the differences between the Chinese sentence and its English version.

（1）那里讲什么语言？

What language is spoken there?

（2）这座桥将在今年年底建成。

The construction of bridge will be completed by the end of this year.

汉语和英语的句子，都有主动语态和被动语态。但在汉语中叙述一种行为的时候，常用主动语态；英语则不然，大量的及物动词可以用被动式，不少相当于及物动词的短语也可以用被动式，因此英语中被动语态的使用频率要高得多。在汉英翻译中，常常需要进行主动语态与被动语态之间的转换。

一、英语和汉语被动语态的主要类型

（一）英语被动语态的主要类型：

1. 无从说出或没有必要说明行为的施行者。

（1）The peace talks were being held in Paris.

和谈那时正在巴黎举行。

（2）You're wanted on the phone.

你的电话。

2. 动作的对象是谈话的中心话题。
   The scientific research plan has already been drawn up.
   科研计划已经拟出来了。
3. 为了强调上下文的连贯、衔接。
   Language is shaped by, and shapes, human thought.
   人的思想形成语言,而语言又影响了人的思想。
4. 出于礼貌,使措辞得当,语气委婉。
   Passengers are requested to fill in the customs declaration form here.
   请旅客在此填写报关表。

(二) 汉语被动语态的主要类型:
汉语被动语态和英语被动语态的表达方式有很大的不同,汉语主要是借助于词汇手段来表达被动语态。这种手段又分为两种:一种是有形式标志的被动式;另一种是没有形式标志的被动式。

1. 带有被动标志的汉语被动句
句子中有一些表示被动意义的助词,如:让、叫、给、被、受、挨、遭、由、加以、予以、为……所、被……所、是……的等等。翻译时,以上助词一般都可以译成英语的被动句。
(1) 这个问题必须予以处理。
    This matter must be dealt with.
(2) 该计划将由一个特别委员会加以审查。
    The plan will be examined by a special committee.

2. 不带被动标记的被动句
除了使用词汇手段表示被动式以外,汉语在很多情况下不用被动的语言结构。这种看似主动的句式,虽然不带任何明显的被动标志,但在主谓关系上却具有被动含义,在语法术语上叫作"当然被动句"。古汉语中这样的句子很多,如"飞鸟尽,良弓藏;狡兔死,走狗烹。"这一语言现象在汉语中使用频繁,大量存在,英译时,常需用被动语态来处理。
(1) 这个任务必须按时完成。
    This task must be fulfilled in time.
(2) 每一分钟都要很好地利用。
    Every minute should be made use of.

二、汉语主动语态译成英语被动语态

汉语多采用主动语态,但在英译中常常需要改用被动语态。语态的变换基于多种原因,概括起来,主要是:

(一) 为了强调接受动作的人或事物的重要性
汉译英时,有时需要将汉语的主动句变换为英语的被动句,即运用被动结构把动作的承受者作为句子的主语来突出它的地位,强调其重要性。
(1) 中美已经建立了外交关系。
    Diplomatic relations have been established between China and the United States of America.

(2) 我国各族人民每年都要热烈庆祝十月一日的国庆节。
National Day is enthusiastically celebrated on Oct. 1 by the Chinese people of all nationalities every year.

(二) 为了加强上下文的连贯性
汉译英时,也常常为了上下文的连贯,使句子之间的衔接紧密自然而运用被动结构。
他出现在台上,观众给予热烈鼓掌。
He appeared on the stage and was warmly applauded by the audience.

(三) 为了使措辞得当,语气委婉
有时为了出于礼貌上的考虑,不说出施事者,尤其是第一人称,也需要在汉译英时将汉语主动语态译成英语被动语态,多见于讲话、通知、请帖等。
(1) 来宾请出示入场券。
Visitors are requested to show their tickets.
(2) 请全系教师于星期三下午两点在会议室集合,听报告。
All teachers of the Department are requested to meet in the conference room at 2:00 p.m. on Wednesday to hear a speech.

(四) 汉语中一些习惯用语需译成被动语态
汉语有很多习惯用语,其中有的是"人们""人家""有人"等作主语;有的看来是无主句,虽然没有形式上的主语,但是在不同的语言环境中,都能表示完整而准确的语义;有的则是句子里的独立结构,如"据悉""应该说""必须指出""已经证明",等等。这类习惯用语,从语态上来说都是主动语态,但译成英语时通常都用被动语态,而且可充分利用英语中以 it 作形式主语的句型。

据说,(有)人说	It is said that...
众所周知,大家知道	It is well known that...
有人指出	It is pointed out that...
据悉	It is learned that...
据估计(预计,计算,预测)	It is estimated (predicted, calculated, projected) that...
必须(应该)承认	It must (should) be admitted that...
无可否认	It cannot be denied that...
已经证明	It has been proved that...
已经举例说明	It has been illustrated that...
由此可见	It will be seen from this that...

(1) 应该教育儿童讲老实话。
Children should be taught to speak the truth.
(2) 发现了错误,一定要改正。
Wrongs must be righted when they are discovered.
(3) 很明显,这项计划应该取消。
It is obvious that the plan should be scraped.
(4) 据谣传,那场事故是由于玩忽职守而造成的。
It is rumored that the accident was due to negligence.

三、汉语被动语态译成英语主动语态

虽然英语中被动语态用得较多,但有时根据英语习惯,汉语被动语态也可译成英语主动语态。

（1）老太太被风吹病了。

The old woman fell ill because of exposure to the wind.

（2）光以此速度一直传播出去,除非中途被什么东西挡住。

Light will go on travelling at this speed until something comes into its way.

练习

翻译下列句子,在必要的时候进行主动语态和被动语态的转换。

1. 人家看见她走出了那个房间。
2. 他们希望有人听听他们的意见。
3. 如果把经费都用到优秀的科研人员身上,就可能有所作为。
4. 口试时,问了十个问题,她全都答对了。
5. 请旅客在此填写报关表(declaration form)。
6. 当你在黑暗中走动时,可能会被椅子绊倒,或者撞在墙上。

Part Three
Simulated Writing

A proposal is an offer or bid to do a certain project for someone. It asks the audience to approve, fund, or grant permission to do the proposed project.

Common Sections in Proposals

Introduction

This section does all of the following things that apply to a particular proposal:

● Indicate that the document to follow is a proposal.

● Refer to some previous contact with the recipient of the proposal or to the source of information about the project.

● Find one brief motivating statement that will encourage the recipient to read on and to consider doing the project.

● Give an overview of the contents of the proposal.

Background on the problem, opportunity, or situation

Often occurring just after the introduction, the background section discusses what has brought about the need for the project—what problem, what opportunity there is for improving things, what the basic situation is.

Benefits and feasibility of the proposed project

Most proposals discuss the advantages or benefits of doing the proposed project. This acts as an argument in favor of approving the project. Also, some proposals discuss the likelihood of the project's success.

Description of the proposed work (results of the project)

Most proposals must describe the finished product of the proposed project.

Method, procedure, theory

This acts as an additional persuasive element; it shows the audience you have a sound, well-thought-out approach to the project. This section also serves as the other form of background some proposals need. It discusses the technical background relating to the procedures or technology to be used in the proposed work.

Schedule

Most proposals contain a section that shows not only the projected completion date but also key milestones for the project.

Qualifications

Most proposals contain a summary of the proposing individual's or organization's qualifications to do the proposed work. This section lists work experience, similar projects, references, training, and education that shows familiarity with the project.

Costs, resources required

Most proposals also contain a section detailing the costs of the project, whether internal or external. With external projects, list the hourly rates, projected hours, costs of equipment and supplies, and so forth, and then calculate the total cost of the complete project. With internal projects, there probably won't be a fee, but you should still list the project costs: for example, hours you will need to complete the project, equipment and supplies you'll be using, assistance from other people in the organization, and so on.

Conclusion

In the final section, you can end by urging the readers to get in touch to work out the details of the project, to remind them of the benefits of doing the project, and maybe to put in one last plug for you or your organization as the right choice for the project.

Sample Reading 1

Proposal: Handbook on Communication and Swallowing Disorders in the Elderly Introduction

The following is a proposal to develop a handbook on communication and swallowing disorders in the elderly, for use by the nursing staff at Elevation Pointe on the Lake. The proposal is based on the RFP announced in the January issue of the American Speech-Language Hearing Association's newsletter. As I know your primary concern is the well-being of your patients, the information given in the handbook will be a valuable resource for your staff. The proposal will provide information regarding the need for the handbook, a description the proposed handbook, and the benefits of the handbook. An outline, information sources, a schedule for completion, qualifications of the author, and costs will also be presented.

Need for the Handbook

Recent changes in the healthcare industry, specifically changes that affect long-term care facilities, have resulted in changes in the provision of therapy services. In the past, most long-term care facilities had access to a speech-language pathologist as a full-time employee or full-time contractor. Currently, many companies have been forced to reduce the hours of their therapy staff. As a result, nurses and nurse aides may not have access to someone who can answer questions about communication and swallowing disorders. In turn, patients may have more difficulty expressing their basic wants and needs and may also suffer unnecessarily from swallowing disorders.

Description of the Handbook

The handbook will address communication and swallowing disorders that are commonly found in long-term care facilities. It will provide basic definitions and a brief list of causes for each type of disorder. Signs or symptoms will be discussed to aid the nursing staff in identifying the disorders in their patients. General recommendations will be given to help the nursing staff to communicate with the patients and to assist patients during mealtimes. If patients are suspected to have any of the disorders, it is recommended that a physician and speech-language pathologist be notified.

Benefits of the Handbook

The proposed handbook can be used as a teaching aid in training nurse aides, and as a reference for nurses and nurse aides who have completed training. The handbook can be used as a reference to answer general questions when a speech-language pathologist is unavailable. In addition, it will provide recommendations on communication and swallowing disorders that would be beneficial to all residents of Elevation Pointe on the Lake.

Handbook Outline

The handbook will provide basic definitions of communication and swallowing disorders that are commonly exhibited by patients in long-term care facilities. Common causes of those disorders will be discussed. An extensive list of signs and symptoms will be given with explanations to aid the nursing staff in identifying patients with these disorders. Finally, general recommendations will be given.

Schedule

The handbook will be completed and delivered to your office on March 16, 1999. The following schedule is a timeline of milestones for completion of the handbook:

Receive permission to begin handbook February 1

Research topics through February 15

Write first draft through March 1

Create graphics finish March 3

Complete first draft finish March 8

Revise first draft finish March 15

Deliver Handbook March 16

Qualifications

As a speech-language pathologist, I have had specialized education and training for assessing and treating individuals with speech, language, and swallowing disorders. A brief summary of my education and experience follows:

Texas license to practice Speech-Language Pathology

Certificate of Clinical Competence by the American Speech-Language Hearing Association

Two years professional experience in long-term care facilities

M.S. Speech Language Pathology GPA 3.85/4.0

B.S. Communication Disorders GPA 3.64/4.0

Cost

The total cost for researching, writing, editing, binding, and printing 100 handbooks is $4,036. A breakdown of the total expenses follows:

Fee for researching, writing, and editing $3,500

Spiral binding with card stock cover $211

Printing $325

Total Expense $4,036

Conclusion

This proposal is based on the requirements listed in your RFP. If you have any changes or suggestions, please contact me. The information provided in the proposed handbook will be a valuable resource for your nursing staff in enabling them to improve daily communication and safety during mealtimes for all of your residents. I look forward to sharing the information I have gained through my formal education and work experience to benefit the nursing staff and residents at Elevation Pointe on the Lake.

Notes

Communication and Swallowing Disorders
交流及吞咽困难

nursing staff 护理人员

speech-language pathologist
言语–语言病理学者

therapy staff 从医人员

license to practice Speech-Language Pathology 言语–语言病理学从医资格

Certificate of Clinical Competence
临床资格证书

Check Your Understanding

Match the comments with each corresponding part of the proposal. (Some of the answers have been given.)

1. Having presented the problem, the writer now goes on to discuss the solution: the handbook. This description of the proposed project is a vital element in any proposal.
2. The proposal ends with cordial words encouraging the readers to get in touch.
3. This part is a list of dates for critical milestones in the project.
4. Having written about the need and about the project that will address that need, the writer now presents the benefits that will be gained from hiring this writer to do the proposed project.
5. This section presents a detailed outline of the proposed handbook.
6. This section contains a "mini-resume" of the author in which she lists four or five of her main qualifications to do this work.
7. This section provides background on the necessity of the proposed project.

8. This section indicates how the writer heard about the RFP, makes some positive comments about the handbook, and provides an overview of the contents of the rest of the proposal that follows.
9. This part deals with the cost of the proposed project.

A. Introduction
B. Need for the Handbook
C. Description of the Handbook
D. Benefits of the Handbook
E. Handbook Outline   5.
F. Schedule
G. Qualifications
H. Cost   9.
I. Conclusion

Sample Reading 2

US Fractured Reservoirs Proposal

Abstract

The purpose of this project is to describe the relationship between basement faults, fractures, and other weak zones, and tight gas sand reservoirs, especially fractured reservoirs. Basement features are often clearly expressed in magnetic and gravity data, and their impact on the sedimentary section can be inferred if the tectonic history of an area is known broadly. Observation shows that many basement features do have impact on the section, but the relationship is poorly understood in detail. We will attempt to discover systematic characteristics in gravity and magnetic expressions that will make such data useful as an inexpensive, predictive tool for exploration for fractured reservoirs. Through geophysical modeling and integration with deep well information, the geological meaning of the geophysical data will be defined. This in turn will be used to identify likely areas of similar structural development in less well-explored areas, resulting in specific analogs and extensions of existing plays and production.

Objectives and Significance

The fundamental goal of this project is to provide support for inexpensive exploration techniques (gravity and magnetics) that will enhance the search for deep gas reservoirs in the United States. The techniques and knowledge gained will be of particular value to the small independent companies that are exploring today. They are not able or willing to afford basic research such as this project, even though it should materially reduce their costs. The final product is expected to be a practical document, designed to help guide exploration at the play level, and in some places, at the prospect level.

The project is expected to result in specific locations that may be construed as leads or extensions of plays, and in some cases analogs to existing production may be defined. The results will support upstream exploration as well as development of fractured-reservoir fields.

State of Resources and Scope

This project would use the existing published gravity and magnetic data base in the United States. In general, this coverage is excellent and adequate for purposes of quantification at small to medium scale, as well as at large scale in some places. No new data acquisition is proposed.

The goal of the project would be to evaluate selected prospective areas of the United States in terms of prospectivity for deep gas reservoirs. This proposal is for in-depth analysis in three major basin areas: The Appalachian, Michigan, and Rocky Mountain Basins (including the Great Basin in Nevada). If you are interested in other areas, let us know and if there is enough interest, other or additional areas will be added to this project.

Approach and Methods

Phase I. Detailed interpretations of gravity and magnetic maps in conjunction with the geologic information in the Gas Atlases will identify fields and regions within basins where basement features appear to affect the deep reservoirs. The tectonics of such areas will be described in as much detail as possible to pin down the expected structural styles (compression, extension, wrench; fracturing related to folding, oblique faulting, etc.).

Phase II. The gravity and magnetic data will then be modeled to identify the most reasonable alternatives for the generating mechanism (e.g., basement fault of what type, basement lithologic contact, mineralogical concentration, etc.). The model study will be integrated with what is known about the geology in existing reservoirs, and predictions will be made about expected conditions away from the known producing fields.

The Final Product

The final product will be a series of interpretation maps, suites of modeled cross-sections, predictive maps showing inferred analogs, and a written report. The report would include some color and film overlays as appropriate with folded maps in a pocket or separate packet. Reproducible copies of all maps are included in participation costs. In addition, all participants will receive a free week (6 days) of confidential consulting, designed to provide more specific information in areas of interest of participating companies. This work (value, $3,000) can be conducted at Gibson Consulting's office or in-house, with the client paying any required travel expenses.

References

Gibson, R.I., 1988, Basement tectonic interpretation of the United States exclusive of Alaska and Hawaii: Proprietary report, 160 p., 29 separate maps.

Gibson, R.I., 1995, Basement tectonics and hydrocarbon production in the Williston Basin: An interpretive overview: Seventh Intl. Williston Basin Symp., pp. 3—9.

Atlas of Major Rocky Mountain Gas Reservoirs (1994)

Atlas of Major Gas Reservoirs in the Appalachian Basin (1993)

Costs

This proposal is submitted as an industry-supported project with participation on a proprietary, non-exclusive basis. Original supporters will enjoy lower costs as well as a 6-month exclusive period, after which time Gibson Consulting may market the project to late participants according to the fee schedule given below.

A minimum of five (5) participants is required for the project to be initiated.

Early Participation. Companies that commit to support the project initially will pay a total of $12,000. Half ($6,000) would be invoiced on commencement of the project (see Schedule, below) with the remainder invoiced upon delivery of the final report.

Late Participation. Companies committing to support the project after work has been underway for 4 months, but before the completion of the project will pay a total of $18,000, with half invoiced on commitment and the remainder on delivery. The report will be available for purchase by other, non-participating companies (six months after delivery to existing participants) at a cost of $25,000. This late purchase price will not be reduced for a minimum of 3 years.

Schedule

This work is anticipated to require seven months to complete.

Statement of Qualifications

The Principal Investigator, Richard I. Gibson, has more than 25 years experience at interpreting gravity and magnetic data for hydrocarbon exploration. He is the only geoscientist in the world who has made detailed, exploration-oriented analyses of five continent-scale gravity or magnetic data sets. ... In addition, Gibson is the author of a map entitled Interpreted Magnetic Basement Terrane Map of the United States, which identifies basement features and delineates major cratonic blocks and intrabasement lithologic contacts.

Other continent-scale interpretation projects accomplished by Gibson include....

Gibson Consulting, a sole proprietorship (small business) of Richard I. Gibson, is based in Cardwell, Montana. We have extensive library resources in-house. We have three computers with CD-ROM readers and writers, scanners, and standard office software (word processor, spreadsheet, database, mapping, graphics, publishing, etc.) installed. Laser and color ink-jet printers, FAX, and copy capabilities are available in-house.

Please refer to our Web site for more information on Gibson Consulting and its products, and to the biographic page for more information on Richard I. Gibson. If questions remain, we can provide more information.

Thank you for considering this proposal.

Fractured Reservoirs 裂缝性储层
basement faults 基底断层
sedimentary section 沉积剖面
tectonic history 构造活动历史
geophysical modeling 地球物理建模

Gas Atlases 天然气分布图
basement lithologic contact 基底岩性接触
mineralogical concentration 矿物浓度
hydrocarbon exploration 碳氢化合物探测

Check Your Understanding

Mark the following statements with T (true) or F (false) according to the proposal.

1. This project will help small independent companies to search for deep gas reservoirs in the

American continent in an inexpensive way.
2. This project will support downstream exploration and development of fractured-reservoir fields.
3. The final product of this project will be a series of interpretation maps, suites of modelled cross-sections, predictive maps showing inferred analogs, and a written report.
4. Supporters have to pay $12,000 when the project starts in order to enjoy lower costs of the products.
5. Richard I. Gibson is both the proprietor and the investigator of the company that is to launch the project.

Follow-up Writing

Complete the following proposal according to the Chinese translation given.
PROPOSAL: HANDBOOK FOR THE M-16A2 RIFLE

Introduction

The following is a proposal to develop a handbook that will cover the operation and maintenance of the M-16A2 rifle. _____1_____（本建议书包括如下内容）the proposed manual, the audience level we are assuming, _____2_____（完成项目的时间表）, our costs and charges, and _____3_____（我们可以保证完成优质使用指南的资格）.

Audience and Purpose

The handbook will be written primarily to purchasers but may also be used by gunsmiths, gun enthusiasts, the military, gun clubs, and anyone else wishing to train people in operation and maintenance of this rifle. No technical knowledge about firearms on the readers' part will be assumed. It will assume that readers have never used any firearm previously. Also, we will develop the handbook at the standard 8th-grade reading level_____4_____
_____（有关该指南的描述）.

This handbook should _____5_____（指导任何有高中学历的人，使其能够操作和保养）on the M-16A2. This handbook will contain graphics; technical background; firing techniques; and information on how to clean, disassemble, and reassemble the rifle. We project _____6_____（该指南的长度为98页）in standard 8-inch by 5-inch format.

Qualifications

Technical writers, Inc. (TWI) qualifications for this handbook are as follows:

● The corporation has eighty years combined experience among six partners.

● TWI _____7_____（已签下十项写作武器使用指南的合同）from Colt Manufacturing.

● Experienced typesetters and artists who can do drawings and charts.

● Five of six partners are experienced with this weapon through military experience. _____8_____（如有需要，可以提供我公司员工的详细简历）.

Costs

We calculate the cost to develop this 98-page manual by assuming _____9_____ (每写一页需要4小时,每小时付费50美元). Editing, graphics, and supervision we calculate at 1 hour per 10 pages at $25.00 per hour:

Writing (4 hrs/pg @ $50.00/hr) 18,800

Editing, graphics, supervision (1 hr/10pgs @ $25.00/hr) 245

TOTAL $19,045

Our company will write, edit, and correct any errors found in the initial draft or in later drafts. This includes correcting technical errors or improving comprehension as requested by your technical staff and developers.

_____10_____ (信息来源)

The bibliography will consist of many military pamphlets. The partners of our corporation have written to friends, who are still in the military, for the latest information and pamphlets. Following are some books we have found to use for research:

1. Ezell, Edward Clinton. The Great Rifle Controversy. Harrisburg: Halsted Press, 1984.

2. Ezell, Edward Clinton. Small Arms Today. Harrisburg: Halsted Press, 1984.

3. Ferber, Steve, ed. All About Rifle Hunting and Shooting in America. New York: Winchester Press, 1977.

More books will be obtained for this research.

Project Checkpoint Dates

The time schedule for this project will be as follows:

March 5 _____11_____ (返还建议书,开始工作)

March 12 Outline section on Introduction completed. Sent to Mr. Jackson for review.

March 19 Outline section on Operation completed. Sent to Mr. Jackson for review. Correct problems in introduction section.

March 26 _____12_____ (完成如何保养部分大纲). Sent to Mr. Jackson for review. Correct problems in other sections.

April 12 Meeting with Mr. Jackson to review possible corrections.

April 19 _____13_____ (将终稿交送) to Mr. Jackson.

Unit Eight

Part Four
Listening

Lead-in

I. Discuss the following topics with your classmates.

1. Do you know something about the British royal family? If yes, say something about it.
2. What do you expect the Queen would address the British people on Christmas Day?

II. Study the following vocabulary before you listen.

evoke	激起	twinkling	闪烁的
touching	感人的	Malta	马耳他(欧洲岛国)
naval	海军的	inspirational	鼓舞人心的
symbol	象征	confront	面对
contain	包含	verse	诗
carol	颂歌	overcome	克服
VJ Day	victory over Japan 太平洋战争胜利日		
veteran	退伍军人	procession	游行队列
Oslo	挪威首都奥斯陆	annual	每年的
Trafalgar Square	伦敦特拉法尔加广场	faith	信仰
represent	代表	Star of Bethlehem	伯利恒之星，圣诞星
topping	圣诞树上的装饰物	stable	马厩
capture	抓住	displaced	无家可归的，被罢黜的
persecuted	受迫害的	unchanging	不变的
revenge	报复	customary	习俗的
curse	诅咒		

While-listening

I. Listen to the recording and supply the missing words.

The Queen's Christmas Speech 2015

At this time of year, few sights __1__ more feelings of cheer and goodwill than the __2__ lights of a Christmas tree.

The popularity of a tree at Christmas is due in part to my great-great grandparents, Queen Victoria and Prince Albert. After this __3__ picture was published, many families wanted a Christmas tree of their own, and the custom soon __4__.

In 1949, I spent Christmas in Malta as a newly-married __5__ wife. We have returned to that island over the years, including last month for a meeting of Commonwealth leaders; and this year I met another group of leaders: The Queen's Young Leaders, an __6__ group, each of them a __7__ of hope in their own Commonwealth communities.

Gathering round the tree gives us a chance to think about the year ahead — I am

183

looking forward to a busy 2016, though I have been warned I may have Happy Birthday sung to me more than once or twice. It also allows us to reflect on the year that has passed, as we think of those who are far away or no longer with us. Many people say the first Christmas after losing a loved one is particularly hard. But it's also a time to remember all that we have to be thankful for.

It is true that the world has had to __8__ moments of darkness this year, but the Gospel of John __9__ a __10__ of great hope, often read at Christmas __11__ services: "The light shines in the darkness, and the darkness has not __12__ it."

One cause for __13__ this summer was marking seventy years since the end of the Second World War. On VJ Day, we honoured the remaining __14__ of that terrible conflict in the Far East, as well as remembering the thousands who never returned. The __15__ from Horse Guards Parade to Westminster Abbey must have been one of the __16__ ever, because so many people wanted to say "thank you" to them.

At the end of that War, the people of Oslo began sending an __17__ gift of a Christmas tree for Trafalgar Square. It has __18__ lightbulbs and is enjoyed not just by Christians but by people of all __19__, and of none. At the very top sits a bright star, to __20__ the Star of Bethlehem.

The custom of __21__ a tree also goes back to Prince Albert's time. For his family's tree, he chose an __22__, helping to remind us that the focus of the Christmas story is on one particular family.

For Joseph and Mary, the circumstances of Jesus's birth — in a __23__ — were far from ideal, but worse was to come as the family was forced to __24__ the country. It's no surprise that such a human story still __25__ our imagination and continues to inspire all of us who are Christians, the world over.

Despite being displaced and __26__ throughout his short life, Christ's __27__ message was not one of __28__ or violence but simply that we should love one another. Although it is not an easy message to follow, we shouldn't be discouraged; rather, it inspires us to try harder: to be thankful for the people who bring love and happiness into our own lives, and to look for ways of spreading that love to others, whenever and wherever we can.

One of the joys of living a long life is watching one's children, then grandchildren, then great grandchildren, help decorate the Christmas tree. And this year my family has a new member to join in the fun!

The __29__ decorations have changed little in the years since that picture of Victoria and Albert's tree first appeared, although of course electric lights have replaced the candles.

There's an old saying that "it is better to light a candle than __30__ the darkness".

There are millions of people lighting candles of hope in our world today. Christmas is a good time to be thankful for them, and for all that brings light to our lives.

I wish you a very happy Christmas.

II. Listen again, stop the recording as necessary, and repeat after the speaker.

Post-listening

Surf the Internet and find more information about the following topic areas. Then prepare a 15-minute oral presentation and deliver it in the class. While preparing the presentation you need to narrow down the topic area and focus on one major point.

1. Queen of UK
2. the role the royal family play in British society

Sample Speech

Closing Speech by Wang Gang, Chairman of EASTICA

Ladies and Gentlemen,

Dear Colleagues,

Thanks to the joint efforts and contribution from all participants, the Second General Conference of EASTICA is going to be closed successfully.

In the past two days, we discussed the future activities of EASTICA, elected new members of the Executive Board, adopted the Resolution and decided the dates and place of the Third General Conference of EASTICA. We have reached agreements on all of these issues, which will be of great significance to EASTICA and to the future archival work of East Asia. Just as Charles Kecskemeti said in his opening speech, old Asia is at a time of dynamic economic development. Archival work should keep pace with this new situation and meet the challenge.

Taking this opportunity, I would like also to express thanks to William Wallach from the Bentley Historical Library of Michigan University and Qiu Xiaowei from the Central Archives of China for their excellent presentation on computer application in archives. I believe these lectures are of great importance to computerization of archives management in East Asia.

We are happy to see that the archival work in East Asia has made great progress. The Okinawa Prefecture Archives of Japan has constructed a modern archival building. The New Archives Building of Hong Kong is going to be completed in two years. The National Archives of Mongolia has built a new archives building. The National Archives of Japan is planning to build a new repository. In China, archives of various kinds have been set up throughout the country. Presently, EASTICA has 7 country/territory members, 2 members of national associations of archivists and 7 institutional members. I believe there will be more archival institutions in East Asia who join EASTICA. Mr. Kecskemeti said that he was very happy to see the rapid progress of EASTICA within this short period of two years, and he will report to Mr. Jean Pierre Wallot, President of ICA about EASTICA.

Here, on behalf of the Organizing Committee of the XIIIth International Congress on Archives, I would like to invite all of you to come to Beijing to attend this conference. I hope to see you all next September in Beijing. On behalf of EASTICA, once again, I would like to express our gratitude to Macao Cultural Institute, to Maria Helena Lima Evora, Director of Macao Historical Archives and her colleagues for their hospitality and very delicate arrangement of this meeting.

Now, I declare the closing of the Second General Conference of EASTICA.

Thank you.

joint efforts 共同努力
Executive Board 执行委员会
reached agreements on 就……达成一致意见
archival work 档案工作

keep pace with 跟上……的步伐，并驾齐驱
computer application 计算机应用
computerization 计算机化
repository 仓库

USEFUL EXPRESSIONS AND PATTERNS:

1. We have come to the end of this conference.
2. We come to the end of a very fruitful set of meetings.
3. I believe that our conference has been a great success. It went smoothly as scheduled.
4. The conference was well organized. I enjoyed it very much and hope I can attend the next conference.
5. Let me begin by thanking you for a wonderfully informative and efficient Oxford conference, I really enjoyed it!
6. We talked a lot, we discussed a lot and we also recommended a lot of things.
7. In these five days the Conference has covered so many important and complex problems in the field of applied linguistics both theoretical and practical.
8. It has truly been inspiring to be here and listen to all the experiences and viewpoints that have been raised from so many different parts of the world.
9. The presentations were very illuminating and informative. And the heated panel discussions were very stimulating and fruitful.
10. I want to thank everybody who took part in the organization.
11. Thanks again for putting on such a super meeting. I learned a lot and had a great time.
12. I would also like to thank the associated institutions and organizational partners of this Conference, who helped us to make known and to implement the project.
13. As the organizer of the conference, I would like to express our sincere thanks to ... for all their support and contributions to this successful Conference.
14. I look forward to seeing many of you in New York in March 2017.

15 Our next conference will be held in Dalian. We will try our best to make the forthcoming gathering another fruitful and pleasant one. I'm looking forward to meeting you then.

16 I wish everybody a good journey home.

17 For now, I wish you all a safe journey back home.

18 And lastly, my friends, see you next year in Shanghai and have a safe trip home.

I. Match the following two columns.

1. 档案管理   A. joint efforts
2. 向……表达谢意   B. keep pace with
3. 迎接挑战   C. express thanks to
4. 并驾齐驱   D. archives management
5. 共同努力   E. meet the challenge

II. Complete the following sentences with the help of the Chinese in the brackets.

1. Before closing, _____ (谨代表) the organizing committee, I want to thank you, Mr. President for making this seminar possible.

2. May I ask you to join me in a toast to _____. (为我们两市的友谊与合作)

3. _____ (我非常感谢有这次机会) to visit this beautiful and affluent county.

4. I wish to have the honor of reciprocating _____. (您的热情招待)

5. As a practical result of this seminar, and before we depart, we could _____. (借此机会为将来做些打算)

6. Please accept my _____. (对这次会议胜利召开表示的祝贺)

7. This conference is a success because of _____. (你们的努力和参与)

8. I wish everybody _____. (返程旅途愉快)

III. Learn to make a closing speech in accordance with the following requirements.

You are responsible for delivering a closing speech. Make a speech with all the following information included.

1. The announcement of the conference ending
2. A summary and evaluation of the conference
3. The appreciation to the organizer, sponsor, attendees, speakers and so on
4. Good wishes to the attendees

Unit Nine

Education

Part One
Reading and Translating

Lead-in

Have you ever heard of the term liberal education? Read the following ten reasons to know more about it.

- A liberal education will involve you in learning how to learn and how to participate actively in learning throughout your life.
- You become more adept at problem solving, both by using sharpened analytical skills and by being able to approach situations from multiple perspectives.
- A liberally educated person feels more comfortable talking with many different people on a variety of topics.
- You become an excellent candidate for specialized and professional training in the health sciences, education, law, business, and graduate programs. In fact, a liberal education forms the base of any successful career.
- You can better perceive the many connections that exist between people, places, and ideas. At the same time, you are more able to appreciate the differences.
- You will be increasingly aware of the many dimensions and influences of the various cultures within our country and throughout the rest of the world.
- You will be better equipped to take a stance on controversial technologies such as genetic engineering and nuclear energy.
- A liberal education frees you from the bounds of this present time and place for the purpose of being able to return to the here and now and see it from a whole new perspective.
- Being a liberally educated person means that you have become more aware of the increasingly inter-dependent and inter-connected community of nations in the world. This is both a matter of survival and personal growth.
- You won't necessarily know more than other people, but you will know better which questions to ask and you will be better able to distinguish between knowledge and wisdom.

Unit Nine

Liberal Education at Harvard in This New Century

Jorge I. Domínguez[1]

1　Liberal education is what remains after you have forgotten the facts that were first learned while becoming educated. This view is especially comforting to professors of a certain age who forget even where they place their glasses but, at Harvard, it has long been influential. Harvard philosopher Alfred North Whitehead put it articulately in an essay first published in 1922. The "really useful training," Whitehead argued, focuses on "general principles." One result is that "in subsequent practice the men will have forgotten your particular details; but they will remember by an unconscious common sense how to apply principles to immediate circumstances."[2]

2　This general view has been a foundation stone of the Harvard College curriculum since President Charles William Eliot introduced the elective system to replace a curriculum of prescribed courses. It is the often-unacknowledged foundation stone of the Core Curriculum, which focuses on "approaches to knowledge" or "modes of thought."[3] It remains a sound basis on which to construct the Harvard College curriculum today.

3　In this essay, I focus only on that portion of a liberal education that can be called "general education," that is, the portion of an undergraduate's time in College spent outside a major or concentration but in some way constrained by some requirements (i.e., not pure electives). A curriculum must be built on courses, and to these I turn first.

4　Harvard College liberal-education courses in a general education program ought to meet four key criteria. The first is that they should foster discernment. Students in such courses should perceive the aesthetic world of the arts and letters; apprehend fundamental ideas, methods, and principles underlying the sciences; recognize and analyze distinctive aspects of social behavior in our world and its past; and be capable of rendering acute judgments and making ethical decisions. Discernment in our century cannot be limited to learning just about the United States or the North Atlantic countries. Our students will live in a world of increasing cosmopolitan experiences and interconnectedness.

5　The second criterion is that these courses should develop creativity. Students should learn to transcend traditional ideas, patterns, and relationships in order to fashion new ones thoughtfully. Professors should encourage originality, exploration, and discovery within and across scholarly

---

[1] Jorge I. Domínguez is the Clarence Dillon Professor of International Affairs in the Department of Government at Harvard University.

[2] Alfred North Whitehead, *The Rhythm of Education* (London: Christophers, 1922), republished in his *The Aims of Education* (New York: The Free Press, 1957, 26).

[3] For a thoughtful history of the process of adopting the Core Curriculum, see Phyllis Keller, *Getting at the Core: Curricular Reform at Harvard* (Cambridge: Harvard University Press, 1982).

disciplines, unafraid to present material that might even seem contradictory. To quote Whitehead, the "justification for a university" requires the "imaginative consideration of learning."[①]

6   Thirdly, such courses should construct and propel the communicative skills of our students. This notion is one of the key features of the penultimate comprehensive review of the College's curriculum in 1945, which sought to make our students capable "to communicate thought."[②] For many disciplines in the physical, life, and behavioral sciences, "thought" is often communicated most effectively through mathematics or statistics. For all disciplines, communication characteristically requires the capacity to write and to speak with some eloquence. In many instances, a language other than the one first learned is an essential to communicate in the cosmopolitan world into whose membership our students should aspire.

7   Finally, general-education courses should be accessible to undergraduates who approach them with varying levels of preparation. The criterion of access leads many colleges to emphasize survey courses. One way to read the one-phrase course labels of possibly new Harvard College Courses that appear in A Report on the Harvard College Curricular Review (2004) is that many will, indeed, be survey courses. But that is not, of course, the only way to make courses accessible to undergraduates who have not studied a subject before. An alternative is to teach highly specialized courses to beginners; the professor can do so, however, only if the course has been designed to entice, inform, motivate, and empower the student to proceed expeditiously and within one semester from ignorance to mastery. This may be what Whitehead may have meant by his second "educational commandment," namely, "What you teach, teach thoroughly."[③]

8   This approach to thinking about courses and the curriculum that follows from it has a number of practical consequences. It makes it unlikely that a good design would be a simple "distributional requirement" scheme that clumps courses into humanities, social sciences, life sciences, and physical sciences. Yes, that is a common design throughout much of higher education in the United States, and it has the advantage of simplicity. It disregards, however, the full dimensions of the criterion of discernment. It takes no explicit steps to develop communicative skills. It is at best agnostic on whether creativity would be fostered. It is virtually condemned to rely exclusively on survey courses to meet the criterion of access. It leaves no obvious place for courses to be developed outside disciplinary departments and thus makes curricular and pedagogical innovation either less likely or merely ornamental. It would be better to adopt a more focused system of specific requirements for students to develop better their mental faculties.

---

① *Getting at the Core: Curricular Reform at Harvard*, 93.

② *General Education in a Free Society* (1945), 8.

③ Whitehead, *The Aims of Education*, 2. His first educational commandment was, "Do not teach too many subjects."

Unit Nine

New Words and Expressions

aesthetic	a.	[iːsˈθetɪk; es-]	美学的,审美的
agnostic	a.	[ægˈnɒstɪk]	不可知论的
apprehend	v.	[ˌæpriˈhend]	领会,理解
articulately	ad.	[ɑːˈtikjulətli, ɑːˈtikjuleitli]	清晰明白地
aspire	v.	[əˈspaɪə]	渴望,立志
clump	v.	[klʌmp]	成群,结块
commandment	n.	[kəˈmɑːndmənt]	戒律
condemn	v.	[kənˈdem]	谴责,声讨
contradictory	a.	[ˌkɒntrəˈdɪkt(ə)rɪ]	矛盾的,反对的
cosmopolitan	a.	[ˌkɒzməˈpɒlɪt(ə)n]	世界性的,世界主义的
criterion	n.	[kraɪˈtɪərɪən]	标准
curriculum	n.	[kəˈrɪkjʊləm]	课程,总课程
discernment	n.	[dɪˈsɜːnm(ə)nt]	识别,洞察力
disregard	v.	[dɪsrɪˈgɑːd]	忽视,不理
distinctive	a.	[dɪˈstɪŋ(k)tɪv]	有特色的,与众不同的
eloquence	n.	[ˈeləkwəns]	口才,雄辩
empower	v.	[ɪmˈpaʊə; em-]	授权
entice	v.	[ɪnˈtaɪs; en-]	诱使,怂恿
ethical	a.	[ˈeθɪk(ə)l]	伦理的,道德的
expeditiously	ad.	[ˌekspɪˈdɪʃəsli]	迅速地,敏捷地
explicit	a.	[ɪkˈsplɪsɪt; ek-]	明确的,清楚的
fashion	v.	[ˈfæʃ(ə)n]	形成,制作
foster	v.	[ˈfɒstə]	培养,养育
influential	a.	[ˌɪnflʊˈenʃ(ə)l]	有影响的,有势力的
originality	n.	[əˌrɪdʒɪˈnælɪtɪ]	创意,独创性
ornamental	a.	[ˌɔːnəˈment(ə)l]	装饰性的
pedagogical	a.	[ˌpedəˈgɒdʒɪkl]	教育学的,教学法的
penultimate	a.	[pɪˈnʌltɪmət]	倒数第二的
perceive	v.	[pəˈsiːv]	感知,察觉
principle	n.	[ˈprɪnsəpl]	原理,原则
propel	v.	[prəˈpel]	推进,驱使
render	v.	[ˈrendə]	实施,致使
scheme	n.	[skiːm]	计划,方案
subsequent	a.	[ˈsʌbsɪkw(ə)nt]	后来的,随后的
transcend	v.	[trænˈsend; trɑːn-]	胜过,超越
unconscious	a.	[ʌnˈkɒnʃəs]	无意识的,失去知觉的

apply...to	将……应用于
lead to	导致
be limited to	局限于

be accessible to	对……来说容易获得的
seek to	试图，设法
at best	最多
other than	而不是
take steps	采取措施

I. Give brief answers to the following questions.

1. What is liberal education?
2. What did Whitehead argue about liberal education?
3. According to Jorge I. Domínguez, what does "general education" refer to?
4. What are the four key criteria Harvard College liberal-education courses in a general education program ought to meet?
5. What capacity is required for all disciplines as far as communicative skills are concerned?
6. What does "distributional requirement" mean? What advantage does it have?

II. Complete the following passage by filling each of the numbered blanks with one or two suitable words using the Chinese in the brackets as the reference.

  This approach to thinking about courses and the curriculum that follows from it has a number of practical __1__（后果）. It makes it unlikely that a good design would be a simple "distributional requirement" __2__（组合）that clumps courses into humanities, social sciences, __3__（生命科学）, and physical sciences. Yes, that is a common design throughout much of higher education in the United States, and it has the advantage of __4__（简易）. It disregards, however, the full dimensions of the __5__（标准）of discernment. It takes no explicit steps to develop communicative skills. It is at best agnostic on whether __6__（创造力）would be fostered. It is virtually condemned to rely exclusively on __7__（概论课程）to meet the criterion of access. It leaves no obvious place for courses to be developed outside __8__（学科的）departments and thus makes curricular and pedagogical __9__（创新）either less likely or merely ornamental. It would be better to __10__（采用）a more focused system of specific requirements for students to develop better their mental faculties.

III. Complete the following sentences with one function word.

1. They will remember by an unconscious common sense how to apply principles _____ immediate circumstances.
2. It remains a sound basis _____ which to construct the Harvard College curriculum today.
3. Students in such courses should be capable _____ rendering acute judgments and making ethical decisions.
4. Professors should encourage originality, exploration, and discovery within and _____ scholarly disciplines, unafraid to present material that might even seem contradictory.
5. In many instances, a language _____ than the one first learned is an essential to communicate in the cosmopolitan world into whose membership our students should aspire.

6. It makes it unlikely that a good design would be a simple "distributional requirement" scheme that clumps courses _____ humanities, social sciences, life sciences, and physical sciences.

IV. Complete the following sentences by translating the Chinese given in the brackets.

1. Over-emphasis on survey courses will _____（使学生失去培养自己创造力的机会）. (lead...to, foster)
2. These criteria put forward by the scientists are not so precise and can be _____ （最多也只能应用在小学生身上）. (apply to, at best)
3. American higher education _____（试图在二者之间做个选择）: whether to concentrate more on survey courses or adopt a more focused system. (seek to)
4. The knowledge of a student should not _____（局限于某一特定的国家或地区）, and should definitely go far beyond that. (be limited to)
5. To answer the call of the scientists, more colleges are _____（立即采取措施用笼统的规则而不是具体的细节来教育学生）. (take steps to, other than)
6. How to _____（使学生学到这些课程）is a problem that has troubled the school authority very much. (render, accessible to)

V. Translate the following sentences into English.

1. 通识教育是忘掉自己最初受教育时学到的事实后剩下的东西。这种观点使上了年纪的教授们尤其欣慰，他们连眼镜放在哪里都想不起来，但是在哈佛，这种观点的影响力由来已久。
2. 学习这些课程的学生应该能够感知文学艺术之美；能够理解这些科学的基本思想、方法及原则；能够辨析古往今来社会中人们行事的突出特征；还能做出敏锐的判断以及合乎伦理的决策。
3. 学生应该学会超越传统的思想、模式和关系，以便在深思熟虑的情况下形成新的思想、模式和关系。教授应该鼓励本学科及跨学科的创新、探索和发现，大胆推出哪怕是可能引起争议的素材。
4. 另一个办法是给初学者上极其专业的课程。但是，只有这门课程设计得可以吸引、告知、激励并授权学生在一学期内突飞猛进，从无知到掌握，教授就可以做到这一点。

VI. Translate the following passage into Chinese.

  This approach to thinking about courses and the curriculum that follows from it has a number of practical consequences. It makes it unlikely that a good design would be a simple "distributional requirement" scheme that clumps courses into humanities, social sciences, life sciences, and physical sciences. Yes, that is a common design throughout much of higher education in the United States, and it has the advantage of simplicity. It disregards, however, the full dimensions of the criterion of discernment. It takes no explicit steps to develop communicative skills. It is at best agnostic on whether creativity would be fostered. It is virtually condemned to rely exclusively on survey courses to meet the criterion of access. It leaves no obvious place for courses to be developed outside disciplinary departments and thus makes curricular and pedagogical innovation either less likely or merely ornamental. It would be better to adopt a more focused system of specific requirements for students to develop better their mental faculties.

Reading B

The Invention Studio: A University Maker Space and Culture[①]

*Craig Forest, Roxanne A. Moore, Amit S. Jariwala,
Barbara Burks Fasse, Julie Linsey, Wendy Newstetter,
Peter Guo, Christopher Quintero
Georgia Institute of Technology Atlanta, GA*

INTRODUCTION

1　　The Engineer of 2020 recognizes that creating, inventing, and innovating are essential skills for engineers (National Research Council 2004). It is the prospect of engaging and cultivating these skills that encourages many undergraduate students to consider studying engineering. However, in standard engineering curricula（课程）, students do not generally create or invent anything tangible until the culminating Capstone（顶点）Design experience. This postponement can be credited to a shift in engineering education that occurred between 1935 and 1965 (Seely 1999, Lamancusa 2006). Engineering curricula changed from hands-on（亲身实践的）, practice-based curricula to theory-based approaches with a heavier emphasis on mathematical modeling. Consequently, many educators, such as the originators of the Conceive-Design-Implement-Operate (CDIO) initiative, (Crawley, Malmqvist, Lucas and Brodeur 2011) have identified industry needs for more capable engineering graduates with traits beyond technical knowledge, including personal maturity, interpersonal skills, and holistic, critical thinking regarding engineering systems (Crawley 2002). As counter-trends have emerged in recent years to re-introduce hands-on learning, some programs have initiated（开始）freshman design experiences (Sheppard and Jenison 1997, Dym, Agogino, Eris, Frey and Leifer 2005). The benefit of such experiences has been demonstrated at the University of Colorado Boulder, for example, where students who participated in an early design experience were retained（保持）at a statistically significantly higher rate than similar groups of engineering students without such introductory experiences (Knight, Carlson and Sullivan 2007). This finding speaks to the potential（潜在的）benefits of practicing creative activities early and often. The overarching goal of Georgia Tech's Invention Studio is to provide a place—a maker space—for students to apply classroom theory to, or simply mess about with, design-build projects, tools, materials, and mentoring（指导）within a community of their own management, independent of curricular requirements, classroom projects, or hierarchical（层级的）structure

---

① Introduction and background are two sections of the full paper entitled "The Invention Studio: A University Maker Space and Culture".

of coursework.

BACKGROUND

2 In order to promote design experiences at the undergraduate level, community maker spaces are gaining popularity at universities. The currently known benefits of these spaces that have been researched appear to be two-fold: the documented benefits of physical modeling and the growth of communities of practice.

3 The Maker Movement originally started outside of universities in the 1990's as a technology-based extension（延伸）of Do-It-Yourself (DIY) culture (Anderson 2012, Anderson 2012). Examples of such non-university "maker spaces" and "gym-like" design/prototyping spaces abound today including Tech-Shops (TechShop 2014) and NextFab Studio (NextFab 2014). In light of（鉴于）the benefits for engineers in terms of both physical modeling and the sense of community, this movement is now merging with the efforts to increase design-build curricula on university campuses. This movement has coupled with dramatic decreases in the price of 3D printers and related "maker" technology (Canessa, Fonda and Zennaro 2013) to drive（推动）development and expansion of maker spaces, resulting in new construction and renovation（革新）of university design facilities since the early 2000's (Lightner, Carlson, Sullivan, Brandemuehl and Reitsma 2000, Carlson and Sullivan 2006, Gedde, Silliman and Batill 2006, Griffin and Cortes 2006, University of Michigan Wilson Student Team Project Center 2013). These spaces, such as CU-Boulder's Integrated Teaching and Learning Laboratory (ITLL), aim to promote hands-on learning for enrolled（登记的）engineering students and support theoretical coursework. Additionally, many such facilities serve as places of outreach（拓展）and engagement with the non-engineering community (CU Boulder ITLL 2013). Other stated goals included enhancing creativity, team-oriented problem solving, and multidisciplinary（多学科的）collaboration skills (Carlson and Sullivan 2006, Griffin and Cortes 2006), goals which address industry needs for graduating engineers to have such skills (Crawley 2002, Lamancusa 2006). These spaces move well beyond traditional machine shops by providing meeting spaces for student design teams and integrating（整合）typical machine shop tools with a wider variety of rapid prototyping（雏形）and low-tech building approaches. The construction of such spaces answers a call to improve American engineering education at the turn of the century (Carlson and Sullivan 2006, Gedde, Silliman and Batill 2006, Griffin and Cortes 2006) and to train engineers to engage increasingly complex challenges (National Research Council 2004).

4 More recently, design spaces have launched（推出）in schools specifically to welcome the hacker and maker cultures that are infiltrating student communities (Laskowski 2010, Collaborative 2012, BUILDS 2013, Studio 2013). Boston University's Association for Computing Machinery (ACM) chapter kicked off BUILDS (Boston University Information Lab & Design Space) in 2010 as a university-sponsored, student-built and run hacker space, open to members who have card access (Laskowski 2010, BUILDS 2013). These spaces and others represent an effort to support "bottom-up" or grassroots student engineering and facilitate（促进）the pursuit（追求）of extracurricular（课外的）personal projects and the exploration of manufacturing techniques.

5 A comparison can be drawn between a notable（值得注意的）instance of a

government-funded, "top-down" approach to updating design education—the Learning Factory curriculum—and the present case of a "bottom-up," student-driven approach—the Invention Studio. The Manufacturing Engineering Education Partnership (MEEP) between Pennsylvania State University, University of Washington, and University of Puerto Rico produced the Learning Factory model for design and manufacturing curriculum in the mid-1990's (Soyster and Lamancusa 1994, Morell, Zayas-Castro and Velez-Arocho 1998, NSF 2006). Enabled by $2.8 million from NSF and ARPA, and through collaboration with Sandia National Laboratories and hundreds of industry partners, the model drove curriculum and facilities（设施）updates at the three universities (Lamancusa, Jorgensen and Zayas-Castro 1997) and, between 1994 and 2006, the model expanded to other schools to reach thousands of students through real-world industry-sponsored projects (Lamancusa and Simpson 2004).

6   The Learning Factory model aimed to serve three stakeholder（利益相关者）groups. First, industry leaders desired more talented, creative, and well-rounded engineers who were better prepared for innovative work. Second, students desired a richer, practice-based curriculum to augment（增加）their theoretical knowledge and make them more competitive in the job market. Third, faculty（全体教员）desired to connect their research with real-world problems and industry needs. Its success in meeting these needs was recognized by the National Academy of Engineering in 2006 (Lamancusa, Zayas, Soyster, Morell and Jorgensen 2008), and its approach is reflected（反映）in many design programs in universities across the country, including Georgia Tech's Design Sequence and Capstone Design course (Georgia Tech 2014).

7   As later sections of this paper make evident, the Invention Studio at Georgia Tech offers a unique alternative for achieving many of the same outcomes as the Learning Factory approach. Without any reliance on grant（拨款）funding, the Invention Studio has grown gradually, over 5 years, to incorporate（合并）ever-increasing facility space and equipment while leveraging a "bottom-up" approach from its beginning to give students primary responsibility for daily operation, maintenance, and equipment training for newcomers. Industry funds which support the Capstone Design course contribute the bulk（大部分）of funding for the Studio, and industry partners have reacted positively to students gaining design and manufacturing skills in a self-driven environment while also working on sponsored projects. Faculty has embraced（拥抱）the Studio as a means of reinforcing fundamental theory from course lectures. Students, in turn, have become well-engaged in the Studio, taking initiatives to improve equipment capabilities and to host（主办）workshops for their peers in specialized design and manufacturing topics.

8   While the Maker Movement is growing across the country and within the university culture, the spaces which house them are under-studied as affordances（承载）for learning in the context of a community of practice. Developing an understanding of these spaces beyond the research already documented about physical modeling and the community of practice is a critical（决定性的）task toward producing guidelines for creating and implementing them in universities, as well as fully understanding the impacts（影响）on student learning.

REFERENCES:

Anderson, C. (2012). *Makers: The New Industrial Revolution,* Crown Business, New York, NY.

Anderson, C. (2012). The New MakerBot Replicator Might Just Change Your World. *Wired Magazine.*

BUILDS. (2013). *About BUILDS* Retrieved June 23, 2014, 2014, from http://builds.cc/about/.

Canessa, E., C. Fonda and M. Zennaro (2013). *Low-cost 3D printing: for science, education & sustainable development,* ICTP.

Carlson, L. E. and J. F. Sullivan (2006). "A Multi-Disciplinary Design Environment." *ASME 2006 International Design Engineering Technical Conferences and Computers and Information in Engineering Conference* 4c: 835—840.

Collaborative, D. E. (2012). "About Design Engineering Collaborative." Retrieved September 4, 2013, 2013, from http://dec.berkeley.edu/about.html.

Crawley, E. F. (2002). Creating the CDIO *syllabus, a universal template for engineering education.* Frontiers in Education, 2002. FIE 2002. 32nd Annual, IEEE.

Crawley, E. F., J. Malmqvist, W. A. Lucas and D. R. Brodeur (2011). The CDIO Syllabus v2.0: An Updated Statement of Goals for Engineering Education. *CDIO Conference.* Technical University of Denmark, Copenhagen.

CU Boulder ITLL. (2013). "About Us." Retrieved September 4, 2013, 2013, from http://itll.colorado.edu/about_us.

Dym, C. M., A. M. Agogino, O. Eris, D. D. Frey and L. J. Leifer (2005). "Engineering design thinking, teaching, and learning." *Journal of Engineeirng Education* 94(1): 103—120.

Gedde, N., S. Silliman and S. Batill (2006). *Lessons Learned From Operating a Multidisciplinary Engineering Learning Center.* ASME 2006 International Design Engineering Technical Conferences and Computers and Information in Engineering Conference. Georgia Tech. (2014). "Georgia Tech Capstone Design Expo." Retrieved 4/17/2014, from http://www.capstone.gatech.edu/.

Griffin, O. H. and S. Cortes (2006). "A Learning Space of, by, and for Engineers: Virginia Tech's Joseph F. Ware, Jr. Advanced Engineering Laboratory." *ASME 2006 International Design Engineering Technical Conferences and Computers and Information in Engineering Conference* 2006: 841—848.

Knight, D. W., L. E. Carlson and J. F. Sullivan (2007). Improving engineering student retention through hands-on, team based, first-year design projects. *International Conference on Research in Engineering. Education.* Honolulu, HI,.

Lamancusa, J. S. (2006). "The Reincarnation of the Engineering 'Shop'." 2006: 849—857.

Lamancusa, J. S., J. E. Jorgensen and J. L. Zayas-Castro (1997). "The learning factory—A new approach to integrating design and manufacturing into the engineering curriculum." *Journal of Engineering Education* 86(2): 103—112.

Lamancusa, J. S. and T. W. Simpson (2004). *The Learning Factory—10 Years of Impact at Penn State.* International Conference on Engineering Education.

Lamancusa, J. S., J. L. Zayas, A. L. Soyster, L. Morell and J. Jorgensen (2008). "2006 Bernard M. Gordon Prize Lecture*: The Learning Factory: Industry-Partnered Active Learning." *Journal of Engineering Education* 97(1): 5—11.

Laskowski, A. (2010). "A Place to Hack or Just Hang." Retrieved September 4, 2013, 2013, from http://www.bu.edu/ today/2010/a-place-to-hack-or-just-hang/.

Lightner, M. R., L. Carlson, J. F. Sullivan, M. J. Brandemuehl and R. Reitsma (2000). "A living laboratory." *Proceedings of the IEEE* 88(1): 31—40.

Morell, L., J. Zayas-Castro and J. Velez-Arocho (1998). The Learning Factory: Implementing ABET 2000 A Hands-On Workshop. University of Puerto Rico Mayaguez, NSF.

National Research Council (2004). The Engineer of 2020: Visions of Engineering in the New Century. Washington, D. C., The National Academies Press.

NextFab. (2014). "NextFab: Philadelphia's 'gym for innovators'." Retrieved 4/17/2014, from www.nextfab.com.

NSF (2006). Learning Factory Receives NAE Gordon Prize.

Seely, B. E. (1999). "The other re-engineering of engineering education, 1900—1965." *Journal of Engineering Education* 89(3): 285—294.

Sheppard, S. D. and R. Jenison (1997). "Freshman engineering design experiences: An organizational framework " *International Journal of. Engineering Education* 13(3): 190—197.

Soyster, A. and J. Lamancusa (1994). TRP: The Manufacturing Engineering Education Partnership. Pennsylvania State University, NSF.

Studio, I. (2013). "About the Studio." Retrieved September 4, 2013, 2013, from http://inventionstudio.gatech.edu/about/. Suwa, M. and B. Tversky (1997). "What do architects and students perceive in their design sketches? A protocol analysis." *Design Studies* 18(4): 385—403.

TechShop. (2014). Retrieved 4/17/2014, from http://techshop.ws/.

University of Michigan Wilson Student Team Project Center. (2013). "About." Retrieved September 4, 2013, 2013, from http://teamprojects.engin.umich.edu/about/.

I. Match the summaries (A–H) on the left column with the number of paragraphs on the right column.

A. The recent development of maker spaces.	Paragraph 1
B. The three stakeholder groups that the Learning Factory model aimed to serve.	Paragraph 2
C. The critical significance to develop an understanding of the maker spaces.	Paragraph 3
D. The primary purpose of the Georgia Tech's Invention Studio.	Paragraph 4
E. The early development of maker spaces.	Paragraph 5
F. The introduction of the Learning Factory curriculum.	Paragraph 6
G. Two benefits of the community maker spaces.	Paragraph 7
H. Brief introduction to the Invention Studio at Georgia Tech.	Paragraph 8

II. Answer the following questions.

1. What industry needs have many educators such as the originators of the CDIO initiative identified?
2. What are the three stakeholder groups that the Learning Factory model aimed to serve?
3. What role have industry partners played in the Invention Studio at Georgia Tech?

Unit Nine

III. Questions for discussion.

1. Do you agree that creating, inventing, and innovating are essential skills for engineers? Why or why not?
2. What can you learn from the Invention Studio at Georgia Tech? What are the implications for engineering education in China?

Part Two
Tips for Translation

合并与切分

Warm-up

1. Compare the three English versions of the given Chinese sentence. Choose the one you think is best and give your reasons.

我有一条出乎意料的好消息,现在要告诉你。

I have a surprising piece of news, and I want to tell you about it.

I have a surprising piece of news, which I will tell you.

I have a surprising piece of news for you.

2. Compare the following Chinese sentence with its English version and discuss what changes have been made during the translation process.

一般说来,典型的金属能导热导电,表面有光泽,具有延展性和可锻性。

Generally speaking, the typical metal conducts electricity and heat. It shows lustrous surface, usually with white, or so-called metallic luster. It is dustile and malleable.

翻译句子时,有时我们可把原文的句子结构整个保存下来或只稍加改变即可;但在不少情况下则必须将原来的句子结构做较大的改变。切分与合并就是改变原文句子结构的两种重要方法。

一、合并

汉语句子的特点是分句较短,承上启下,层次分明,要求言简意赅,直接明快,不用或少用曲折隐晦的表达手法。表达一个复杂的概念,汉语一般不采用扩展句子某个成分的方法,而是用一些短句,逐点逐层交代清楚。

英语句子一般比较长,而且结构往往十分繁琐,因为句子的各种成分都可以附有不同形式的修饰成分,如单词、短语、从句等等,有时还要穿插独立结构、插入语等等。但由于关系代词、介词和连词等的纽带作用,任何复杂的英语长句分析起来仍然线索清楚,主从关系分明,不致造成误解。

汉译英时,根据英语习惯,有时需要将汉语的几个句子合并成一个英语句子,或将汉语的一个句子译成英语的一个分句,或将汉语的分句译成英语词组或单词,这些处理方法统称为合并。合并的方法主要有以下两种：

(一) 使用英语连接词进行合并

汉语中的句子，有时前一句话提到一件事，后一句话接着谈这件事，两句话又都不长，或者两个句子之间联系十分紧密，已经构成了主从关系，英译时即可利用连接词（包括连词、关系代词、关系副词等）进行合并。例如：

他和史密斯先生谈过话。史密斯向他担保，凡是能够做到的都将竭尽全力去做。

He had talked to Mr. Smith, who assured him that everything that could be done would be done.

(二) 使用英语非连接词进行合并

汉语句子中的分句之间必然有着一定的语义联系，这就构成了合并的语义基础。有时，可将其中一个分句转成一个修饰词（副词或形容词）并移到另一个分句中起修饰作用；有时则可添加一个介词，将两个分句中的动宾意义连接起来或表示伴随；另外，有些条件或原因状语从句可以紧缩成英语中的名词或名词词组，充当译文中的主语。

1. 利用英语名词或名词词组进行合并。例如：

但是，如果该地区再次发生战争，显然会使国际关系处于紧张状态。

But another round of war in the region clearly would put strains on international relations.

2. 利用英语副词进行合并。例如：

当时，友谊商店只对外宾开放，不对内宾开放。

At the time the friendship store was exclusively open to foreign visitors.

3. 利用英语形容词进行合并。例如：

重复建设比较严重，造成了一些浪费。

There was much wasteful duplicate construction.

4. 利用英语介词或介词短语进行合并。例如：

年满十八岁的公民，都有选举权和被选举权。依照法律被剥夺选举权和被选举权的人除外。

All citizens who have reached the age of eighteen have the right to vote and to stand for election, with the exception of persons deprived of these rights.

二、切分

鉴于汉语松散句多这一特点，在很多情况下，译者应考虑将两句汉语合并为一句英语。但也有一些时候，由于汉语句子的结构比较松散，一个句子里存在不少并列分句或并列成分，而又没有连接词把它们之间的逻辑关系明显地表现出来。为了照顾到英语句子结构严谨的习惯，需要把汉语原文的一句话译成两句或更多句，也就是对原句进行切分。

(一) 汉语句子如前半句说明一方面情况，后半句说明另一方面的情况，英译时即可进行切分，译文会更清晰，明快。例如：

把右手放在热水里，把左手放在冷水里。

Put your right hand in the hot water. Put your left hand in the cold water.

Unit Nine

（二）汉语中有些句子是先总说，后分述，即先用几个字概括地提一下，然后再详细地加以说明，像"拿……来说""比如……"，译成英语时，一般可在句子开头部分断句，也就是将最前面总说或概括部分单独译成一句。例如：

拿我们这些人来说，很多人每年都有一些进步。

Take for example those of us present here. Many of us make some progress each year.

（三）汉语中有些句子是先分述，后总说，即先详细地把事情说清楚，然后简单地加以概括，也可能是一种评论，也可能是得出的结论。这样的句子译成英语时，一般要在句子结尾部分断句，即将最后的总结或判断部分单独译成一句。例如：

本工艺具有造型速度快，生产效率高，工艺性能优良，综合经济效益高，劳动条件好等优点，引起了世界铸造工作者的关注。

This technology has the advantages of great moulding speed, high production efficiency, fine technological performances, excellent overall economic results and good labor conditions. Therefore, it has attracted the attention from foundry businesses all over the world.

（四）汉语中有些句子意思的层次较多，所含信息很多，译成一句英语句子后可能会显得更长，信息十分拥挤，切分后译文会更清晰，也更符合英语习惯。

(1) 她很有才智、雄心勃勃、工作努力，还善于解决问题。(两句合一)

She is intelligent, ambitious and hard-working. She is also good at solving problems.

(2) 我把椅子挪过去坐下，开始两脚分开，但我突然觉得这样显得不尊重，太不拘礼节，便把两膝并拢，把双手随便地放在膝盖上。

I pulled up a chair and sat down. I sat with my legs wide apart at first. But this struck me as being irreverent and too familiar. So I put my knees together and let my hands rest loosely on them.

练习

1. 根据汉语句子的意思按括号中给出的要求完成对应的英语句子。

(1) 我遇到了一个问题。当我要出席会议时，这个问题越发明显了。

I had a problem, _____ became clearly obvious just as I was to appear at the meeting.（填关系代词）

(2) 我们认识到，中国的长期现代化计划以发展经济为重点，这是可以理解的，也是必要的。

We recognize that China's long-term modernization program _____ and _____ emphasizes economic growth.（填副词）

(3) 这家小工厂经过技术改造，发展飞快，使人感到惊讶不已。

This small factory underwent a technological renovation, thus developing with _____ speed.（填形容词）

(4) 黎明时分，大雾弥漫，细雨蒙蒙。

Daybreak comes _____ thick mist and drizzle.（填介词）

(5) 肯尼迪遇刺时，基辛格认为，如果肯尼迪再任一届总统的话，大概不是立大功，就是闯大祸。

At the time of Kennedy's assassination, Kissenger felt that _____ would have either led to greatness or to disaster.（填名词短语）

2. 比较下面每组句子并判断每一句英译文分别对原句进行了哪一类切分处理。
   (1) 门没锁上,她走了进去,呆呆地坐了下来,极度的衰弱几乎使她无力挪动她那红肿的双脚。

   The door was unlocked. She went inside and sat in a stupor. She was near collapse, barely able to move her swollen feet.

   (2) 今年不同,战争费用估计只要用去年的一半。

   This year it will be different. It is estimated that the outlays for war will come to only half last year's figure.

   (3) 人们必须通过对现象的分析和研究,才能了解到事物的本质,因此需要科学。

   It is by analyzing and studying the appearance of a thing that people come to know its essence. Hence the need for science.

   (4) 本文扼要地叙述了用来制造单块电路的各种工艺及其优缺点。

   The various process which may be used in fabricating a monolithic circuit are briefly reviewed. The advantages and disadvantages of each process are enumerated.

Part Three
Simulated Writing

Abstract

摘要又称概要、内容提要。摘要是以提供文献内容梗概为目的,不加评论和补充解释,简明、确切地记述文献重要内容的短文。其基本要素包括研究目的、研究方法、结果和结论。具体地讲就是研究工作的主要对象和范围、采用的手段和方法、得出的结果和重要结论。摘要应具有独立性和自明性,并且拥有与文献同等量的主要信息,也就是,不阅读全文,就能获得必要的信息。

摘要有短有长,短的只有一句话,长的有好几段,但一般说来在学术期刊上发表的论文摘要都不宜过长,通常在100~150词左右,更确切地说,约为原文长度的1%~5%(有的期刊规定摘要平均长度为全文的3%~5%)。

英文摘要应该用简洁、明确的语言,将论文的"目的(Purposes)",主要的研究"过程(Procedures)"及所采用的"方法(Methods)",由此得到的主要"结果(Results)"和得出的重要"结论(Conclusions)"表达清楚。如有可能,还应尽量提一句论文结果和结论的应用范围和应用情况。也就是说,要写好英文摘要,作者必须回答好以下几个问题:

1. 本文的目的或要解决的问题 (What I want to do?)
2. 解决问题的方法及过程 (How I did it?)
3. 主要结果及结论 (What results did I get and what conclusions can I draw?)
4. 本文的创新、独到之处 (What is new and original in this paper?)

英文摘要的写作并没有一成不变的格式,但一般来说,英文摘要是对原始文献不加诠释或评论的准确而简短的概括,并要求它能反映原始文献的主要信息。英文摘要的各部分写作一般分别有以下要求：

1. 目的 (What I want to do?)

主要说明作者写作此文的目的，或本文主要解决的问题。一般来说，一篇好的英文摘要，一开头就应该把作者本文的目的或要解决的主要问题非常明确地交代清楚。必要时，可利用论文中所列的最新文献，简要介绍前人的工作，但这种介绍一定要极其简练。

2. 过程与方法 (How I did it?)

主要说明作者工作过程及研究方法，也应包括众多的便捷条件、使用的主要设备和仪器。在英文摘要中，过程与方法的阐述起着承前启后的作用。开头交代了要解决的问题 (What I want to do)之后，接着要回答的自然就是如何解决问题(How I did it)，而且，最后的结果和结论也往往与研究过程及方法是密切相关的。在说明过程与方法时，应结合（指向）论文中的公式、实验框图等来进行阐述，这样可以既给读者一个清晰的思路，又可以产生一种可信的感觉。

3. 结果和结论(What results did I get and what conclusions can I draw?)

结果和结论部分代表着文章的主要成就和贡献，论文有没有价值，值不值得读者阅读，主要取决于你所获得的结果和所得出的结论。因此，在写作结果和结论部分时，一般都要尽量结合实验结果或仿真结果的图、表、曲线等来加以说明，使结论部分言之有物，有根有据，只有这样，论文的结论才有说服力。如有可能，在结尾部分还可将论文结果和他人最新研究结果进行比较，以突出论文的主要贡献和创新、独到之处。

通过对摘要的语言结构进行分析研究，得出了摘要语言的几个突出特点：(1) 谓语动词很简单而句子的其余成分却十分复杂；(2) 大量使用be动词（主要用来陈述定义或表示"什么是什么"的陈述句)和have（主要用来叙述事物具有某种或某些特征）的各种变化形式作谓语动词；(3) 使用不提及人的陈述句，因此广泛使用被动句，使用主动句也尽量回避使用第一人称。

USEFUL EXPRESSIONS AND PATTERNS:

1 Research objectives

- The purpose of this paper is...
- The primary goal of this research is...
- The intention of this paper is to survey...
- The overall objective of this study is...
- In this paper, we aim at...
- The chief aim of the present work is to investigate the features of...
- The work presented in this paper focuses on several aspects of the following...
- The problem we have outlined deals largely with the study of...
- With his many years' research, the author's endeavor is to explain why...
- The primary object of this fundamental research will be to reveal the cause of...
- The main objective of our investigation has been to obtain some knowledge of...
- With recent research, the author intends to outline the framework of...
- The author attempted the set of experiments with a view to demonstrating certain phenomena...

- The experiment being made by our research group is aimed at obtaining the result of...
- The experiment on... were made in order to measure the amount of...

2. Procedures & Methods
- The method used in our study is known as...
- The technique we applied is referred to as...
- The procedure they followed can be briefly described as...
- The approach adopted extensively is called...
- Detailed information has been acquired by the authors using...
- This is a working theory which is based on the idea that...
- The fundamental feature of this theory is as follows ...
- The theory is characterized by...
- The experiment consisted of three steps, which are described in...
- The test equipment which was used consisted of...
- Included in the experiments were...
- The winch is composed of the following main parts:
- We have carried out several sets of experiments to test the validity of...
- They undertook many experiments to support the hypothesis which...
- Recent experiments in this area suggested that...
- A number of experiments were performed to check...
- Examples with actual experiment demonstrate...
- Special mention is given here to...
- The formula is verified by...
- We also supply...

3. Results & Conclusions
- In conclusion, we state that...
- In summing up it may be stated that...
- It is concluded that...
- The results of the experiment indicate that...
- The studies we have performed showed that...
- The pioneer studies that the authors attempted have indicated that...
- All our preliminary results throw light on the nature of...
- As a result of our experiments, we concluded that... this fruitful work gives explanation of...
- The author's pioneer work has brought about a discovery of...
- These findings of the research have led the author to the conclusion that...
- The data obtained appear to be very similar to those reported earlier by...
- The author has satisfactorily come to the conclusion that...

Sample Reading

Through a study of website design practice, we observed that website designers design sites at different levels of refinement—site map, storyboard, and individual page—and that designers sketch at all levels during the early stages of design. However, existing web design tools do not support these tasks very well. Informed by these observations, we created DENIM, a system that helps website designers in the early stages of design. DENIM supports sketching input, allows design at different refinement levels, and unifies the levels through zooming. We performed an informal evaluation with seven professional designers and found that they reacted positively to the concept and were interested in using such a system in their work.

website design	网站设计
site map	地位级图
storyboard	情节串连图板

Check Your Understanding

Answer the following questions.

1. What is the problem observed by the researchers?
2. What have the researchers done to solve the problem?
3. What have the researchers found about the DENIM?

Follow-up Writing

Complete the following abstract with the information given in the brackets.

　　Modern management is essentially about managing people as well as processes in a rapidly changing environment. __1__（作者提出了）the factors which make "strategic management" effective. A dominant factor is the organization climate which, in turn, __2__（由……决定）the quality of managers and the availability of alternatives. __3__（为了改善）the organization climate in which strategic management can be effective, the quality of the managers is a crucial factor. The scope for alternatives also proves an important constraint.

　　__4__（作者建议）that the assessment of effects for management should include the use of consultants and the role of formal procedure. __5__（结论是）that the correct judgment and optimal operation of the essential factors will enhance the effectiveness of strategic management in general.

Part Four
Listening

Lead-in

I. Discuss the following topics with your classmates.
   1. Do you know something about STEM education? If yes, say something about it.
   2. What inspires you to further your study for the Master of Engineering?

II. Study the following vocabulary before you listen.

STEM	science, technology, engineering and mathematics 的首字母缩略语
NASA	美国国家航空和宇宙航行局(National Aeronautics and Space Administration)
spark	发动,激起
take to	喜欢,开始从事
aspiring	有抱负的
marvel	对……感到惊异
mission	使命
spacewalk	太空行走
aerospace	航空航天空间
creativity	创造力
artistic	艺术的
straightforward	直截了当的,坦率的
yield	出产,产生
originally	最初,起初
assurance	保证,保险
hazard	危险
nitty-gritty	事实真相,本质
cascade	像瀑布般冲下或倾泻
inherent	内在的,固有的
flexibility	灵活性
informed	消息灵通的,见多识广的
knowledgeable	知识渊博的,有知识的
combustion	燃烧,氧化
automobile	汽车
relevant	相关的,切题的

Unit Nine

While-listening

I. Listen to the recording and supply the missing words.

Making STEM Matter for the Next Generation of Astronauts and Engineers

Former NASA astronaut and Raytheon engineer Robert Curbeam explains what sparked his interest in science and how to inspire the next generation of STEM leaders.

As an aspiring scientist in Baltimore in the 1970s, Robert Curbeam would stand at the end of his street and __1__ at NASA's Skylab space station when he could see it __2__ in the sky. Decades later, as an astronaut, he would see space __3__ and put his STEM skills to use installing and repairing equipment on the International Space Station during several __4__. Curbeam, 51, participated in three NASA spaceflights and was the first astronaut to complete four __5__ during a single mission. He retired from the space agency in 2007 and now serves as vice president for mission __6__ for Massachusetts-based __7__ and defense company Raytheon. Curbeam recently spoke with U.S. News about what __8__ his early interest in science and engineering and how to inspire the next generation of STEM leaders.

What inspired you to study engineering?	When I was growing up, my mom was a __9__ teacher and I really, really took to it. When I started looking at colleges, I found out that I really had a __10__ interest in engineering. Also, when I was in middle school, I had a very good friend... he and I used to spend a lot of time together trying to __11__ a better car or a better plane, things like that. To us it just seemed like it made sense that there were so many things that didn't change about the car for so __12__ that we could do it better at age 12 or 13.
What kept you interested?	It was creativity mixed with mathematics. When you do design work, it's never __13__. It almost approaches being art-like, an __14__ kind of thing, where creativity and the way you think about the problem sometimes will __15__ a different design than someone would __16__ think.
How did you use that engineering training in your work at NASA?	There were two ways, actually. The first is the actual operation of a spacecraft. That's not to say that without a __17__ degree you couldn't do that. It just makes it easier to operate the spacecraft and understand the interaction between all of the __18__. I also used my engineering degree after the Columbia accident because I was on the safety and mission assurance team that was evaluating all of the __19__ analyses...for the space shuttle system. At that point you really get to the nitty-gritty of how the systems work, where the hazards are, what kinds of interfaces the different systems have and their __20__, and how maybe a failure in one can cause a cascading failure in others.

What do you see ahead in terms of the future of space travel and research?	The thing that excites me is we're finally to that stage where you can have an interaction of both __21__ systems and purely machine systems. We can take the best of the remotely __22__ or driven vehicles, which is their persistence, their ability to operate in very __23__ environments, along with your human-driven or -piloted vehicles, vehicles that we would actually put people in, and their inherent __24__ and responsiveness. At the end of the day, we're going to need a lot of very, very smart and informed and __25__ people in the next generation to help us continue to push that forward. Although we sit here and we're very, very worried about the short term—how do we get people that are __26__ to do the jobs we have now? — we also have to think a generation away: How are we going to make sure that we have the people to do that work in 2030, 2040, 2050?
How do we attract that next generation of astronauts and engineers to the STEM disciplines?	I think the most important thing is to make it __27__ . Learning about how, for instance, combustion worked was very interesting to me because I saw it every day. I understood that was the key to the automobile, __28__ to how airplanes flew. By the same token, if you want to get kids interested and keep them interested in the STEM fields, you have to make it relevant. I really don't care what the __29__ to $3x+2y=1$ is, but if you tell me that that equation will help me solve the problem of how much grain I need to buy for how many horses to keep them __30__ for the next winter, then it becomes relevant.

II. Listen again, stop the recording as necessary, and repeat after the speaker.

Post-listening

Surf the Internet and find more information about the following topic areas. Then prepare a 15-minute oral presentation and deliver it in the class. While preparing the presentation you need to narrow down topic area and focus one major point.

1. STEM education
2. Introduction to a university in English speaking country

Part Five
Speaking

Academic Report

Sample Report (Part 1)

Hello everyone and welcome. I am Benjamin Ricketson, from Michigan University. Thank you all for coming to this presentation. Today I will present on the complexities of psychological stress. Since psychological stress is a complex concept, I will be giving you a brief overview. There are many different ways to define stress. But for me this one is the best: Psychological stress is a normal reaction to a threat or to a disturbing change in the environment. There are things that cause psychological stress. The things that cause it are things like other people, our own thoughts and emotions or physical changes in the environment, such as heat and cold.

...

Small doses of daily stress are not unhealthy at all. Stress is part of life, and our bodies are adapted to it. Of course, sometimes the down time for recovery may not come and the on/off switch for the stress response can get stuck in the "on" position. This brings up the fact that we may face a blend of both short and long-term stress.

In the classic definition a short-term, or acute, stress is what happens when we must respond immediately to a threatening situation like a near miss in traffic. And as people we all face long-term or cumulative stress. This type of stress is stress that occurs over a long period of time and is a result of situations that do not present an easy or quick solution like the everyday events of modern life—things like overdue bills, an undependable car, or troubles at home.

Also, you can have very intense long-term stress called adversity. These are things like illnesses or deaths in the family. What many people have told me is that what wears them out is being under a lot of stress for a long period of time. And they are right because carrying a heavy burden of long-term stress tends to have worse effects on health than just the occasional short burst of stress.

Now, let's look at how stress affects our physical health. The first thing we need to do is to talk about the immediate bodily changes that occur when we feel threatened. The stress response can lead to some physical symptoms that can make life unpleasant such as nausea, a racing heart with palpitations, profuse sweating, rapid breathing, dizziness, muscle tremors, and sensory changes.

During the stress response the levels of certain nerve transmitters shift in the brain. This can lead to psychological and emotional changes under stress such as fear, anxiety, and anger. You can become tense. You can become increasingly irritable or jittery and jumpy or others feel sorrow and anguish under stress. Plus when there's extreme stress you can feel like you're losing control, worry about being criticized, or feel like you're going mad.

...

Let's look at what happens to the mind under stress. Your senses become much sharper when you're stressed out. And also under stress you'll find you can become forgetful. It becomes much harder to concentrate. Your thinking may slow down and you'll probably experience difficulty in thinking analytical thoughts. You can get confused, and you may have trouble making decisions. Additionally, fear-related changes can cause everyday facts to slip away. You can become more vigilant and distractible. And there tends to be a loss of objectivity and perspective.

Sample Report (Part 2)

Now, let's switch gears and talk about how to turn off the stress response and return to a calm state. Dr. Herbert Benson named this calming physical reaction the relaxation response. It is our "off switch." During the relaxation response as we recover from the stress of the day, our blood pressure goes down, our heart will slow to a normal rate, we'll stop breathing so fast, and we will calm down emotionally. The relaxation response is why a normal load of daily stress does not affect our health, for it helps us to recover.

But, people who suffer from chronic stress that is not relieved by periods of relaxation are more at risk for negative effects on their health than someone who suffers an isolated episode of even intense stress and has time to recover. Chronic stress is a known risk and contributing factor to many physical diseases. Why is this? Long-term stress results in chronic, day-to-day activation of the stress response. Over time this chronic arousal of the body knocks the body's systems out of balance.

However, usually stress by itself, is not enough to cause disease. Let's look at an example. An acute stressor like an argument can trigger a heart attack in someone who's predisposed to heart disease. But researchers believe that it's the chronic everyday stress over the years that lead to the coronary artery blockages. Stress-related chemicals, such as epinephrine can also irritate the tissues that carry the heart's electrical activity and can cause irregular heartbeats in people with underlying heart disease. Although hypertension has other risk factors, chronic stress is one and can contribute to genetic hypertension in people who have the right genetic predisposition. The risk of infection is higher when a person is suffering from chronic stress because the stress-related increase of the cortisol hormone suppresses their immune system. Finally, the gastrointestinal system is not immune to the effects of chronic stress either and a disorder called irritable bowel syndrome is related to psychological stress.

So what can we do to control stress? First, we are not helpless against the effects of stress. There are ways to turn off the stress response and turn on the calming relaxation response. Second, remember, we all possess innate stress buffers. These buffers can prevent ahead of time the negative effects of stress.

Right now we'll learn ways to strengthen our innate prevention factors. Our number one stress buffer is coping skills. Coping skills are automatic mental ways in which we deal with stress. Our coping styles color the way we think and therefore feel about a situation. Here are four main coping styles. Some types of styles are going to automatically fit a certain situation better than others.

The first coping type is called appraisal focused coping, meaning people who seek and interpret the meaning in events. The second type of coping is problem-focused coping, finding practical solutions to problems. The third type of coping is emotion-focused coping, meaning to regulate your emotion under situations. Everyone has their automatic coping style. It's important to know that coping skills can be learned and they are taught by counselors and psychologists. Therefore, if you think about it and you find you tend to use just one kind, you can learn others and therefore come up with a more flexible coping strategy.

The second innate stress buffer is psychological resilience. Resilience is the universal human capacity to face, overcome and even be strengthened by experiences of adversity. How we respond to stress is partly rooted in our personalities. There are people who have naturally hard personalities. They tend to engage the world in very positive ways. They feel like they have the ability to influence the outcome of events. And they tend to see crises and challenges as opportunities for growth. It is currently believed that skills that lead to increased resilience can be taught.

The third stress buffer is social support...

The fourth and final stress buffer is self-care strategies such as exercise and good diet and adequate sleep. It's been found the physically harmful effects of chronic stress can be reduced by moderate exercise. A balanced diet helps keep stress from becoming distress. Our diet affects our blood chemistry, weight, energy levels and reserves. So remember, even though it seems simple, you can fight stress by doing such things as eating right, sleeping, and exercising.

That's the end of my presentation. Thank you.

palpitation	心悸	nerve transmitter	神经递质
jittery	神经过敏的	predisposed to heart disease	先天性心脏病
coronary artery blockages	冠状动脉堵塞	epinephrine	肾上腺素
genetic hypertension	遗传性高血压	cortisol hormone	皮质醇荷尔蒙
immune system	免疫系统	gastrointestinal system	胃肠系统
irritable bowel syndrome	肠易激综合症	stress buffers	缓压器
psychological resilience	心理弹性		

USEFUL EXPRESSIONS AND PATTERNS:

1. I am Benjamin Ricketson, from Michigan University.
2. Thank you all for coming to this presentation.
3. Today I will present on the complexities of psychological stress.
4. Since psychological stress is a complex concept, I will be giving you a brief overview.
5. There are many different ways to define stress.
6. Psychological stress is a normal reaction to a threat or to a disturbing change in the environment.
7. The things that cause it are...

⑧ This brings up the fact that we may face a blend of both short and long-term stress.

⑨ In the classic definition a short-term, or acute, stress is...

⑩ This type of stress is stress that occurs over a long period of time and is a result of situations that do not present an easy or quick solution like the everyday events...

⑪ Also, you can have very intense lone-term stress called adversity.

⑫ They are right because carrying a heavy burden of long-term stress tends to have worse effects on health than just the occasional short burst of stress.

⑬ Now, let's look at how stress affects our physical health.

⑭ The first thing we need to do is to talk about the immediate bodily changes that occur when we feel threatened.

⑮ This can lead to psychological and emotional changes under stress such as fear, anxiety, and anger.

⑯ Let's look at what happens to the mind under stress.

⑰ Now, let's switch gears and talk about how to turn off the stress response and return to a calm state.

⑱ Chronic stress is a known risk and contributing factor to many physical diseases.

⑲ The relaxation response is why a normal load of daily stress does not affect our health.

⑳ Long-term stress results in chronic, day-to-day activation of the stress response.

㉑ Let's look at an example.

㉒ Right now we'll learn ways to strengthen our innate prevention factors.

㉓ Our number one stress buffer is coping skills.

㉔ Here are three main coping styles.

㉕ The first coping type is called appraisal focused coping, meaning people who seek and interpret the meaning in events.

㉖ The second type of coping is problem-focused coping, finding practical solutions to problems.

㉗ The second innate stress buffer is psychological resilience.

㉘ The fourth and final stress buffer is self-care strategies such as exercise and good diet and adequate sleep.

I. Listen to the report and answer the following questions.

1. According to the speaker, what is the best definition of psychological stress?
2. List three items that can cause psychological stress.
3. How can we define a short-term stress?
4. What is intense long-term stress called?
5. Which one poses more danger to our health, a heavy burden of long-term stress or the occasional short burst of stress?
6. What physical changes are likely to occur when we are under intense stress?
7. What is the cause of psychological and emotional changes under stress such as fear, anxiety, and anger?
8. What changes are likely to occur to the mind when we are under stress?
9. Why doesn't a normal load of daily stress affect our health?

10. Name a few diseases that may result from chronic stress.
11. What can our innate stress buffers do?
12. How many major coping skills with stress do we have?
13. What is psychological resilience?
14. What is the last stress buffer introduced by the speaker?

II. **Match the following sentences with the corresponding patterns of organization. Some of the answers have been given.**

1. Psychological stress is a normal reaction to a threat or to a disturbing change in the environment.
2. This can lead to psychological and emotional changes under stress such as fear, anxiety, and anger.
3. The relaxation response is why a normal load of daily stress does not affect our health, for it helps us to recover.
4. Long-term stress results in chronic, day-to-day activation of the stress response.
5. Let's look at an example. An acute stressor like an argument can trigger a heart attack in someone who's predisposed to heart disease.
6. Resilience is the universal human capacity to face, overcome and even be strengthened by experiences of adversity.
7. Stress-related chemicals can also irritate the tissues that carry the heart's electrical activity and can cause irregular heartbeats in people with underlying heart disease.
8. Here are four main coping styles. The first coping type is called appraisal focused coping, meaning people who seek and interpret the meaning in events. The second type of coping is problem-focused coping, finding practical solutions to problems....
9. The fourth and final stress buffer is self-care strategies such as exercise and good diet and adequate sleep.
10. Carrying a heavy burden of long-term stress tends to have worse effects on health than just the occasional short burst of stress.
11. This is things like illnesses or deaths in the family.
12. Chronic stress is a known risk and contributing factor to many physical diseases.

A. definition (定义法)　　　　　　　　　　　　　6
B. cause and effect (因果关系法)　　　　　　　　2
C. classification (分类法)
D. exemplification (举例法)　　　　　　　　　　2
E. comparison and contrast (对比法)

III. **Give a presentation on the latest development in your field. Be sure to use simple language to explain the technical terms so that the layman can understand you without much difficulty.**

Unit Ten

Environment

Part One
Reading and Translating

Lead-in

Transport affects everyone, every day. The Transport sector is a major contributor to air pollution and climate emissions, impact set to increase with an expected tripling of the global car fleet.

Guiding Principles for Sustainable Transportation

Principle 1: Access
People are entitled to reasonable access to other people, places, goods and services.

Principle 2: Equity
Nation states and the transportation community must strive to ensure social, interregional and inter-generational equity, meeting the basic transportation-related needs of all people including women, the poor, the rural, and the disabled.

Principle 3: Health and Safety
Transportation systems should be designed and operated in a way that protects the health (physical, mental and social well-being) and safety of all people, and enhances the quality of life in communities.

Principle 4: Individual Responsibility
All individuals have a responsibility to act as stewards of the natural environment, undertaking to make sustainable choices with regard to personal movement and consumption.

Principle 5: Integrated Planning
Transportation decision makers have a responsibility to pursue more integrated approaches to planning.

Principle 6: Pollution Prevention
Transportation needs must be met without generating emissions that threaten public health, global climate, biological diversity or the integrity of essential ecological processes.

Principle 7: Land and Resource Use

Transportation systems must make efficient use of land and other natural resources while ensuring the preservation of vital habitats and other requirements for maintaining biodiversity

Principle 8: Fuller Cost Accounting

Transportation decision makers must move as expeditiously as possible toward fuller cost accounting, reflecting the true social, economic and environmental costs, in order to ensure users pay an equitable share of costs.

Reading A

Businesses Delivering the Most Coveted Perk: a Better Commute

Lisa Palmer [1]

1 Imagine that, starting tomorrow, half your company's employees stopped driving to work. The benefits would start accruing almost immediately: less pollution, less real estate needed for parking spaces, improved quality of life and much more. So how do companies do it and, given all these benefits, why aren't more jumping onboard?

2 Google — which this week rebranded itself as Alphabet — may not have been the first company to offer shuttles to its employees, but the size and growth of its shuttle program have made it the most prominent, for better or for worse.

3 The company started its own bus service in 2004 to shuttle roughly 150 employees from their San Francisco homes to the Googleplex in Mountain View, California. Today, 6,400 of Alphabet's 11,000 Bay Area employees use the corporate fleet of 140 biodiesel-fueled buses to get to work each day. While the buses have been met with protests since 2013 for fuelling gentrification in the form of skyrocketing housing costs, the buses have succeeded in keeping cars off the road.

4 Private busing is not an option for most companies, but a variety of tools — from social media to long term planning — can reduce the number of single-driver cars employees put on the road, according to Susan Hunt Stevens, the founder and chief executive of WeSpire, a 35-person tech firm in Boston that offers an interactive, web-based platform to help companies motivate employees to change their habits, get onboard with company sustainability goals and measure outcomes. Commuting programs are among the most sought-after initiatives, she said.

5 Roughly 47,000 employees of companies using the WeSpire platform participate in programs to drive less, Stevens said. In total, they have taken more than 58,000 commuting-related actions — whether carpooling to work, taking public transportation, or telecommuting and holding virtual meetings.

---

[1] Lisa Palmer is a freelance journalist based in Maryland and a fellow at the National Socio-Environmental Synthesis Center.

6   Stevens modeled the WeSpire platform after the work of behavior change research scientist BJ Fogg of Stanford University. According to Fogg's behavior model, three elements — motivation, ability and a trigger — must converge for a behavior to change. Company sustainability initiatives are the motivation. WeSpire's game mechanics platform helps with the trigger. Employees, then, are left to work on developing their ability to overcome barriers — sometimes perceived, sometimes all too real — to an alternative commute.

7   "Where do I get the bus? Where do I transfer? How much does it cost? In many places, the lack of ability to even find commuting options is very real," Stevens said. "We hear, 'I don't have access to alternative options. There's no public transit. No vanpools.'"

8   Stevens said that the key to getting employees to drive less is improving their ability to find options and getting them to try something just once. "When they find out the non-driving option is doable, we task them to try it once a month, then once a week, and so on. Some people move to every day quickly," she said.

9   In Boston and elsewhere, companies are increasingly relocating to be closer to transit or to where their employees live, even encouraging them to work from home. Adobe, for instance, left its $44m facility along a major suburban tech corridor outside of Boston for smaller digs closer to the city and nearer public transport, while providing its employees with a work-from-home option.

10   "Companies stand to have a competitive advantage in thinking about getting workers to their location in a way that does not require driving," Stevens said. "Cars are not the first choice for millennials. [Companies] need to think about how to support a workforce that doesn't want to drive. It's good for the environment, but frankly [it's also] good for business."

11   Marriott International announced earlier this year that it plans to move its headquarters from Bethesda, Maryland, over the next few years to a location in the region that would better appeal to younger workers. Slightly more than 2,000 people work at the corporate headquarters. Marriott chief executive Arne Sorenson told the Washington Post in March that it is "essential we be accessible to metro" and located in a more urban area. Currently, the closest Washington DC metro rail stop is three miles away from Marriott headquarters.

12   Integrating economics, social behavior and environmental sustainability trends, such as the desire for companies to move closer to public transit and city centers, can improve policy development.

13   Gerrit-Jan Knaap, professor and director of the National Center for Smart Growth at the University of Maryland, wonders what will happen long term if more companies follow Marriott's lead. It's a question that has been on his mind since developing a model for the region covering Baltimore to Washington DC to understand how behavior preferences and state policies will impact the future trends in development, transportation, land use and the environment.

14   Knaap said that forecasting sustainable development involves tracking the interplay of large scale phenomena. Factoring in regional development, gas prices, greenhouse gas incentives, preferences for where millennials live, transportation choices and where highways get built are all helpful in deciding where to locate businesses and where future infrastructure development may fall short.

15   "The future, 20 years from now, with respect to travel choices, will be much different than it is today," Knaap said, adding that the choices beyond the automobile — even if we're talking about driverless cars or car sharing services like Zipcar — should be expected and factored into sustainability planning. Modeling regional trends and transportation preferences, he said, presents an opportunity to forecast the effects of policies on the development of infrastructure that can be expected to last for 50 to 100 years, and determine what improvements are needed for a more sustainable future.

16   Until that happens, WeSpire's Stevens said that companies can build momentum by increasing their employees' capabilities to drive less. She added that successful nudges to improve low-carbon transportation have included preferential parking for electric or hybrid vehicles and carpools, as well as company benefits such as subsidies and pre-tax purchasing options for public transportation. She also said it's important to understand regional differences: what works in Boston won't work in Atlanta. But the failures, such as punitive pricing for driving, or asking employees to pay for parking, are universally bad motivators.

17   Getting people to stop driving to work ultimately means overcoming obstacles. Safety nets, like as having Zipcars available to employees for emergencies curb fears of being stranded. But for some, obstacles such as waiting for infrequent shuttles or transit stand in the way of important family and personal time. "Those 30 minutes can mean the difference of having time to get to an exercise class or read your kid a bedtime story," Stevens said.

New Words and Expressions

accrue	v.	[əˈkruː]	产生；自然增长或利益增加
alternative	adj.	[ɔːlˈtɜːnətɪv; ɒl-]	供选择的；选择性的
barrier	n.	[ˈbærɪə]	障碍物，屏障；界线
biodieselfuel	adj.	[ˈbaɪəʊdiːzl]	生物柴油燃料的
carpool	v.	[ˈkɑːpuːl]	合伙使用汽车
commute	n.	[kəˈmjuːt]	通勤
converge	v.	[kənˈvɜːdʒ]	汇聚，聚集
corridor	n.	[ˈkɒrɪdɔː]	走廊
coveted	adj.	[ˈkʌvitid]	令人向往的
curb	v.	[kɜːb]	控制，抑制
dig	n.	[dɪg]	住所，寓所
gentrification	n.	[ˌdʒentrɪfɪˈkeɪʃən]	中产阶级化
infrastructure	n.	[ˈɪnfrəstrʌktʃə]	基础设施；公共建设
initiative	n.	[ɪˈnɪʃɪətɪv; -ʃə-]	举措
integrate	v.	[ˈɪntɪgreɪt]	整合
interactive	adj.	[ɪntərˈæktɪv]	交互式的；相互作用的
mechanic	n.	[mɪˈkænɪk]	结构
millennials	n.	[mɪˈlenɪəls]	千禧一代
momentum	n.	[məˈmentəm]	势头

motivate	v.	[ˈməʊtɪveɪt]	刺激；激发……的积极性
nudge	n.	[nʌdʒ]	说服；推动
obstacle	n.	[ˈɒbstək(ə)l]	障碍，干扰
perceive	v.	[pəˈsiːv]	感觉，感知，认知
perk	n.	[pɜːk]	特殊待遇
prominent	adj.	[ˈprɒmɪnənt]	突出的，杰出的，卓越的
protest	n.	[ˈprəʊtest]	抗议
punitive	adj.	[ˈpjuːnɪtɪv]	惩罚性的
roughly	adv.	[ˈrʌfli]	粗略地
shuttle	n.	[ˈʃʌt(ə)l]	穿梭巴士，公共汽车
skyrocket	v.	[ˈskaɪrɒkɪt]	飞涨，突然高升
sought-after	adj.	[ˈsɔːt ˌæftə]	受欢迎的，很吃香的
strand	v.	[strænd]	使陷于困境
subsidy	n.	[ˈsʌbsɪdi]	补贴，津贴，补助金
suburban	adj.	[səˈbɜːb(ə)n]	郊区的，城郊的
telecommuting	n.	[ˈtelɪkəˌmjuːtɪŋ]	远程办公；远程交换

appeal to	对……有吸引力
be left to	由……来决定
for better or for worse	不管怎样
have access to	可以利用/接触到……
help with	有助于……
in the form of	以……的形式
meet with	遭受……
succeed in doing	成功地做了……
with respect to	关于/至于……

I. **Give brief answers to the following questions.**

1. What benefits would be if company's employees stopped driving to work mostly?
2. What's the function of the platform offered by WeSpire for companies?
3. What are the three elements for a behavior to change in participating in commute program?
4. What is the key to getting employees to drive less?
5. What factors are helpful in deciding where to locate businesses and where future infrastructure development may fall short?
6. What should be included for successful nudges to improve low-carbon transportation?

II. **Complete the following passage by filling each of the numbered blanks with one suitable word using the Chinese in the brackets as the reference.**

  Until that happens, WeSpire's Stevens said that companies can ___1___ （建立） momentum by increasing their employees' ___2___ （能力） to drive less. She added that successful nudges to improve ___3___ （低碳） transportation have included ___4___ （优先的） parking for electric or hybrid vehicles and carpools, as well as company benefits such as subsidies and pre-tax purchasing options for public ___5___ （交通）. She also said it's important to understand ___6___ （地区的）differences: what works in Boston won't work in Atlanta. But the failures, such as punitive pricing for driving, or asking employees to pay for parking, are universally bad ___7___ （激励因素）.

　　Getting people to stop driving to work ___8___ （根本上）means overcoming ___9___ （障碍）. Safety nets, like as having Zipcars available to employees for emergencies ___10___ （控制）fears of being stranded. But for some, obstacles such as waiting for infrequent shuttles or transit stand in the way of important family and personal time. "Those 30 minutes can mean the difference of having time to get to an exercise class or read your kid a bedtime story," Stevens said.

III. Complete the following sentences with one function word.

1. Google — which this week rebranded itself as Alphabet — may not have been the first company to offer shuttles to its employees, but the size and growth of its shuttle program have made it the most prominent, for better _____ for worse.

2. While the buses have been met _____ protests since 2013 for fuelling gentrification in the form of skyrocketing housing costs, the buses have succeeded _____ keeping cars off the road.

3. Stevens modeled the WeSpire platform after the work of behavior change research scientist BJ Fogg of Stanford University. According to Fogg's behavior model, three elements — motivation, ability and a trigger — must converge _____ a behavior to change.

4. Employees, then, are left _____ work on developing their ability to overcome barriers — sometimes perceived, sometimes all too real — to an alternative commute.

5. She added that successful nudges _____ improve low-carbon transportation have included preferential parking for electric or hybrid vehicles and carpools, as well as company benefits such as subsidies and pre-tax purchasing options for public transportation.

6. "The future, 20 years from now, _____ respect to travel choices, will be much different than it is today," Knaap said.

IV. Complete the following sentences by translating the Chinese given in the brackets.

1. _____
（农场之旅和其他与农业相关的体验常常能够更好地吸引城市居民）, because, as Dawn Hegland notes, "A lot of people aren't connected to where their food comes from.

2. _____
（不管怎样，麦当劳不再是一个化学实验室）of secretcompounds designed to embalm us from the inside than any other processed foodmaker. (for better or for worse, no more)

3. As a result, _____
（这些组织要自己制定规则）, and this inevitably draws criticism from the global health community. (be left to, set)

4. In China, _____
   （五亿人不能接触到新鲜干净的水）, and this is why the majority of people have to drink bottled water or buy water purifiers. (have access to)

5. _____
   （这个中心将有助于危机管理）in situations such as outbreaks, drought, floods, and natural disasters. (help with)

6. Environmentalist is the one concerned about environmental quality especially of the human environment _____
   （关于对污染的控制）. (with respect to)

V. Translate the following sentences into English.

1. 本周更名为Alphabet的谷歌公司也许并不是最早为员工提供班车接送服务的公司，但是无论怎样，其班车项目的规模和增长却使得它成为业界最突出的企业。

2. 自从他为整个巴尔的摩到华盛顿地区开发了一个能够更好地理解人们的行为偏好和州政策如何影响未来发展、交通、土地利用和环境的模型，这个问题就一直萦绕在他心中。

3. 地区发展、原油价格、诱发温室效应气体的产生等因素对于企业的办公选址和未来哪些基础设施会出现不足都起到了决定作用。

4. 克纳普(Knaap)说：“未来二十年，交通选择将会与今天大不相同”，未来将会有更多令人期待的不同于现有机动车的选择，甚至包括我们现在所讨论的无人驾驶机动车或者类似美国Zipcar公司的汽车共享服务，未来的可持续发展规划都应该将这些考虑在内。

VI. Translate the following passage into Chinese.

In Boston and elsewhere, companies are increasingly relocating to be closer to transit or to where their employees live, even encouraging them to work from home. Adobe, for instance, left its $44m facility along a major suburban tech corridor outside of Boston for smaller digs closer to the city and nearer public transport, while providing its employees with a work-from-home option.

"Companies stand to have a competitive advantage in thinking about getting workers to their location in a way that does not require driving," Stevens said. "Cars are not the first choice for millennials. [Companies] need to think about how to support a workforce that doesn't want to drive. It's good for the environment, but frankly [it's also] good for business."

Marriott International announced earlier this year that it plans to move its headquarters from Bethesda, Maryland, over the next few years to a location in the region that would better appeal to younger workers. Slightly more than 2,000 people work at the corporate headquarters. Marriott chief executive Arne *Sorenson* told the *Washington Post* in March that it is "essential we be accessible to metro" and located in a more urban area. Currently, the closest Washington DC metro rail stop is three miles away from Marriott headquarters.

Unit Ten

Reading B

Why Is Fracking Bad?
Adam Vaughan

1　　You don't have to look hard for stories of people who think fracking(水力压裂)is bad. There are the two children in Pennsylvania who were given a lifelong gagging order(缄口令)over talking about fracking after a settlement with an oil and gas company. A woman in north Texas experienced nosebleeds, nausea(恶心)and headaches after drilling started near her home. And in Barnhart, Texas, people blame fracking for the town running out of water.

2　　Even advocates for the industry admit to examples of people having views near their homes obscured(遮蔽,掩盖)by fracking rigs popping up, or of their homes being devalued by fracking.

3　　Some countries, such as France and Germany, think it's bad enough to warrant banning, though the latter is considering lifting its moratorium(暂停,中止). New York State banned it, citing risks to public health.

4　　Yet there is nothing inherently bad about fracking, or hydraulic fracturing(水压致裂). The technique is a way of extracting natural gas, which is mostly methane(沼气), from shale rock(页岩)formations that are often deep underground. It involves pumping water, chemicals and usually sand underground at high pressure to fracture shale — hence the name — and release the gas trapped within to be collected back at the surface.

5　　The technology has transformed the US energy landscape in the last decade, owing to the combination of high-volume fracking — 1.5m gallons of water per well, on average — and the relatively modern ability to drill horizontally into shale after a vertical well(直井)has been drilled.

6　　In the US, up to 30,000 new wells were drilled and fracked between 2011 and 2014. In the UK, not a single well has been drilled and fracked completely — the only attempt to date, near Blackpool in 2010, was halted(停止)halfway after being linked to minor earthquakes.

7　　Weighing up whether fracking is bad depends on how you define "bad".

8　　Fracking has given America gas prices that are far cheaper than in Europe, created hundreds of thousands if not millions of jobs, and has almost doubled crude(原油)production over the last seven years. Some claim it can even take the credit for America's falling greenhouse(温室)gas emissions(排放), though recent research suggests that may have had more to do with the recession(衰退)than a switch from polluting coal to cleaner gas.

9　　What most critics point to, of course, are the potential health and environmental impacts. Concerns include contamination(污染物)of water supplies, seismic(地震的)activity caused by the fracking itself but mostly by the injection of wastewater deep underground, and fears that the gas glut from fracking threatens to hinder the development of emissions-free renewable sources of power, such as wind and solar. Then there are fears over the venting(排放)and flaring(燃烧)of methane, industrialisation of rural areas and noise from lorries.

10 There is also a huge debate — too big to cover in detail here — over whether fracking is bad news for the climate, since it unlocks a whole new source of fossil fuels(化石燃料)and some academics say it has emissions even worse than coal once methane leaks (a powerful greenhouse gas) have been factored in. Others argue it is good news, as gas produces around half the carbon emissions of coal, which it is displacing in some parts of the world.

11 In many cases in the US, where fracking got up and running before regulation caught up, the local environmental impacts are not just theoretical but well-documented.

12 The US Environmental Protection Agency (EPA) which, in a recent report on fracking's impact on water, cleared the industry of "widespread" and "systematic" pollution of drinking water, still lists some egregious(惊人的,过分的)examples. There can be problems with the well casings — an issue that is not specific to fracking, and which can affect conventional drilling — such as one incident in Bainbridge, Ohio, where inadequate casing saw natural gas move into drinking water aquifers(蓄水层).

13 Sometimes the water that returns to the surface after a frack gets spilled, such as when 2.9m gallons spilled from a broken pipeline in North Dakota and "impacted surface and groundwater", in the largest volume spill recorded by the EPA. Since the state's shale boom took off around 2006, 18m gallons of oil and toxic(有毒的)wastewater have been spilled between January 2006 to October 2014, a New York Times investigation found.

14 By comparison, even the exploratory phase of fracking for shale in the UK has yet to get off the ground, or under it. But august British organisations say it can be done safely — provided it's done properly.

15 "I think the shale gas thing has suffered from a lack of high quality public engagement [in the UK]. That is down to industry, government, public bodies, so it [the debate over risks] is unfortunately dominated by social media and press releases and stuff like that, which can skew(歪曲,曲解)the issues," says a spokesman for the Royal Academy of Engineering, which produced an influential report saying fracking should go ahead in the UK provided it's well-regulated.

16 "If carried out to industry best standard, with close regulation, then the risks can be managed to an acceptable level," he said.

17 Similarly, the UK's health watchdog cleared fracking of health risks in a report, saying it was safe if properly regulated.

18 It's not all been plain sailing in the UK though. An environment department report, which the government fought to keep secret, suggested house prices near shale wells could fall and insurance costs might rise. The shale industry's impact on British democracy has also come to the fore, with a leaked letter showing the chancellor, George Osborne, intervening(介入)personally to fast-track the industry's development.

19 And the UK's ability to regulate the industry properly has been questioned too, with Cuadrilla failing to report a deformed well in Lancashire to government officials for six months. The company has also breached(违背,违反)previous planning permissions, drilling beyond a cut-off date designed to protect wintering birds.

20　　Mike Bradshaw, professor of global energy at Warwick Business School and researcher at the UK Energy Research Centre, says what is needed above all in the UK is a more informed debate. He blames both the industry and the media for the current level of public mistrust over fracking.

21　　"This is an industrial activity just like any industrial activity, and like all sources of energy it has environmental impacts. Whether those environmental impacts are greater than other industrial activity is a case for planners and industry," he says.

22　　But ironically (讽刺地) the only way Britons will find out if fracking is bad or not for them, he says, will be for more drilling to take place. Until then, we won't know whether people will accept it, or whether the gas and oil trapped within British shale is even commercially viable (可行的) to extract.

23　　"I'm not saying that there are not risks. There are risks. They are well understood and clearly identified. What we don't know is the scale of the risks until we carry out drilling in the UK."

24　　Ultimately, it may just be too early to say if fracking is bad — and what's bad for one country might not be for another.

I.　**Match the summaries on the left column to the seven parts of the article with the number of paragraphs on the right column.**

　　A. The current situation of fracking in the UK and the reasons for why it is like this.　　1. (Paragraphs 1—3)

　　B. The development of fracking in the US.　　2. (Paragraphs 4)

　　C. The concrete documentation of the environment impact of fracking in the US.　　3. (Paragraphs 5—6)

　　D. The debate of fracking's advantages and disadvantages.　　4. (Paragraphs 7—10)

　　E. Mike Bradshaw's opinions on fracking that it's too early to say fracking is bad.　　5. (Paragraphs 11—13)

　　F. The negative opinions of the public on fracking.　　6. (Paragraphs 14—19)

　　G. Brief introduction to fracking technique.　　7. (Paragraphs 20—24)

II.　**Answer the following questions.**
　　1. What is fracking technique according to the text?
　　2. What benefits does fracking give to US?
　　3. What do most critics point to on fracking?

III.　**Questions for discussion.**
　　1. What is fracking and why is it controversial?
　　2. Do you agree that fracking is bad? Why or why not?

Part Two
Tips for Translation

科技文本的翻译

Warm-up

Read the following paragraphs, compare and comment on the writing styles.

1. This morning when I first caught sight of the unfamiliar whitened world, I could not help wishing that we had snow oftener, that English winters were more wintry. How delightful it would be, I thought, to have months of clean snow and a landscape sparkling with frost instead of innumerable gray featureless days of rain and raw winds.

2. The efforts that have been made to explain optical phenomena by means of the hypothesis of a medium having the same physical character as an elastic solid body led, in the first instance, to the understanding of a concrete example of a medium which can transmit transverse vibrations, and at a later stage to the definite conclusion that there is no luminiferous medium having the physical character assumed in the hypothesis.

科技文体是随着科学技术的发展而形成的独立的文体形式,包括描述、探讨自然科学各专业的著作、论文、实验报告,科技实用手段(包括仪器、仪表、机械、工具等)的结构描述和操作说明等,涉及自然科学各个专业的题材。由于科技文本种类繁杂,信息量丰富,科技翻译以准确传递信息,再现原文信息功能为最终目标。

汉语和英语的科技文本用词都非常严谨,行文规范,注重客观性,而且描述一般不带个人感情色彩,有准确、正式、逻辑严密等特点。汉译英时,我们应当留心科技英语的特点,根据英语的习惯译出忠实而又地道的英文。

一、科技英语的特点

科技英语(English for Science and Technology,简称EST)是从事科学技术活动时所使用的英语,是英语的一种变体(科技文体)。由于其内容、使用域和语篇功能的特殊性,也由于科技工作者长期以来的语言使用习惯,科技英语形成了自身的一些特点,在许多方面有别于日常英语、文学英语等语体。这些特点主要表现在词汇和句法两个层面上:

(一)词汇层面

1. 专业术语多。专业术语指某一学科领域所特有或专用的语汇,其词义常不为专业外读者所明白。这些专业术语的特点是:(1)词形较长,大多含有源于拉丁语、希腊语和法语的词根、词缀。这类词语的语义范围较为狭窄,意义较为明确固定,符合科技英语准确明晰的要求。如semisomnus(半昏迷),autoradiography(自动射线照相术)等。(2)多复合词。人们常常通过各种构词方法创造出一些复合词来表示科技发展中出现的新事物,如radiophotography (无线电传真),anti-armored fighting vehicle missile(反装甲车导弹)等。(3)多缩略词。为使用便利和节省时间,科技英语同经贸英语一样,也有许多缩略词,如FM (frequency

modulation 调频), telesat (telecommunications satellite 通讯卫星)等。

2. 准专业术语和词汇多。准专业词汇指的是那些在不同学科中都存在但意义所指不同的词汇，其中有相当数量的词汇属于普通常用词汇。如 frame 一词在日常英语中指"框架"，而在机械原理中指"机架"，在电讯技术中又作"帧"或"镜头"解。

(二) 句法层面

1. 多名词化结构。为使行文简洁，科技英语中多用表示动作或状态的抽象名词或起名词作用的 V-ing 形式以及名词短语结构。如 the transmission and reception of images of moving objects by radio waves（通过无线电波来发射和接收活动物体的图像）；the generation of heat by friction（摩擦生热）等。

2. 介词词组连用多。为了较为简练地反映各事物（即句子成分）之间的时空、所属、因果等逻辑关系，科技英语中介词词组（短语）连用较多。例如：The action of air on an airplane in flight at low altitude is greater than that at high altitude.（空气对于低空飞行飞机的作用力大于高空飞行的飞机。）

3. 多长句和逻辑关联词(logic connectors)。科技英语中虽然大量使用名词化词语、名词短语结构以及悬垂结构来压缩句子长度，但是为了将事理充分说明，也常常使用一些含有许多短语和分句的长句，同时还常使用许多逻辑关联词，如 hence, accordingly, however, also, on the contrary, as a result, furthermore, finally, in short 等，以使行文逻辑关系清楚、层次条理分明。

4. 多用一般现在时和完成时。这两种时态之所以在科技英语中常见，是因为前者可以较好地表现文章内容的无时间性，说明文章中的科学定义、定理、公式不受时间限制，任何时候都成立；后者则多用来表述已经发现或获得的研究成果。

5. 多被动语态。英语中的被动语态要比汉语中的多，在各种文体中都是这样，在科技英语中尤为突出。国外有学者统计，在物理、化学、工程类教科书里，英语中的谓语至少三分之一是被动态。这是因为科技文章侧重叙事推理，强调客观准确。第一、二人称使用过多，会造成主观臆断的印象，因此尽量使用第三人称叙述，采用被动语态。

总之，科技英语以客观事物为中心，在用词上讲究准确明晰，论述上讲究逻辑严密，表述上则力求客观，行文上追求简洁通畅，修辞以平实为范，辞格用得很少，句式显得单一少变，语篇中有许多科技词汇和术语以及公式、图表、数字、符号，句子长而不乱。

二、汉语科技文本的翻译原则

要做好汉语科技文本的翻译工作，译者应时刻牢记科技英语的特点，使译文符合科技英语文体的特征和表达习惯。

(一) 注意术语翻译的准确性

科技英语专业术语性强，专业术语语义具有严谨性和单一性，要求译者除了有较高的汉英语言水平外，还需掌握一定的专业知识。平时应当阅读与所译材料同类的英文材料，留心其中的专业术语和表达方法。例如：

国内外研究认为，饮茶对治疗慢性肾炎、肝炎和原子辐射都有一定效果。

Tea as a beverage is considered by researchers all over the world to ameliorate chronic nephritis, hepatitis and atomic radiation.

（二）注意汉语动态语言向英语静态语言的转换

科技英语大量使用抽象名词和介词，尤其是名词化结构，使语言呈明显的静态倾向。汉语动词则没有形态变化的约束，使用起来十分简便，因而在汉语文本中出现频繁，使得科技汉语在一定程度上呈动态倾向。汉译英时，译者应注意将汉语的动态语言转换成英语的静态语言。

（1）阿基米德最先发现固体排水的原理。

Archimedes first discovered the principle of displacement of water by solid bodies.

（2）应用科学直接研究如何将理论科学中可行的定律用于生活实践，用于加强人类对周围世界的控制，从而导致新技术、新工艺和新机器的产生。

Applied science, on the other hand, is directly concerned with the application of the working laws of pure science to the practical affairs of life, and to increasing man's control over his environment, thus leading to the development of new techniques, processes and machines.

（三）注意时态多采用一般现在时

科技英语主要叙述普遍真理，描述工作原理、实验效果与结论、物质特性和功能，因此，内容具有相对稳定性和持久性。除了描述科学史实时需使用过去时，科技英语通常大量使用一般现在时。汉译英时，要特别注意这种时态的运用。例如：

根据近代科学分析研究，饮茶确有清热降火、消食生津、利尿除病、提神醒脑、消除疲劳、恢复体力等功效。

Modern scientific research shows that tea helps dissipate internal heat and ameliorate digestion, micturition and secretion of saliva. It refreshes one, helps him regain physical energy and relieve him of fatigue.

译文采用一般现在时态，突出所述内容的科学性。

（四）注意原句中的主动语态常常要转换成英语的被动语态和非人称句

科技英语较少使用人称句，大量使用被动语态，以突出科技文本侧重叙事和推理的特点；而汉语习惯使用主动语态，被动句出现频率较低，汉译英时译者需要在语态方面进行必要的转换。例如：

炒钢的原料是生铁。把生铁加热到液态或半液态，靠鼓风或撒入精矿粉，使硅、锰、碳氧化，让碳量降低到钢的成分范围。

The raw material of puddling steel is cast iron, which is first heated to a liquid or semi-liquid state. The silicon, manganese and carbon ore are then oxidized by wind blowers or the addition of fine ore powder so that the carbon content is lowered to within the limits of steel composition.

原文采用大量的无主句，介绍钢铁冶炼的过程，这种主动语态的使用比较符合汉语习惯。译文则将这些无主句译成被动句，既避免添加任何人称主语，又使读者的注意力集中在冶炼过程上，体现了内容的客观性和规范性。

（五）注意灵活使用定语从句、分词短语等，并增添必要的衔接手段以保证译文的逻辑性和语义的连贯

科技英语重视叙事的逻辑性、层次感和论证手段，因此多长句、复合句，而且语句平衡匀

密,句长而不累赘、迂回,句子间连接紧密。相比之下,汉语科技文本尽管也要求叙述准确,推理严谨,逻辑性突出,但由于汉语句式多流散形,出现大量零散句,容易造成形散神聚的效果。所以汉译英时,应注意采取必要的措施保证语句的逻辑层次和连贯性。例如:

通常炼铁的地方也炼钢。因此,现代炼钢厂是一个配套的整体,从运进原料到生产各种类型的铸铁与钢材;有的送往其他工厂进一步加工处理,有的就制成成品,如工字钢及其他一些成材。

Steel is usually made where the iron ore is smelted, so that the modern steelworks forms a complete unity, taking in raw materials and producing all types of cast iron and steel, both for sending to other works for further treatment, and as finished products such as joists and other consumers.

练习

1. 根据科技英语的特征用所给单词的正确形式填空。
   (1) 地球绕轴自转,引起昼夜的变化。(rotate)
   The _____ of the earth on its own axis causes the change from day to night.
   (2) 阿基米德最先发现固体排水的原理。(displace)
   Archimedes first discovered the principle of _____ of water by solid bodies.
   (3) 自从机床采用数控以来,生产率大大地提高了。(adopt; raise)
   Since numerical control _____ at machine tools, the productivity _____ greatly.
   (4) 从较长时间的临床应用看来,我们认为人体皮肤是做视网膜脱离手术的比较理想的填充材料。(judge)
   _____ from the results of long-term clinical application, human skin is a satisfactory implant material for retinal detachment surgery.

2. 根据科技英语特征修改下列英译文。
   (1) 现决定将垂直测斜仪V15的钻孔作为初次试验,以测试该施工方法的可行性。
   We decided that we should use the drilling for vertical inclinometer V15 as a trial to test the feasibility of the construction method.
   (2) 控制系统采用最佳化切头切尾,减少切损,提高成品收得率约0.4%。
   The control system adopts the optimized head and tail cutting. It reduces the cutting loss. It also increases the finished product recovery rate by 0.4%.
   (3) 第二期世界银行贷款总额为130万美元,用于购置设备的经费111.5万美元,图书采购、培训、技术服务等各项为18.5万美元。
   The total amount of the loan from the World Bank for the second time is 1,300,000 dollars. The use of it is as follows: 1,115,000 dollars is used to purchase equipment. The expense in buying books, training staff members and technical service is 185,000 dollars altogether.

Part Three
Simulated Writing

Citations

　　任何一个科学问题的提出或者一项科研成果的取得都是在前人研究的基础上发展起来的。众所周知,撰写论文是进行科学研究的初步尝试,一篇文章或一本著作在撰写过程中,一般都需要参考其他有关文献,因此在写作过程中,往往要引用他人著作、论文中的观点、材料和方法等作为自己论文的根据。引文就是借鉴前人研究成果的一种方法,它是任何一项学术写作中不可缺少的一部分。

　　引文的作用对于一篇文章来说有很多,它可以充实文章的内容,可以用具有权威性的思想观点来代替自己想要表达的观点。同时,广泛、深入、详细的阅读意味着作者阅读了大量不同类型的研究,这能够让读者们知道该研究是科学地建立在前人研究基础之上的,作者很好地利用了这些文献资料,并对其进行消化、吸收和总结,这无疑增加了一项研究的严谨性和可靠性。另外,引文还可以避免剽窃,它代表了作者是否正确对待了原文作者的知识产权。

　　引文样式(citation style)是多种多样的,而目前在国际上主要分为MLA和APA两种。APA格式来源于美国心理学会(American Psychological Association)出版的《美国心理学会出版物手册》,后逐渐成为一种广为接受的研究论文撰写格式。MLA格式来源于美国现代语言学会(Modern Language Association)出版的《MLA格式指南》。APA格式偏重人文学科,而MLA格式则偏重自然科学学科,这两种格式规范都规定了文中引文和参考文献的不同标注样式。

　　作者在进行研究写作时,不仅要在自己的文章中标注引文,同时也要在文章的最后附加这些引文的具体信息,即参考文献。因此,引文在一篇文章中可以体现为两个方面,一是文中引文(in-text citation),二是参考文献引文(reference citation)。

　　(一) 文中引文
　　文中引文通常可以分为两大类,一类是直接引用(direct citation),另一类是间接引用(indirect citation)。

　　直接引用,即抄录原文,不删除和增加任何内容,无论从文字上还是标点符号上,所引用内容必须与原文保持完全一致,并且要在引用的文字前后加引号,插在作者写作的内容中,以表示原文引用。

　　间接引用,即论文的写作者运用自己的语言将原文所表达的意思概括表述出来。比如,作者可以改述原文,这种方法适用于引用时想要保持和原文一样长度的情况;作者也可以总结原文,这种方式适用于原文篇幅较长,而作者想要简练地表达;原意引用也可以是综合概括,这种方式则适用于想要引用的内容较复杂地分散在不同的原作中,而作者想要将它们综合在一起进行概括。

　　具体来看,文中引文主要有以下几种形式:
　　1. 融入式引用(Integral Citation),即作者名字出现在原文的句子中,是原文句法成分的一部分。例如：

APA

According to the U.S. Census Bureau (2001), "There are an estimated 32.8 million people of Hispanic origin living in the United States (P.23)".

MLA

Wordsworth stated that Romantic poetry was marked by a "spontaneous overflow of powerful feelings" (263).

2. 非融入式引用(Non-Integral Citation)，即作者的名字没有出现在原文的句子中，但是要标注在括号的引文注释中。例如：

APA

The origins of the concept of literacy are typically tied to the rise of organized education (Sandhu, 2005, p. 218).

MLA

Romantic poetry is characterized by the "spontaneous overflow of powerful feelings" (Wordsworth 263).

3. 综合引用(Synthesizing Citation)，即需要概括、总结并引用来自多个来源文献的观点。例如：

APA

There is a growing body of research investigating ways to enhance readiness to change eating disorder behaviors (Cockell, Geller,& Linden,2002, 2003; Williams & Srikameswaran,2001; Treasure & Schmidt, 1998).

MLA

... as has been discussed elsewhere (Burke 3; Dewey 21).

（二）参考文献引文

任何一篇研究论文或者一部研究著作的最后都应附上参考文献以表明文中引文的出处，即列出作者在论文撰写过程中参考、借鉴过的重要文献资料的主要信息。与文中引文相同，不同的引文样式下，参考文献的撰写也不尽相同，这里主要介绍在APA和MLA两种样式下，主要出版物形式的参考文献写作格式，如著书、编著、期刊论文、著作篇章、网络资源等。

1. APA样式下的参考文献格式[①]

（1）作者的写作格式

任何一种出版物形式的第一作者都按照"姓氏，名字首字母"的顺序来写作。

Berndt, T. J. (2002). Friendship quality and social development. *Current Directions in Psychological Science, 11*, 7—10.（单作者）

Wegener, D. T., & Petty, R. E. (1994). Mood management across affective states: The hedonic contingency hypothesis. *Journal of Personality and Social Psychology, 66*, 1034—1048. （双作者）

Kernis, M. H., Cornell, D. P., Sun, C. R., Berry, A., Harlow, T., & Bach, J. S. (1993). There's more to self-esteem than whether it is high or low: The importance of stability of self-es-

---

① 该部分的格式与举例均来源于由美国普渡大学网上写作实验室所提供的开源素材(https://www.library.cornell.edu/research/citation/mla)和由美国康奈尔大学图书馆提供的开源素材 (https://www.library.cornell.edu/research/citation/mla)

teem. *Journal of Personality and Social Psychology, 65*, 1190—1204.（三至七个作者）

Miller, F. H., Choi, M. J., Angeli, L. L., Harland, A. A., Stamos, J. A., Thomas, S. T., . . . Rubin, L. H. (2009). Web site usability for the blind and low-vision user. *Technical Communication, 57*, 323—335.（七个以上作者）

（2）著书基本格式

基本格式：Author, A. A. (Year of publication). *Title of work: Capital letter also for subtitle.* Location: Publisher.

Kidder, T. (1981). *The soul of a new machine.* Boston, MA: Little, Brown & Company.

Frank, R. H., & Bernanke, B. (2007). *Principles of macro-economics* (3rd ed.). Boston, MA: McGraw-Hill/Irwin.

（3）编著基本格式

基本格式：Author, A. A. (Eds.). (Year of publication). *Title of work: Capital letter also for subtitle.* Location: Publisher.

Duncan, G. J., & Brooks-Gunn, J. (Eds.). (1997). *Consequences of Growing Up Poor.* New York, NY: Russell Sage Foundation.（编著：选集或论文集）

（4）编著中析出的篇章基本格式

基本格式：Author, A. A., & Author, B. B. (Year of publication). Title of chapter. In A. A. Editor & B. B. Editor (Eds.), *Title of book* (pages of chapter). Location: Publisher.

O'Neil, J. M., & Egan, J. (1992). Men's and women's gender role journeys: A metaphor for healing, transition, and transformation. In B. R. Wainrib (Ed.), *Gender issues across the life cycle* (pp. 107—123). New York, NY: Springer.

（5）学术期刊论文

基本格式：Author, A. A., Author, B. B., & Author, C. C. (Year). Title of article.*Title of Periodical, volume number*(issue number), pages.

Scruton, R. (1996). The eclipse of listening. *The New Criterion, 15*(3), 5—13.

Harlow, H. F. (1983). Fundamentals for preparing psychology journal articles. *Journal of Comparative and Physiological Psychology, 55*, 893—896.

（6）网络资源

基本格式：Author, I. (year). *Title of document.* Retrieved from url

Health Canada. (2009). *AIDS awareness among IDUs on Vancouver's Downtown East Side.*（网站）

Mansour, N. (2009). Science-technology-society (STS): A new paradigm in science education. *Bulletin of Science, Technology and Society, 29*, 287—301. doi: 10.1177/0270467609336307（仅供在线阅览的期刊论文）

对于电子期刊论文来说，若有DOI号码，则应该在最后写上DOI号码；如果没有则要写上论文检索的网页地址。

2. MLA样式下的参考文献格式[①]

（1）作者的写作格式。

任何一种出版物形式下的第一作者都按照"姓氏，名字"的顺序来写作。

Nabokov, Vladimir. *Lolita.* New York: Putnam, 1955. Print.（单作者）

[①] 该部分的格式与举例均来源于由美国普渡大学网上写作实验室所提供的开源素材(https://owl.english.purdue.edu/owl/resource/747/1/)和由美国康奈尔大学图书馆提供的开源素材 (https://www.library.cornell.edu/research/citation/apa)

Cross, Susan, and Christine Hoffman. *Bruce Nauman: Theaters of Experience*. New York: Guggenheim Museum; London: Thames & Hudson, 2004. Print.(双作者)

Lowi, Theodore, Benjamin Ginsberg, and Steve Jackson. *Analyzing American Government: American Government, Freedom and Power*. 3rd ed. New York: Norton, 1994. Print.(三作者)

Gilman, Sander, et al. *Hysteria beyond Freud*. Berkeley: U of California P, 1993. Print.(三个以上作者)

(2) 著书基本格式

基本格式:Lastname, Firstname. *Title of Book*. Place of Publication: Publisher, Year of Publication. Medium of Publication.

Cross, Susan, and Christine Hoffman. *Bruce Nauman: Theaters of Experience*. New York: Guggenheim Museum; London: Thames & Hudson, 2004. Print.(著书)

(3) 编著基本格式

基本格式:Lastname, Firstnames, eds. *Title of Book*. Place of Publication: Publisher, Year of Publication. Medium of Publication.

Hill, Charles A., and Marguerite Helmers, eds. *Defining Visual Rhetorics*. Mahwah, NJ: Lawrence Erlbaum Associates, 2004. Print.

(4) 编著中析出的篇章基本格式

基本格式: Lastname, First name. "Title of Essay." *Title of Collection*. Ed. Editor's Name(s). City of Publication: Publisher, Year. Page range of entry. Medium of Publication.

Ahmedi, Fauzia Erfan. "Welcoming Courtyards: Hospitality, Spirituality, and Gender." *Feminism and Hospitality: Gender in the Host/Guest Relationship*. Ed. Maurice Hamington. Lanham: Lexington Books, 2010. 109—24. Print.

(5) 学术期刊论文

基本格式:Author(s). "Title of Article." *Title of Journal* Volume.Issue (Year): pages. Medium of publication.

Matarrita-Cascante, David. "Beyond Growth: Reaching Tourism-Led Development." *Annals of Tourism Research* 37.4 (2010): 1141—63. Print.

Laing, Jennifer, and Warwick Frost. "How Green Was My Festival: Exploring Challenges and Opportunities Associated With Staging Green Events." *International Journal of Hospitality Management* 29.2 (2010): 261—7. Print.

(6) 网络资源

基本格式:Editor, author, or compiler name (if available). *Name of Site*. Version number. Name of institution/organization affiliated with the site (sponsor or publisher), date of resource creation (if available). Medium of publication. Date of access.

The Purdue OWL Family of Sites. The Writing Lab and OWL at Purdue and Purdue U, 2008. Web. 23 Apr. 2008.(网站)

Dolby, Nadine. "Research in Youth Culture and Policy: Current Conditions and Future Directions." *Social Work and Society: The International Online-Only Journal* 6.2 (2008): n. pag. Web. 20 May 2009.(仅供在线阅览的期刊论文)

Sample Reading

1. Science education now takes into account the role that science and technology play in shaping social processes of knowledge-making (Mansour, 2009, p. 289).
2. According to some, dreams express "profound aspects of personality" (Foulkes 184), though others disagree.
3. Cullen concludes, "Of all the things that happened there / That's all I remember" (11—12).
4. Sandhu (2005) discusses the origins of the concept of literacy (p. 212).
5. Critical literacy can be defined as "a set of practices that allow learners to change their wor(l)ds" (Lal, 2008, p. 27).
6. Citation is central to the social context of persuation as it can both provide justification for arguments and demonstrate the novelty of one's position(Gilber,1976; Berkenkotter & Huckin, 1995).

Please read the citations above and fill in the squares to figure out their citation kinds, type, style and pattern.

Number	Type		Style		Pattern		
	Direct Citation	Indirect Citation	APA	MLA	Integral	Non-Integral	Synthesizing
1							
2							
3							
4							
5							
6							

Follow-up Writing

Please write the reference according to the given information and citation type.

1. Book Author: Paula Gillespie, Neal Lerner
   Year:2000
   Title: The Allyn and Bacon Guide to Peer Tutoring
   Location: Boston
   Publisher: Allyn
   Medium of Publication:*Print*

Type: MLA

2. Book Author: Thomas Kuhn
   Year: 1962
   Title: The structure of scientific revolutions
   Location: Chicago, IL
   Publisher: University of Chicago
   Type: APA

3. Article Author: Miller, P.S.
   Year: 1998
   Title: Genetic discrimination in the work place
   Journal: Journal of Law, Medicine, and Ethics
   Volume: 26
   Issue: 2
   Pages: 189—197
   Type: APA

4. Article Author: Alaknanda Bagchi
   Year: 1996
   Title: Conflicting Nationalisms: The Voice of the Subaltern in Mahasweta Devi's *Bashai Tudu*
   Journal: *Tulsa Studies in Women's Literature*
   Volume: 15
   Issue: 1
   Pages: 41—50
   Medium of Publication: *Print*
   Type: MLA

Part Four
Listening

Lead-in

I. Discuss the following topics with your classmates.

1. What environmental problems are there in your city?
2. In your opinion, how can we grow fresh air?

II. **Study the following vocabulary before you listen.**

allergic	对……过敏的
IIT	美国伊利诺伊理工学院(Illinois Institute of Technology)
TERI	印度Tata能源研究院(Tata Energy Research Institute)
NASA	美国国家航空和宇宙航行局(National Aeronautics and Space Administration)
Areca palm	散尾葵
Mother-in-Law's Tongue	虎尾兰
money plant	黄金葛
botanical	植物学的
convert	使转变
vermi manure	施肥
sterile	无菌的
hydroponics	水栽培,水耕法
formaldehyde	甲醛
volatile	挥发的
occupant	居住者
probability	概率
New Delhi	新德里(印度的首都)
irritation	刺激
incidence	影响
respiratory	呼吸的
asthma	哮喘
replicate	复制
Mahatma Gandhi	圣雄甘地

While-listening

I. **Listen to the recording and supply the missing words.**

How to Grow Fresh Air

Some 17 years ago, I became __1__ to Delhi's air. My doctors told me that my __2__ capacity had __3__ down to 70 percent, and it was killing me. With the help of IIT, TERI, and learnings from NASA, we __4__ that there are three basic green plants, __5__ green plants, with which we can grow all the fresh air we need __6__ to keep us healthy. We've also found that you can __7__ the fresh air requirements into the building, while __8__ industry indoor air-quality standards.

The three plants are Areca palm, Mother-in-Law's Tongue and money plant. The botanical names are in front of you. Areca palm is a plant which removes CO_2 and removes it into __9__. We need four shoulder-high plants per person, and in __10__ of plant care, we need to wipe the leaves every day in Delhi, and __11__ once a week in cleaner-air cities. We had to __12__ them in vermi manure, which is __13__, or hydroponics, and take them outdoors every three to four months. The second plant is Mother-in-law's Tongue, which is again a very common plant, and we call it a bedroom plant, because it converts CO_2 into oxygen at night. And we need six to eight waist-high plants per person. The third plant is money plant, and this is again a very common plant; __14__ grows in hydroponics. And this __15__ plant removes formaldehydes and other volatile chemicals.

With these three plants, you can grow all the fresh air you need. In fact, you could be in a bottle with a __16__ on top, and you would not die at all, and you would not need any fresh air. We have tried these plants at our own building in Delhi, which is a 50,000-__17__-feet, 20-year-old building. And it has close to 1,200 such plants for 300 __18__. Our studies have found that there is a 42 percent __19__ of one's blood oxygen going up by one percent if one stays indoors in this building for 10 hours. The __20__ of India has discovered or published a study to show that this is the __21__ building in New Delhi. And the study showed that, __22__ to other buildings, there is a reduced incidence of eye irritation by 52 percent, respiratory systems by 34 percent, headaches by 24 percent, lung impairment by 12 percent and asthma by nine percent. And this study has been published on September 8, 2008, and it's __23__ on the government of India website.

Our experience points to an amazing increase in human __24__ by over 20 percent by using these plants. And also a reduction in energy __25__ in buildings by an __26__ 15 percent, because you need less fresh air. We are now __27__ this in a 1.75-million-square-feet building, which will have 60,000 indoor plants.

Why is this important? It is also important for the environment, because the world's energy requirements are __28__ to grow by 30 percent in the next __29__. 40 percent of the world's energy is taken up by buildings __30__, and 60 percent of the world's population will be living in buildings in cities with a population of over one million in the next 15 years. And there is a growing preference for living and working in air-conditioned places. "Be the change you want to see in the world," said Mahatma Gandhi. And thank you for listening.

II. Listen again, stop the recording as necessary, and repeat after the speaker.

Post-listening

Surf the Internet and find more information about the following topic areas. Then prepare a 15-minute oral presentation and deliver it in the class. While preparing the presentation you need to narrow down topic area and focus one major point.
1. Smog in China.
2. Economic development and environment protection.

Part Five
Speaking

Job Routines

Sample Dialogue

A journalist is interviewing Mr. Smith, a top businessman.

Journalist: When do you get up?

Mr. Smith: I usually get up about five, and go for a jog before breakfast. I have breakfast around 6:30. Then I have time to read the papers.

Journalist: Which papers do you take?

Mr. Smith: Well, the *Financial Times*, *The Times* and *The Independent*. I don't exactly read them from cover to cover!

Journalist: No, of course not.

Mr. Smith: Well, after the papers, I leave for the office. I'm behind my desk by 7:30. The first job of the day is the post. My secretary sorts out those letters which need immediate attention. Then round about 9:00, I have a daily meeting with my deputy. We run through the agenda for the day.

Journalist: What's a typical day like?

Mr. Smith: Well, there is no such thing as a typical say, but I have regular morning meetings with my Finance and Sales Directors. Of course I travel abroad a lot, and then I keep up-to-date by telephone.

Journalist: What about lunch?

Mr. Smith: I try to have lunch in the company canteen as often as possible. But, of course, sometimes I have lunch out with customers or the bank manager!

Journalist: What about the afternoons?

Mr. Smith: If I'm in the country, I often go down to our plant and see how things are going. We have weekly management committee meetings on Friday afternoon. Then of course there are monthly board meetings, usually the first Monday of the month.

Journalist: When do you finish work?

Mr. Smith: Round seven. Then, if there's nothing on in the evening, I'll go home. More often than not, there's a dinner engagement. My wife comes to quite a lot of these, so at least we see each other.

Journalist: When do you get to bed?

Mr. Smith: Rarely before midnight. I always read a book for half an hour before going to sleep.

Journalist: Right, thank you Mr. Smith...

Unit Ten

Sample Monologue

A secretary is introducing her job routine:

I've been working at this company for three years. I start work at nine. It's not bad, but the office is very far from where I live, so it takes me about two hours to commute, When I get to work I have a cup of coffee and open the mail. There's usually quite a lot of that. My boss usually arrives at 9:30 or 10 o'clock, unless he's away, visiting a client. We go over his schedule and he dictates a few letters to me. By the time I've typed them up it's about 11 o'clock. I don't have fixed coffee break, but there's a coffee machine in the office, so I can get one whenever I want. The second half of the morning is usually quite hectic. We get a lot of calls and faxes from clients. I usually have lunch between 12:30 and 1:30, but it depends whether we're busy and whether I can get away. There's a shop across the road which makes sandwiches and delivers them. Sometimes I phone them and order a sandwich, and eat it at my desk. The afternoon is usually more interesting than the morning. My boss usually asks me to make some phone calls or translate some documents for him. Sometimes I sit in on meetings with clients. I usually finish work at 6 o'clock, but I sometimes stay later if my boss asks me to.

go for a jog	慢跑,跑步
from cover to cover	从头看到尾
sort out	整理
daily meeting	每日例会
run through	浏览
regular morning meetings	每天上午例会
keep up-to-date by telephone	通过电话了解公司的最新情况
weekly management committee meetings	管理委员会的周会
monthly board meetings	董事会的月会
there is nothing on	没有安排
more often than not	多数情况下
dinner engagement	晚餐约会
open the mail	打开邮件
visit a client	拜访客户
type up	打字完毕
fixed coffee break	固定的喝咖啡休息时间
sit on meetings	开会讨论

USEFUL EXPRESSIONS AND PATTERNS:

1 I usually get up about five, and go for a jog before breakfast.

② I have breakfast around 6:30. Then I have time to read the papers.
③ After the papers, I leave for the office.
④ I'm behind my desk by 7:30.
⑤ I start work at nine.
⑥ The first job of the day is the post.
⑦ I try to have lunch in the company canteen as often as possible.
⑧ I usually finish work at 6 o'clock.
⑨ I always read a book for half an hour before going to sleep.
⑩ In the morning I usually read the mail, dictate letters to my secretary and make a few phone calls.
⑪ I take a break at about 11 o'clock and have a coffee.
⑫ I break for lunch at 12:30.
⑬ Then I'm back in the office again from 1:30 to 5:30.
⑭ We normally have meetings in the afternoon.
⑮ I live quite far from the office and it takes me a long time to get home, especially when the traffic is bad.

I. Role-play the sample dialogues.

II. Match the following two columns.

1. 从头看到尾　　　　　　　　　　A. keep up-to-date by telephone
2. 董事会的月会　　　　　　　　　B. sit on meetings
3. 固定的茶歇　　　　　　　　　　C. run through
4. 浏览　　　　　　　　　　　　　D. sort out
5. 多数情况下　　　　　　　　　　E. monthly board meetings
6. 整理　　　　　　　　　　　　　F. fixed coffee break
7. 通过电话了解公司的最新情况　　G. from cover to cover
8. 拜访客户　　　　　　　　　　　H. more often than not
9. 开会讨论　　　　　　　　　　　I. visit a client

III. Complete the following dialogues by making sentences with the help of the key words given in brackets.

1. A: When do you get up?
   B: (usually, six, alarm clock, go off).
   A: Do you have breakfast straight away?
   B: (no, first, go for a run).
2. A: What do you do after breakfast?
   B: (read papers, The Guardian or The Independent).
   A: When do you leave for the office?
   B: (usually, eight, behind my desk, 8:30).
3. A: What do you do first?
   B: (sort through, mail, first).

A: Do you usually stay in the office?
B: (no, go out, sometimes, travel abroad).

IV. Learn to communicate in the situation given below.

Student A: a friend of B.
Student B: a new come secretary of a company.
A and B are talking about the secretary's office routines.
The following points can be referred to in your conversation:
type letters
take minutes at board meetings
sort through the mails
distribute mail
translate some documents

Key to the Exercises

Unit One   Cross-Cultural Communication

Part One   Reading and Translating

Reading A

I. Give brief answers to the following questions.
   1. They want to determine where they were looking in a picture and how long they focused on a particular area.
   2. Shown a photograph, North American students of European background paid more attention to the object in the foreground of a scene, while students from China spent more time studying the background and taking in the whole scene.
   3. Nisbett thinks that Chinese and European Americans perceive the world differently because of cultural differences: Chinese live in a socially complicated society where harmony is highly valued, while westerners are individualists who pay less attention to other people.
   4. The Japanese.
   5. Because these tests show that cultural differences extend to low level perceptual processes such as how people control their eyes.
   6. They have found differences in eye movements between Asians and Westerners in reading.

II. Complete the following passage by filling each of the numbered blanks with one or two suitable words using the Chinese in the brackets as the reference.
   1. paying less attention to
   2. goes back to
   3. developed a system of irrigated agriculture
   4. share water
   5. individual farms
   6. perception
   7. the property of gravity
   8. the property of floating
   9. related to
   10. long before

III. Complete the following sentences with one function word.
   1. in   2. on   3. to   4. to   5. on   6. beyond

IV. Complete the following sentences by translating the Chinese given in the brackets.
   1. explore in depth the contribution of complicated enterprise business rules
   2. harmony between man and the environment
   3. Positive employees outperform negative employees

240

Key to the Exercises

4. reinforce and repair these old residential buildings
5. the company needed to focus on mobile
6. things will be more likely to go your way

V. Translate the following sentences into English.

1. Nisbett illustrated this with a test asking Japanese and Americans to look at pictures of underwater scenes and report what they saw. The Japanese gave 60 percent more information on the background and twice as much about the relationship between background and foreground objects as Americans.
2. The Americans looked at the object in the foreground sooner—a leopard in the jungle for example—and they looked at it longer. The Chinese had more eye movements, especially on the background and back and forth between the main object and the background.
3. Asians live in a more socially complicated world than we do. They have to pay more attention to others than we do. We are individualists. We can be bulls in a china shop, they can't afford it.
4. The researchers, led by Richard Nisbett, tracked the eye movements of the students—25 European Americans and 27 native Chinese—to determine where they were looking in a picture and how long they focused on a particular area.

VI. Translate the following passages into Chinese.

1. 亚洲人和北美人观察世界的方式的确是不同的。密歇根大学的研究人员指出,在观看相片时,欧洲裔的美国学生更多注意前景物体,而中国学生则用更长的时间来研究背景,感受整幅画面。
2. 马萨诸塞大学艾摩斯特分校的凯勒卡夫评论说:"这些试验结果的惊人之处在于他们表明文化差异可以延伸到诸如如何控制眼球移动之类的低层次感知过程。这些结果暗示我们的文化背景直接决定了我们如何来观察和探索世界。"

Reading B

I. Match the topics below to the eight paragraphs of the main part in the article.
Monochronic and Polychronic Time Orientations: Paragraph 2, 3, 4, 5
Future Orientation: Paragraph 6
Present Orientation: Paragraph 7, 8
Past Orientation: Paragraph 9

II. Answer the following questions.

1. Past-oriented cultures believe strongly in the significance of prior events.
2. Present-oriented cultures.
3. Future-oriented cultures.

Part Three Simulated Writing

Follow-up Writing
Complete the following resumé with the information given below.
1. Good interpersonal, supervisory and team building skills
2. Hard-working, dedicated professional
3. proactive
4. Excellent English language skill in both writing and speaking
5. Played instrumental role

6. promoted providing excellent service

7. employee of the month

8. Won several customer service and sales awards

Part Four Listening

While-listening

I. Listen to the recording and supply the missing words.

1. sign of farewell	2. duty payments	3. poison
4. an arm's length	5. respect	6. foreign visitors
7. guided tours	8. rare	9. cluster
10. conditioned	11. blindness	12. ignorance
13. 1979	14. 55	15. upper hand

Part Five Speaking

II. Match the following two columns.

1. E   2. H   3. A   4. G   5. F   6. C   7. D   8. B

III. Complete the following dialogues by making sentences with the help of the key words given in brackets.

1. A: Here are the quotations you asked for.

   B: Let's take a look at your prices.

2. A: When can I have your C.I.F. firm offer?

   B: Our offer remains open for 3 days.

3. A: Is this your C.I.F. quotation?

   B: All the quotations are subject to our final confirmation.

IV. Learn to communicate in the situation given below.

A: Welcome to the Shanghai Machinery Company Inc. I'm Li Gang, the Sales Manager.

B: Hi, Mr. Li. My name is John Smith. I'm from Seattle, USA. I'm in charge of the supply department of the Pacific Trading Company Ltd.

A: I'm very pleased to meet you, Mr. Smith. Please sit down and allow me to introduce our company and its products.

B: Thank you. I have read your brochure and am very impressed by your scope of business, especially the variety of machine tools you manufacture. I believe my customers will like your new products. If you don't mind, I'd like to make an inquiry. Here's the list of our interested machine tools. I'd like to hear your lowest quotations C. I. F. Seatle.

A: Thank you for your inquiry. We can supply you with all the required tools on the list. Here's my C. I. F. US Pacific Coastal City price list. We may adjust the prices according to the quantity you want.

B: Well, Mr. Chen, your prices are not very competitive. My demand is bulk, but of course I'll have to reduce the quantity of my intended purchase substantially with your offer.

A: As I said earlier, Mr. Smith, our prices are adjustable according to the quantity of your requirement. If our offer is the only thing that bothers you, you can look around and call again for another discussion of our quotations.

B: I sure will. Nice meeting you. Anyway, I'll call home about your quotations and come back tomorrow with your decision.

Key to the Exercises

A: That's fine. See you tomorrow then.
B: Bye.

Transcripts

Our culture has caused most Americans to assume not only that our language is universal but that the gestures we use are understood by everyone. We do not realize that waving good-bye is the way to summon a person from the Philippines to one's side, or that in Italy and some Latin-American countries, curling the finger to oneself is a sign of farewell.

Those private citizens who sent packages to our troops occupying Germany after World War II and marked them GIFT to escape duty payments did not bother to find out that "Gift" means poison in German. Moreover, we like to think of ourselves as friendly, yet we prefer to be at least 3 feet or an arm's length away from others. Latinos and Middle Easterners like to come closer and touch, which makes Americans uncomfortable.

Our linguistic and cultural blindness and the casualness with which we take notice of the developed tastes, gestures, customs and languages of other countries, are losing us friends, business and respect in the world.

Even here in the United States, we make few concessions to the needs of foreign visitors. There are no information signs in four languages on our public buildings or monuments; we do not have multilingual guided tours. Very few restaurant menus have translations, and multilingual waiters, bank clerks and policemen are rare. Our transportation systems have maps in English only and often we ourselves have difficulty understanding them.

When we go abroad, we tend to cluster in hotels and restaurants where English is spoken. The attitudes and information we pick up are conditioned by those natives - usually the richer - who speak English. Our business dealings, as well as the nation's diplomacy, are conducted through interpreters.

For many years, America and Americans could get by with cultural blindness and linguistic ignorance. After all, America wastes the most powerful country of the free world, the distributor of needed funds and goods.

But all that is past. American dollars no longer buy all good things, and we are slowly beginning to realize that our proper role in the world is changing. A 1979 Harris poll reported that 55 percent of Americans want this country to play a more significant role in world affairs; we want to have a hand in the important decisions of the next century, even though it may not always be the upper hand.

Unit Two Social Networking

Part One Reading and Translating

Reading A
I. Give brief answers to the following questions.
  1. He canceled his MySpace account.
  2. It allows users to create profiles, swap message and share photos, for example.
  3. He lectures students knowing when, where and for what purpose technology is most appropriate.
  4. It is one phenomenon when people may post anything from unflattering photos to online threats to others.
  5. It concluded that faceless communication was seen as a supplement to everyday interactions, not a replacement.
  6. He thinks that social networking can be an "extremely effective" way to publicize events to large groups and even to help build a sense of community on campus.

II. Complete the following passage by filling each of the numbered blanks with one or two suitable words using the Chinese in the brackets as the reference.

1. dominate
2. released
3. ongoing
4. survey
5. majority
6. Web surfing
7. warier
8. posting
9. forwarded
10. data stream

III. Complete the following sentences with one function word or phrase.

1. the goal of
2. where
3. to some degree
4. go across
5. for instance
6. By and large

IV. Complete the following sentences by translating the Chinese given in the brackets.

1. phasing out his writing on the Internet in the meantime of preparing for his final exams
2. when the novelty weared off
3. a bad news was hitting home
4. trying to find a way out, he met up with another friend
5. have topics to begin with
6. get over our fear to fail

V. Translate the following sentences into English.

1. It's one of a few signs, he says, that some members of the tech generation are starting to see the value of quality face time.
2. As the novelty of their wired lives wears off, they're also getting more sophisticated about the way they use such tools as social networking and text and instant messaging — not just constantly using them because they're there.
3. He points out the students he's seen walking across campus, holding hands with significant others while talking on cell phones to someone else. He's also observed them in coffee shops, surrounded by people, but staring instead at a computer screen.
4. Privacy issues also are hitting home, most recently when students discovered that personal updates on their Facebook pages were being automatically forwarded to contacts they didn't necessarily want to have the information.

VI. Translate the following passage into Chinese.

  19岁的大二学生米勒说:"见过很多网友之后,我发现,脸书网上的优秀个人资料甚至能使一个令人讨厌的人变得吸引人。"

  同时,他也不喜欢用手机短信功能。虽然手机短信能更快地发送问候信息,也能及时地改变行程,避免约在嘈杂的演唱会现场。

  米勒也说:"短信使社交变得容易。"

  他的一些朋友会用短信取消晚上的约会,这样做可以避免做出过多解释。另外,他还看到一些人为了避免当面或电话中被拒绝的尴尬,就用短信来做出邀请。

  他还说:"我们这一代需要克服这种害怕拒绝的心理。"

Reading B

I. Match the summaries on the left column to the seven parts of the article with the number of paragraphs on the right column.

  A. 2 B. 1 C. 5 D. 7 E. 4 F. 3 G. 6

II. Answer the following questions.
  1. There are 4 steps in total.
  2. One reason is that you will avoid forgetting some less-obvious digital accounts or assets that you didn't initially include on your list. The other reason is to ensure you add the answers to any security questions you created to verify your login identities.
  3. Because you should keep it secure in order to prevent theft, whether monetary or identity and to prevent unauthorized access.

Part Two Tips for Translation

比较下列汉语句子及其英语译文,说明每组句子分别主要反映了汉语和英语哪一方面的差异。
1. 汉语的意合特征和英语的形合特征(汉语多短句和分句,英语多长句和从句)
2. 英汉语词序的不同(定语)
3. 汉语的后重心 v.s.英语的前重心
4. 汉语的后重心 v.s.英语的前重心
5. 英汉语句序的不同(条件状语从句)
6. 汉语的主动 v.s.英语的被动

Part Three Simulated Writing

Check Your Understanding
Answer the following questions according to the above instruction manual.
1. The heater must be located in an area where leakage of the tank or connections will not result in damage to the area adjacent to the heater or to lower floors of the structure.
2. It should be closed.
3. We should use elbows, nipples and unions as shown in the diagrams.
4. After the installation of all water lines, open the main water supply valve and fill the heater. Open several hot water faucets to allow air to escape from the system while the heater if filling. When water passes through the faucets, close them and check for possible leaks in the system.
5. Increasing the thermostat setting above the preset temperature may cause severe burns and consume excessive energy. Hotter water increases the risk of scald injury.
6. Contact manufacturer for replacement information.

Follow-up Writing
The following is part of a digital camera instruction manual; complete it with the information given below.
1. Turn on your PC to start Windows
2. The main window of the Utility appears
3. Open the folder where you installed the application software
4. Double-click the "Dimage Image Viewer Utility" software application Icon
5. Set the digital camera to the computer connection mode
6. Start the "Dimage Image Viewer Utility" application software
7. Select the folder where Image files are stored
8. Image files in the selected folder are read

Part Four Listening

While-listening

I. Listen to the recording and supply the missing words.

1. terrorism	2. phase	3. self-declared
4. launch	5. launched	6. terrorists
7. reach out	8. recruit	9. opened fire on
10. contest	11. strike	12. vigilant
13. online	14. disrespectful	15. watch for
16. engagements	17. countering	18. frankly
19. urge	20. progress	21. security
22. militants	23. against	24. concerning
25. phenomenon	26. gone viral	27. worse
28. across	29. attack	30. threats

Part Five Speaking

II. Match the following two columns.
   1. F 2. H 3. A 4. C 5. E 6. B 7. D 8. I 9. G

III. Read through this outline of the responses of three applicants to the same questions asked of them in an interview. Consider their answers carefully.
   1. ill-prepared; unsure; under confident
   2. confident and prepared; has done some research; modest but sure of him/ herself
   3. arrogant; an upstart (presumptuous); not interested in the job
   4. The answer is open.

Transcripts

A top Obama administration official says the fight against terrorism has entered what he calls a new phase. Homeland Security Secretary Jeh Johnson spoke to ABC News on Sunday. He said groups like the self-declared Islamic State are successfully using social media to interest new members or to launch attacks in the United States. His comments followed reports that federal law enforcement officials have launched hundreds of investigations to identify likely terrorists nationwide. Mr. Johnson says the terrorist threat has changed because of the successful use of social media by the Islamic State. He says the group has shown the ability to reach out and recruit members in the United States.

Police shot and killed two gunmen after they opened fire on a security officer outside Curtis Culwell Center in Garland, Texas, Monday, May 4, 2015. The center was hosting a contest for Prophet Muhammad cartoons. "Because of the use of the Internet, we could have little, or no, notice in advance of an independent actor (attacker) attempting to strike. And so that's why law enforcement at the local level needs to be ever more vigilant, and we're constantly reminding them to do that." Mr. Johnson says federal, state and local law enforcement officials are cooperating more closely now than they were before the terrorist attacks of September 11, 2001.

Last week, the head of the Federal Bureau of Investigation warned there might be thousands of Islamic State followers online in the United States. FBI Director James Comey said it is not easy to know who among them is a threat. Earlier this month, two gunmen attacked what has been called a 'free speech' event in Garland, Texas.

The event's organizers offered a $10,000 prize for the best cartoon of Islam's Prophet Mohammad. For Muslims, any image of the Prophet is considered disrespectful. The gunmen were killed in an exchange of gunfire with police. Mr. Comey said the FBI had warned the Garland police to watch for the two men hours before the attack.

Secretary Johnson says federal officials are fighting social media recruitment efforts by talking to members of the Muslim community in the United States. "Since I've been secretary, I have personally participated in engagements with community leaders in the Islamic community and elsewhere. I've been to New York, Boston, Minneapolis, Chicago, Los Angeles and other places where I personally meet with community leaders about countering violent extremism in their communities. That has to be part of our efforts in this new phase." Mr. Johnson admits the Islamic State seems to be effective in its communications. He says Muslim communities must help federal, state and local officials fight the recruiting efforts. "It has to come from Islamic leaders who, frankly, can talk the language better than the federal government can and so, when I meet with community leaders, Islamic leaders, it's one of the things we urge them to do. Some have begun it. We've seen some good progress, but there's a lot more than can be done."

Mr. Johnson supported the decision by U.S. military officials to increase security at bases across the country. The FBI had warned that Islamist militants could attack troops or local police. Michael McCaul is the chairman of the House Homeland Security Committee. He told Fox News on Sunday there had been an increase in threats against local police and military bases in the US. "We're seeing these on an almost daily basis. It's very concerning. I'm over here with the French counter-terrorism experts on the Charlie Hebdo case (trying to learn) how we can stop foreign fighters coming out of Iraq and Syria to Europe. But then, we have this phenomenon in the United States where they (terrorists) can be activated by the Internet. And, really, terrorism has gone viral."

Representative McCaul says the possible threat from terrorism is worse than the FBI has said it is. He says the United States faces two threats: one from fighters leaving the Middle East, and the other from thousands across the country who will attack when the Islamic State sends a message on the Internet. He warns that threats from the terrorists will increase because of the many failed states in the Middle East and North Africa.

Unit Three   Work

Part One   Reading and Translating

Reading A

I. Give brief answers to the following questions.
1. What distinguishes the helpful consequences from the harmful is the intention behind what is said, how the information is perceived and acted on, and the length of time it is allowed to spread and fester.
2. According to Nicholas DiFonzo, "The common denominator seems to be fear — we're afraid of what this person in the organization will do to us; we're afraid of how the engineering department is going to get more money and we in marketing are going to get less money; we're afraid of what this rival company is doing — and so we spread rumors about them."
3. It's the kind of information you have to hear through the grapevine: what the organizational norms are, who you should approach and who you should not approach, and who gets paid what, the kind of information that is often secret.
4. Projecting our own feelings of inadequacy on others by putting them down rids us of our bad feelings and makes us feel superior. Gossip allows us to retaliate against perceived unfairness, act out passive-aggressive and envious feelings and redress power imbalances. People revert to gossip when they believe they cannot confront an issue directly.

5. It is the negative gossip most people enjoy more because it makes us feel better about ourselves and reassures us, because we are not the subject of it.
6. It acts as a safety valve for grievances, allowing pent-up feelings to be released in a way that minimizes potential damage.

II. Complete the following passage by filling each of the numbered blanks with one suitable word using the Chinese in the brackets as the reference.
1. entertain   2. destroy   3. spread   4. unfairness
5. hatred   6. anxieties   7. affected   8. adequate
9. decisions   10. uncertainty

III. Complete the following sentences with one function word.
1. at   2. In   3. of   4. from
5. by   6. for

IV. Complete the following sentences by translating the Chinese given in the brackets.
1. make us reluctant to open up to new things and people
2. If they're opposed to this jobs bill
3. you've made the mistake of projecting your outlook on to others' behavior
4. revert to the older work
5. have had an affair with someone
6. One of the main reasons people mess up their lives

V. Translate the following sentences into English.
1. The common denominator seems to be fear — we're afraid of what this person in the organization will do to us; we're afraid of how the engineering department is going to get more money and we in marketing are going to get less money; we're afraid of what this rival company is doing — and so we spread rumors about them.
2. Studies have shown that while rumors reduce trust in management and harm the attitudes of staff, they do not necessarily affect productivity.
3. Although rumor often holds some truth, people's interpretation of events tends to avoid complexity and personal responsibility, and is often directed towards an individual, a department or an outside rival.
4. Gossip, as opposed to rumor, is often about social networking and bonding and can be entertaining, irresistible and even witty. Because it is so pleasurable, people tend not to consider the harm it causes.

VI. Translate the following passage into Chinese.
　　八卦和谣言是办公室生活的一部分——它们让人们获得娱乐和信息，让人际关系更加密切，但它们也能败坏名声、摧毁信任、造成不良心态，甚至降低生产率。
　　结果有益的八卦和谣言与结果有害的，其区别在于背后的意图，信息给人何种印象、促成何种行动，以及信息被允许传播和发酵的时长。
　　除了提供非正式的交流网络，八卦和谣言为人们眼中的不公和权力不平衡，或者嫉妒、怨恨、无聊，乃至仇恨等情感提供了心理空间。当人们无法与一个问题或者一个人正面对抗的时候，与同事闲聊成了一种发泄郁闷的方式。出现改变和不确定性的时期，比如机构发生重组、领导人变更或进行并购时，人们的焦虑情绪会增强。
　　这些状况会使人们担心自己将受到何种影响。谁会得到晋升或者被降职，谁会失去饭碗或者职位发生变动，谁的薪酬又会是多少？

Key to the Exercises

在管理层公布的信息不足的情况下，人们会自然而然地提出各种说法来填补这一空白。高管们做决策花的时间越长，人们就会越焦虑，就越会有更多谣言来填补真空，试图为这种不确定找到合理解释。

Reading B
I. Match the companies with the description according to the article.
1. C 2. G 3. A 4. F 5. B 6. D 7. E

II. Answer the following questions.
1. At InfoBeans, managers feared that workers' inefficiency would lead to financial losses and client defections. So it began to use a software system called Buddy to measure work.
2. In the office of the future, you will always know what you are doing and how fast you are doing it.
3. We have pedometers to measure how far we walk, apps to monitor our blood pressure, stress level, the calories we're taking in, the calories we're burning.

Part Two Tips for Translation

练习
翻译下列各句，注意词的选择。
1. He is deeply engrossed in medical research.
2. That chap is infatuated with fame and gain.
3. May I use your telephone?
4. Excuse me, excuse me! (Please let me pass.)
5. He dedicated his whole life to serving the people.

Part Three Simulated Writing

Check Your Understanding

Supply the missing information in the following table according to the sample of invitation for Bids you have just read.
1. China International Tendering Company
2. November 26, 2005
3. ITC991508
4. 1543-PRC
5. Asian Development Bank
6. Tongchuan Environment Improvement Project
7. Xi'an Xijiao Cogeneration Plant
8. Electric Feed Water Pump
   110kv Electric Equipment
   Circulating Water Pump & Raw Water Pump
9. between 9:00 a.m.—11:00 a.m. and 1:30—4:00 p.m. (Beijing Time) starting from November 26, 2005 (Sunday and Holidays expected)
10. Room 514
    China International Tendering Company
    Jiuling Building (North Wing)
    No. 21 Xi San Huan Bei Lu
    Beijing, 100089

11. RMB 1,000

12. at or before 9:30 a.m. (Beijing Time) on January 18, 2006

Follow-up Writing

Complete the following Invitation for Bids by filling in the following items in proper places.

Invitation for Bids (IFB)

Date: <u>August 28, 2006</u>

Loan No: <u>4325 CHA</u>

Bid No: <u>CMC991511</u>

1. The Government of the People's Republic of China (PRC) has received a loan from <u>the World Bank</u> in various currencies towards the cost of <u>The Pipeline at Jetty Project</u>. It is intended that part of the proceeds of this credit will be applied to eligible payments under the Contract(s) for <u>tubing and welded line pipe</u>.

2. The procurement agent — <u>CMC International Tendering Company</u> (hereinafter referred to as <u>CMC-ITC</u>) for and on behalf of the buyer — The World Bank Loan Projects Management Center of the State Forestry Administration of the People's Republic of China invites sealed bids from eligible bidders for the supply of the following goods: tubing, welded line pipe.

3. Interested eligible bidders may obtain further information from and inspect the bidding documents at the office of CMC-ITC:

   Address: <u>Rm 2110, West Wing Of Sichuan Mansion, 1 Fuchengmenwai Dajie, Beijing 100037, China</u>

   Tel: <u>(86-10) 68991383</u> Fax: <u>(86-10) 68991366</u>

4. A complete set of bidding documents may be purchased by any interested bidder on the submission of a written application to the above address between <u>8:30 and 11:00 a.m. /1:30 and 4:00 p.m. starting from August 28, 2006 (except Sundays and holidays) at the above address and</u> upon payment of nonrefundable fee of <u>RMB 1,000 or US$ 120</u> for one set of bidding documents.

5. Bids must be delivered to the above office <u>at or before 10:30 a.m. (Beijing Time) on October 12, 2006</u> and must be accompanied by a security of not less than 2% of the total bid price.

6. Bids will be opened in the presence of bidders' representatives who choose to attend <u>at 10:30 a.m. on October 12, 2006</u> at the address given below:

   Rm 2110, the West Wing of Sichuan Mansion

   　1 Fuchengmengwai Dajie, Beijing 100037, China

   　　Procurement Agent: CMC International Tendering Company

   　Mailing Address: 2110, West Wing of Sichuan Mansion

   　1 Fuchengmenwai Dajie, Beijing 100037, China

   　Tel: (0086-10) 68991383 Fax: (0086-10) 68991366

Part Four Listening

While-listening

I. Listen to the recording and supply the missing words.

1. growing	2. remotely	3. small	4. number
5. estimated	6. vision	7. organization	8. majority
9. support	10. concern	11. employees	12. appeals
13. prefer	14. stapler	15. acceptable	16. location
17. technology	18. resource	19. organizations	20. operational

Key to the Exercises

21. maintenance	22. viewable	23. conference	24. utilization
25. growing	26. areas	27. dimension	28. physically
29. opportunities	30. challenges		

Part Five Speaking

II. Match the following two columns.
   1. F   2. H   3. A   4. C   5. E   6. B   7. G   8. D   9. K   10. L   11. I   12. J

III. Complete the following dialogues by making choices from the sentences given.
   1. D   2. B   3. E   4. A   5. C

IV. Read the dialogue given below and translate the sentences into English. Refer to Useful Expressions and Patterns if necessary.
   1. We now have a new Quality Assurance program.
   2. We will have to terminate the contract and find a new supplier.
   3. We also have a good reputation. And that reputation is built upon reliability and good relationships with our customers.
   4. This will damage our reputation in the market place and it's very embarrassing for us.
   5. We are prepared to allow you a special discount of 5% to compensate for the trouble we have caused.

Transcripts

The Workplace of the Future Is Still the Office

Every time I read about the future of work, I see a focus almost entirely on remote work, virtual workplaces and stories of people working from coffee shops. Yes, overall, this is a rapidly growing trend, increasing by over 60% in recent years. I personally have worked remotely for almost two decades, but in general this is still pretty infrequent. What we need to realize is that the overall number is still quite small. According to Global Workplace Analytics' *State of Telework in the U.S.* and based on the U.S. Census Bureau, the total number of people who work solely from home is still only around 3 million.

On the other hand, those who work only part of their time from home, or on the road, are estimated to be a much larger 45% of all U.S. jobs. So, the idea of organizations with most of their employees working from practically anywhere they want is still a distant vision for the broader economy. More accurately, the idea of a significantly virtual organization with no need for office space, or everyone sitting in co-working spaces, is not the reality for the majority of companies. And it won't be for a while, if ever.

While you will need to support more remote workers, the hybrid office-plus-remote worker scenario will continue to be the biggest concern for office, IT and HR managers. The pros and cons of what this does for employees aside, consider the complexity in managing resources for such situations.

In one view, you could gain some efficiencies by sharing office rooms, or desks. That idea appeals to office managers more than employees—what employee wouldn't prefer people to not mess around with their desk space, files, or stapler just as they have left them?

Yet, "mobility desks" or offices are gaining popularity in larger companies. What makes this more acceptable is a mind shift away from the primary view of "my office" as a specific location in their company building, to seeing it more as a virtual space they access from a laptop or smartphone.

This shift from the physical to virtual is made possible by technology: powerful laptops or mobile devices, high speed wireless networks, VPNs, enterprise portals, and, most of all, employee resource management tools in software.

I recently spoke to Elizabeth Dukes, co-author of Wide Open Workspace, and EVP & CMO at iOffice, Inc. on how organizations are managing resources in this hybrid future.

Office and Facilities Managers today are typically responsible for all the resources that keep the office running and employees operational: coordinating office space use, assigning and tracking laptops and personal assets, managing common resources such as network printers and devices, keeping office supply inventory, building maintenance, the mailroom chase, etc.

In a connected business, these are easily accessible and viewable by the employee through the intranet portal, to see how much they have used as well as to request and track resources—e.g., every time you need to book a conference room, find quick directions to a local office in another town, have a package shipped to a salesperson, etc. Similarly, it is critical to operations all around to see utilization of any of these resources, forecast the demand for resources as the organization grows, moves or pivots.

As mentioned in the beginning, while new forms such as co-working is a growing trend, it is still far from the norm. According to Ms. Dukes, this seems to be growing faster in the tech centers of the West and East coast, and less so in other areas of the U.S. While large companies have an undeniable need to manage facilities, she also sees growth in mid-market organizations.

The analytics from facilities management software offer a new dimension of capabilities and issues. Propinquity—the outcomes of being physically near others—is gaining more significance as more start moving towards remote work. This is the property of collaborating in a physical office space that creates new serendipities and opportunities that you don't really get when working entirely virtual or remote. Without it, you don't run into your peers, or come across new challenges and ideas that may lead to new ideas, collaboration or innovation.

Unit Four Lifestyle

Part One Reading and Translating

Reading A

I. Give brief answers to the following questions.
  1. Dorian Grey is a character in Oscar Wilde's 1890 novel *The Picture of Dorian Gray*. It refers to the big differences between the real books and ebooks that we are reading.
  2. We are seen to be reading prize-winning novels, Edwardian-green Virago Classics, or orange Penguin Classics.
  3. What we are really reading is something like harrowing first-person accounts of abuse, marshmallowy love stories, gritty killings, true crime, contemporary commuting-based psychodramas with "girl" and "train" in the title.
  4. Because it's the place you hide what you are really reading, the place where your basest instincts and truest, rawest, subconscious urges settle like slime at the bottom of a forbidding lake.
  5. Slime at the Bottom of a Forbidding Lake.
  6. The author suggests us to liberate ourselves and read what we want aboveboard.

II. Complete the following passage by filling each of the numbered blanks with one suitable word using the Chinese in the brackets as the reference.

  1. embrace   2. wrought   3. amulets   4. blood-soaked

5. admit	6. strain	7. venerable	8. reclaim
9. overripe	10. sorcery		

III. Complete the following sentences with one function word.

   1. out, up   2. to   3. to   4. to, on   5. for   6. on

IV. Complete the following sentences by translating the Chinese given in the brackets.

   1. it allowed core patents in digital photography to languish
   2. does this hypocrite really believe, in his heart
   3. resolutely avoiding the social round
   4. exquisitely sensitive sensors
   5. Regular exercise and meditation
   6. at any time to reclaim memory

V. Translate the following sentences into English.

   1. A recent list of Waterstones top-selling paper books of 2015, compared with the top 20 ebooks purchased from Amazon in the same period, has revealed the gulf between what we are seen to be reading and what we're really reading.

   2. The hardbacks are what we feel we ought to buy, or better yet give as gifts, which show our high-mindedness while ensuring that we pass the reading burden on to someone else.

   3. Meanwhile, copies of untouched prize-winning novels languish on our shelves, impressive but remote, like an exhibition of Elizabeth Taylor's evening dresses.

   4. We pay for hardback editions of thoughtful, exquisitely written meditations on something or other, which took years to write.

VI. Translate the following passage into Chinese.

      这就是事实：我们手中捧着精致的散文集，散文中塑造了精致的人物和他们的个人、社会、文化生活；而我们脑中感兴趣的却是狂欢作乐，男欢女爱，神秘护符和浸血尸体。我想，人们是时候脱掉Kindle给我们的伪装，承认已承受这种双重生活已久。或许人们应该将那些庄重珍贵的作品上传至电子阅读器中，再将它们小心翼翼地存放在抽屉里，并转身忘掉，然后在希斯罗机场5号航站楼的WH Smiths书店里肆无忌惮的购买我们真正想读的。

      优秀的文学作品可以留作我们的退休读物，如果那时自然资源紧张，还可以作为燃料烧掉。而在此同时，我们需要释放自己，收回痛苦的回忆、腐朽的伪君子的中世纪长剑、魔法铺位，还有限制级的浪漫幻想，并骄傲地将它们付之一炬。

Reading B

I. Match the summaries (A—J) on the left column with the number of paragraphs on the right column.

A. Paragragh10	B. Paragraph 8	C. Paragraph 6	D. Paragraph 9	E. Paragraph 2
F. Paragraph 7	G. Paragraph 5	H. Paragraph 3	I. Paragraph 4	J. Paragraph 1

II. Answer the following questions.

   1. Flavour is the paramount issue in beer.
   2. The new UCB aims to "promote and protect the interests of British craft brewers, their beers and beer enthusiasts."
   3. Because, for example, people cannot restrict craft beer to a list of ingredients, or people cannot define craft beer in terms of how it is packaged.

Besides, tell a craft brewer you cannot do something and, invariably, they will come back next week with a flavour-packed beer that proves you can. Craft beer is antithetical to rules.

Part Two Tips for Translation

练习

翻译下列句子，根据需要增补适当的词语。

1. I was very glad to have received your letter.

2. She covered her face with her hand, as if to protect her eyes.

3. Please fill in this form, and give it to me when you have finished.

4. Supper is served at 6 p.m.

5. We must make a comprehensive analysis of a problem before it can be properly solved.

6. Three cobblers with their wits combined equal Zhuge Liang the master mind.

Part Three Simulated Writing

Check Your Understanding

Match the items listed in the following two columns.

1. E   2. D   3. J   4. B   5. C   6. A   7. F   8. H   9. I   10. G

Follow-up Writing

Complete the following Company Profile with the information given below.

The Textron Company

  Textron Inc. is one of the world's largest and most successful multi-industry companies. Founded in 1923, we have grown into a network of businesses with total revenues of $10 billion, and more than 37,000 employees in nearly 33 countries, serving a diverse and global customer base. Headquartered in Providence, Rhode Island, Textron is ranked 190th on the FORTUNE 500 list of largest U.S. companies. Organizationally, Textron consists of numerous subsidiaries and operating divisions, which are responsible for the day-to-day operation of their businesses.

Part Four Listening

While-listening

I. Listen to the recording and supply the missing words.

1. fringe	2. highlight	3. divisions	4. culinary
5. scratch	6. naturalist	7. loaf	8. fibres
9. flavours	10. naturalist	11. lettuce	12. emphasis
13. fizzy	14. keen	15. sustain	16. nourish
17. consequences	18. ingredients	19. corresponding	20. refrigeration
21. occasionally	22. array	23. ecology	24. dwells
25. vanished	26. specialities	27. biocultural	28. nutrients
29. industrialised	30. standardised		

Key to the Exercises

Part Five Speaking

II. Complete the following dialogue by translating Chinese into English orally.

1. it has shown a great market potential
2. we enjoy good relations with all the wholesalers, chain stores and distributors in Canada
3. promote the sales of our products
4. If we are granted the sole agency
5. Our agents in other areas usually get a 10% commission
6. we need to do a lot of work and spend a lot of money on the sales promotion
7. you will not supply your product to any other buyer

III. Learn to communicate in the situation given below.

A: Mr. Anderson, did you receive our letter of last week?

B: You mean the letter about the agency? Yes, I did, and I read it carefully. I'm very glad that you chose us to be your sole agent in Eastern Europe. But frankly, I still have some questions.

A: I invited you here to discuss just this question in detail. You see, we have been expanding our business globally ever since the company restructuring. We are now looking to the American and Western European markets, both of which are very demanding. So we are thinking of entrusting our products to some established local dealers there, and we are thinking of you. So I wonder if you'd be willing to take the job?

B: I'd be more than willing. Actually I'm quite confident I'd be a good agent. We have a lot of experience in marketing your products. What's more, we have business contacts all over Eastern Europe. I don't foresee much difficulty in pushing the sales of your products.

A: I'm glad to hear that. Then let me propose an annual sales volume of 10, 000 pieces for three years. Is this all right?

B: Though we have done very well in this line, 10, 000 dozen is still a bit too much for us, I think. Last year we sold 8,000 pieces. So let's start with 8, 000 pieces.

A: Mr. Anderson, you know very well that our petrochemical products sell well on your market. Acting as our agent, it will be much easier for you to control the whole market, because we'll stop our supply to other dealers. We don't think you'll have any difficulties in fulfilling this sales figure.

B: Well, how about the commission? Such a big turnover deserves a good return, don't you think so?

A: In order to facilitate your sales, we can allow you an extraordinary 8% commission for the first year and 5% for the other two years. What do you think?

B: The commission rate is reasonable. I'll take it.

A: Good. One more thing, we'd like you to send us a detailed report on your market condition every three months.

B: No problem. We will do that.

A: Well, I'm glad that we have agreed on the major points.

B: Me too. What about other terms?

A: Well, I have a blank agreement here. Other terms and conditions will be the same as those on this agreement. Maybe you can take it back and have a look while I prepare for the formal agreement. If you have further doubts about those terms, we can discuss them. Otherwise, we'll sign the agreement next time we meet. What do you say to this?

B: Couldn't be better.

A: Then shall we meet again at 6:30 tomorrow evening at the China Grand Hotel?

B: Fine.

Transcripts

Humanity's Relationship with Cookery Is Unique—and Shouldn't Be Lost

Before Michael Pollan came along, eating as a form of politics was a fringe activity. Dubbed the "liberal foodie intellectual" by the New York Times, the American activist and author has spent the last two decades writing bestselling books, such as "In Defence of Food" (2008) and "The Omnivore's Dilemma" (2006), in an effort to popularise cooking and highlight the defects of the food industry and the rich world's bad eating habits.

Mr Pollan's latest book, "Cooked", is divided into four sections: fire, water, air and earth. Although something of an authorly conceit, these divisions allow him to explore a range of culinary topics from the joy of making soufflés that rise to why bacteria are needed in fermentation. He also returns to a conundrum he has previously described as the "cooking paradox": why it is that people now spend less time preparing food from scratch and more time reading about cooking or watching cookery programmes on television.

Mr Pollan explores the same way a naturalist might, by studying the animals, plants and microbes involved in cooking, and delving into history, culture and chemistry. With help from experts he masters the "whole hog" barbecue, a loaf of bread and the cooking pot. He describes the remarkable transformations that take place in the humble saucepan, where fibres are broken down, seeds softened and rendered edible, plants detoxified, and flavours brought together from far-flung taxonomic kingdoms.

Side by side with Mr Pollan the naturalist is the author as activist. Although the fruit and vegetable areas of supermarkets have grown ever bigger over the past two decades, cooking has expanded to take in heating up a tin of soup, microwaving ready-meals and frozen pizzas or breaking open a bag of mixed lettuce leaves. Mr Pollan places great emphasis on the work of Harry Balzer, an expert on food, diet and eating patterns in America. Collecting data from thousands of food diaries, Mr Balzer concludes that, since the 1980s, fewer and fewer people have been cooking their evening meal. (The most popular meal in America, at lunch and dinner, is a sandwich accompanied by a fizzy drink.)

Mr Pollan is keen for this trend to be reversed and his book is a hymn to why people should be enticed back into the kitchen. Cooking, he believes, creates bonds between humans and the web of living creatures that sustain and nourish them. Turning away from this means that foods that are tasty and healthy (as bread once was) are being taken off the menu with far-reaching consequences. Industrially produced food almost always trades in quality ingredients for higher amounts of sugar, salt and fat—with a corresponding rise in levels of obesity.

Before refrigeration, bad food often killed people. Bacteria, such as E. coli, occasionally still do. In recent decades a great deal of research has been done on the array of good microbes humans carry within them and which they need in order to stay healthy. "Cooked" is particularly informative about the rapidly moving scientific frontier of microbial ecology and how, in a post-Pasteurian world, the live-culture foods which used to make up a large part of the human diet are good for people and for the microbes that live inside the gut.

The book dwells on fermented foods, for example. These have largely vanished from supermarkets but many cultures have developed such specialities, including Malaysiantempoyak, (fermented durian fruit), Russian kefir (similar to yogurt) and Mexican pozole (a maize stew). Even bread, cheese and chocolate all depend on harnessing the power of microbes. These invisible forces travel alongside humans, Mr Pollan says, in a "dance of biocultural symbiosis", cleverly transforming, sterilising or even adding nutrients.

Mr Pollan recognises that cooking today is very different from what it was in his grandmother's time, and that decades from now even a limited desire to cook may be seen as quaint. This would be a shame. Real cooking (not just heating up) allows people to create, to put their own values into food, to escape the industrialised eating that has created health crises all over the world. Cooking is part of being human. The alternative is to evolve into passive consumers of standardised commodities that promise more than they deliver. Best of all, argues Mr Pollan, cooking makes people happy.

Key to the Exercises

Unit Five   Ethics

Lead-in

1. The cause for concern is that the building Dr. X designed could potentially topple in strong winds.
2. Large number of the building's owners and occupants.
3. The building occupants could be maimed or killed. The buildings would be ruined. Dr. X's professional reputation and career would certainly be ruined and he could also face imprisonment and civil lawsuits.
4. Certainly if the building collapsed and people died, Dr. X would be guilty of many counts of murder. There are likely many laws and regulations that would also apply. Likely the code of ethics for Dr. X's profession holds its members responsible for ensuring public safety.
5. Dr. X can go to the building owners and inform them of the problem and of what needs to be done in order to fix the skyscraper.
6. Certainly by informing the owners as soon as possible Dr. X will minimize the severity of the consequences. Dr. X should also carefully review his calculations to determine how/why he made the error in the first place. This will allow him to make sure that he doesn't make the same mistake again in the future.

Part One Reading and Translating

Reading A

I. Give brief answers to the following questions.
1. Anthropocentric positions find it problematic to articulate what is wrong with the cruel treatment of nonhuman animals, except to the extent that such treatment may lead to bad consequences for human beings. / Anthropocentric perspective assigns intrinsic value to huaman beings alone.
2. Biocentrism states that nature does not exist simply to be used or consumed by humans, but that humans are simply one species amongst many, and that because we are part of an ecosystem, any actions which negatively affect the living systems of which we are a part, adversely affect us as well, whether or not we maintain a biocentric worldview.
3. Deep ecology describes itself as "deep" because it persists in asking deeper questions concerning "why" and "how" and thus is concerned with the fundamental philosophical questions about the impacts of human life as one part of the ecosphere, rather than with a narrow view of ecology as a branch of biological science, and aims to avoid merely anthropocentric environmentalism, which is concerned with conservation of the environment only for exploitation by and for humans purposes, which excludes the fundamental philosophy of deep ecology.
4. "Instrumental value" is the value of things as means to further some other ends, whereas the "intrinsic value" is the value of things as ends in themselves regardless of whether they are also useful as means to other ends.
5. Ecofeminism, a pluralistic, nonhierarchical, relationship-oriented philosophy that suggests how humans could reconceive themselves and their relationships to nature in nondominating ways, is proposed as an alternative to patriarchal systems of domination.
6. Environmental racism is inequitable distribution of environmental hazards based on race.

II. Complete the following passage by filling each of the numbered blanks with one suitable word using the Chinese in the brackets as the reference.

1. domination   2. responsibilities   3. appropriate
4. promotes   5. encounters   6. scarcity

7. isolated   8. reject   9. neutral
10. objectivity

III. Complete the following sentences with one function word.
   1. for   2. on   3. with   4. to   5. in   6. to

IV. Complete the following sentences by translating the Chinese given in the brackets.
   1. will choose to assign to its former unit
   2. In a strict sense, at the expense of huge long-term interests
   3. From the standpoint of expense
   4. along with the associated long-term costs
   5. regardless of the consequences
   6. It sends a strong signal to refrain from imposing unfair restrictions to trade

V. Translate the following sentences into English.
   1. Many traditional western ethical perspectives, however, are anthropocentric or human-centered in that either they assign intrinsic value to human beings alone or they assign a significantly greater amount of intrinsic value to human beings than to any nonhuman things such that the protection or promotion of human interests or well-being at the expense of nonhuman things turns out to be nearly always justified.
   2. Biocentrists believe that all species have inherent value, and that humans are not "superior" in a moral or ethical sense.
   3. The philosophy emphasizes the interdependence of organisms within ecosystems and that of ecosystems with each other within the biosphere.
   4. According to ecofeminist philosophy, when people see themselves as related to others and to nature, they will see life as bounty rather than scarcity, as cooperation rather than isolated egos.

VI. Translate the following passage into Chinese.
   生物中心论者认为，自然的存在不仅仅是被人类利用和消费，他们认为人类只不过是众多物种之一。正因为我们是这个生态系统的一部分，我们自身任何能够破坏我们生存体系的行为，也可以对我们产生坏的影响。无论我们是否是生物中心论者，事实就是如此。生物中心论者认为，所有物种都具有内在价值，并且，无论从道德还是伦理意义上讲，人类并不比其他生物"高级"。保罗　泰勒是早期生物中心论倡导者之一，坚信生物中心论是"对自然敬畏的态度"，因此人类应该致力于寻求尊重人类自身福利和所有生物的内在价值的生活方式。

Reading B

I. Match the philosophers or psychologists with their claims or ideas mentioned in the article.
   A. Socrates____4____
   B. James Rest 1, 3
   C. Lawrence Kohlberg 2, 5, 6

II. Answer the following questions.
   1. In a recent editorial, the *Wall Street Journal* announced that ethics courses are useless because ethics can't be taught.
   2. Most psychologists today would agree with Socrates on that ethics can be taught.
   3. The person at the postconventional level stops defining right and wrong in terms of group loyalties or norms. Instead, the adult at this level develops moral principles that define right and wrong from a

Key to the Exercises

universal point of view. The moral principles of the postconventional person are principles that would appeal to any reasonable person because they take everyone's interest into account.

Part Two Tips for Translation

翻译下列句子,根据需要省略适当的词语。

1. This was a complete lie.
2. They are close (bosom) friends.
3. A proton has a positive charge and an electron a negative charge, but a neutron has neither.
4. People use science to understand and change nature.
5. For many years there has been serious unemployment in that country.

Part Three Simulated Writing

Check Your Understanding
Match the items listed in the following two columns.

1. G   2. I   3. J   4. K   5. E   6. D   7. M
8. C   9. L   10. F 11. H 12. A 13. N 14. B

Follow-up Writing
Complete the following Patent with the information given below.

1. 3,694,513
2. Sept. 26,1972
3. DIRECT NITRATION OF ALKYPHENOLS COMPOUND
4. Stephen W. Tobey, Sudbury, Mass. 01766; Marilyn Z. Lourandos, Ashland, Mass. 01721
5. The Dow Chemical Company, Midland, Mich.
6. June 8, 1970
7. 44,666
8. 260/622R
9. C07c 79/24
10. 260/622
11. Howard T. Mars
12. Griswold & Burdick, Herbert D. Knudsen & C. E. Rehberg

Part Four Listening

While-listening
I. Listen to the recording and supply the missing words.

1. individuals   2. Basically   3. controversies   4. concerned   5. maximize   6. involves
7. resolve   8. respond   9. included   10. varied   11. extent   12. focus

II. Match the following terms with their related items.

1. D, F   2. A, C, E   3. B

III. Listen to the passage again, and answer the following questions based on the passage.
1. Ethics is the word that refers to morals, values, and beliefs of the individuals, family or the society.
2. Common morality, personal morality and professional ethics.

Part Five Speaking

II. Match the following two columns.
1. F　　2. H　　3. A　　4. C　　5. E　　6. B　　7. G　　8. D

III. Complete the following dialogues by making sentences with the help of the key words given in brackets.
1. B: This is certainly a wise strategy.
   B: I wish to extend our thanks to your help.
2. B: the imported technology shall be integrated, precise and reliable
   B: the expenses should be fair and reasonable
3. B: We suggest the rate come down to 3% of the net sales price.
   B: finish the feasibility report and the draft contract first

IV. Learn to communicate in the situation given below.
A: From the visit I can see that your company has very good machinery and equipment. But in order to compete in the world market and occupy a leading place in petrochemical industry, you need to improve your designs.
B: Yes, you are quite right. We realize that we need to improve the designs of our products in order to upgrade them to the advanced world level. We would highly appreciate your technological cooperation.
A: I'm glad to cooperate with you. I think what I can do is to provide you with our designs and send your 2 or 3 technicians for a certain period at the beginning stage during our cooperation.
B: That is excellent! I know that you have provided your technological know-how to quite a number of car factories in the world.
A: Yes, any country, or any enterprise benefits from imported advanced technology.
B: That is true. I'm sure with your help our products will reach the advanced world level very quickly.
A: I hope so, too.

Transcripts

Ethics

Ethics is the word that refers to morals, values, and beliefs of the individuals, family or the society. The word has several meanings. Basically it is an activity and process of inquiry. Secondly, it is different from non-moral problems, when dealing with issues and controversies. Thirdly, ethics refers to a particular set of beliefs, attitudes, and habits of individuals or family or groups concerned with morals. Fourth, it is used to mean 'morally correct'.

The study on ethics helps to know the people's beliefs, values, and morals, learn the good and bad of them, and practice them to maximize their well-being and happiness. It involves the inquiry on the existing situations, form judgments and resolve the issues. In addition, ethics tells us how to live, to respond to issues, through the duties, rights, responsibilities, and obligations. In religion, similar principles are included, but the reasoning on procedures is limited. The principles and practices of religions have varied from to time to time (history), region (geography, climatic conditions), religion, society, language, caste and creed. But ethics has grown to a large extent beyond the barriers listed above. In ethics, the focus is to study and apply the principles and practices, universally.

Three Types of Ethics or Morality

As ethical commitment is core of professionalism, we must know more on the ethics, especially to professional ethics. How do professional ethics differ from other types of ethics, such as philosophical ethics, business ethics and personal ethics? We begin discussion on the three types of ethics or morality.

1. Common Morality

Common morality is the set of moral beliefs shared by all. It is the basis for the other types of morality. In ethics or morality, we usually think of such principles as Ahimsa (no harm physically or mentally to or killing others or even suicides), Satyam (no lies and break of promises), Contentment (no greed, cheating or stealing) etc. We don't question these principles.

2. Personal Morality

Personal ethics or personal morality is the set of moral beliefs that a person holds. Our personal moral beliefs mostly and closely run parallel to the principles of common morality, such as ahimsa, satyam and contentment. But our personal moral beliefs may differ from common morality in some areas, especially where common morality appears to be unclear or in a state of change. Thus, we may oppose abortion, even though common morality may not be clear on the issue.

3. Professional Ethics (Role Morality)

Professional ethics is the set of standards adopted by professionals. Every profession has its professional ethics: medicine, law, pharmacy etc. Engineering ethics is the set of ethical standards that applies to the engineering profession.

Unit Six　Technology

Part One Reading and Translating

Reading A

I. Give brief answers to the following questions.
  1. He/She wants the doctor to pay attention to him/her, not the computer.
  2. Health care is the only industry that has managed to lose productivity while going digital. Because the reality is that the more "digital" physicians go, and the longer they use software, the less satisfied they become.
  3. No, it will not. Because we need to bring together the intelligence of doctors, nurses, patients, hospitals, laboratories, insurers and everyone else who contributes to the continuum of care.
  4. It means that through focusing on delivering EMRs that provide rich clinical information, it will still allow doctors to be fully present at meaningful moments of care.
  5. It is to simplify every process where clinicians are presented with an overwhelming number of choices.
  6. The goal is to prompt providers to gather the data they need to gather in the least intrusive way.

II. Complete the following passage by filling each of the numbered blanks with one or two suitable words using the Chinese in the brackets as the reference.

1. quest	2. tactics	3. simplify	4. clinicians
5. overwhelming	6. plugged into	7. aggregate	8. byzantine
9. reimbursement	10. intrusive		

III. Complete the following sentences with one function word.
1. Yet   2. regardless   3. continuum   4. aliment
5. hassle   6. launching

IV. Complete the following sentences by translating the Chinese given in the brackets.
1. effectively plug into an electric power
2. managed to be a clinician
3. An overwhelming number of things have gone digital
4. in the wild
5. launch overwhelming attacks against civilians
6. in disconnected software don't know if a student has an adverse reaction to a new teacher

V. Translate the following sentences into English.
1. Worse, much of this activity is routine census taking, driven by insurers and regulators who assume digitization makes it easy to gather statistical data, regardless of whether it contributes to the quality of care.
2. The reality is that the more "digital" physicians go, and the longer they use software, the less satisfied they become.
3. We need to bring together the intelligence of doctors, nurses, patients, hospitals, laboratories, insurers and everyone else who contributes to the continuum of care.
4. In our quest to make the EMR smarter, one of our primary tactics is to simplify every process where clinicians are presented with an overwhelming number of choices.

VI. Translate the following passage into Chinese.
很多病人的病例文档都是在断网的软件上记录的。这些记录并不知道病人是否会对某种药有不良反应。当同样的病人一周之后去看另外一个医生时，会就相似的病症一直补充类似的营养或进行各种检测。期望分离的电子病历智能化就像是你喜欢James Brown的音乐时，会希望你的CD唱片机自动播放Isaac Hayes的音乐一样。但是，目前的电子病例却并不像你最喜欢的电子音乐服务那样是联网的。在过去4年里，我的公司Athenahealth，一直致力于重新想象电子病例。我们想要把上面提到的技术麻烦解决掉，使之对医生更有用，对病人伤害性更小。虽然还处于尚未完成阶段，但是我们一直在努力和进步。最终，我们聚焦于实现电子病例在能提供丰富的病例信息的同时，还能允许医生对病人充分进行有意义的呵护。换句话说，我们相信科技一定会让医生发挥医生的职能。

Reading B

I. Match the summaries (A—E) on the left column to the five parts of the article with the number of paragraphs on the right column.
A. 3   B. 1   C. 2   D. 5   E. 4

II. Answer the following questions.
1. 3D printing in the term's original sense refers to processes that sequentially deposit material onto a powder bed with inkjet printer heads. More recently the meaning of the term has expanded to encompass a wider variety of techniques such as extrusion and sintering based processes. Technical standards generally use the term additive manufacturing for this broader sense.
2. (1) Boeing has already used 3D printing to make more than 22,000 parts used on civilian and military aircraft flying today. (2) The medical industry has taken advantage of 3D printing's ability to make unique objects that might otherwise be tough to build using traditional methods. (3) The U.S. military has deployed 3D printing labs to Afghanistan as a way to speed up the pace of battlefield innovation and

Key to the Exercises

rapidly build whatever soldiers might need onsite. (4) NASA has looked into 3D printing for making replacement parts aboard the International Space Station and building spacecraft in orbit. (5) A separate NASA project has investigated the possibility of building lunar bases for future astronauts by using moon "dirt" known as regolith.

3. Most 3D printers can only print objects using a specific type of material—a serious limitation that prevents 3D printers from creating complex objects such as an Apple iPhone. The 3D printing boom could eventually prove disruptive in both a positive and negative sense.

Part Two Tips for Translation

翻译下列句子，注意黑体部分词类的转换。

1. I am no drinker, nor smoker.
2. The government called for the establishment of more technical schools.
3. I am so grateful to my father for his continuous encouragement during my childhood.
4. He has long been used to last-minute decisions.
5. We felt no difficulty in solving this problem.
6. It was a very informative meeting.
7. He was between sheets by eleven.
8. The development of scientific research in our country is characterized by the combination of theory with practice.

Part Three Simulated Writing

Check Your Understanding

Match the items listed in the following two columns.
1. F 2. H 3. A 4. I 5. D 6. C 7. J 8. E 9. G 10. B

Follow-up Writing

Complete the following abstract with the information given below.

1. 26 April 2006 (Wednesday)
2. 3:00 p.m.
3. Conference Room, 48/F, Immigration Tower, Wan Chai, Hong Kong
4. Prof. HO Kin Chung, Chairman; Mr. CHAN Chi Chiu, Vice-Chairman, Director of Water Supplies; Prof. TSO Wung Wai, The Chinese University of Hong Kong; Dr. CHAN Hon Fai, Cinotech Consultants Limited; Ms. LEE Yoke Shum, Sam World Wide Fund for Nature Hong Kong
5. The Chairman expressed special thanks to the retired founding Chairman, Mr FANG Hung, Kenneth
6. Confirmation of the Minutes of Last Meeting
7. Matters Arising
8. Publication of Water Quality Data
9. Any Other Business
10. the meeting was adjourned at

Part Four Listening

While-listening

I. Listen to the recording and supply the missing words.

1. telephone	2. car	3. changes	4. definitely
5. automotive	6. self-driving	7. mainstream	8. 2025
9. violating	10. operators	11. self-driving	12. Autopilot
13. brake	14. steer	15. pedal	16. slow down
17. lanes	18. avoid	19. trusting	20. perfectly
21. error	22. Traffic	23. smoothly	24. limits
25. operate	26. raised	27. transport	28. feature
29. costly	30. priced		

Part Five Speaking

II. Match the following two columns.

1. G 2. H 3. D 4. E 5. C 6. B 7. A 8. F

III. Below is what was said in a meeting of the Board of Directors of a bus company, "Crazy Bus Company."
Complete the dialogue with the help of the Chinese information given.

1. Do we have any comments

2. the problem is

3. I agree

4. What do the rest of you think about that

5. Let's now get on to Item 1

6. I absolutely agree

7. Are we all agreed then

8. now let's move on to Item 2

9. will you start the advertising process for ex-racing drivers

10. My pleasure

11. that ends today's meeting

Transcripts

Will Your Next Car Drive Itself?

You know how much your telephone has changed over the past 10 years? Your car will change even more than that in the next 10 years. One of the big changes is that cars will drive themselves. Some day you may not need to drive a car. You will just tell the car where you want to go and it will drive itself. "We definitely have the technology for it now," says Andrew Poliak of automotive technology supplier QNX. "We expect self-driving cars to be a mainstream thing between 2020 and 2025." The American company Google has been working on a self-driving automobile for years. These cars are already on the roads in the United States, mainly in California. Google cars are truly self-driving. These cars have no steering wheels or pedals.

Will Your Next Car Drive Itself?

Last week, police ordered one of Google's cars to stop for driving too slowly on a public road. The car was not violating any law, so no one was punished. But police did speak with the operators of the vehicle. According to Google, its self-driving cars have been driven nearly 2 million kilometers. That is equal to the distance the average person drives in 90 years.

So far, no Google self-driving car has gotten a traffic ticket. Some of them have been in accidents when other cars hit them.

Another American company, Tesla, added an "Autopilot" feature to its cars last month. Tesla put the feature, a computer software program, in cars that were built after September 2014.

With the Autopilot turned on, the vehicle drives itself. The car will speed up, slow down, brake and steer by itself. You can take over driving any time by turning the steering wheel or touching a pedal. Your car will slow down if the vehicle in front of you gets closer. It will turn at bends and change lanes if you use the turn signal. The car uses sensors to know when lane changing is safe and whether it should speed up or slow down. Tesla Autopilot takes over driving at speeds over 29 kilometers per hour when you press a button twice. Autopilot is made for cross-country driving. It keeps you in the lane and helps you avoid hitting other cars. Autopilot does not work as well on local roads. It will not stop at a red light or stop sign or turn at intersections.

Reporter Carolyn Nicander Mohr tried the Autopilot feature of a Tesla earlier this month. She had a hard time trusting the car to do what it should do. She thought about disabling the Autopilot feature many times during her trip. She wanted to take control at every bend in the road and hit the brake when the car in front of her slowed down. Yet the car drove perfectly.

Advantages of Self-Driving Cars

Safety

According to The Auto Insurance Center, 81% of car crashes result from human error. Many lives could be saved if cars drove more safely without human drivers. With fewer accidents, insurance costs may be lower for self-driving cars than other vehicles.

Efficiency

In a self-driving car, you would not have to be worried about talking on the phone or sending a text message. You could do other things while getting to where you need to go.

Traffic may be reduced. Cars could flow more smoothly, with fewer cars on the road during busy times. Fewer accidents mean improving traffic conditions, and reducing delays, repairs and injuries. Speed limits could rise with more people using self-driving cars. When self-driving cars prove they can operate at higher speed limits, speed limits could be raised.

Self-driving cars could drive people who are unable to drive themselves. They could travel without depending on others. Businesses could use self-driving cars to bring goods to your home. Order food and have a self-driving car transport it. Send the store your shopping list and wait for the store's self-driving car to bring your order to you.

Criticism of Self-Driving Cars

Cost

Self-driving cars may cost a lot more than other cars. The self-driving feature may first be offered on the most costly cars. Lower priced vehicles may take longer to offer the feature.

But the cost of technology usually drops over time. Expect that self-driving cars could become less costly in the future.

Unit Seven Health

Part One Reading and Translating

Reading A

I. Give brief answers to the following questions.

1. The ancient Greeks were first to make the point. Shakespeare raised the prospect too. Lord Byron believes that we of the craft are all crazy. The notion of the tortured artist is a stubborn meme. It states that creativity is fuelled by the demons that artists wrestle in their darkest hours.
2. Scientists in Iceland report that genetic factors that raise the risk of bipolar disorder and schizophrenia are found more often in people in creative professions.
3. Stefansson believes that a small overlap between the biology of mental illness and creativity is fascinating. It means that a lot of the good things we get in life, through creativity, come at a price. It tells me that when it comes to our biology, we have to understand that everything is in some way good and in some way bad.
4. It's the romantic notion of the 19th century, that the artist is the struggler, aberrant from society, and wrestling with inner demons.
5. Rothernberg found no evidence between mental illness and creativity. He suspects that studies which find links between creativity and mental illness might be picking up on something rather different.
6. Because nearly all mental hospitals use art therapy, many patients are attracted to artistic positions and artistic pursuits after coming out of the hospital.

II. Complete the following passage by filling each of the numbered blanks with one suitable word using the Chinese in the brackets as the reference.

1. genes   2. alter   3. culminate   4. diagnosis
5. mental   6. straddling   7. support   8. Creativity
9. risk   10. population

III. Complete the following sentences with one function word.

1. over   2. on   3. in
4. at   5. on   6. to

IV. Complete the following sentences by translating the Chinese given in the brackets.

1. cast an eye over the room
2. draw on his own talent, courage and creativity to get over the difficulties in life
3. culminated in success
4. pick up on the humour in his remark
5. straddles two cultures
6. conceded that Nancy made a right decision

V. Translate the following sentences into English.

1. Stefansson believes that scores of genes increase the risk of schizophrenia and bipolar disorder. These may alter the ways in which many people think, but in most people do nothing very harmful.
2. The scientists drew on genetic and medical information from 86,000 Icelanders to find genetic variants that doubled the average risk of schizophrenia, and raised the risk of bipolar disorder by more than a third.

3. Most of the artist's creative flair, then, is down to different genetic factors, or to other influences altogether, such as life experiences, that set them on their creative journey.
4. But the fact is that many people who have mental illness do try to work in jobs that have to do with art and literature, not because they are good at it, but because they're attracted to it.

VI. Translate the following passage into Chinese.

　　斯蒂芬森教授认为即使精神疾病和创造力之间联系很小，这一发现也是吸引人的。他说："这意味着在生活中，我们获得美好的事物的同时，也是要付出代价的。这告诉我们，当谈及生物学时，我们应当明白其积极面和消极面。"
　　但是美国哈佛大学精神病学专家罗滕伯格教授不相信这一事实，他认为没有合适的证据可以证实精神疾病和创造力之间的联系。他说："艺术家是社会中的斗争者，他们偏离常规，总是和内心的恶魔做斗争，这是十九世纪以来浪漫主义的观点。以艺术家梵高为例，他碰巧患有精神疾病又极富创造力。对我来说，这件事的对立面更有意思：有创造力的人不是有精神疾病，而他们的思考过程当然是与众不同的。"

Reading B

I. Match the summaries (A—J) on the left column with the number of paragraphs on the right column.
　A. Paragraph 6　B. Paragraph 8　C. Paragraph 9　D. Paragraph 1　E. Paragraph 10
　F. Paragraph 3　G. Paragraph 2　H. Paragraph 7　I. Paragraph 5　J. Paragraph 4

II. Answer the following questions.
1. Long working hours, shift work, work-family conflict, high job demands and low job control are harmful for workers' health.
2. High job demands raised the odds of a physician-diagnosed illness by 35 percent. Long work hours increased mortality by nearly 20 percent.
3. A healthy workplace is associated with greater productivity. It would presumably lower the costs for employer-provided health insurance and health-care related taxes.

Part Two Tips for Translation

请根据给出的汉语句子填写出对应英语句子中缺少的词或词组。所需要的词性已在括号中给出。
1. missed
2. safely
3. indecisive
4. beyond
5. far from

Part Three Simulated Writing

Check Your Understanding
Answer the following questions.
1. CrazyOne Electronics Ltd. has experienced difficulty in recruiting suitable employees.
2. Human Resources Manager of the CrazyOne Electronics Ltd.
3. Three. Green's Communications Inc., The Abacus People, and Software Creators Reservoir.
4. A Webmaster, a CFO and 5 Programmers.

Follow-up Writing

Complete the following report with the words given below. Be sure to use the correct form of each word.

(1) aim   (2) summarize   (3) recommend   (4) Findings
(5) approached   (6) identified   (7) Conclusion   (8) Recommendations

Part Four Listening

While-listening

I. Listen to the recording and supply the missing words.

1. estimated	2. impact	3. debate	4. complex
5. personally	6. biology	7. guilty	8. conference
9. habits	10. behavior	11. break	12. encourage
13. preventing	14. toughest	15. unrefined	16. obesity
17. satisfy	18. Commercially	19. amounts	20. diet
21. foster	22. precedent	23. cigarette	24. ancestors
25. diet	26. radically	27. indigenous	28. modern
29. combination	30. intervention		

Part Five Speaking

II. Match the following two columns.

  1. F   2. H   3. A   4. C   5. E   6. B   7. G   8. D

III. The following is the opening speech by Dr Yaacob Ibrahim, Minister for the Environment and Water Resources in Singapore, at the 1st IWA-ASPIRE Conference, at Pan Pacific Hotel. Fill in the blanks with the following expressions.

   1. warm welcome
   2. so many of you
   3. for organizing a conference
   4. managing our water resources
   5. key to success
   6. a robust exchange of views
   7. a fruitful discussion
   8. as many of you as possible
   9. sustainable water resources
   10. to declare

IV. Complete the following speech by translating the Chinese into English.

   1. made important contribution to the progress of human civilization
   2. accept my warm congratulations
   3. the friendly exchanges between our peoples
   4. economic globalization and the information network
   5. No culture can flourish in isolation
   6. achieve economic prosperity and social progress

Key to the Exercises

Transcripts

For the last 15 years, Plymouth, England has held a symposium on obesity. It's estimated that more than half the city's adults are overweight or obese. The rest of Britain is not fairing much better.

Professor Jonathan Pinkney said: "No one health issue has the most impact on human health, or engenders more debate about how to tackle it, than obesity." Pinkney, a professor of Endocrinology and Diabetes, took part in the annual Plymouth Symposium on Obesity, Diabetes and Metabolic Syndrome on May 21st.

He said: "obesity is a complex issue that involves more than calorie intake. I personally feel that this is such a wide field. There are so many issues. There's politics. There's biology. There's everything you can imagine. There's the food industry. And I think that sometimes we're all a bit guilty of just maybe concentrating on one of those areas. And you can go to a conference anywhere in the world where they spend days just talking about bariatric surgery or fizzy drinks. So, I think it's right to talk about everything under one umbrella." He thinks that many issues are concerned with source.

Going to the source means how eating habits are formed. Poor eating habits can be a learned behavior passed down by parents to their children. "I think a lot of things start very early in life. You know, it's difficult to break the habits of a lifetime, isn't it?" he said. "Solving the problem," he said, "is a lot harder than simply trying to encourage prevention. There isn't a kind of medical way to prevent the problem. It really does look as if it's down to politics, policy, marketing, food industry and preventing children from being exposed to all of this. And I think that's the toughest thing that we face in the world. It's very, very difficult." Professor Pinkney said too many unrefined carbohydrates were to blame for much of the obesity epidemic. He said that they didn't satisfy a person's hunger for long and people ate their next meal sooner.

"Commercially produced processed food with large amounts of carbohydrates — sweeteners, short acting carbohydrates — and it just sets us up to fail. And I think there are big problems with carbohydrates in the Western diet," he said. While it may be difficult to foster better eating habits, Pinkney said: "there is precedent for large scale behavior change. Other things have changed. I mean one really interesting thing, I think, was what's happened over cigarette smoking. And how people complained about not being able to smoke in pubs and restaurants and have to go outside. But it didn't take very long for that to translate into clear health benefits. So, you know, maybe you can get these things through in time, little by little."

"Some lessons," he said, "can be learned from our hunter-gatherer ancestors. The hunter-gatherers going right back to last Ice Age and before that would have had a diet that was rich in complex, sort of, fiber kind of carbohydrates. There would be protein in it now and again. But it didn't have all the sugar. So, the diet that is, of course, followed by traditional peoples is radically different." He said studies of indigenous peoples took a step back from modern health problems." A combination of prevention methods, medical intervention and political will be needed to stop the obesity epidemic.

Unit Eight Celebrity

Part One Reading and Translating

Reading A

I. Give brief answers to the following questions.
   1. John Nash is a mathematician, an economist, and a professor at Princeton University, whose game theory won him 1994 Nobel Prize in economics. He is the original character in the movie A Beautiful Mind.
   2. Nasar is the writer of Nash's biography of the same name with the movie.

3. The mathematician John Forbes Nash Jr. attended graduate school at Princeton, where he was arrogant, childish, and brilliant. His doctoral thesis on the so-called "Nash equilibrium" revolutionized economics. Over time, he began to suffer delusions. He was hospitalized for paranoid schizophrenia, administered insulin shock therapy, and released. Afterward, Nash became a mysterious, ghostlike figure at Princeton. Eventually, through the support of his loving wife, his friends, and the force of his own will, he experienced a dramatic remission. In 1994, he won the Nobel Prize in economics, and to this day he keeps an office at Princeton.

4. Nasar herself believes that the filmmakers have "invented a narrative that, while far from a literal telling, is true to the spirit of Nash's story."

5. Among the many important events from Nash's life, the filmmakers dropped his homosexual experiences, an illegitimate child and divorce.

6. He said he was not inclined to give speeches, but he has three things to say. First he hoped that getting the Nobel would improve his credit rating because he really wanted a credit card. Second, he said that one is supposed to say that one is glad he is sharing the prize, but he wished he had won the whole thing because he really needed the money badly. Third, Nash said that he had won for game theory and that he felt that game theory was like string theory, a subject of great intrinsic intellectual interest that the world wishes to imagine can be of some utility.

II. Complete the following passage by filling each of the numbered blanks with one or two suitable words using the Chinese in the brackets as the reference.

1. inclined   2. getting   3. credit rating   4. supposed
5. badly   6. string theory 7. intrinsic   8. utility
9. skepticism 10. funny

III. Complete the following sentences with one function word.
1. for   2. to   3. by   4. On   5. to   6. with

IV. Complete the following sentences by translating the Chinese given in the brackets.
1. foster care does not correspond to
2. is supposed to play a critical role
3. filed for bankruptcy
4. peter out over time
5. paying tribute to Dong and Wang, both of whom possessed superb medical skills and high medical ethics during their stay in Gansu for medical aid.
6. is inclined to increase

V. Translate the following sentences into English.
1. Nash also made a sexual overture toward John Milnor, a fellow mathematician with whom Nash lived one summer while working for the RAND Corporation think tank in Santa Monica, Calif.
2. In 1954, Nash was arrested for indecent exposure in a bathroom in Santa Monica, which cost him his position at RAND.
3. Though single, Nash was unwilling to care for Eleanor or John, and John had to be placed in foster care for a time.
4. Nash was still ill at the time and thought John Stier would play "an essential and significant personal role in my personal long-awaited 'gay liberation,'" according to a letter Nash wrote to a friend.

Key to the Exercises

VI. Translate the following passage into Chinese.

当然,电影中的一些部分绝对有问题——人物削减,场景压缩,事件美化,但是这些粗制滥造的地方大多是可以谅解的,因为把一本近400页的书压缩成一部2小时的传记电影的确有难度。Nasar本人认为电影拍摄者改编了剧本,尽管与书相差甚远,但是可以说是忠于原著中纳什的精神的。但是与改编原著相比更加恼人的是电影摄制人故意漏掉了一些内容,其中包括重要的方面。

Reading B

I. Match the summaries below with the thirteen paragraphs of the article.
   A. 2   B. 4   C. 1   D. 13   E. 10   F. 5   G. 7   H. 8   I. 6   J. 3   K. 11   L. 9   M. 12

II. Answer the following questions.
   1. The longing for love, the search for knowledge, and unbearable pity for the suffering of mankind.
   2. A series of protests and a 1940 judicial decision which found him morally unfit to teach at the College.
   3. He became a prime organizer of the first Pugwash Conference, which brought together a large number of scientists concerned about the nuclear issue.

Part Two Tips for Translation

翻译下列句子,在必要的时候进行主动语态和被动语态的转换。
1. She was seen to go out of the room.
2. They want to be listened to.
3. If the funds are used on excellent scientific researchers, then it is possible to achieve something.
4. She was asked ten questions in the oral exam and answered every one of them correctly.
5. Passengers are requested to fill in the customs declaration form here.
6. You will probably fall over a chair or walk into the wall when you try to move about in the dark.

Part Three Simulated Writing

Check Your Understanding
Sample Reading 1
Match the comments with each corresponding part of the proposal. (Some of the answers have been given.)
A. 8   B. 7   C. 1   D. 4   F. 3   G. 6   I. 2

Sample Reading 2
Mark the following statements with T (true) or F (false) according to the proposal.
1. T   2. F   3. T   4. F   5. T

Follow-up Writing
Complete the following proposal according to the Chinese translation given.
 1. This proposal contains information on the contents of
 2. our schedule to complete this project
 3. our qualifications to produce a high-quality finished handbook
 4. about description of the handbook
 5. enable any person with a high school diploma to operate and perform preventive maintenance
 6. the length of the handbook to be 98 pages

271

7. has won ten other contracts for weapons handbooks

8. Detailed resumes of our staff are available upon request.

9. 4 hours of writing time per page at $50.00 per hour

10. Information Sources

11. Proposal returned, begin work

12. Outline section on Maintenance completed

13. Completed copy sent

Part Four Listening

While-listening

I. Listen to the recording and supply the missing words.

1. evoke	2. twinkling	3. touching	4. spread
5. naval	6. inspirational	7. symbol	8. confront
9. contains	10. verse	11. carol	12. overcome
13. thankfulness	14. veterans	15. procession	16. slowest
17. annual	18. five hundred	19. faiths	20. represent
21. topping	22. angel	23. stable	24. flee
25. captures	26. persecuted	27. unchanging	28. revenge
29. customary	30. curse		

Part Five Speaking

I. Match the following two columns.
   1. D   2. C   3. E   4. B   5. A

II. Complete the following sentences with the help of the Chinese in the brackets.

1. on behalf of

2. the friendship and cooperation between our two cities

3. I greatly appreciate this opportunity

4. your warm reception

5. use this opportunity to plan something for the future

6. congratulations on a successful conference

7. your efforts and participation

8. a good journey home

III. Learn to make a closing speech in accordance with the following requirements.
   You are responsible for delivering a closing speech. Make a speech with all the following information included.
   Honorary Mr. President,
   Dear Colleagues and Friends,
   Ladies and Gentlemen,
   We are soon closing this workshop which has been a great success.
   　We have enjoyed the advanced professional program as well as the interesting introduction to your high prestige company. Also we have had possibilities to join some unforgettable evenings with colleagues and there is still one more evening gathering in our program.

From our side we can only say that everything was successful, professional and especially international guests received the most wonderful Chinese hospitality.

I want to thank everybody who took part in the organization work.

As a practical result of this workshop, and before our departure—we could use this opportunity to plan something for the future. For example, bilateral agreements between companies can help a lot in the joint venture. I am very happy about the discussions which we had this afternoon on this topic.

Before closing, on behalf of Organizing Committee, I want to thank you, Mr. President, for making this workshop possible. I want also to thank you, Mr. Wu Zhongming, for hosting all of us both during the daytime and in the evenings. I want to thank everyone who has worked for our workshop and made it a success.

We will all go home with good memories of this meeting and I hope that some day in the future I can be the host for all of you in my country.

I wish everybody a good journey home, wherever you live, but before that I know we shall spend one more relaxing evening together.

Thank you for joining the seminar and for your support and cooperation with us.

Transcripts

The Queen's Christmas Speech 2015

At this time of year, few sights evoke more feelings of cheer and goodwill than the twinkling lights of a Christmas tree.

The popularity of a tree at Christmas is due in part to my great-great grandparents, Queen Victoria and Prince Albert. After this touching picture was published, many families wanted a Christmas tree of their own, and the custom soon spread.

In 1949, I spent Christmas in Malta as a newly-married naval wife. We have returned to that island over the years, including last month for a meeting of Commonwealth leaders; and this year I met another group of leaders: The Queen's Young Leaders, an inspirational group, each of them a symbol of hope in their own Commonwealth communities.

Gathering round the tree gives us a chance to think about the year ahead — I am looking forward to a busy 2016, though I have been warned I may have Happy Birthday sung to me more than once or twice. It also allows us to reflect on the year that has passed, as we think of those who are far away or no longer with us. Many people say the first Christmas after losing a loved one is particularly hard. But it's also a time to remember all that we have to be thankful for.

It is true that the world has had to confront moments of darkness this year, but the Gospel of John contains a verse of great hope, often read at Christmas carol services: "The light shines in the darkness, and the darkness has not overcome it."

One cause for thankfulness this summer was marking seventy years since the end of the Second World War. On VJ Day, we honoured the remaining veterans of that terrible conflict in the Far East, as well as remembering the thousands who never returned. The procession from Horse Guards Parade to Westminster Abbey must have been one of the slowest ever, because so many people wanted to say "thank you" to them.

At the end of that War, the people of Oslo began sending an annual gift of a Christmas tree for Trafalgar Square. It has five hundred lightbulbs and is enjoyed not just by Christians but by people of all faiths, and of none. At the very top sits a bright star, to represent the Star of Bethlehem.

The custom of topping a tree also goes back to Prince Albert's time. For his family's tree, he chose an angel, helping to remind us that the focus of the Christmas story is on one particular family.

For Joseph and Mary, the circumstances of Jesus's birth — in a stable — were far from ideal, but worse was to come as the family was forced to flee the country. It's no surprise that such a human story still captures our imagination and continues to inspire all of us who are Christians, the world over.

Despite being displaced and persecuted throughout his short life, Christ's unchanging message was not one of revenge or violence but simply that we should love one another. Although it is not an easy message to follow, we shouldn't be discouraged; rather, it inspires us to try harder: to be thankful for the people who bring love and happiness into our own lives, and to look for ways of spreading that love to others, whenever and wherever we can.

One of the joys of living a long life is watching one's children, then grandchildren, then great grandchildren, help decorate the Christmas tree. And this year my family has a new member to join in the fun!

The customary decorations have changed little in the years since that picture of Victoria and Albert's tree first appeared, although of course electric lights have replaced the candles.

There's an old saying that "it is better to light a candle than curse the darkness".

There are millions of people lighting candles of hope in our world today. Christmas is a good time to be thankful for them, and for all that brings light to our lives.

I wish you a very happy Christmas.

Unit Nine   Education

Part One Reading and Translating

Reading A

I. Give brief answers to the following questions.

1. Liberal education is what remains after you have forgotten the facts that were first learned while becoming educated.

2. Whitehead argued that the "really useful training" focuses on "general principles." One result is that "in subsequent practice the men will have forgotten your particular details; but they will remember by an unconscious common sense how to apply principles to immediate circumstances."

3. "General education" refers to the portion of an undergraduate's time in College spent outside a major or concentration but in some way constrained by some requirements.

4. Harvard College liberal-education courses in a general education program ought to meet the following four key criteria. The first is that they should foster discernment. The second criterion is that these courses should develop creativity. Thirdly, such courses should construct and propel the communicative skills of our students. Finally, general-education courses should be accessible to undergraduates who approach them with varying levels of preparation.

5. For all disciplines, communication characteristically requires the capacity to write and to speak with some eloquence. In many instances, a language other than the one first learned is an essential to communicate in the cosmopolitan world into whose membership our students should aspire.

6. "Distributional requirement" is a simple scheme that clumps courses into humanities, social sciences, life sciences, and physical sciences. It has the advantage of simplicity.

II. Complete the following passage by filling each of the numbered blanks with one or two suitable words using the Chinese in the brackets as the reference.

    1. consequences   2. scheme   3. life sciences   4. simplicity

5. criterion	6. creativity	7. survey courses	8. disciplinary
9. innovation	10. adopt		

III. Complete the following sentences with one function word.
1. to   2. on   3. of   4. across   5. other   6. into

IV. Complete the following sentences by translating the Chinese given in the brackets.
1. lead the students to the loss of the opportunity to foster their creativity
2. applied to pupils at best
3. seeks to make a choice between the two
4. be limited to a specific country or region
5. taking immediate steps to train students with general principles other than particular details
6. render these courses accessible to the students

V. Translate the following sentences into English.
1. Liberal education is what remains after you have forgotten the facts that were first learned while becoming educated. This view is especially comforting to professors of a certain age who forget even where they place their glasses but, at Harvard, it has long been influential.
2. Students in such courses should perceive the aesthetic world of the arts and letters; apprehend fundamental ideas, methods, and principles underlying the sciences; recognize and analyze distinctive aspects of social behavior in our world and its past; and be capable of rendering acute judgments and making ethical decisions.
3. Students should learn to transcend traditional ideas, patterns, and relationships in order to fashion new ones thoughtfully. Professors should encourage originality, exploration, and discovery within and across scholarly disciplines, unafraid to present material that might even seem contradictory.
4. An alternative is to teach highly specialized courses to beginners; the professor can do so, however, only if the course has been designed to entice, inform, motivate, and empower the student to proceed expeditiously and within one semester from ignorance to mastery.

VI. Translate the following passage into Chinese.
　　这种看待课程的方法和随之形成的课程体系产生了一些实际的结果。证明了一个好的设计不太可能将课程分类为人文科学、社会科学、生命科学和物理科学这样简单的"分配需求"方案。没错，那是一个贯穿美国高等教育的普遍设计，好处就是简单易行。然而，这一设计忽视了洞察力标准的全面性，同时也没有采取明确的措施发展沟通技能，创造力是否得到了培养也完全不得而知。事实上，这一设计因为完全依赖概论课程去满足学生的修课需求而备受谴责。该设计没有在学科之外的院系为课程留出明显的空间，因此使得课程和教学改革不太可行或者仅仅是形同虚设。一个更好的方法就是采用一种满足学生具体要求的、更有针对性的体系来使学生的心智更好地得到发展。

Reading B

I. Match the summaries (A—H) on the left column with the number of paragraphs on the right column.

A. paragraph 4	B. paragraph 6	C. paragraph 8	D. paragraph 1
E. paragraph 3	F. paragraph 5	G. paragraph 2	H. paragraph 7

II. Answer the following questions.
1. Many educators, such as the originators of the CDIO initiative have identified industry needs for more capable engineering graduates with traits beyond technical knowledge, including personal maturity, interpersonal skills, and holistic, critical thinking regarding engineering systems.

2. The Learning Factory model aimed to serve three stakeholder groups. First, industry leaders desired more talented, creative, and well-rounded engineers who were better prepared for innovative work. Second, students desired a richer, practice-based curriculum to augment their theoretical knowledge and make them more competitive in the job market. Third, faculty desired to connect their research with real-world problems and industry needs.

3. Industry partners have reacted positively to students gaining design and manufacturing skills in a self-driven environment while also working on sponsored projects.

Part Two Tips for Translation

1. 根据汉语句子的意思按括号中给出的要求完成对应的英语句子。

   (1) which

   (2) understandably; necessarily

   (3) surprising

   (4) with

   (5) a second term

2. 比较下面每组句子并判断每一句英译文分别对原句进行了哪一类切分处理。

   句1和句4属于第四类切分,即汉语句子意思的层次较多,所含信息较多。

   句2属于第二类切分,即汉语句子先总说,后分述。

   句3属于第三类切分,即汉语句子先分述,后总说。

Part Three Simulated Writing

Check Your Understanding

Answer the following questions.

1. Existing web design tools do not support different levels of tasks very well.
2. They created DENIM, a system that helps web site designers in the early stages of design.
3. They found that seven professional designers reacted positively to the concept and were interested in using DENIM in their work.

Follow-up Writing

Complete the following abstract with the information given in the brackets.

1. The author presents
2. is determined by
3. To improve
4. The author suggests
5. It is concluded

Part Four Listening

While-listening

I. Listen to the recording and supply the missing words.

| 1. marvel | 2. floating | 3. firsthand | 4. missions |
| 5. spacewalks | 6. assurance | 7. aerospace | 8. sparked |

Key to the Exercises

9. chemistry	10. keener	11. design	12. long
13. straightforward	14. artistic	15. yield	16. originally
17. technical	18. systems	19. hazard	20. interactions
21. human	22. piloted	23. harsh	24. flexibility
25. knowledgeable	26. qualified	27. relevant	28. key
29. answer	30. alive		

Part Five Speaking

I. Listen to the report and answer the following questions.
1. Psychological stress is a normal reaction to a threat or to a disturbing change in the environment.
2. Other people, our own thoughts and emotions or physical changes in the environment.
3. A short-term, or acute, stress is what happens when we must respond immediately to a threatening situation like a near miss in traffic.
4. It's called adversity.
5. A heavy burden of long-term stress.
6. Nausea, a racing heart with palpitations, profuse sweating, rapid breathing, dizziness, muscle tremors, and sensory changes.
7. The shift of levels of certain nerve transmitters.
8. Your senses become much sharper; you can become forgetful. It becomes much harder to concentrate. You thinking may slow down and you'll probably experience difficulty in thinking analytical thoughts. You can get confused, and you may have trouble making decisions. You can become more vigilant and distractible. And there tends to be a loss of objectivity and perspective.
9. Because we have the relaxation response which helps us to recover from stress.
10. Coronary artery blockage, hypertension, irritable bowel syndrome.
11. They can prevent the negative effects of stress ahead of time.
12. Three.
13. Psychological resilience is the universal human capacity to face, overcome and even be strengthened by experiences of adversity.
14. Self-care strategies such as exercise and good diet and adequate sleep.

II. Match the following sentences with the corresponding patterns of organization. Some of the answers have been given.
A. 1, 6   B. 2, 3, 12   C. 8, 9   D. 2, 5, 11   E. 10

Transcripts

Making STEM Matter for the Next Generation of Astronauts and Engineers

Former NASA astronaut and Raytheon engineer Robert Curbeam explains what sparked his interest in science and how to inspire the next generation of STEM leaders.

As an aspiring scientist in Baltimore in the 1970s, Robert Curbeam would stand at the end of his street and marvel at NASA's Skylab space station when he could see it floating in the sky. Decades later, as an astronaut, he would see space firsthand and put his STEM skills to use installing and repairing equipment on the International Space Station during several missions. Curbeam, 51, participated in three NASA spaceflights and was the first astronaut to complete four spacewalks during a single mission. He retired from the space agency in

2007 and now serves as vice president for mission assurance for Massachusetts-based aerospace and defense company Raytheon. Curbeam recently spoke with U.S. News about what sparked his early interest in science and engineering and how to inspire the next generation of STEM leaders. Excerpts:

What inspired you to study engineering?

When I was growing up, my mom was a chemistry teacher and I really, really took to it. When I started looking at colleges, I found out that I really had a keener interest in engineering. Also, when I was in middle school, I had a very good friend…[and] he and I used to spend a lot of time together trying to design a better car or a better plane, things like that. To us it just seemed like it made sense that there were so many things that didn't change about the car for so long that we could do it better at age 12 or 13.

What kept you interested?

It was creativity mixed with mathematics. When you do design work, it's never straightforward. It almost approaches being art-like, an artistic kind of thing, where creativity and the way you think about the problem sometimes will yield a different design than someone would originally think.

How did you use that engineering training in your work at NASA?

There were two ways, actually. The first is the actual operation of a spacecraft. That's not to say that without a technical degree you couldn't do that. It just makes it easier to operate the spacecraft and understand the interaction between all of the systems. I also used my engineering degree after the [2003 space shuttle] Columbia accident because I was on the safety and mission assurance team that was evaluating all of the hazard analyses... for the space shuttle system. At that point you really get to the nitty-gritty of how the systems work, where the hazards are, what kinds of interfaces the different systems have and their interactions, and how maybe a failure in one can cause a cascading failure in others.

What do you see ahead in terms of the future of space travel and research?

The thing that excites me is we're finally to that stage where you can have an interaction of both human systems and purely machine systems. We can take the best of the remotely piloted or driven vehicles, which is their persistence, their ability to operate in very harsh environments, along with your human-driven or -piloted vehicles, vehicles that we would actually put people in, and their inherent flexibility and responsiveness. At the end of the day, we're going to need a lot of very, very smart and informed and knowledgeable people in the next generation to help us continue to push that forward. Although we sit here and we're very, very worried about the short term—how do we get people that are qualified to do the jobs we have now? — we also have to think a generation away: How are we going to make sure that we have the people to do that work in 2030, 2040, 2050?

How do we attract that next generation of astronauts and engineers to the STEM disciplines?

I think the most important thing is to make it relevant. Learning about how, for instance, combustion worked was very interesting to me because I saw it every day. I understood that that was the key to the automobile, key to how airplanes flew. By the same token, if you want to get kids interested and keep them interested in the STEM fields, you have to make it relevant. I really don't care what the answer to $3x+2y=1$ is, but if you tell me that that equation will help me solve the problem of how much grain I need to buy for how many horses to keep them alive for the next winter, then it becomes relevant.

Key to the Exercises

Unit Ten Environment

Part One Reading and Translating

Reading A

I. Give brief answers to the following questions.
  1. The benefits would be less pollution, less real estate needed for parking spaces, improved quality of life and much more.
  2. It can help companies motivate employees to change their habits, get onboard with company sustainability goals and measure outcomes.
  3. They are motivation, ability and a trigger. Company sustainability initiatives are the motivation. WeSpire's game mechanics platform helps with the trigger. Employees, then, are left to work on developing their ability to overcome barriers.
  4. The key to getting employees to drive less is improving their ability to find options and getting them to try something just once.
  5. Factoring in regional development, gas prices, greenhouse gas incentives, preferences for where millennials live, transportation choices and where highways get built are all helpful in deciding where to locate businesses and where future infrastructure development may fall short.
  6. Successful nudges to improve low-carbon transportation have included preferential parking for electric or hybrid vehicles and carpools, as well as company benefits such as subsidies and pre-tax purchasing options for public transportation.

II. Complete the following passage by filling each of the numbered blanks with one suitable word using the Chinese in the brackets as the reference.
  1. build   2. capabilities   3. low-carbon   4. preferential
  5. transportation 6. regional   7. motivators   8. ultimately
  9. obstacles   10. curb

III. Complete the following sentences with one function word.
  1. or   2. with, in   3. for   4. to   5. to   6. with

IV. Complete the following sentences by translating the Chinese given in the brackets.
  1. Farm tours and other agriculture-based experiences can often better appeal to urban residents
  2. For better or for worse, McDonald's is no more a chemical laboratory
  3. organisations are left to set their own rules
  4. 500 million people do not have access to fresh, clean water
  5. The centre will help with crisis management
  6. with respect to the control of pollution

V. Translate the following sentences into English.
  1. Google — which this week rebranded itself as Alphabet — may not have been the first company to offer shuttles to its employees, but the size and growth of its shuttle program have made it the most prominent, for better or for worse.
  2. It's a question that has been on his mind since developing a model for the region covering Baltimore to Washington DC to understand how behavior preferences and state policies will impact the future trends in

development, transportation, land use and the environment.
3. Factoring in regional development, gas prices, greenhouse gas incentives, preferences for where millennials live, transportation choices and where highways get built are all helpful in deciding where to locate businesses and where future infrastructure development may fall short.
4. "The future, 20 years from now, with respect to travel choices, will be much different than it is today," Knaap said, adding that the choices beyond the automobile — even if we're talking about driverless cars or car sharing services like Zipcar — should be expected and factored into sustainability planning.

VI. Translate the following passage into Chinese.

在波士顿和其他地方，越来越多的公司将办公地点迁移到离交通运输系统或者员工居住地很近的地方，甚至有些公司还鼓励员工在家里工作。拿Adobe公司来说，它搬离了原位于波士顿近郊主要技术地带的办公地点，该处的公司设备和设施价值44,000,000美元。由于能够为公司员工提供在家中办公的选择，Adobe公司搬到了一处离城市公共交通非常近的一处很小的办公寓所。

史蒂文斯说："很多公司的选址都考虑到自己的员工无须开车便可以到达工作地点这一因素，这也是很多公司坚持遵守的竞争优势。"此外，他还认为："对于在新千年工作的人来说，开车上班并不是第一选择。因此，公司需要考虑如何支持那些不希望开车上班的员工。这不仅对于环境有好处，同时对于公司的发展也大有益处。"

美国万豪国际集团在2015年初宣布公司计划在未来几年内将其总部由马里兰州的贝塞斯达搬到能够更好吸引年轻员工的地区，而该总部的员工大概有2000多人。集团董事长苏安励在3月时告诉《华盛顿邮报》记者，对于公司来说，办公地点在接近地铁站的城市区域十分重要。目前在华盛顿，距离万豪国际总部最近的地铁站仅有三英里。

Reading B

Match the summaries on the left column to the seven parts of the article with the number of paragraphs on the right column.
A. 6   B. 3   C. 5   D. 4   E. 7   F. 1   G. 2

II. Answer the following questions below.
1. The technique is a way of extracting natural gas, which is mostly methane, from shale rock formations that are often deep underground. It involves pumping water, chemicals and usually sand underground at high pressure to fracture shale — hence the name — and release the gas trapped within to be collected back at the surface.
2. Fracking has given America gas prices that are far cheaper than in Europe, created hundreds of thousands if not millions of jobs, and has almost doubled crude production over the last seven years. Some claim it can even take the credit for America's falling greenhouse gas emissions.
3. What most critics point to are the potential health and environmental impacts which include contamination of water supplies, seismic activity caused by the fracking itself, fears that the gas glut from fracking threatens to hinder the development of emissions-free renewable sources of power and fears over the venting and flaring of methane, industrialisation of rural areas and noise from lorries.

Part Two Tips for Translation

1. 根据科技英语的特征用所给单词的正确形式填空。

   (1) rotation

   (2) displacement

   (3) was adopted; has been raised

(4) Judged

2. 根据科技英语特征修改下列英译文。
   (1) 原译文使用了人称主语,不符合科技英语一般语法特征。可改为:It has been decided that the drilling for vertical inclinometer V15 should be used initially to test the feasibility of the construction method.
   (2) 原译文使用主动语态,连贯性和衔接性差。可改为:The way to cut head and tail optimally is adopted in the control system to reduce the cutting loss, resulting in an increased recovery rate of the finished product by 0.4%.
   (3) 原译文的信息不准确,语篇结构松散,欠连贯。可改为:The total amount of the WB (World Bank) loan of Phase II is 1.3 million US dollars, of which 1.115 million is for the equipment purchase, and 0.185 million for book purchase, technical training, technical service and miscellaneous items.

Part Three Simulated Writing

Sample Reading

Please read the citations above and fill in the squares to figure out their citation kinds, type, style and pattern.

Number	Type		Style		Pattern		
	Direct Citation	Indirect Citation	APA	MLA	Integral	Non-Integral	Synthesizing
1		✓	✓			✓	
2	✓			✓		✓	
3	✓			✓	✓		
4		✓	✓		✓		
5	✓		✓			✓	
6		✓	✓				✓

Follow-up Writing

Please write the reference according to the given information and citation type.

1. Gillespie, Paula, and Neal Lerner. The Allyn and Bacon Guide to Peer Tutoring. Boston: Allyn, 2000. Print.

2. Kuhn, T. (1962). The structure of scientific revolutions. Chicago, IL: University of Chicago.

3. Miller, P.S. (1998). Genetic discrimination in the work place. Journal of Law, Medicine, and Ethics, 26(2), 189—197.

4. Bagchi, Alaknanda. "Conflicting Nationalisms: The Voice of the Subaltern in Mahasweta Devi's Bashai Tudu." Tulsa Studies in Women's Literature 15.1 (1996): 41—50. Print.

Part Four Listening

While-listening

I. Listen to the recording and supply the missing words.

1. allergic	2. lung	3. gone	4. discovered
5. common	6. indoors	7. reduce	8. maintaining
9. oxygen	10. terms	11. perhaps	12. grow
13. sterile	14. preferably	15. particular	16. cap
17. square	18. occupants	19. probability	20. government
21. healthiest	22. compared	23. available	24. productivity
25. requirements	26. outstanding	27. replicating	28. expected
29. decade	30. currently		

Part Five Speaking

II. Match the following two columns.
 1. G   2. E   3. F   4. C   5. H   6. D   7. A   8. I   9. B

III. Complete the following dialogues by making sentences with the help of the key words given in brackets.
 1. B: Usually at six. At least my alarm clock goes off at six.
    B: No, I don't have breakfast straight away, first I go for a run.
 2. B: After breakfast I read the papers, such as *The Guardian* or *The Independent*.
    B: I usually leave for the office about eight and I'm behind my desk by 8:30.
 3. B: I sort through the mail fist.
    B: No, I usually go out. Sometimes I even travel abroad.

IV. Learn to communicate in the situation given below.
 A: I've heard that you have some problems about your work.
 B: Oh, I just seemed to have too many things to do and I'm not accustomed to them yet.
 A: Well, Could you tell me what your typical day is like?
 B: I start work at nine. It's not bad, but the office is very far form where I live, so it takes me about two hour to commute.
 A: What do you usually do in the morning?
 B: The mornings are usually quite hectic. I have to type letters for the Finance and Sales departmental managers. I'm always asked to sort through mails and distribute them to different departments. There is usually quite a lot of that. I also get a lot of calls and faxes from clients.
 A: It sounds too busy to have a lunch.
 B: I usually have lunch between 12:30 and 1:30, but it depends whether we're busy.
 A: How about the afternoons?
 B: My boss usually asks me to translate some documents for him. At times I have to take minutes at board meetings.
 A: Then when do you finish your work?
 B: I usually finish work at 6 o'clock, but I sometimes stay later if my boss asks me to.

Key to the Exercises

Transcripts

How to Grow Fresh Air

Some 17 years ago, I became allergic to Delhi's air. My doctors told me that my lung capacity had gone down to 70 percent, and it was killing me. With the help of IIT, TERI, and learnings from NASA, we discovered that there are three basic green plants, common green plants, with which we can grow all the fresh air we need indoors to keep us healthy. We've also found that you can reduce the fresh air requirements into the building, while maintaining industry indoor air-quality standards.

The three plants are Areca palm, Mother-in-Law's Tongue and money plant. The botanical names are in front of you. Areca palm is a plant which removes CO_2 and converts it into oxygen. We need four shoulder-high plants per person, and in terms of plant care, we need to wipe the leaves every day in Delhi, and perhaps once a week in cleaner-air cities. We had to grow them in vermi manure, which is sterile, or hydroponics, and take them outdoors every three to four months. The second plant is Mother-in-law's Tongue, which is again a very common plant, and we call it a bedroom plant, because it converts CO_2 into oxygen at night. And we need six to eight waist-high plants per person. The third plant is money plant, and this is again a very common plant; preferably grows in hydroponics. And this particular plant removes formaldehydes and other volatile chemicals.

With these three plants, you can grow all the fresh air you need. In fact, you could be in a bottle with a cap on top, and you would not die at all, and you would not need any fresh air. We have tried these plants at our own building in Delhi, which is a 50,000-square-feet, 20-year-old building. And it has close to 1,200 such plants for 300 occupants. Our studies have found that there is a 42 percent probability of one's blood oxygen going up by one percent if one stays indoors in this building for 10 hours. The government of India has discovered or published a study to show that this is the healthiest building in New Delhi. And the study showed that, compared to other buildings, there is a reduced incidence of eye irritation by 52 percent, respiratory systems by 34 percent, headaches by 24 percent, lung impairment by 12 percent and asthma by nine percent. And this study has been published on September 8, 2008, and it's available on the government of India website.

Our experience points to an amazing increase in human productivity by over 20 percent by using these plants. And also a reduction in energy requirements in buildings by an outstanding 15 percent, because you need less fresh air. We are now replicating this in a 1.75-million-square-feet building, which will have 60,000 indoor plants.

Why is this important? It is also important for the environment, because the world's energy requirements are expected to grow by 30 percent in the next decade. 40 percent of the world's energy is taken up by buildings currently, and 60 percent of the world's population will be living in buildings in cities with a population of over one million in the next 15 years. And there is a growing preference for living and working in air-conditioned places. "Be the change you want to see in the world," said Mahatma Gandhi. And thank you for listening.